Plug-in PHP
100 POWER SOLUTIONS

Robin Nixon

New York   Chicago   San Francisco
Lisbon   London   Madrid   Mexico City
Milan   New Delhi   San Juan
Seoul   Singapore   Sydney   Toronto

Cataloging-in-Publication Data is on file with the Library of Congress

McGraw-Hill books are available at special quantity discounts to use as premiums and sales promotions, or for use in corporate training programs. To contact a representative, please e-mail us at bulksales@mcgraw-hill.com.

Plug-in PHP: 100 Power Solutions

1234567890   DOC DOC   109876543210

ISBN   978-0-07-166659-6
MHID   0-07-166659-1

Sponsoring Editor Wendy Rinaldi	**Technical Editor** Todd Meister	**Composition** Glyph International
Editorial Supervisor Jody McKenzie	**Copy Editor** Mike McGee	**Illustration** Glyph International
Project Manager Vipra Fauzdar, Glyph International	**Proofreader** Bev Weiler	**Art Director, Cover** Jeff Weeks
Acquisitions Coordinator Joya Anthony	**Indexer** Karin Arrigoni **Production Supervisor** George Anderson	**Cover Designer** Pehrsson Design

For Julie

Contents at a Glance

1	Building a Development Server	1
2	Using the Plug-ins	27
3	Text Processing	33
4	Image Handling	59
5	Content Management	87
6	Forms and User Input	111
7	The Internet	141
8	Chat and Messaging	175
9	MySQL, Sessions, and Cookies	207
10	APIs, RSS, and XML	235
11	Incorporating JavaScript	277
12	Diverse Solutions	309
	Index	335

Contents

Acknowledgments xxiii
Introduction xxv

1   Building a Development Server **1**
Windows XP, Windows Vista, and Windows 7 2
    Reinstalling Zend Server CE 8
    Upgrading Zend Server CE 8
    Windows Security Alerts 8
    After Installation 8
    Uninstalling 11
    Document Root 12
Ubuntu and Debian Linux 12
    Uninstalling 14
    After Installation 15
    Document Root 16
Fedora, RHEL, and CentOS Linux 16
    Installing MySQL 16
    Uninstalling 16
    Document Root 17
Other Versions of Linux 17
    Installing MySQL 17
    Uninstalling 17
    Document Root 17
Mac OS X 10.4 Plus on Intel Chips 18
    Document Root 20
    Uninstalling 21
Mac OS X 10.3 21
    Document Root 24
Configuring Error Handling in Zend Server CE 25
And Now You're Set to Go 25

2   Using the Plug-ins **27**
Using include 28
    include_once 28
Using require 29
    require_once 29
Include Scope 29
Correctly Inserting PHP code 30
    Inserting HTML 31
    Including PHP Files from Other Servers 32

3   Text Processing **33**
Plug-in 1: Wrap Text 34
   About the Plug-in 35
   Variables, Arrays, and Functions 35
   How It Works 35
   How to Use It 36
   The Plug-in 36
Plug-in 2: Caps Control 37
   About the Plug-in 38
   Variables, Arrays, and Functions 38
   How It Works 38
   How to Use It 39
   The Plug-in 39
Plug-in 3: Friendly Text 39
   About the Plug-in 40
   Variables, Arrays, and Functions 40
   How It Works 41
   How to Use It 42
   The Plug-in 42
Plug-in 4: Strip Whitespace 43
   About the Plug-in 44
   Variables, Arrays, and Functions 44
   How It Works 44
   How to Use It 45
   The Plug-in 45
Plug-in 5: Word Selector 45
   About the Plug-in 46
   Variables, Arrays, and Functions 46
   How It Works 46
   How to Use It 46
   The Plug-in 47
Plug-in 6: Count Tail 47
   About the Plug-in 48
   Variables, Arrays, and Functions 48
   How It Works 48
   How to Use It 49
   The Plug-in 49
Plug-in 7: Text Truncate 49
   About the Plug-in 50
   Variables, Arrays, and Functions 50
   How It Works 50
   How to Use It 51
   The Plug-in 51
Plug-in 8: Spell Check 51
   About the Plug-in 52
   Variables, Arrays, and Functions 52
   How It Works 52
   How to Use It 54
   The Plug-in 54

Plug-in 9: Remove Accents 55
   About the Plug-in 56
   Variables, Arrays, and Functions 56
   How It Works 56
   How to Use It 56
   The Plug-in 56
Plug-in 10: Shorten Text 57
   About the Plug-in 57
   Variables, Arrays, and Functions 57
   How It Works 57
   How to Use It 58
   The Plug-in 58

4   Image Handling **59**
Installing the GD Library 60
Plug-in 11: Upload File 60
   About the Plug-in 61
   Variables, Arrays, and Functions 61
   How It Works 61
   How to Use It 62
   The Plug-in 64
Plug-in 12: Resize Image 64
   About the Plug-in 65
   Variables, Arrays, and Functions 65
   How It Works 65
   How to Use It 65
   The Plug-in 66
Plug-in 13: Make Thumbnail 66
   About the Plug-in 67
   Variables, Arrays, and Functions 67
   How It Works 67
   How to Use It 68
   The Plug-in 68
Plug-in 14: Image Alter 68
   About the Plug-in 69
   Variables, Arrays, and Functions 70
   How It Works 70
   How to Use It 70
   The Plug-in 70
Plug-in 15: Image Crop 71
   About the Plug-in 71
   Variables, Arrays, and Functions 72
   How It Works 72
   How to Use It 72
   The Plug-in 73
Plug-in 16: Image Enlarge 73
   About the Plug-in 74
   Variables, Arrays, and Functions 74
   How It Works 75
   How to Use It 75
   The Plug-in 75

Plug-in 17: Image Display 76
About the Plug-in 76
Variables, Arrays, and Functions 77
How It Works 77
How to Use It 77
The Plug-in 78
Plug-in 18: Image Convert 78
About the Plug-in 79
Variables, Arrays, and Functions 79
How It Works 79
How to Use It 79
The Plug-in 79
Plug-in 19: Gif Text 80
About the Plug-in 81
Variables, Arrays, and Functions 81
How It Works 81
How to Use It 82
The Plug-in 82
Plug-in 20: Image Watermark 83
About the Plug-in 83
Variables, Arrays, and Functions 84
How It Works 84
How to Use It 85
The Plug-in 85

5 Content Management **87**
Plug-in 21: Relative to Absolute URL 88
About the Plug-in 89
Variables, Arrays, and Functions 89
How It Works 89
How to Use It 90
The Plug-in 90
Plug-in 22: Get Links from URL 90
About the Plug-in 91
Variables, Arrays, and Functions 91
How It Works 91
How to Use It 92
The Plug-in 92
Plug-in 23: Check Links 92
About the Plug-in 93
Variables, Arrays, and Functions 93
How It Works 93
How to Use It 94
The Plug-in 94
Plug-in 24: Directory List 95
About the Plug-in 96
Variables, Arrays, and Functions 96
How It Works 96
How to Use It 97
The Plug-in 97

Plug-in 25: Query Highlight 98
    About the Plug-in 98
    Variables, Arrays, and Functions 98
    How It Works 98
    How to Use It 99
    The Plug-in 100
Plug-in 26: Rolling Copyright 100
    About the Plug-in 101
    Variables, Arrays, and Functions 101
    How It Works 101
    How to Use It 101
    The Plug-in 101
Plug-in 27: Embed YouTube Video 101
    About the Plug-in 101
    Variables, Arrays, and Functions 102
    How It Works 102
    How to Use It 102
    The Plug-in 103
Plug-in 28: Create List 103
    About the Plug-in 104
    Variables, Arrays, and Functions 104
    How It Works 104
    How to Use It 104
    The Plug-in 105
Plug-in 29: Hit Counter 105
    About the Plug-in 105
    Variables, Arrays, and Functions 105
    How It Works 106
    How to Use It 106
    The Plug-in 107
Plug-in 30: Referer Log 108
    About the Plug-in 108
    Variables, Arrays, and Functions 108
    How It Works 108
    How to Use It 109
    The Plug-in 109

6 Forms and User Input **111**
Plug-in 31: Evaluate Expression 112
    About the Plug-in 112
    Variables, Arrays, and Functions 112
    How It Works 113
    How to Use It 114
    The Plug-in 114
Plug-in 32: Validate Credit Card 114
    About the Plug-in 114
    Variables, Arrays, and Functions 115
    How It Works 115
    How to Use It 116
    The Plug-in 116

Plug-in 33: Create Captcha 118
About the Plug-in 118
Variables, Arrays, and Functions 119
How It Works 119
How to Use It 120
The Plug-in 121
Plug-in 34: Check Captcha 122
About the Plug-in 123
Variables, Arrays, and Functions 123
How It Works 123
How to Use It 123
The Plug-in 124
Plug-in 35: Validate Text 124
About the Plug-in 124
Variables, Arrays, and Functions 125
How It Works 125
How to Use It 126
The Plug-in 127
Plug-in 36: Validate E-mail 128
About the Plug-in 128
Variables, Arrays, and Functions 129
How It Works 129
How to Use It 129
The Plug-in 129
Plug-in 37: Spam Catch 130
About the Plug-in 130
Variables, Arrays, and Functions 130
How It Works 131
How to Use It 131
The Plug-in 131
Plug-in 38: Send E-mail 131
About the Plug-in 132
Variables, Arrays, and Functions 132
How It Works 132
How to Use It 133
The Plug-in 133
Plug-in 39: BB Code 134
About the Plug-in 134
Variables, Arrays, and Functions 135
How It Works 135
How to Use It 135
The Plug-in 136
Plug-in 40: Pound Code 137
About the Plug-in 137
Variables, Arrays, and Functions 137
How It Works 137
How to Use It 138
The Plug-in 139

7   The Internet **141**
   Plug-in 41: Check Links 142
      About the Plug-in 142
      Variables, Arrays, and Functions 143
      How It Works 143
      How to Use It 143
      The Plug-in 144
   Plug-in 42: Get Title from URL 144
      About the Plug-in 144
      Variables, Arrays, and Functions 145
      How It Works 145
      How to Use It 145
      The Plug-in 145
   Plug-in 43: Auto Back Links 145
      About the Plug-in 146
      Variables, Arrays, and Functions 146
      How It Works 146
      How to Use It 147
      The Plug-in 147
   Plug-in 44: Create Short URL 148
      About the Plug-in 148
      Variables, Arrays, and Functions 149
      How It Works 149
      How to Use It 150
      The Plug-in 150
   Plug-in 45: Use Short URL 151
      About the Plug-in 151
      Variables, Arrays, and Functions 151
      How It Works 152
      How to Use It 152
      The Plug-in 153
   Plug-in 46: Simple Web Proxy 154
      About the Plug-in 155
      Variables, Arrays, and Functions 155
      How It Works 155
      How to Use It 157
      The Plug-in 158
   Plug-in 47: Page Updated? 159
      About the Plug-in 160
      Variables, Arrays, and Functions 160
      How It Works 160
      How to Use It 161
      The Plug-in 162
   Plug-in 48: HTML To RSS 163
      About the Plug-in 164
      Variables, Arrays, and Functions 164
      How It Works 164
      How to Use It 165
      The Plug-in 166

Plug-in 49: RSS to HTML 168
    About the Plug-in 168
    Variables, Arrays, and Functions 169
    How It Works 169
    How to Use It 169
    The Plug-in 170
Plug-in 50: HTML to Mobile 170
    About the Plug-in 172
    Variables, Arrays, and Functions 172
    How It Works 172
    How to Use It 173
    The Plug-in 173

8 Chat and Messaging **175**
Plug-in 51: Users Online 176
    About the Plug-in 176
    Variables, Arrays, and Functions 177
    How It Works 177
    How to Use It 177
    The Plug-in 178
Plug-in 52: Post to Guestbook 178
    About the Plug-in 178
    Variables, Arrays, and Functions 179
    How It Works 179
    How to Use It 180
    The Plug-in 180
Plug-in 53: Get Guestbook 181
    About the Plug-in 181
    Variables, Arrays, and Functions 181
    How It Works 182
    How to Use It 182
    The Plug-in 183
Plug-in 54: Post to Chat 183
    About the Plug-in 184
    Variables, Arrays, and Functions 185
    How It Works 185
    How to Use It 186
    The Plug-in 188
Plug-in 55: View Chat 189
    About the Plug-in 190
    Variables, Arrays, and Functions 190
    How It Works 190
    How to Use It 192
    The Plug-in 193
Plug-in 56: Send Tweet 194
    About the Plug-in 194
    Variables, Arrays, and Functions 194
    How It Works 195
    How to Use It 195
    The Plug-in 196

Plug-in 57: Send Direct Tweet 196
    About the Plug-in 196
    Variables, Arrays, and Functions 197
    How It Works 197
    How to Use It 197
    The Plug-in 197
Plug-in 58: Get Tweets 198
    About the Plug-in 198
    Variables, Arrays, and Functions 199
    How It Works 199
    How to Use It 199
    The Plug-in 200
Plug-in 59: Replace Smileys 200
    About the Plug-in 201
    Variables, Arrays, and Functions 201
    How It Works 201
    How to Use It 201
    The Plug-in 202
Plug-in 60: Replace SMS Talk 203
    About the Plug-in 203
    Variables, Arrays, and Functions 204
    How It Works 204
    How to Use It 204
    The Plug-in 205

9 **MySQL, Sessions, and Cookies** **207**
Plug-in 61: Add User to DB 208
    About the Plug-in 209
    Variables, Arrays, and Functions 209
    How It Works 209
    How to Use It 211
    The Plug-in 214
Plug-in 62: Get User from DB 214
    About the Plug-in 215
    Variables, Arrays, and Functions 215
    How It Works 215
    How to Use It 215
    The Plug-in 216
Plug-in 63: Verify User in DB 216
    About the Plug-in 217
    Variables, Arrays, and Functions 217
    How It Works 217
    How to Use It 217
    The Plug-in 218
Plug-in 64: Sanitize String and MySQL Sanitize String 219
    About the Plug-ins 219
    Variables, Arrays, and Functions 219
    How They Work 219
    How to Use Them 220
    The Plug-ins 221

Plug-in 65: Create Session 221
About the Plug-in 222
Variables, Arrays, and Functions 222
How It Works 222
How to Use It 222
The Plug-in 223
Plug-in 66: Open Session 223
About the Plug-in 224
Variables, Arrays, and Functions 224
How It Works 224
How to Use It 224
The Plug-in 224
Plug-in 67: Close Session 225
About the Plug-in 225
Variables, Arrays, and Functions 225
How It Works 225
How to Use It 226
The Plug-in 226
Plug-in 68: Secure Session 226
About the Plug-in 227
Variables, Arrays, and Functions 227
How It Works 227
How to Use It 227
The Plug-in 228
Plug-in 69: Manage Cookie 228
About the Plug-in 229
Variables, Arrays, and Functions 229
How It Works 229
How to Use It 229
The Plug-in 230
Plug-in 70: Block User by Cookie 230
About the Plug-in 231
Variables, Arrays, and Functions 231
How It Works 231
How to Use It 232
The Plug-in 233

10   APIs, RSS, and XML 235
Plug-in 71: Create Google Chart 236
About the Plug-in 237
Variables, Arrays, and Functions 237
How It Works 238
How to Use It 239
The Plug-in 240
Plug-in 72: Curl Get Contents 241
About the Plug-in 241
Variables, Arrays, and Functions 242
How It Works 242
How to Use It 242
The Plug-in 242

Plug-in 73: Fetch Wiki Page 243
    About the Plug-in 244
    Variables, Arrays, and Functions 244
    How It Works 245
    How to Use It 247
    The Plug-in 247
Plug-in 74: Fetch Flickr Stream 249
    About the Plug-in 249
    Variables, Arrays, and Functions 249
    How It Works 250
    How to Use It 251
    The Plug-in 251
Plug-in 75: Get Yahoo! Answers 252
    About the Plug-in 252
    Variables, Arrays, and Functions 253
    How It Works 253
    How to Use It 254
    The Plug-in 255
Plug-in 76: Search Yahoo! 256
    About the Plug-in 256
    Variables, Arrays, and Functions 257
    How It Works 257
    How to Use It 258
    The Plug-in 259
Plug-in 77: Get Yahoo! Stock News 259
    About the Plug-in 260
    Variables, Arrays, and Functions 261
    How It Works 261
    How to Use It 262
    The Plug-in 263
Plug-in 78: Get Yahoo! News 264
    About the Plug-in 265
    Variables, Arrays, and Functions 265
    How It Works 266
    How to Use It 266
    The Plug-in 267
Plug-in 79: Search Google Books 268
    About the Plug-in 268
    Variables, Arrays, and Functions 269
    How It Works 270
    How to Use It 270
    The Plug-in 272
Plug-in 80: Convert Currency 272
    About the Plug-in 273
    Variables, Arrays, and Functions 274
    How It Works 274
    How to Use It 275
    The Plug-in 275

11   Incorporating JavaScript **277**

Plug-in 81: Ajax Request 278
   About the Plug-in 279
   Variables, Arrays, and Functions 279
   How It Works 279
   How to Use It 279
   The Plug-in 280

Plug-in 82: Post Ajax Request 280
   About the Plug-in 281
   Variables, Arrays, and Functions 281
   How It Works 281
   How to Use It 282
   The Plug-in 284

Plug-in 83: Get Ajax Request 285
   About the Plug-in 285
   Variables, Arrays, and Functions 285
   How It Works 286
   How to Use It 286
   The Plug-in 287

Plug-in 84: Protect E-mail 287
   About the Plug-in 287
   Variables, Arrays, and Functions 288
   How It Works 288
   How to Use It 289
   The Plug-in 289

Plug-in 85: Toggle Text 290
   About the Plug-in 290
   Variables, Arrays, and Functions 290
   How It Works 291
   How to Use It 291
   The Plug-in 292

Plug-in 86: Status Message 292
   About the Plug-in 293
   Variables, Arrays, and Functions 293
   How It Works 293
   How to Use It 293
   The Plug-in 294

Plug-in 87: Slide Show 295
   About the Plug-in 295
   Variables, Arrays, and Functions 295
   How It Works 296
   How to Use It 296
   The Plug-in 297

Plug-in 88: Input Prompt 299
   About the Plug-in 299
   Variables, Arrays, and Functions 300
   How It Works 300
   How to Use It 301
   The Plug-in 301

Plug-in 89: Words from Root 302
   About the Plug-in 303
   Variables, Arrays, and Functions 303
   How It Works 303
   How to Use It 303
   The Plug-in 304
Plug-in 90: Predict Word 304
   About the Plug-in 305
   Variables, Arrays, and Functions 305
   How It Works 305
   How to Use It 306
   The Plug-in 306

12   Diverse Solutions **309**
Plug-in 91: Get Country by IP 310
   About the Plug-in 310
   Variables, Arrays, and Functions 310
   How it Works 311
   How to Use It 311
   The Plug-in 312
Plug-in 92: Bypass Captcha 312
   About the Plug-in 313
   Variables, Arrays, and Functions 313
   How It Works 313
   How to Use It 313
   The Plug-in 314
Plug-in 93: Get Book from ISBN 314
   About the Plug-in 314
   Variables, Arrays, and Functions 315
   How It Works 315
   How to Use It 315
   The Plug-in 315
Plug-in 94: Get Amazon Sales Rank 316
   About the Plug-in 316
   Variables, Arrays, and Functions 317
   How It Works 317
   How to Use It 317
   The Plug-in 318
Plug-in 95: Pattern Match Word 318
   About the Plug-in 319
   Variables, Arrays, and Functions 319
   How It Works 319
   How to Use It 320
   The Plug-in 320
Plug-in 96: Suggest Spelling 320
   About the Plug-in 320
   Variables, Arrays, and Functions 321
   How It Works 321
   How to Use It 322
   The Plug-in 323

Plug-in 97: Google Translate 324
  About the Plug-in 324
  Variables, Arrays, and Functions 325
  How It Works 325
  How to Use It 325
  The Plug-in 326
Plug-in 98: Corner Gif 327
  About the Plug-in 327
  Variables, Arrays, and Functions 328
  How It Works 328
  How to Use It 328
  The Plug-in 329
Plug-in 99: Rounded Table 330
  About the Plug-in 331
  Variables, Arrays, and Functions 331
  How It Works 331
  How to Use It 331
  The Plug-in 332
Plug-in 100: Display Bing Map 332
  About the Plug-in 333
  Variables, Arrays, and Functions 333
  How It Works 333
  How to Use It 333
  The Plug-in 334

Index **335**

Acknowledgments

Thanks to everyone who worked with me on this book, particularly Wendy, Todd, Joya, Mike, Vipra, and Melinda, without whom this book simply would not be the same. In fact, the whole team at McGraw-Hill is a pleasure to work with and I thank you all for your, kindness, intelligent insights, and support.

Introduction

PHP is an open-source (and therefore free) scripting language for creating dynamic web pages. Since its creation in 1995, its popularity has grown to more than double that of the previously most used scripting language, Perl.

In fact, PHP is now in the top five most popular and most used languages according to a majority of surveys, which is hardly surprising because it is provided with most web hosting accounts, is easy to integrate into web pages, is extremely fast (given that it is interpreted), and it has built-in links to MySQL, the world's most popular open-source database program.

Because it was written by and for programmers, PHP comes with an extensive library of features and functions that may baffle a beginner. But it is possible to use just a small core subset of these to create most of the dynamic content a webmaster could need, which is precisely what this book demonstrates.

Plug-in PHP is aimed squarely at web site owners who have learned basic HTML and PHP and are interested in doing more with their sites. For example, you may wish to create member areas protected by usernames and passwords, or want to write a simple Guestbook and so on. Using *Plug-in PHP*, you will learn how to do all these things and much more using very simple ready-made PHP.

It is never assumed that you already know something, so you are taken through each subject step by step with full explanations, making sure you never have to go elsewhere to find the information you need. This book also purposefully ignores more advanced topics such as object-oriented programming. Instead, the code samples look very much like a cross between simple C and Basic. Elegant, tight structures that more advanced programmers might appreciate are set aside in preference for more understandable code, where the flow from any point to any other is as obvious as possible.

All of the plug-ins and examples are written in a complete and ready-to-use form that you can type into your own web pages. Even if you have almost no knowledge of programming, you can still make full use of the book, which can be dipped into as required since each chapter is mostly self-contained. This means that wherever you have a problem on your web site you can simply refer to the relevant chapter, which should be all you need to solve it.

To help you get up and running with these plug-ins, the first chapter walks you through how to set up your own web development server on a PC, Mac, or Linux computer, while the second shows how best to integrate the plug-ins into your own programs.

About PHP

PHP was originally developed in 1994 by Rasmus Lerdorf to replace a set of Perl scripts he had been using to maintain his personal web site. The acronym originally stood for Personal Home Page, but when he released a version to the public the following year it was recursively retitled PHP: Hypertext Processor.

Even in the early days, Lerdorf intended that PHP should be flexible and easily expandable, through rewrites of the language parser. This has remained a key ethos of the project to this day, with numerous extension libraries available through the PEAR (PHP Extension and Application Repository) add-on.

Even without these extensions, PHP comes supplied with hundreds of ready-made functions—many more than in most other programming languages—making it a very rich development platform. No doubt this is a contributing factor towards its current popularity, being installed on a third of all web servers, and behind only C++, C, and Java in usage for web development.

There are many reasons to use PHP for web development. These include its incredible speed, which is even more remarkable given that it's an interpreted language, its ease of use and interoperability with the MySQL database, and the fact that it's almost always installed on any computer running the Apache web server.

Prior to PHP, the most used scripting language was PERL, which was developed by Larry Wall in 1987. Originally intended as a general scripting language to automate report processing on Unix, it was adopted by many web developers too, and remains quite popular today. But, unlike PHP, PERL was never designed specifically for use on web sites, whereas PHP was written from the ground up with web development in mind, which may account for the fact that PHP is now more than twice as popular as PERL.

Regarding learning and using the language, PHP is reasonably similar to other well-known languages such as C, Java, and Perl, whereas ASP uses Visual Basic (although ASP.net supports other languages). What's more —ASP is built on the COM architecture, whereas PHP is not constrained this way and runs much faster.

From a performance point of view, PHP is extremely fast and can support millions of accesses a day. According to Zend Technologies (*www.zend.com*), the writers of the main engine that PHP uses, PHP often outperforms the competition. Unlike Microsoft's ASP (Active Server Pages), PHP is available on multiple platforms and, because it is free (open source software), it can be implemented at little cost other than that of the hardware it runs on.

Interestingly a quick check at Google for the searches "filetype:php" and "filetype:asp" returns 7.4 billion PHP pages and 1.8 billion ASP pages on the web. That's a ratio of over four to one in favor of PHP.

You may be surprised at some of the sites that use PHP as their backbone because you probably know many of them. Here's a list of just five top web sites that use PHP for some or all of their site's programming:

- **Yahoo!**   A popular search engine (see Figure 1)
- **Facebook**   A social networking site
- **Wikipedia**   A collaborative encyclopedia
- **Photobucket**   A photo sharing service
- **Digg**   A technology news bookmarking site

FIGURE 1   Yahoo! is possibly the best-known web company that uses PHP extensively.

Actually, Yahoo! shouldn't be too much of a surprise because Rasmus Lerdorf has worked at the company as a Distinguished Engineer since 2002.

So why is PHP so popular? There are three main reasons. First, PHP integrates seamlessly with HTML. Even if you know next to no programming, it's very easy to rename your *.html* files to *.php* and they will automatically become PHP programs, albeit ones that display themselves as an HTML page. But then, whenever you need a little dynamic functionality, you can drop in a quick line of PHP code, like the following snippet, which will display the day of the week:

```
<?php echo date("l"); ?>
```

Second, it's easy to learn. With a few simple PHP functions under your belt, almost without knowing it, you're already a PHP programmer. Add in `for` loops and a couple of other constructs and you can very quickly start making your own dynamic web sites.

Third, there's excellent support from the PHP programming community and books such as this. Just type "help PHP" into Google and you'll be presented with a staggering 125 million search results.

What This Book Provides

Having access to all of PHP's functions isn't very useful when you need to quickly put together a project to a tight deadline, because the functions typically provide very specific functionality. Even PEAR plug-ins are not always the complete solution either, since they usually take time to learn and still must be wrapped in PHP code of your own devising.

That's where this book comes into its own, because it provides 100 ready-to-go plug-ins you can simply drop into your programs and use, normally with a simple, single call. Of course, because all projects are different I only provide the bare bones needed and leave layout and styling to the absolute minimum. This leaves you free to grab a plug-in, insert it into your own program, and then tailor it to your exact requirements.

The types of plug-ins supplied offer quick and simple solutions to a very wide range of problems including processing text in a variety of ways, uploading and manipulating images, server content management, form handling, user input validation, chat and messaging, user authentication and security, integration with third-party web sites, and much more besides.

With them you can avoid having to reinvent the wheel each time you need a new feature, because the chances are that the module you need (or one very similar) can be found in this book as a plug-in. And even if it isn't, because each and every plug-in is broken down into component parts and explained in detail, you should find you can cherry-pick code segments from different plug-ins to build your own.

About the Plug-ins

All of this book's plug-ins are ready-to-run and can be either typed in if you don't have Internet access, or you can download them from *www.pluginphp.com* (see Figure 2) where they are stored as both individual plug-ins and also grouped into larger collections by theme. For example, all the authentication and security plug-ins can be found in the file security.php.

When you visit the web site, you can navigate through the plug-ins chapter by chapter, and also view the PHP program code highlighted in color for clarity. From there, you can copy, paste, or download individual plug-ins, groups, or the whole collection directly to your computer.

What Is and Isn't Included

Although the first aim of this book is to provide newcomers to PHP with a comprehensive resource of functions and routines to draw on, it has a secondary goal, which is to help you move up to the next level and to create your own programming toolkit. Therefore every plug-in is thoroughly documented and explained in detail, and advice is given on ways to improve and extend them, as well as how to adapt them to your own requirements.

To aid with this, I have attempted to stick with a basic subset of PHP functions so you can familiarize yourself with them as you work through the book. Except for cases where it is unavoidable, I have also steered clear of advanced techniques such as object-oriented programming (OOP), so most of the plug-ins work (and can be explained) in a procedural manner. Of course, OOP is powerful and, if you don't already use it, you really should learn it because you'll find your productivity rate increases substantially.

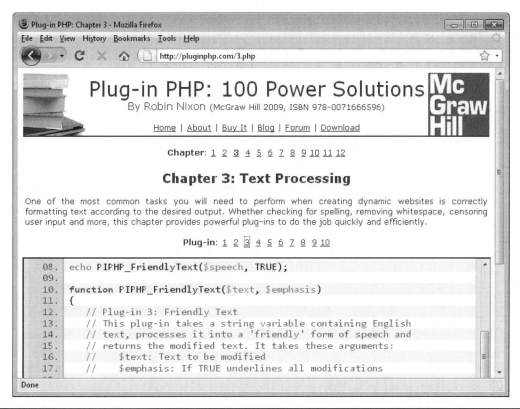

FIGURE 2   All the plug-ins from this book can be downloaded from *www.pluginphp.com*.

And while this book isn't a programming manual or a teaching guide, I do hope that by reading through the plug-in explanations, rather than just including them in your projects, you'll pick up a number of tips and tricks that many programmers take years to discover, and by osmosis you will learn more about the PHP programming language.

Plug-in License

You are free to use any of the plug-ins in this book in your own projects, and may modify them as necessary, without attributing this book—although if you do so, it will always be appreciated.

However, you may not sell, give away, or otherwise distribute the plug-ins themselves in any manner, whether printed or in electronic format, without the written permission of the publisher.

Companion Web Site

A companion web site (at *www.pluginphp.com*) accompanies this book, where all 100 plug-ins are available to download, along with example code for you to experiment with. The site also includes useful extras such as an 80,000-word dictionary and a geo-location IP data file.

The web site is best used in conjunction with this book. As you read a chapter, call it up on the web site, too, and you can list each plug-in on screen with color-highlighted syntax. This makes it very easy to see the structure of each program.

When you wish to, you can click a link to copy and paste a particular plug-in right into your own programs. Or, if you prefer, you can download all of the plug-ins to your computer from where you can pick the one(s) to upload to your own web site.

To help you with accessing them, the plug-ins are all stored in groups of ten per file, each file having a certain theme, such as image manipulation or text processing, and so on. You can then copy and paste from these files, or use a PHP `include` command to incorporate them in your own programs.

There is also a blog where you can keep up to date with the latest developments, as well as a forum where you can share your experiences and ask for assistance if you need it.

CHAPTER 1

Building a Development Server

When creating plain HTML web sites, it's easy to develop them on a personal computer because no web server is needed to serve up the pages. You simply load them into your browser and display them. The same goes for JavaScript and even Flash.

However, when it comes to PHP it's a whole different ball game because you need a number of new programs, such as the PHP parser and interpreter, and a web server to take the output from PHP and return HTML pages. Plus, if you'll be accessing any data, you'll also need a database program such as MySQL.

Until a few years ago, your only simple choice was to find a hosting company that would set you up with a server with all these options already in place. Alternatively, if you were an expert, you could install each of these items separately and configure them to work with each other, a process often fraught with many hours of tweaking and hair pulling before everything would work correctly.

Recently, however, a number of WAMP, MAMP, and LAMP packages have sprung up. Respectively, these stand for Windows/Mac/Linux, Apache, MySQL, and PHP and they provide an integrated installation environment to automatically configure the various elements to properly interact with each other. Even so, some of them still needed a bit of tweaking on less-than-standard installations.

Early 2009, though, saw the release of Zend Server CE from Zend, the company behind PHP itself. The CE stands for Community Edition, which means it's free and community supported, and it's truly a quality product. While not as powerful as the original Zend Server, which was designed for running and managing business-critical PHP applications in production, it's absolutely perfect to use as a development platform, and is available for all of the following:

- Windows XP, service pack 2
- Windows Vista (excluding Starter)
- Windows 7
- Most flavors of Linux
- Mac OS X 10.4 plus running on Intel chips

Zend Server CE comes with everything you need, including Apache and PHP (and with a little configuring, MySQL, too) and is very easy to install. However, because the process varies by platform, I have divided its installation into different sections here. So please choose the one relevant to your computer.

Windows XP, Windows Vista, and Windows 7

To install the program on a Windows machine, you need to visit the following URL and download the Windows installation file (see Figure 1-1): *www.zend.com/en/products/server/downloads-all*.

Once you have downloaded the installation file, which should be around 50MB in size, you will have an executable file in your downloads folder with a filename such as *ZendServer-CE-php-5.2.10-4.05-Windows_x86.exe*, depending on the version. To begin installation just

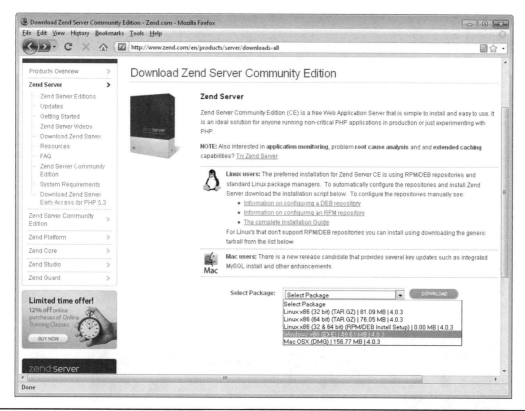

FIGURE 1-1   Downloading the Windows Zend Server CE installation program

double-click the file. If you are running Windows Vista or Windows 7, and a User Account Control box such as that displayed in Figure 1-2, click Yes to continue.

If you have already installed Zend Server CE and are now installing a newer version, another confirmation box will appear from the installer itself (see Figure 1-3). In this case, click Yes to continue.

FIGURE 1-2
If prompted by User Account Control, click Yes to confirm installation.

FIGURE 1-3
Click Yes when the
Zend installer asks
if you wish to
continue.

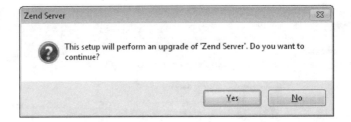

The screen in Figure 1-4 will appear. Click the Next button to continue.

After a while, the installer will have gathered enough information to continue with the installation and you will be prompted to agree to the terms of the End-User License Agreement (see Figure 1-5).

Next you are asked whether the program should perform a Typical, Full, or Custom installation (see Figure 1-6). Select Custom at this point so your setup will agree with the one described in this chapter. You can always re-install again later with different options if you need to.

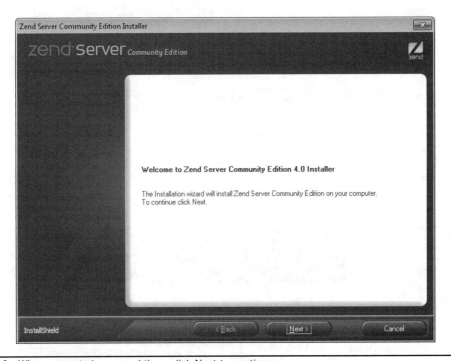

FIGURE 1-4   When prompted a second time, click Next to continue.

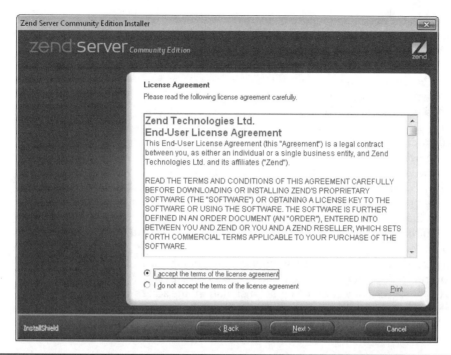

FIGURE 1-5   You must agree to the license agreement to be able to install Zend Server CE.

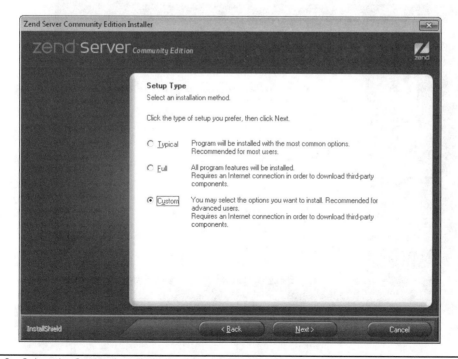

FIGURE 1-6   Select the Custom installation option and then click Next.

Having told the installer you need a custom installation, you must now set an option to ensure that MySQL gets installed as well. To do this, scroll down through the list of components (shown in Figure 1-7) until, near the end, you see MySQL Server. Click its checkbox, and then click Next.

You will be asked whether you wish to install an Apache Web Server or configure an existing IIS server (see Figure 1-8). The latter option will be disabled if IIS is not installed. I recommend you choose the Apache option anyway, at least until you have verified that the plug-ins in this book work correctly for you. You can also choose where to install the program (by default it will be *C:\Program Files\Zend*). If you choose to change this, then you will also need to remember to use the appropriate directory to access this folder when the path name is referenced later in this chapter and elsewhere in the book.

If, at the next screen, you are prompted for the web server port number, leave the default value of 80 which will be offered, and click Next. When finished with these initial settings, you'll be presented with a confirmation screen where you can review them (see Figure 1-9). If they are not correct, click the Back button and amend them; otherwise, click the Install button.

During installation, you may be shown the dialog in Figure 1-13 (see the Windows Security Alerts section). You must click Allow Access for Apache for the installation to work properly. Upon successfully completing the installation, the screen in Figure 1-10 will display. Here you can choose whether to create a Desktop shortcut before clicking Finish.

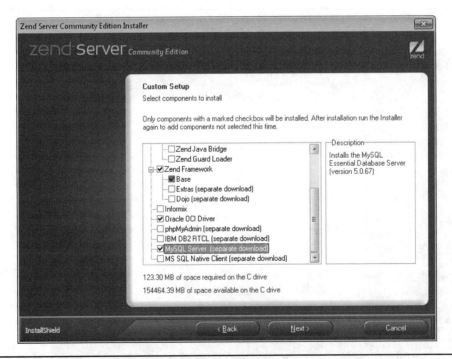

FIGURE 1-7   Select the MySQL Server checkbox before continuing.

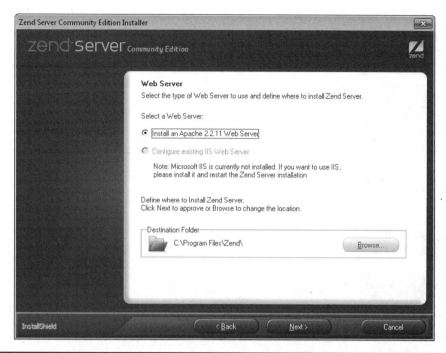

FIGURE 1-8 Here you can tell the installer to install an Apache web server and where to install the Zend server.

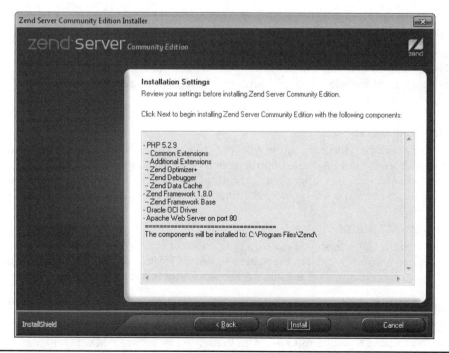

FIGURE 1-9 Review the installation settings before proceeding.

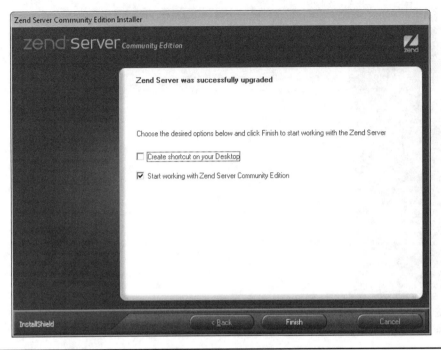

FIGURE 1-10 Upon completion, you can decide whether to create a Desktop shortcut.

Reinstalling Zend Server CE

If you have already installed Zend Server CE and are reinstalling it, either to change the installation options, or to repair a faulty install, you will be presented with the screen in Figure 1-11 (instead of the one mentioned earlier), where you can also choose to uninstall the program if you wish.

Upgrading Zend Server CE

The process of upgrading the program to a newer version is much quicker than an initial installation, comprising only a single main screen, as shown in Figure 1-12. Note the warning issued here, that once upgraded you cannot roll back to an earlier version. You will not see this screen if you are only reinstalling the same version as is already installed.

Windows Security Alerts

If, at any point during installation, you receive a Windows Security Alert, such as the one in Figure 1-13, asking whether to unblock the Apache server, click Allow Access (on Windows Vista and 7) or Unblock (on Windows XP) to grant full access to Zend Server CE and its components.

After Installation

Once Zend Server CE has been successfully installed, your web browser will open and you'll be asked to enter a password to use with the setup (see Figure 1-14). If you are

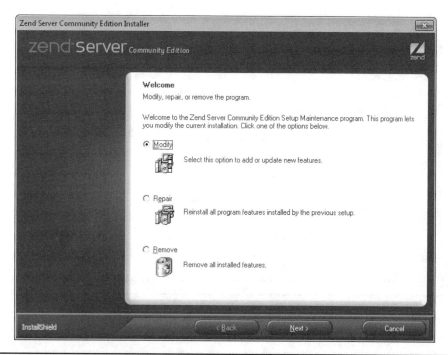

FIGURE 1-11 By rerunning the installation program, you can modify, repair, or remove Zend Server CE.

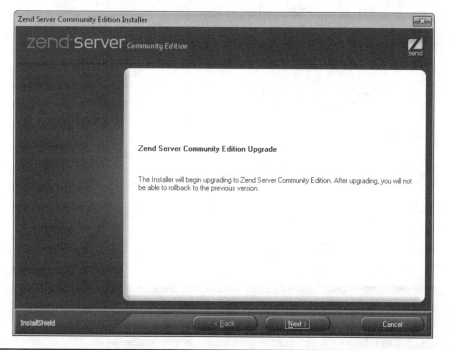

FIGURE 1-12 Upgrading Zend Server CE is even easier than installing it.

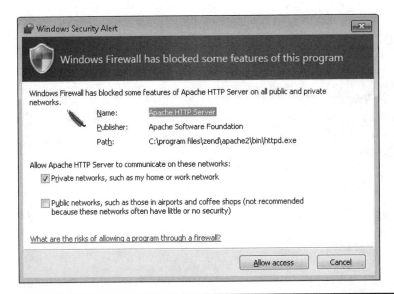

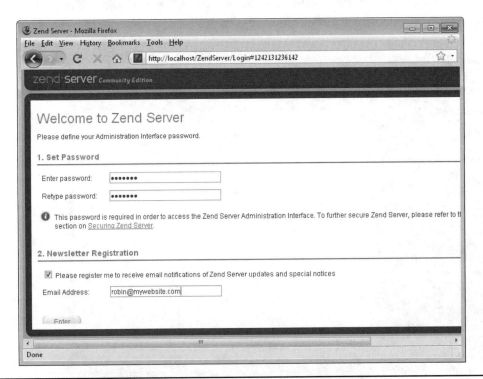

FIGURE 1-14   Before using Zend Server CE, you must choose a password for accessing it.

reinstalling or upgrading, you'll simply be asked to confirm the previous password you created. You can also enter your e-mail address if you'd like to receive the Zend newsletter.

CAUTION *If you will be forwarding HTTP requests from the Internet to your server (not recommended permanently but useful for granting a colleague temporary access to a project in progress), then it's particularly important that you choose a very secure password.*

Now you are set up and ready to go, and the screen shown in Figure 1-15 will display in your browser. From this screen you can control various aspects of your Zend Server CE installation.

You can verify that everything is working correctly by entering *http://localhost* into your web browser. The result should look like Figure 1-16.

Uninstalling

To uninstall Zend Server CE, from the Start Menu select All Programs | Zend Server Community Edition | Uninstall Zend Server.

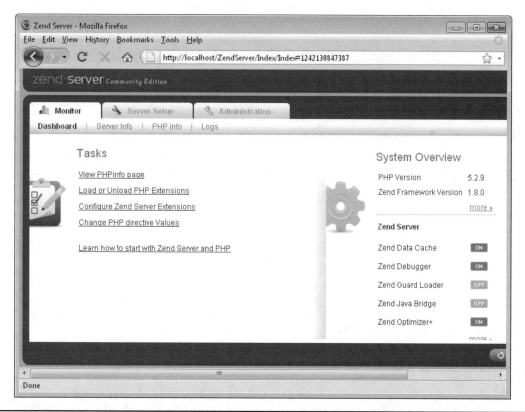

FIGURE 1-15   After installation, your browser will open up a control window for Zend Server CE.

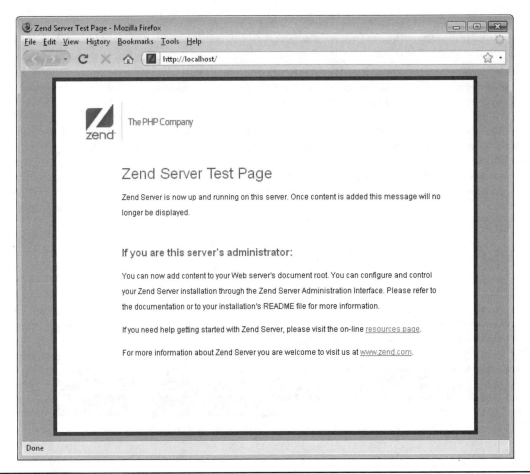

FIGURE 1-16   Everything installed correctly if you can see this page when you enter http://localhost.

Document Root

By default, your document root (the place where all your HTML and PHP files should be stored) is *c:\Program Files\Zend\Apache2\htdocs*. If you find that you cannot edit or save files into it, you will need to modify the folder's permission settings. You may find it convenient to create a shortcut to this folder by navigating to it, right clicking (and holding) on the *htdocs* folder, and dragging it to the Desktop. Once you release the mouse button, you can then select Create Shortcuts Here.

Ubuntu and Debian Linux

On Ubuntu or Debian Linux, you will need to install the MySQL program separately if you don't have it already. It's very easy to do because it uses Aptitude, a front end to the Advanced Packaging Tool (APT) system.

Just open up the Terminal by selecting Applications | Accessories | Terminal and
entering the following two commands, the first of which ensures you are running as root,
while the second installs the server. If you are prompted for your password, enter it. At the
end of the installation, you may be prompted to enter a root password as in Figure 1-17,
which, like all the following Linux screen grabs, is from Ubuntu Linux.

```
sudo -i
apt-get install mysql-server
```

You are now ready to install Zend Server CE itself. The process takes a few commands
to set up because you must follow several steps. First, staying in the Terminal window, you
need to change to the */etc/apt* folder and then edit the file *sources.list* by typing the following
(assuming you are still logged in as root after installing MySQL):

```
cd /etc/apt
nano sources.list
```

TIP *If you are using Debian Linux rather than Ubuntu, and Nano is not your default text editor,
you should alter the second line of the preceding code according to the editor you use. Or you can
install Nano first by entering the command:* `apt-get install nano`.

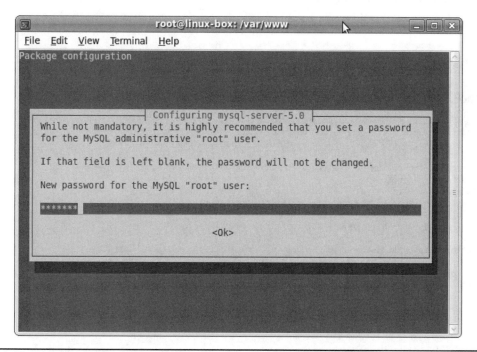

FIGURE 1-17   It's recommended you enter a password for the MySQL root user.

Once the file is open, scroll down and add the following line to the end of the file so it looks like Figure 1-18. When done, press CTRL-X, followed by Y and then press RETURN to save the modified file:

```
deb http://repos.zend.com/zend-server/deb server non-free
```

Now you must fetch Zend's repository public key so the installation file can be verified once downloaded and, having set up these various items, you should also update Aptitude. So, enter the following two commands, noting that the option in the middle, which looks like -O-, is an uppercase letter O sandwiched between two minus signs, or dashes:

```
wget http://repos.zend.com/deb/zend.key -O- |apt-key add -
aptitude update
```

Finally, you are ready to install Zend Server CE itself with the following command (see Figure 1-19):

```
aptitude install zend-server-ce-php-5.2
```

Uninstalling

Should you encounter any problems, or decide for any other reason to uninstall the program, you can issue the following command:

```
aptitude remove '~nzend.*-ce'
```

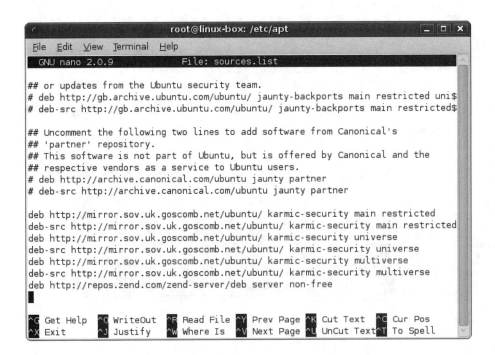

FIGURE 1-18   Using Nano to add a new line to *sources.list*

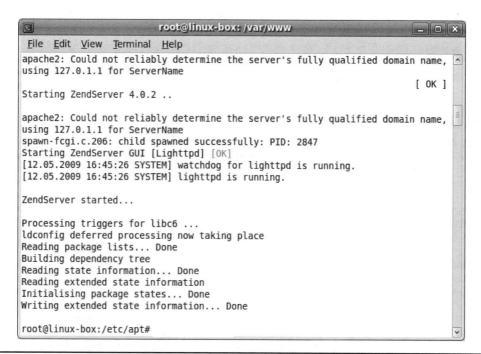

FIGURE 1-19   The installation of Zend Server CE is successful.

After Installation

The last thing you need to do in order to verify whether Zend Server CE has actually installed correctly is to test out the web server by entering the URL *http://localhost* into your browser. If everything is correct, you should get a terse message similar to the one in Figure 1-20. You can now enter the Admin interface by entering *http://localhost:10081* into your browser.

FIGURE 1-20   Enter *http://localhost* into your browser to ensure that the web server is running.

Document Root

By default, the document root—the place where all your HTML and PHP files should be saved to make them visible to a web browser—is */var/www*. If you find that you cannot edit or save files into it, you will need to modify the folder's permission settings.

Fedora, RHEL, and CentOS Linux

To install Zend Server CE on one of these versions of Linux, the first thing you must do is set up the repository for downloading the package by entering the following lines into your favorite text editor, and then save it using the path and filename */etc/yum.repos.d/zend.repo*:

```
[Zend]
name=Zend Server CE
baseurl=http://repos.zend.com/zend-server/rpm/$basearch
enabled=1
gpgcheck=0
[Zend_noarch]
name=Zend Server CE - noarch
baseurl=http://repos.zend.com/zend-server/rpm/noarch
enabled=1
gpgcheck=0
```

Now you can use Yum, or any other tool that supports the RPM packaging format, to handle installations. So, to install the program, run the command:

```
yum install zend-server-ce-php-5.2
```

Finally, to clean your package's cache and ensure the retrieval of updates from the Web, run this command:

```
yum clean all
```

Installing MySQL

To ensure you also have access to MySQL on the server, use Yum to install both the MySQL command-line tool and the server. You also need to enable and start the MySQL server and set the root password. To do all this, enter the following commands, replacing 'mypassword' with a password of your choice, and making sure you keep the quotation marks, or it won't work:

```
yum -y install mysql mysql-server
/sbin/chkconfig mysqld on
/sbin/service mysqld start
mysqladmin -u root password 'mypassword'
```

Uninstalling

Should you encounter any problems or decide for any other reason to uninstall Zend Server CE, you can issue the following commands:

```
zendctl.sh stop
yum -y remove zend-server-ce-php-5.2 && yum -y remove 'rpm -qa|grep
zend|xargs'
```

Document Root

Your document root (the place to store all HTML and PHP files to make them visible to a web browser) is *var/www/html*. You can verify that the install was successful by visiting *http://localhost* in your web browser and checking for a Zend success message page.

Other Versions of Linux

For all other versions of Linux, such as SUSE, you will need to download, extract, and install the installation tarball. Visit the following URL in your browser and download either the 32-bit or the 64-bit tarball for your setup:

www.zend.com/en/products/server/downloads-all

Once downloaded, you should have a file of about 65MB with a name similar to *ZendServer-CE-php-5.2.10-4.0.5-linux-glibc23-i386.tar.gz*, depending on the version downloaded. So, first you need to make sure you have root privileges and type:

```
tar -xzvf ZendServer-CE-php-5.2.10-4.0.5-linux-glibc23-i386.tar.gz
```

This will create a new folder in which the extracted files are stored. Change to that directory and start the installation by typing the following two lines:

```
cd ZendServer-CE-php-5.2.10-4.0.5-linux-glibc23-i386
./install.sh
```

When prompted, accept the default of */usr/local* for the installation path.

Installing MySQL

If you also need to install MySQL from a tarball, be aware that the installation has several parts to it, including unpacking and moving files, creating users and groups, configuring, initialization, permissions, and more. Therefore, it is beyond the scope of this book and I would instead refer you to an excellent online guide at *www.devside.net/guides/linux/mysql*.

Uninstalling

Should you encounter any problems, or decide for any other reason to uninstall the program, you can issue the following commands:

```
/usr/local/zend/bin/zendctl.sh stop
rm -rf /usr/local/zend
```

Document Root

Your document root (the place to store all HTML and PHP files to make them visible to a web browser) is */usr/local/zend/Apache2/htdocs*. If you find you cannot edit or save files into it, you will need to modify the folder's permission settings. You can verify that the install was successful by visiting *http://localhost* in your web browser and checking for a Zend success message page.

Mac OS X 10.4 Plus on Intel Chips

To install Zend Server CE on a Mac powered by an Intel processor, visit the Zend web site at the following URL:

www.zend.com/en/products/server/downloads-all

Then select the Mac OS X DMG file for downloading (see Figure 1-21).

The file you download will be about 140MB in size and will have a filename similar to *ZendServer-CE-php-5.2.10-4.0.5-darwin8.6-i386.dmg*, depending on the version. Once it has finished downloading, double-click the file to mount the disk image and you'll see the *ZendServer.pkg* icon, which you should also double-click to start the installation (see Figure 1-22).

At this point, you will be told a few things (which you should read) and asked a number of simple questions about the installation. Once you've responded to them, all you'll be prompted for is your password (see Figure 1-23). Enter it and the installation will commence.

FIGURE 1-21   Download the Zend Server disk image directly from the web site.

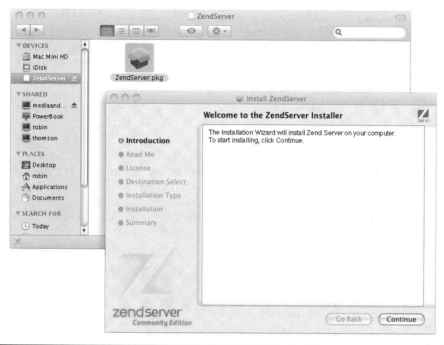

FIGURE 1-22   Double-click *ZendServer.pkg* to commence the package installation.

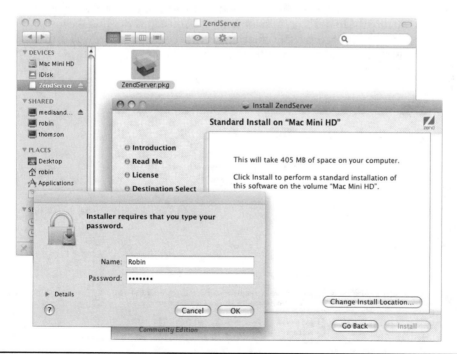

FIGURE 1-23   After a series of prompts, questions, and answers, enter your password to begin installation.

By default, Zend Server CE Apache runs on port 10088 and is available at *http://localhost:10088/* in order to avoid collisions with any existing web server. To save having to append port numbers to your localhost URLs, I recommend you change this if you can. To do this, you need to call up the Terminal utility and enter the following three commands:

```
sudo -i
cd /usr/local/zend/apache2/conf
nano httpd.conf
```

If you are asked for your password by the sudo command, enter it. When the *httpd.conf* file has loaded into the text editor, use the cursor keys to scroll down about 40 lines or so until you get to the one that reads Listen 10088. Replace the 10088 with 80. Afterward, press CTRL-X, followed by Y, and then press RETURN to save the modified file (see Figure 1-24).

Bear in mind that if you do this, you must also uninstall or otherwise disable any version of Apache you already have on your Mac. At the very least, turn it off by typing:

```
apachectl stop
```

Having done that, you will then need to restart the Zend Apache server by entering the following command:

```
/usr/local/zend/apache2/bin/apachectl restart
```

Document Root

Your document root (the place to store all HTML and PHP files to make them visible to a web browser) is */usr/local/zend/Apache2/htdocs*. If you find you cannot edit or save files into it, you will need to modify the folder's permission settings. You can verify that the installation works correctly and the port used is 80 by entering *http://localhost* into your web browser. If all worked well, you'll see the Zend Server Test Page.

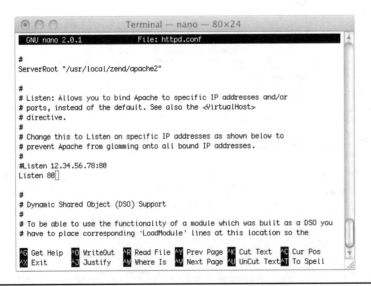

FIGURE 1-24   To restore its default port, change Apache to listen on port 80.

Should you need to access it, the Zend Administration Interface is accessible at *http://localhost:10081*, or you can always run */Applications/ZendServer*. The first time you use it you'll be asked to create a password and choose whether to opt into receiving the newsletter.

Uninstalling

Should you encounter any problems, or decide for any other reason to uninstall the program, issue the following commands to totally remove it, along with any files you've modified or added to the installation:

```
/usr/local/zend/bin/zendctl.sh stop
rm -rf /usr/local/zend
```

Mac OS X 10.3

Older Macs will generally use the Power PC processor and are therefore incompatible with Zend Server CE. Also, even if you have an Intel Mac, it still won't work with Zend Server CE unless it is running version 10.4 or higher of OS X. An alternative setup is also available, called MAMP, which will do the job for you, as long as you are running OS X 10.3. To install it, enter *http://mamp.info/en/downloads/* into your web browser and, on the right-hand side of the screen, select either the Intel or the PowerPC installer. If you are in doubt as to which processor your Mac uses, choose the Universal Binary (see Figure 1-25).

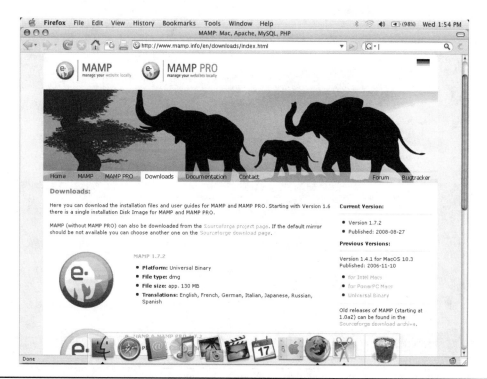

FIGURE 1-25 Downloading the MAMP installer

If you have difficulties accessing the *mamp.info* web site, you may wish to download the installer from the Source Forge web site at http://sourceforge.net/project/showfiles. php?group_id=121134. The latest version (currently 1.7.2) will show by default, but just click the link entitled "mamp" under the "Package" heading to see all previous ones. Next click the 1.4 link to open up the i386, PPC, and Universal installers for version 1.4.1.

Once the approximately 110MB download is complete, unarchive the new zip file using Stuffit Expander (or a similar utility) to create a disk image with the file extension *.dmg*. Double-click the extracted disk image to mount it, and a window will open up in which you must drag and drop the large MAMP icon into the Applications folder alias (see Figure 1-26).

You can now double-click the MAMP program within the *Applications/MAMP* folder to start the servers. Unless you configure your Mac to do this on each startup, you'll have to run the MAMP each time you intend to use it. Once it starts, wait a moment and the green lights should appear for both the Apache and MySQL servers (see Figure 1-27).

Unfortunately, by default, MAMP doesn't use standard ports, so you must perform a final configuration task before the system is ready to use. To do this, click the Preferences button in the MAMP window, followed by the Ports tab, and then change the Apache port from 8888 to 80, and the MySQL port from 8889 to 3306. To do this, click Set To Default Apache And MySQL Ports, and then click OK (see Figure 1-28). The two servers will then automatically restart and you may be asked for your password. Once you've done this, these preferences will stay in place until you change them.

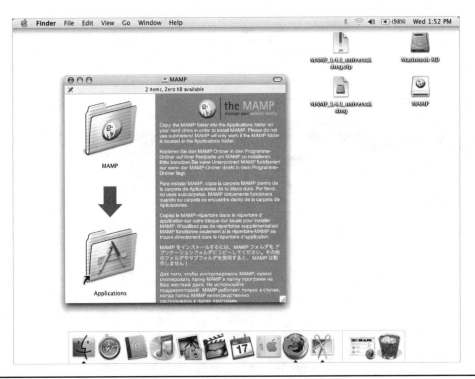

FIGURE 1-26   Drag and drop the MAMP icon into the Applications folder alias.

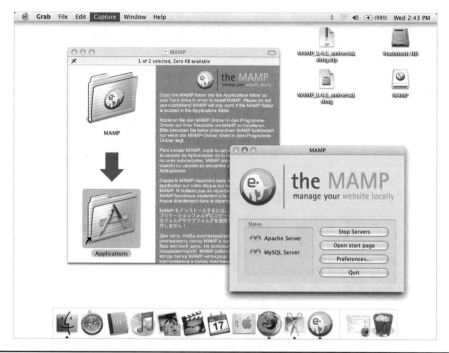

FIGURE 1-27   After running MAMP, both the MySQL and Apache green lights should appear.

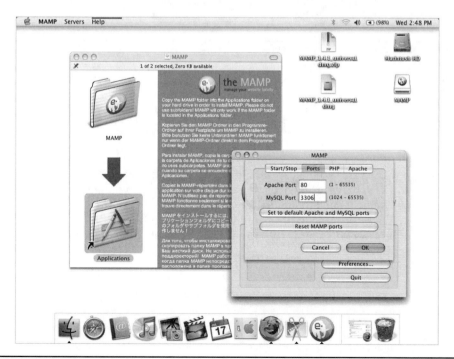

FIGURE 1-28   You must configure MAMP to use the correct Apache and MySQL ports.

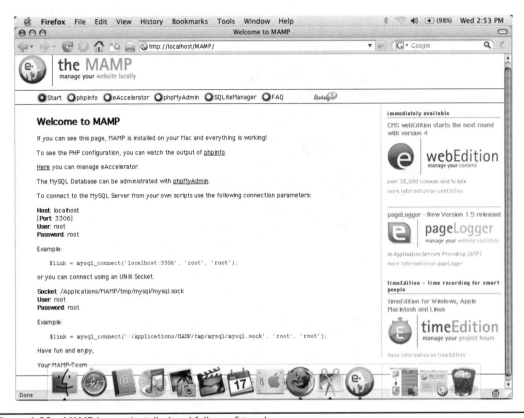

FIGURE 1-29   MAMP is now installed and fully configured.

Everything should now be fully installed, which you can verify by entering *http://localhost/MAMP* into a web browser to call up the main configuration page (see Figure 1-29).

Document Root

The document root (the place where you should store your PHP and HTML files to make them accessible to a web browser) is */Applications/MAMP/htdocs/*. If you find you cannot edit or save files into it, you will need to modify the folder's permission settings. By default, there may not be an *index.html* file in it, so until you put something there, typing *http://localhost* into your browser will simply call up a blank "Index of" directory listing, followed by the server description.

Configuring Error Handling in Zend Server CE

Before you move onto the plug-ins, to ensure that PHP will report all errors in Zend Server CE, you need to perform a final configuration step by going to one of *http://localhost/ZendServer* on Windows, *http://localhost/MAMP* on a Mac, or *http://localhost:10081* on Linux and entering your password, then selecting Server Setup | Directives | Error Handling and Logging and clicking the On check box for *display_errors*.

And Now You're Set to Go

If you have successfully configured either Zend Server CE or MAMP, you're now ready to start incorporating the plug-ins from this book into PHP programs running on your web development server. Using the advice given in the following chapter, you'll learn how you can type them in, copy and paste them, download them from the web site at *http://pluginphp.com*, or simply include them with a PHP statement.

CHAPTER 2

Using the Plug-ins

How you choose to include the plug-ins in your own programs is entirely up to you, but two main techniques can be used. The first of these is to simply copy a plug-in from the companion web site for this book and paste it directly into your program. This is a method that is simple and easy to use when working on small projects because your program and the plug-ins it uses are all there in a single file, ready to edit as necessary.

But once you start to write larger projects (and more of them), you'll begin to find it wasteful to keep copying the plug-ins to each new program file. What's more, whenever you tweak a plug-in, if you want the latest version, you'll need to find the program that contains it and copy it from there. Worse than that, every time you come up with another improvement you'll need to edit every instance of it across your code if you want all your projects to benefit from it.

Obviously this is no way to run a railroad, so I recommend that from the start, if you aren't already, you get used to saving all your plug-ins into one or more separate program files that can be included into your code with simple directives. This means you'll only ever have a single instance of each plug-in to update, which will then be reflected in all projects that include it.

PHP supplies two main methods for including files: `include` and `require`.

Using include

As you would expect, the `include` command takes a filename as a parameter and includes it, like this:

```
include "myfunctions.php";
```

This tells the PHP interpreter to fetch the specified file and loads its contents in as if it had been typed into the current program file. In the preceding example, *myfunctions.php* must reside in the current folder. If you keep your include files elsewhere, you need to provide either a relative or the full path to the file like this:

```
include "/usr/local/apache/htdocs/includes/myfunctions.php";
```

That was a Unix/Linux/Mac path. In Windows, an include statement might look like this:

```
include "c:\phpfunctions\myfunctions.php"
```

This creates a slight problem though, because every time PHP encounters this particular `include` statement it will load the file in again. This takes up more memory than is necessary and is slow and inefficient. What's more, any functions already defined will be redefined, which is not allowed, and will generate an error message. To overcome this difficulty, you can use the `include_once` command instead, described in the following section.

include_once

When you use `include_once`, each time PHP is asked to include a file it will check whether the file has already been loaded into memory and, if so, it will ignore the request. For this reason, I recommend you use `include_once` instead of `include`.

But this still isn't always the best solution, because `include` and `include_once` don't care whether the file requested actually exists. If it doesn't, the commands simply get ignored and a warning error message is displayed, while the program execution continues. Now this is fine if the file to be included contains non-essential code that is not absolutely necessary for your program to run, or if you always include a file of ready-made functions just to be sure they are available but you aren't currently calling any of them. As soon as you do need access to one of these functions, if the include file hasn't been loaded into memory, you'll be presented with unsightly error messages that may only crop up on specific events relating to the current state of program flow, such as when an infrequently used function gets called up.

The solution to this is the `require` command, discussed next.

Using require

When you use the `require` command instead of `include`, PHP will return an error and halt program execution if it cannot locate the requested file. This is usually preferable to using either `include` or `include_once`, because every time the program runs you will get a fatal error if the file cannot be found, rather than only in cases where a function in the include file is accessed. This enables you to correct the problem (probably a mistyped filename or incorrect path) before you release your project to the general public.

But, as they say, that's not the whole story. Just like with `include`, each time PHP encounters a `require` command it will reload the requested file into memory. This, as previously discussed, is not a good idea. So the final (and in my opinion best) solution is to use the `require_once` command, explored next.

require_once

Like its counterpart, `include_once`, `require_once` will only ever load in a single copy of a file, no matter how often that file is requested. But, unlike `include`, it will also generate an error if it can't find the file requested.

So there you have it, `require_once` provides the best of both worlds and is the ideal way to include files in your PHP programs. It is therefore the recommended method used throughout this book.

Include Scope

When you include a file, it is inserted exactly at the point of the `include` or `require` statement (or the `include_once` or `require_once` statement). This is intentional, so you can choose the *scope* of the included code.

To understand this, let's take a look at what is meant by scope. For example, in the following code snippet, the variable `$fred` has global scope because it is declared outside of any functions. This means that all parts of the program, whether inside or outside of functions, have access to this variable and can read and change its value. This includes functions, as long as a function is told to treat the variable as global using the `global` keyword:

```php
<?php // Example 1: Illustrating scope
$fred = "X";
test();
echo "Test 2: [fred: $fred] [jane: $jane]<br />";
```

FIGURE 2-1
The variable $jane
only has local
scope and cannot
be referenced
outside the
function test().

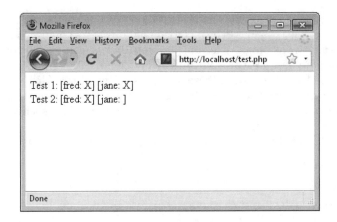

FIGURE 2-1
The variable $jane only has local scope and cannot be referenced outside the function test().

```
function test()
{
    $jane = "X";
    global $fred; // Allow access to global variable
    echo "Test 1: [fred: $fred] [jane: $jane]<br />";
}
?>
```

While $fred has global scope, the variable $jane only has local scope because it is declared within the function test(), and only that function can read or change its value. The output from this code can be seen in Figure 2-1.

As you would expect, Test 1, an echo statement within the function test(), shows that from inside that function both the variables $jane and $fred can have their values read—indicated by the letter X that was assigned to them. But from outside the function, Test 2 is unable to retrieve the value assigned to $jane, and so no X is displayed.

In just the same way, if you include another PHP file outside of any functions (usually right at the start of a file), its variables and functions will be accessible from anywhere in that file. But if you choose to include it from within a function, then only that function can access the file's contents. This latter case is a very special one and you are unlikely to use it yourself or encounter it often in other people's code.

So another rule to adopt when including the plug-ins from this book is to remember to include them right at the start of a file (so you can tell at a glance whether the include has been made) and not from inside any functions.

Correctly Inserting PHP code

When a file is included, PHP interpretation stops at the start of the included file and recommences at its end. This means that, by default, all included files will be treated as plain HTML, unless you ensure they have surrounding <?php ... ?> tags, the same way your main program does. If you leave these tags out of an included PHP program, then a bunch of garbled program code will be displayed in the browser. Not only is this messy, but anyone can view this code and see how your program works (or at least is supposed to work).

On the other hand, there are times when you don't want to only include PHP program code. For example, sometimes you may have a fixed set of HTML tags and/or text that you use in various places on a web site. In which case, it's a simple matter to write them once, save them in a file, and just include them as and when needed.

Inserting HTML

Let's take the case of a very simple HTML file called *file.html*, with the following contents:

```
<h1>This is a headline</h1>
<p>This is some body text</p>
```

This is not a complete HTML file with document headings and so on. Rather, it's a snippet containing just a couple of tags of HTML to include, which can be done by altering Example 1, adding a require statement as follows:

```
<?php // Example 2: Including an HTML file
$fred = "X";
test();

require "file.html";

echo "Test 2: [fred: $fred] [jane: $jane]<br />";

function test()
{
    $jane = "X";
    global $fred;
    echo "Test 1: [fred: $fred] [jane: $jane]<br />";
}
?>
```

The output from running this code can be seen in Figure 2-2. Now you may be wondering what a require statement was doing in this code when I strongly advised to only use require_once for including PHP files. Well, the reason is because PHP code is not being included here. Rather, some HTML tags and text are being inserted into the program at the current position, and it's possible that we may wish to include it more than once. If require_once had been used, then it could only be inserted a single time.

FIGURE 2-2
Inserting an HTML file into a program

In addition to immediately including an HTML file within your program, you can also assign its contents to a variable, as in the following statement which loads the contents of *file.html* into the string variable $html (something you might need to do prior to modifying and/or displaying the HTML):

```
$html = require "file.html";
```

Another use for including HTML this way could be for pulling in advertisements at the right locations. When you do this, it means you can change advertisements as frequently as you like by simply editing the included file and not touching your program code; this technique is especially useful for advertising programs such as Google AdSense.

Including PHP Files from Other Servers

You can also include a PHP file from another server, as long as that server is configured to return the PHP file itself—and not execute it and return the result of doing so. To do this, enter the full URL to the file like this:

```
require "http://otherserver.com/functions.php";
```

However, you must be aware that if you can include such a program file over the Web, then so can anyone else, meaning they can also view its contents, which creates a potential security risk. It's much better to make sure you store all PHP files you will be needing on your own server. It also means that if the other site is ever down, your program will not be affected.

CAUTION *Even if you are certain that there is no current risk with a remote PHP file, you should be aware that such a file is at the control of the remote server's administrator and, if that's not you, then it could be changed or compromised at any time without your say so.*

Now that you have a means to easily include the plug-ins in this book within your programs, you're all set to go. The remaining chapters explain how they work (so you can modify them as necessary), and how to use them, and provides plenty of examples. A handy breakdown of all variables, arrays, and functions used by each is also included.

CHAPTER 3

Text Processing

A lthough many web sites have video and other multimedia capabilities, the most fundamental part of almost all web sites remains the information contained within its text. This first batch of plug-ins concentrates on providing a range of functions to facilitate manipulating and presenting text in the most suitable way.

Whether you wish to control word wrapping, use of upper- and lowercase, spelling and grammar, text length, unwanted words and characters, or other textual features, there's a plug-in here that will do the job. Some of these plug-ins are so useful they are themselves used by other plug-ins in this book.

PLUG-IN 1 Wrap Text

You can make text wrap in a browser in various ways, including using tables, iframes, and textareas, but sometimes you need absolute control over the wrapping in terms of the number of characters at which the wrap should occur, regardless of whether the user resizes their browser window.

Using this plug-in, it's easy to pass a string of text and have it wrapped using <br /> tags. What's more it can also indent the start of each new paragraph by an amount of your choosing. Figure 3-1 shows the opening paragraphs of Charles Dickens' *Oliver Twist*, with a wrap width of 71 characters and a paragraph indent setting of 5 characters.

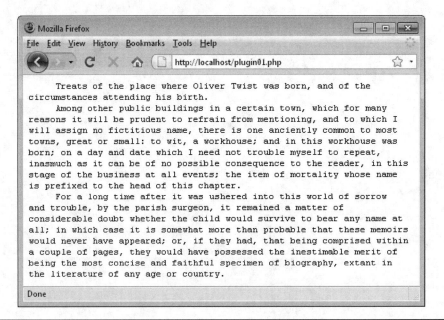

FIGURE 3-1   Setting text to wrap at a fixed width is a breeze with the Wrap Text plug-in.

About the Plug-in

This plug-in takes a string variable containing any text and adds `<br />` and ` ` tags in the right places to make the text wrap and indent paragraphs. It takes these arguments:

- **$text**   A string variable containing the text to be wrapped
- **$width**   An integer representing the character at which to force word wrapping
- **$indent**   An integer representing the number of characters by which to indent each paragraph start

Variables, Arrays, and Functions

$wrapped	String variable containing the wrapped text to be returned
$paragraphs	Array containing the separate paragraphs as determined by \n characters
$paragraph	String containing an individual paragraph being processed
$words	Array of all words in a paragraph
$word	String containing the current word being processed
$len	Numeric variable containing the length of the current line
$wlen	Numeric variable containing the length of the next word to be processed

How It Works

The plug-in works by first splitting the text passed to it into separate paragraphs using the PHP `explode()` function with an argument of \n, which is the newline character. What this function does is return an array of substrings based on splitting the original string each time a \n is encountered. The function returns these paragraphs in the array $paragraphs.

A `foreach` loop is then entered passing $paragraphs as the input, and then each iteration of the loop places one paragraph at a time into the string variable $paragraph.

NOTE   *Notice the singular form of the variable name $paragraph, with no "s" on the end. This is a convention I use throughout this book—the plural form of a name being for an array, and the singular form of the same name used for an element extracted from that array.*

Next a check is made to see whether paragraphs must be indented. If so, $indent will have a value greater than zero and so the `str_repeat()` function is used to add $indent number of non-blank spaces to the string $wrapped, which contains the wrapped text to be returned.

Now it's time to extract all the words in the current paragraph by using the `explode()` function again, but this time splitting the text up at each space. The resulting list of words is placed in the array $words. Then, before proceeding into processing the words, the variable $len, which monitors the length of the current line, is set to whatever value $indent has, so that the length of the first line is correctly initialized.

Another `foreach` loop is now used to iterate through the words, assigning each element in the array $words in turn to the string variable $word. Then, the first action taken in the loop is to make a note of the length of the word in the variable $wlen.

Next an `if ... else` pair of tests checks whether, if added together, the current line length, `$len`, plus the current word length, `$wlen`, would be less than the required width, `$width`. If so, then the word is appended to `$wrapped`, followed by a space, and then `$len` is updated accordingly.

If adding the word to the current line would have made it too long, then the `else` part of the test is executed. Here any space character previously added to `$wrapped` is now unnecessary and is removed by a quick call to `rtrim()`, which removes whitespace from a string's tail. Then, a `<br />` tag followed by a newline character (to help make viewing the page source clearer) and a space are appended to `$wrapped`, followed by `$word` (which is now on a new line). The `<br />` is used because a `\n` does not add a line break to HTML output. The value of `$len` is then updated to reflect this.

Once the inner loop has completed executing, `rtrim()` is again called to remove any extra space added. But it isn't needed now, so a `<br />` tag and newline are appended to `$wrapped` to signify reaching the end of a paragraph.

Once the outer loop has also completed, the text has been fully processed and so the value in `$wrapped` is returned to the calling code.

How to Use It

To transform unwrapped text into wrapped, call the function like this:

```
echo PIPHP_WrapText($message, 80, 5);
```

Here `$message` is the text to be wrapped, `80` is the character at which to force the wrapping, and `5` is the number of characters by which to indent the start of each paragraph. If you don't want indenting, just set the third parameter to zero.

The Plug-in

```php
function PIPHP_WrapText($text, $width, $indent)
{
    $wrapped    = "";
    $paragraphs = explode("\n", $text);

    foreach($paragraphs as $paragraph)
    {
        if ($indent > 0) $wrapped .= str_repeat(" ", $indent);

        $words = explode(" ", $paragraph);
        $len   = $indent;

        foreach($words as $word)
        {
            $wlen = strlen($word);

            if (($len + $wlen) < $width)
            {
                $wrapped .= "$word ";
                $len     += $wlen + 1;
            }
            else
```

```
        {
            $wrapped = rtrim($wrapped);
            $wrapped .= "<br />\n$word ";
            $len     = $wlen;
        }
    }

    $wrapped = rtrim($wrapped);
    $wrapped .= "<br />\n";
}

    return $wrapped;
}
```

Caps Control

PLUG-IN 2

When dealing with user input, you will often come across people who keep their Caps Lock key permanently enabled, which can make reading what they write difficult on the eye. It also looks like they are shouting. To diminish or entirely remove this problem, use this plug-in, which also supports three other upper- and lowercase text transformations. Figure 3-2 shows these four transformations applied to a poem by Lewis Carroll.

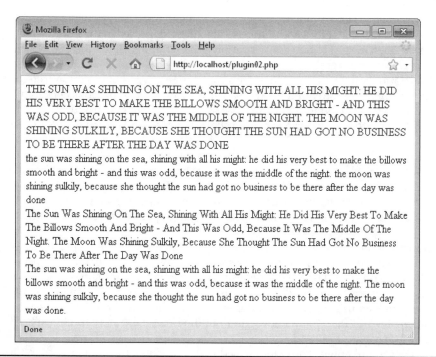

FIGURE 3-2   Converting all caps or other nonstandard text to a more readable form using the Caps Control plug-in

About the Plug-in

This plug-in takes a string variable containing any text and transforms its case according to the second parameter. It takes these arguments:

- **$text**   A string variable containing the text to be transformed
- **$type**   A string containing the type of transformation to make:
  "u" –Capitalize all letters
  "l" –Set all letters to lowercase
  "w"–Capitalize the first letter of every word
  "s" –Capitalize the first letter of every sentence

Variables, Arrays, and Functions

$newtext	String variable containing transformed text
$words	Array of all words in the text
$word	String containing the current word being processed
$sentences	Array of all sentences in the text
$sentence	String containing the current sentence being processed

How It Works

This plug-in is based around a four-way switch statement, the first two elements of which are extremely simple in that if the style of transform requested (passed in the $type variable) is either "u" or "l", then the text to transform is simply passed through either the strtoupper() or strtolower() functions and then returned.

If the transformation type is "w", then the string variable $newtext is initialized to the empty string; it will be used to build the transformed string to be returned. Then, all the words in the text are extracted into the array $words using the function explode(), which is set to split $text into smaller strings at each space character and return the result in an array.

Next a foreach loop iterates through all the elements in $words, placing them one at a time in the string variable $word, from where they are first converted to lowercase using strtolower(), and then the first letter of the word is converted to uppercase using the ucfirst() function. After this, a space is added back to the end of each word. Once $newtext has been constructed, any extra space that was appended is removed using the rtrim() function and the string is returned.

If the transformation type is "s", then $newtext is initialized to the empty string and all the sentences are extracted into the array $sentences using the explode() function. From here they are processed one at a time, using a foreach loop, into the string variable $sentence, which is then converted to lowercase using strtolower(). Any preceding whitespace is removed using ltrim(), and then the first character of the sentence is set to uppercase using the ucfirst() function. After building $newtext, any trailing space is removed and the string is returned.

In the case of an unknown type being passed to this function, the final line will return the original string unchanged.

How to Use It

You use the plug-in by calling it up in one of the four following ways:

```
echo PIPHP_CapsControl($text, "u");
echo PIPHP_CapsControl($text, "l");
echo PIPHP_CapsControl($text, "w");
echo PIPHP_CapsControl($text, "s");
```

The $text argument should contain the string to transform, while the second argument should be one of the four letters shown (in lowercase).

The Plug-in

```
function PIPHP_CapsControl($text, $type)
{
    switch($type)
    {
        case "u": return strtoupper($text);

        case "l": return strtolower($text);

        case "w":
            $newtext = "";
            $words   = explode(" ", $text);
            foreach($words as $word)
                $newtext .= ucfirst(strtolower($word)) . " ";
            return rtrim($newtext);

        case "s":
            $newtext   = "";
            $sentences = explode(".", $text);
            foreach($sentences as $sentence)
                $newtext .= ucfirst(ltrim(strtolower($sentence))) . ". ";
            return rtrim($newtext);
    }

    return $text;
}
```

PLUG-IN 3

Friendly Text

Sometimes when you have text to post on a web site, it can be quite dry and unexciting. Although there's not much you can do about that (apart from completely rewriting it), at least you can make it read better by converting it into as friendly a form as possible. This is achieved by using contractions. For example, replacing *you have* with *you've* or *it is* with *it's* is easier to read and more like the way we speak in everyday life, and this code takes that concept to the extreme.

Figure 3-3 shows an excerpt from one of Winston Churchill's speeches, which now flows a lot better, although I admit, the original has a certain punchiness and power that's lost in

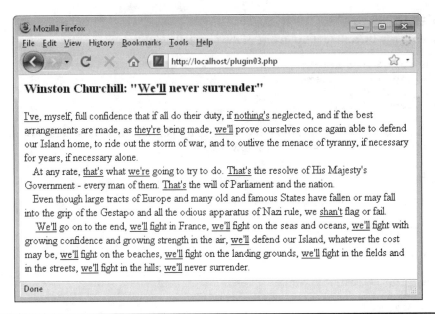

FIGURE 3-3   The Friendly Text plug-in is used to convert a famous speech with the underline option enabled for testing.

the conversion. Still, it shows you can leave this plug-in running on your server and it will almost always produce proper readable English.

This is also a good example of why plug-ins are so useful, because you probably could write this code quite easily yourself, but actually sitting down and working out all the various parts of the rules of the English language (and all its exceptions) is quite time-consuming. Thankfully, though, I've done all that work for you.

About the Plug-in

This plug-in takes a string variable containing English text, processes it into a "friendly" form of speech, and returns the modified text. It takes these arguments:

- **$text**   A string variable containing the text to be modified
- **$emphasis**   A Boolean value which, if TRUE, underlines all modifications

Variables, Arrays, and Functions

$misc	Array containing pairs of strings to find and substitute
$nots	Array of words that can preface the word *not*
$haves	Array of words that can preface the word *have*
$who	Array of pronouns and question words
$what	Array of common verbs that can be contracted

$contractions	Array of the contracted forms of $what
$j, $k	Integer loop counters
$from, $to	Strings to convert from and to
$u1, $u2	Strings containing start and end underline tags if $emphasis is true
$f, $t, $s, $e	Various arguments passed to the function PIPHP_FT_FN1()
$uf, $ut	String variable copies of $f and $t with their initial letters capitalized
$1, $2	String variables containing the matches found by preg_replace()
PIPHP_FT_FN1()	Function to perform the string replacements

How It Works

This plug-in takes as an argument a string of text which it then modifies and returns. The original text is not changed by the process. It performs five passes through the text to change different types of English.

The first pass iterates through the $misc array, stepping two elements at a time. It searches for the first element and, if found, replaces it with the second. The $misc array contains a set of unusual contractions that don't follow the normal English rules, which is one reason why the program gets them out of the way first.

The second pass works through the $nots array and checks whether any of the words in it are followed by the word *not*. If so, it contracts them so that, for example, *did not* becomes *didn't*.

In the third pass, the $haves array is processed in an identical manner to the $nots array, except that pairs of words such as *should have* become *should've*.

Pass four uses a pair of nested loops to iterate through the $who array of pronouns and similar words, and then iterate through the $what array of words that follow directly after them in the plug-in and can be contracted. If matches are made, then the contraction to use is looked up in $contractions and applied. So, for example, *he has* will become *he's*.

The final pass, at the end of the main function, looks for all instances of the word *is* with another word and a space in front of it, and when it finds any it contracts the two together so that, for example, *Paul is* would become *Paul's*.

The second function in this code, PIPHP_FT_FN1(), is only used by the plug-in. It takes the four arguments $f, $t, $s, and $e, which in order contain a string to change from, what to change it to if found, the string to search within, and whether to emphasize any changes by underlining them. It does all this by using regular expressions within the PHP preg_replace() function. It repeats each match and replace twice; the second time to catch strings beginning with capital letters.

NOTE *The function PIPHP_FT_FN1() uses an obscure name since it has no real use anywhere other than as a partner function to PIPHP_FriendlyText(). Where partner functions can be useful in their own right, they are given a more memorable name, such as the ones for PIPHP_SpellCheck(), PIPHP_SpellCheckLoadDictionary(), and PIPHP_SpellCheckWord(), which appear a little further on in this chapter, in plug-in 8.*

How to Use It

To transform any text (including text with HTML) using this plug-in, call the main function in the following way:

```
$oldtext = "Let us go for a picnic. I hope it will not rain.";
$newtext = PIPHP_FriendlyText($oldtext, TRUE);
```

The first parameter holds the string to be modified. This will not be changed. Instead, a new string containing the transformed text will be returned by the function. The second parameter can be either FALSE or TRUE, which will cause all changes to be underlined. This can be useful for debugging purposes.

In this example, the value of $newtext becomes "Let's go for a picnic. I hope it won't rain."

The Plug-in

```
function PIPHP_FriendlyText($text, $emphasis)
{
    $misc = array("let us", "let's", "i\.e\.", "for example",
        "e\.g\.", "for example", "cannot", "can't", "can not",
        "can't", "shall not", "shan't", "will not", "won't");
    $nots = array("are", "could", "did", "do", "does", "is",
        "had", "has", "have", "might", "must", "should", "was",
        "were", "would");
    $haves = array("could", "might", "must", "should", "would");
    $who = array("he", "here", "how", "I", "it", "she", "that",
        "there", "they", "we", "who", "what", "when", "where",
        "why", "you");
    $what = array("am", "are", "had", "has", "have", "shall",
        "will", "would");
    $contractions = array("m", "re", "d", "s", "ve", "ll", "ll",
        "d");

    for ($j = 0 ; $j < sizeof($misc) ; $j += 2)
    {
        $from = $misc[$j];
        $to   = $misc[$j+1];
        $text = PIPHP_FT_FN1($from, $to, $text, $emphasis);
    }

    for ($j = 0 ; $j < sizeof($nots) ; ++$j)
    {
        $from = $nots[$j] . " not";
        $to   = $nots[$j] . "n't";
        $text = PIPHP_FT_FN1($from, $to, $text, $emphasis);
    }

    for ($j = 0 ; $j < sizeof($haves) ; ++$j)

    {
        $from = $haves[$j] . " have";
```

```
        $to   = $haves[$j] . "'ve";
        $text = PIPHP_FT_FN1($from, $to, $text, $emphasis);
    }

    for ($j = 0 ; $j < sizeof($who) ; ++$j)
    {
        for ($k = 0 ; $k < sizeof($what) ; ++$k)
        {
            $from = "$who[$j] $what[$k]";
            $to   = "$who[$j]'$contractions[$k]";
            $text = PIPHP_FT_FN1($from, $to, $text, $emphasis);
        }
    }

    $to = "'s";
    $u1 = $u2 = "";

    if ($emphasis)
    {
        $u1 = "<u>";
        $u2 = "</u>";
    }

    return preg_replace("/([\w]*) is([^\w]+)/", "$u1$1$to$u2$2",
        $text);
}

function PIPHP_FT_FN1($f, $t, $s, $e)
{
    $uf = ucfirst($f);
    $ut = ucfirst($t);

    if ($e)
    {
        $t  = "<u>$t</u>";
        $ut = "<u>$ut</u>";
    }

    $s   = preg_replace("/([^\w]+)$f([^\w]+)/", "$1$t$2",  $s);
    return preg_replace("/([^\w]+)$uf([^\w]+)/", "$1$ut$2", $s);
}
```

PLUG-IN 4 Strip Whitespace

A few of the plug-ins in this book are really short and sweet, and at just a single line of code, this is one of them. But although it's tiny, it packs a punch because it can clean up the messiest text by removing all the whitespace in a string such as extra spaces, tabs, newlines, and so on.

Figure 3-4 shows part of the U.S. Declaration of Independence as it might appear if read in from a poor quality reprint by some optical character recognition software, followed by the result of running the text through this plug-in.

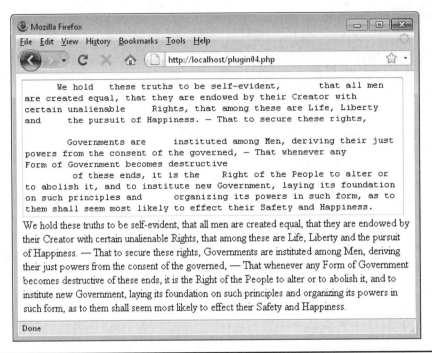

FIGURE 3-4   Unsightly whitespace can seriously mess up some text, but this plug-in will remove it for you.

Although browsers generally ignore whitespace, if the text is displayed using the `<pre>` tag or placed in a form element such as a `<textarea>` (as used in Figure 3-4) then all the whitespace will be apparent.

About the Plug-in

This plug-in takes a string variable containing any text and removes all the whitespace. It requires a single argument:

- **$text**   A string variable containing the text to be modified

Variables, Arrays, and Functions

- None

How It Works

The plug-in makes use of the regular expression feature built into PHP. What it does is search for the text within the two forward slash characters `,/`, and then replaces any it finds with a single space. Between the slashes is the simple string `\s+`, which means find any section of whitespace that is one or more characters in length. The `\s` stands for a whitespace character and the + indicates that the preceding character should appear one or more times in the search. The actual string passed to the `preg_replace()` function is modified and then returned to the calling code.

How to Use It

To use this plug-in, call the function in the following manner, where `$text` is the string to be cleaned up:

```
echo PIPHP_StripWhitespace($text);
```

The Plug-in

```
function PIPHP_StripWhitespace($text)
{
    return preg_replace('/\s+/', ' ', $text);
}
```

5 Word Selector

Quite often you will find you need to somehow highlight chosen words within a web page—for example, when a user arrives from a search engine, you may wish to highlight the search terms they used to help them find what they are looking for. Other times, you might *not* want certain words to appear, such as profanities or other terms you wish to prevent your users from posting.

This plug-in is powerful enough to handle both of these cases because you simply decide on the relevant words and what should happen to them. Figure 3-5 shows a few words highlighted within a section of the U.S. Declaration of Independence.

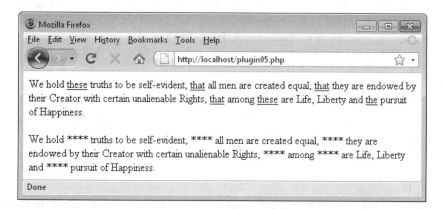

FIGURE 3-5 Using the Word Selector plug-in, you can highlight selected words or censor unwanted ones.

About the Plug-in

This plug-in takes a string variable containing the text to process and an array containing words to be highlighted, as well as a parameter defining the type of highlighting. These are the arguments:

- **$text**   A string variable containing the text to be modified
- **$matches**   An array containing words to highlight
- **$replace**   A string representing the action to perform on matching words. If it is any of "u", "b", or "i", then matching words will be highlighted using one of the following: underline, bold face, or italic; otherwise, matching words are replaced with the contents of $replace.

Variables, Arrays, and Functions

$match	String containing the current word being matched

How It Works

The plug-in starts iterating through the $matches array of supplied words one at a time, using a switch statement to decide whether any matches found should be highlighted in underline, bold, or italic font (if $replace contains one of "u", "b", or "i").

In the case of highlighting a word, the preg_replace() function is called, passing the following three elements to it:

1. ([^\w]+) looks for any sequence of one or more non-word characters, followed by...
2. ($match) ... the current word being matched, followed by...
3. ([^\w]+) ... another sequence of one or more non-word characters

Using this pattern, it's possible to extract individual words by checking for one or more non-word characters on either side of the 2nd parameter ($match).

The brackets enclosing each of these parts tell PHP to save the matches found for use in the replace part of the function, where they can be inserted using the values $1, $2, and $3, each representing the values in the order they appear in the brackets.

When a match is found, the replace string inserts the non-word characters before the match ($1), followed by <$replace>, which will be one of <u>, <b>, or <i>, followed by the word found ($2), followed by </$replace> to close the tag that was opened, finally followed by the non-word characters after the match ($3).

In the case of a string of text having been passed in $replace, rather than one of "u", "b" or "i", the same initial match is made except that $match doesn't have brackets around it because we won't be needing to save a copy of the match, as it will be replaced. Therefore, the replace section is simpler in that it just replaces the entire match with the value in $replace.

How to Use It

To use this function, you should provide the text to be checked, an array of words to match, and a string to either replace or highlight matched words. For example, to underline a given set of words, you could use the following line of code:

```
echo PIPHP_WordSelector($text, array("cat", "dog"), "u");
```

If the list of words is long, you probably would not want to create an array on the fly and instead would pre-populate an array first, using code such as these two lines:

```
$words = array("rat", "fish", "cat", "dog", "rabbit");
echo PIPHP_WordSelector($text, $words, "u");
```

To blank out or censor a set of words, you specify a replace string that is none of "b", "u", or "i". For example, the following line replaces all the words in the array $words that are found in $text with four asterisks:

```
echo PIPHP_WordSelector($text, $words, "****");
```

The Plug-in

```
function PIPHP_WordSelector($text, $matches, $replace)
{
    foreach($matches as $match)
    {
        switch($replace)
        {
            case "u":
            case "b":
            case "i":
                $text = preg_replace("/([^\w]+)($match)([^\w]+)/",
                    "$1<$replace>$2</$replace>$3", $text);
                break;

            default:
                $text = preg_replace("/([^\w]+)$match([^\w]+)/",
                    "$1$replace$2", $text);
                break;
        }
    }

    return $text;
}
```

---

6 Count Tail

Displaying a date in the format "23 November" or "March 12" isn't really that friendly, and you may wish to use the better flowing "23rd November" and "March 12th". In fact, there are many places where you use numbers, and they would look better displayed with one of "st", "nd", "rd", or "th" following, such as in the sentence "You're our 124,362nd" visitor, rather than "You are visitor 124,362," and so on. Figure 3-6 shows using this plug-in to add the correct suffix to all the numbers between 0 and 100.

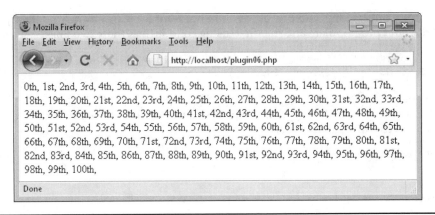

FIGURE 3-6   Using this plug-in makes it easy to add "st", "nd", "rd", and "th" automatically to numbers.

About the Plug-in

This plug-in takes a number as input and then returns that number with a suffix of one out of "st", "nd", "rd", or "th". It takes a single argument:

- **$number**   The number on which to append a suffix

Variables, Arrays, and Functions

$nstring	String variable created from $number
$pointer	Numeric variable that points into $nstring
$digit	Single character string extracted from $nstring
$suffix	String representing the suffix to append

How It Works

In order to operate on individual digits of the given number, it is first turned into a string using the *cast* keyword (string) and stored in $nstring. This is because, although PHP is a loosely typed language and does its best to automatically change the type of a variable according to how it is accessed, it cannot be relied upon to make the change correctly in this instance, where numbers would have to be treated as strings, which are then treated as arrays. Thus, the forced change of type using the cast statement.

Next the numeric variable $pointer is defined with a value derived from the length of $nstring - 1. This means it will also point at (or index into) the final character in $nstring. Using $pointer, the variable $digit is then set to the value of the final digit in the number. The string variable $suffix is then set to the default value "th", the most common suffix.

With all the variables initialized, a test is made to see whether $pointer has a value of 0. In other words, is $number a single-digit number less than 10? A second part of the test then takes the case of $pointer being greater than zero (therefore, $number is 10 or higher), and if it is, tests whether the second to last digit is *not* the number 1.

The reason for this test is that any number ending in 1, 2, or 3 usually requires the suffix "st", "nd", or "rd" *unless* the previous digit is a 1, in which case the suffix must be "th", as in 11th, 12th, and 13th.

If it isn't an exception case, the switch statement sets $suffix to one of the three lesser common suffixes if the last digit is a 1, 2, or 3. Otherwise, you will recall, $suffix was already set to "th" by default.

Finally, the number is returned with the correct suffix appended.

How to Use It

To add a suffix to a number, just call the plug-in by passing the number, like this:

```
echo PIPHP_CountTail(123);
```

So, for example, to create the output shown in Figure 3-6, you could use the following:

```
for ($j = 0 ; $j < 101 ; ++$j) echo PIPHP_CountTail($j) . ", ";
```

The Plug-in

```
function PIPHP_CountTail($number)
{
    $nstring = (string) $number;
    $pointer = strlen($nstring) - 1;
    $digit   = $nstring[$pointer];
    $suffix  = "th";

    if ($pointer == 0 ||
       ($pointer > 0 && $nstring[$pointer - 1] != 1))
    {
        switch ($nstring[$pointer])
        {
            case 1: $suffix = "st"; break;
            case 2: $suffix = "nd"; break;
            case 3: $suffix = "rd"; break;
        }
    }

    return $number . $suffix;
}
```

7 Text Truncate

Have you noticed how the results provided by the Google search engine always neatly display snippets of information from each web site, without truncating text mid-word? Now you can cut long strings short in a similar manner using this plug-in, as shown by the screen shot in Figure 3-7, which illustrates three snippets from the first paragraph of Charles Dickens' *A Tale of Two Cities*.

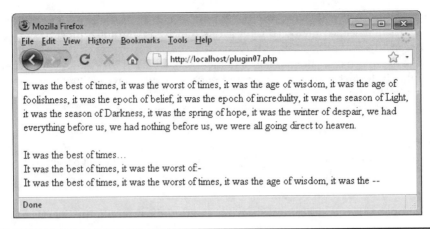

About the Plug-in

This plug-in takes a string variable containing text to truncate, the maximum number of characters to allow in the new string, and a symbol or string to follow the truncated text, to show what has been done. It takes these arguments:

- **$text**   A string variable containing the text to be modified
- **$max**   A numeric variable representing the maximum number of characters allowed
- **$symbol**   A string variable to follow the new text

Variables, Arrays, and Functions

$temp	Temporary copy of the string variable $text after initial truncating
$last	Numeric variable pointing to the final space character in $temp

How It Works

The truncation process has several parts. The first is a hard truncation down to the maximum size allowed by $max. This is done using the substr() function. Next the strrpos() function is used to find the final space in the newly truncated string. Once determined, the new string is again truncated at this new position.

In the case of the Google search engine, this would be most of the process but I decided it's unsightly to leave punctuation or another non-word character as the final character in the new string, so preg_replace() is called up to remove any non-word character that may be there. Only then is the new string returned, with the value of $symbol attached to it's end.

How to Use It

To use this plug-in, pass it some text to truncate, the maximum number of allowed characters, and a symbol or string to attach to the end of the truncated string, like this:

```
echo PIPHP_TextTruncate($text, 90, " --");
```

You can choose any character or string for $symbol (or even the empty string) such as the useful HTML entity …, which displays an ellipsis made up of three periods—the standard notation to indicate that some text is missing.

The Plug-in

```
function PIPHP_TextTruncate($text, $max, $symbol)
{
    $temp = substr($text, 0, $max);
    $last = strrpos($temp, " ");
    $temp = substr($temp, 0, $last);
    $temp = preg_replace("/([^\w])$/", "", $temp);
    return "$temp$symbol";
}
```

PLUG-IN 8 Spell Check

There's a spell checking module available for PHP called *pspell*, but if it's not already installed on your server, it needs downloading, installing, and configuring before you can use it. However, if you want to ensure your code will work on any server, this plug-in provides a reasonably fast spell checker based on a dictionary of over 80,000 words, which is supplied on the companion web site for this book (*http://pluginphp.com*) along with the plug-ins.

Figure 3-8 again shows a paragraph from Dickens' *A Tale of Two Cities*, but this time some deliberate spelling errors have been introduced, which have been caught by the plug-in.

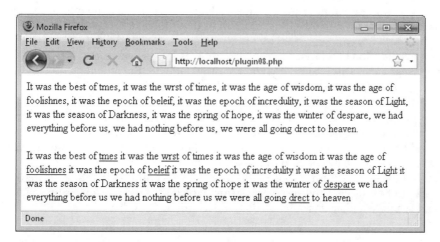

FIGURE 3-8 Checking user input for spelling is easily accomplished with this plug-in.

About the Plug-in

This plug-in takes a string variable containing text to spell check, along with a variable to determine how the resulting text should be displayed. It requires these arguments:

- **$text**   A string variable containing the text to be modified
- **$action**   A string variable which should contain a single letter text formatting tag

Variables, Arrays, and Functions

`$filename`	String variable containing the path and name of the dictionary file to load
`$dictionary`	Array containing all the dictionary words
`$newtext`	String variable containing the transformed text
`$matches`	Array containing the results from the `preg_match()` calls
`$offset`	Numeric variable pointer to the next word to check
`$word`	String variable containing the current word
`PIPHP_SpellCheckLoadDictionary()`	Function to load in the dictionary
`PIPHP_SpellCheckWord()`	Function to check a single word
`$top, $bot, $p`	Temporary variables used by `PIPHP_SpellCheckWord()` to perform a binary search of the dictionary

How It Works

With this plug-in you get two for the price of one, because the main function, `PIPHP_SpellCheck()`, relies on another function, `PIPHP_SpellCheckWord()`, to check individual words, and you can call `PIPHP_SpellCheck()` on its own, too.

The very first thing the main function does is load the dictionary file into the array `$dictionary`. This file is on the web site and will be downloaded along with the plug-in. It comprises over 80,000 words separated by \r\n (carriage return and line feed) pairs. If you have your own collection of words, you can also use it as long as you make sure there's a \r\n pair between each. This is also why you are provided with the function PHP_SpellCheckLoadDictionary(), so you can specify the path and filename for such a file.

With the dictionary loaded into an array by using the `explode()` function, $text has a space character appended to it. This is so the following code has a guaranteed non-word character at the end so a match can be made on the final word. Then, the two variables $newtext and $offset are initialized. Respectively, they contain the transformed text and a pointer to the next word to be checked in the string $text.

The heart of the system comprises a while loop, which continues iterating through each word in $text until it reaches the end of the string, which the loop recognizes by checking $offset and seeing whether it is still less than the length of $text.

Within the loop, each word is extracted in turn using the preg_match() function with a three-part regular expression:

1. [^\w]* This looks for zero or more non-word characters, followed by…

2. ([\w]+) … one or more word characters (a-z, A-z, or 0-9), followed by…

3. [^\w]+ … one or more non-word characters

In part 2, above, the regular expression segment is surrounded by brackets, which means that particular value will be saved in the array element $matches[1][0], and its length in $matches[1][1]. The whole matched string, comprising all three parts, is saved in the array element $matches[0][1], and the length of this value is saved in $matches[0][1].

Provided with these values, the string variable $word is assigned just the part 2 match, which is the word to be spell checked. Then $offset, the pointer to the next word to be checked, is incremented by the length of the full matched string, so as to jump over any non-word characters. The code is then ready to process the following word the next time round the loop.

In the meantime, the newly extracted word is passed to the function PIPHP_SpellCheckWord(), along with the dictionary array to use, in $dictionary. The return value from this function is either TRUE if the word is found or FALSE if it isn't. Depending on the value returned, the word is added to $newtext either with or without highlighting tags. Once execution exits from the loop, the text has been fully checked and so $newtext is returned, after passing it through the rtrim() function to remove the final space that was added at the function start.

The function PIPHP_SpellCheckLoadDictionary() is next. It simply loads in the specified text file, explodes it into an array by splitting it at all the \r\n pairs, and then returns the new array.

Finally, there's the function PIPHP_SpellCheckWord(). This takes the arguments $word and $dictionary and then returns either TRUE or FALSE depending on whether or not the word is in the dictionary. This is done by means of a binary search in which the $dictionary array is continually bisected until a word is found, or is found to be missing. In a dictionary of 80,000 words or so, it will take no more than about 17 iterations maximum to drill down to where a word is (or should be), which is an order of magnitude faster than checking every word in the dictionary. By the way, this search relies on having a fully sorted list of words, so if you use your own word list, make sure you sort it alphabetically first.

The way the plug-in performs the binary search is to say "Is the word I'm looking for in the top half or bottom half of this section of words?" Then, the loop goes around again splitting whichever half it determines the word to be in, asking the same question. This continues until the word is either found or determined not to be in the dictionary.

The variables that control this divide-and-conquer method are $bot and $top, which represent the start and end positions to search between within the $dictionary array. Initially they are set to the first and last elements. Then, $bot is moved up or $top is moved down by taking the midway point between the two values and assigning that to a pivotal numeric variable called $p, right in the middle. If the word is greater than the one at position $p, then $bot is moved up past that word. If the word is lower than the one at position $p, then $top is dropped below that position.

If at any point the word at position $p in the $dictionary array is the same as $word, then a match has been found and the value TRUE is returned. Otherwise, the process continues and eventually $top and $bot will pass each other and $bot will have a value higher than $top, because all the words in the dictionary have been checked, at which point the loop exits and the value FALSE is returned because no match was made.

How to Use It

To use the main function and have any misspelled words highlighted with underlines, you call it like this:

```
echo PIPHP_SpellCheck($text, "u");
```

This will check the words in $text against all the dictionary words and highlight any that are not recognized. You can replace the "u" with "i" or "b" for italic or bold if you prefer.

If you wish to spell check a single word, perhaps to support interactive spell checking, you must make sure you have loaded the dictionary in before calling the PIPHP_SpellCheckWord() function. Ideally, place the call to the function to do this somewhere at the start of your PHP file so you know for sure it has been loaded when you make a call. To load a dictionary file, use a command such as this:

```
$dictionary = PIPHP_SpellCheckLoadDictionary("dictionary.txt");
```

Make sure you provide the correct file and pathname. If you are using the supplied plug-in from the web site, then *dictionary.txt* will be in the same directory as the plug-in.

Then, to spell check an individual word, call the function like this:

```
$result = PIPHP_SpellCheckWord($word, $dictionary);
```

It will return TRUE if the word is recognized, or FALSE if it isn't.

The Plug-in

```
function PIPHP_SpellCheck($text, $action)
{
    $dictionary = PIPHP_SpellCheckLoadDictionary("dictionary.txt");
    $text       .= ' ';
    $newtext     = "";
    $offset      = 0;

    while ($offset < strlen($text))

    {
        $result = preg_match('/[^\w]*([\w]+)[^\w]+/',
            $text, $matches, PREG_OFFSET_CAPTURE, $offset);
        $word   = $matches[1][0];
        $offset = $matches[0][1]  + strlen($matches[0][0]);

        if (!PIPHP_SpellCheckWord($word, $dictionary))
            $newtext .= "<$action>$word</$action> ";
        else $newtext .= "$word ";
    }
```

```
    return rtrim($newtext);
}

function PIPHP_SpellCheckLoadDictionary($filename)
{
    return explode("\r\n", file_get_contents($filename));
}

function PIPHP_SpellCheckWord($word, $dictionary)
{
    $top = sizeof($dictionary) -1;
    $bot = 0;
    $word = strtolower($word);

    while($top >= $bot)
    {
        $p =    floor(($top + $bot) / 2);
        if      ($dictionary[$p] < $word) $bot = $p + 1;
        elseif ($dictionary[$p] > $word) $top = $p - 1;
        else    return TRUE;
    }

    return FALSE;
}
```

PLUG-IN 9 Remove Accents

When you have data that is accented with diacritics such as the letter "é", you sometimes need to convert this data to plain ASCII but still be able to read it. The solution is to replace all the diacritic characters with standard ones using this plug-in. Figure 3-9 shows some French text before and after running the plug-in.

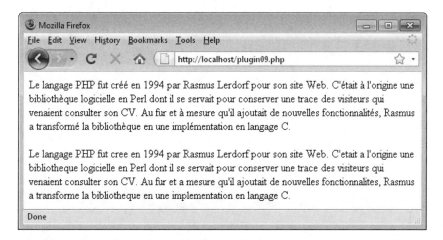

FIGURE 3-9 Part of the French Wikipedia entry for PHP before and after running it through this plug-in

About the Plug-in

This plug-in takes a string variable containing accented text and returns a non-accented version. It requires this argument:

- **$text**   A string variable containing the text to be modified

Variables, Arrays, and Functions

$from	Array containing a list of accented characters
$to	Array containing non-accented versions of $from

How It Works

This plug-in uses the str_replace() function to replace the characters in the string $text that match those in the array $from with their non-accented counterparts in the array $to.

In PHP, you can use str_replace() either to substitute single items or, as here, complete arrays of strings, with each array having 55 characters. If, for example, the character at location 23 is matched in the array $from, then the character at location 23 in the array $to is substituted. The substituted text is then returned.

How to Use It

To transform accented text to non-accented text, call up the plug-in as follows:

```
echo PIPHP_RemoveAccents($text);
```

The Plug-in

```
function PIPHP_RemoveAccents($text)
{
    $from = array("ç", "æ", "œ", "á", "é", "í", "ó", "ú", "à", "è",
                  "ì", "ò", "ù", "ä", "ë", "ï", "ö", "ü", "ÿ", "â",
                  "ê", "î", "ô", "û", "å", "e", "i", "ø", "u", "Ç",
                  "Æ", "Œ", "Á", "É", "Í", "Ó", "Ú", "À", "È", "Ì",
                  "Ò", "Ù", "Ä", "Ë", "Ï", "Ö", "Ü", "Ÿ", "Â", "Ê",
                  "Î", "Ô", "Û", "Å", "Ø");

    $to =   array("c", "ae", "oe", "a", "e", "i", "o", "u", "a", "e",
                  "i", "o", "u", "a", "e", "i", "o", "u", "y", "a",
                  "e", "i", "o", "u", "a", "e", "i", "o", "u", "C",
                  "AE", "OE", "A", "E", "I", "O", "U", "A", "E", "I",
                  "O", "U", "A", "E", "I", "O", "U", "Y", "A", "E",
                  "I", "O", "U", "A", "O");

    return str_replace($from, $to, $text);
}
```

 **Shorten Text**

Sometimes, when you want to display the URL on a web page, it can be so long it looks untidy and messes up your layout. Of course, you can come up with suitable text for a hyperlink instead of showing the URL, but what about when a user posts a web address to your web site?

This plug-in has a simple solution because it shortens any long URLs (or other strings) by removing the middle and only keeping the two ends. Figure 3-10 shows a long URL text string followed by a version shortened by this plug-in.

You should note that when used on URLs, the shortened text is *only* for the displayed part of an HTML link and not the actual link itself, which must remain unchanged; the plug-in's main use is for reducing the space that the text of a link takes up on a web page.

About the Plug-in

This plug-in takes a string variable containing a long URL (or other string) and returns a shortened version. It takes these arguments:

- **$text** A string variable containing the text to be modified
- **$size** A numeric variable containing the new string size
- **$mark** A string variable containing a character sequence to mark the part that was removed

Variables, Arrays, and Functions

$len	Numeric variable containing the length of the original string
$a	String variable containing the left-hand part of the new string
$b	String variable containing the right-hand part of the new string

How It Works

This plug-in first notes the length of the original string, and if the new required length is not smaller, simply returns the original string since there's no shortening to do.

FIGURE 3-10 Shortening URLs or other strings is easily done with this plug-in.

Otherwise, the left portion of the new string is created by copying half the number of characters that are to be in the new string from the left of the original string using the substr() function. The result is then stored in $a. The right-hand portion is similarly derived by taking half the number of characters required for the new string from the right of the original string.

This is not quite true. Actually the left and right halves are each one character less than half the required size of the new string to allow for inserting the $mark string to signify the part of the string that has been removed.

The three parts—$a, $mark, and $b—are then assembled and returned.

How to Use It

To shorten a URL (or other string), call the plug-in like this, where $text is the string to shorten, 60 is the new maximum size, and /-/-/ is the marker to signify the portion of the string that was removed:

```
echo PIPHP_ShortenText($text, 60, "/-/-/");
```

The new shorter string will be displayed. You can replace the marker shown with any string of your choosing.

The Plug-in

```
function PIPHP_ShortenText($text, $size, $mark)
{
    $len = strlen($text);
    if ($size >= $len) return $text;

    $a = substr($text, 0, $size / 2 -1);
    $b = substr($text, $len - $size / 2 + 1, $size/ 2 -1);
    return $a . $mark . $b;
}
```

CHAPTER 4

Image Handling

HTML and CSS have developed to such an extent that the depth and variety of features available to a web developer have never been greater. But when it comes to images and manipulating them there's not a lot you can do, other than resize them in-browser (not a true resize, more of a squash or a stretch) and add borders. True, using JavaScript you can overlay one image on another and blend them by making one image semi-transparent, but that's about the extent of it.

That's where PHP comes to the rescue, thanks to the GD library of image functions, which most implementations of PHP now include by default. For example, the recommended Zend Server CE from Chapter 1 already has GD enabled, as does the Mac MAMP setup.

Installing the GD Library

If you are running a different PHP installation and these plug-ins won't work because GD isn't available, then you need to add it. On Ubuntu and Debian Linux, you can install GD from the terminal with the following commands:

```
sudo -i
apt-get install php5-gd
/etc/init.d/apache2 restart
```

And on Fedora Linux you enter (as root):

```
yum install php-gd
```

On other setups, you'll need to read the PHP documentation for your operating system and usually recompile PHP with GD using the `--with-gd` option.

For further details on the GD library, including installation and usage, please visit *http://php.net/manual/en/book.image.php*. Otherwise, let's get onto the next batch of ten plug-ins.

PLUG-IN 11   Upload File

A major service offered by many web sites is the facility for users to upload files and images. For example, you may wish to let your users create avatars or upload photos they have taken. Or perhaps you need to support the uploading of Word, Excel, or other types of files. Using this plug-in you can enable this feature, while retaining the security of your web site. Figure 4-1 shows the result of uploading an image file called *test.jpg*.

FIGURE 4-1   The Upload File plug-in is easy to use and provides lots of information and error checking.

About the Plug-in

This plug-in takes the name of a form field used to upload a file to a web server and returns the uploaded file in a string. Upon success, it returns a two-element array, the first value of which is zero and the second is the uploaded file. On failure, a single element array is returned with one of these values: −1 = upload failed; −2 = wrong file type; −3 = file too large; 1 = file exceeds upload_max_filesize as defined in *php.ini*; 2 = file exceeds the MAX_FILE_SIZE directive in the HTML form; 3 = file was only partially uploaded; 4 = no file was uploaded; 6 = PHP is missing a temporary folder; 7 = failed to write file to disk; 8 = file upload stopped by extension. The plug-in takes these arguments:

$name   String containing the form field name given to the uploaded file

$filetypes   Array containing the supported file (mime) types

$maxlen   Integer representing the maximum allowable file size

Variables, Arrays, and Functions

$_FILES	System array containing the uploaded file information
$temp	String containing a temporary copy of the uploaded file

How It Works

Once a file has been received by the web server, it's stored in a temporary location and a system array called $_FILES is populated with various details about the file, as follows:

$_FILES['file']['name']   The original name of the file on the client machine

$_FILES['file']['type']   The mime type of the file (such as "image/jpeg")

$_FILES['file']['size']   The size, in bytes, of the uploaded file

$_FILES['file']['tmp_name']   The temporary filename of the file in which the uploaded file was stored on the server

$_FILES['file']['error']   Any error code associated with this file upload

In this plug-in, the form field name used to upload the file is passed to the function in $name, which is used in place of 'file' as shown earlier. To check whether a file was successfully uploaded, the first thing the plug-in does is see whether $_FILES[$name]['name'] has a value. If so, a file has been uploaded. Otherwise, an error value of −1 is returned.

Next the $filetypes array of allowable file (or mime) types is compared with the type in $_FILES[$name]['type'], using the in_array() function. If it isn't one of the allowed types, then the plug-in returns a value of −2.

Then, the maximum allowed file length in $maxlen is compared with $_FILES[$name]['size'], and if the file is too large, an error value of −3 is returned. After this, $_FILES[$name]['error'] is tested, and if it has a value greater than 0, an error was encountered and the proper error value is returned.

In all these cases, the function actually returns an array of three elements, only the first of which contains the error value. The second two elements are set to NULL, as they will only return data upon a successful file upload.

After passing all the tests, the uploaded file is loaded into the variable $temp from its temporary location, pointed to by $_FILES[$name]['tmp_name'], and a value of 0 is returned in the first element of the array (meaning the function was successful). The file type and the file itself are then returned in the other two elements.

How to Use It

To use this plug-in you need to offer an HTML upload form similar to this:

```
<form method="post" action="upload.php"
    enctype="multipart/form-data">
<input type="file" name="test" />
<input type="submit" value="Upload" /></form>
```

Here the form has been set to post its input to the PHP program *upload.php* using the encoding type of multipart/form-data. The program uploaded to can be any of your choosing, even the current PHP program, but the encoding type must be as shown or the upload will fail.

The next line tells the browser that a file needs to be uploaded and that its name, as sent to the server, should be test. In fact, the web browser will normally also send the name of the file as it is stored on the local computer, but as explained a little later, it's a security risk to rely on that information. A malicious person could create a web form of their own, with altered details designed to send spoof filenames to your web server in the hope of saving a file on it by which they can compromise the server. This plug-in therefore totally ignores the original filename and uses only the form field name as an identifier.

The final line creates a submit button with the label "Upload" and closes the form. When they click the Browse button created by the form, users can then navigate their local file system to locate and upload a file to the server.

When you call up the plug-in, all you need to do is pass it the field name used in the form, an array of acceptable file (or mime) types, and the maximum allowable file length. Everything else is taken care of for you. When the function returns to the calling code, it will either pass an error code, or it will return the uploaded file, which you can save (if you wish) to the server's hard disk.

The following code creates an array of two mime types in $allowed: for the regular and progressive kinds of JPEG images. Then, the plug-in is called and the returned array is stored in $result. If the first element of $result, $result[0], is non-zero, there was an error and a message will be displayed, otherwise the returned file, stored in $result[2], is saved to the disk as *test.jpg*. If you need to know it, the type of the uploaded file is also available in $result[1].

```
$allowed = array("image/jpeg", "image/pjpeg");
$result = PIPHP_UploadFile("test", $allowed, 100000);
if ($result != 0) echo "There was an error"
else file_put_contents($result[2], "test.jpg");
```

If the plug-in had accepted the supplied filename instead (in $_FILES['file']['name']), then users could upload a name such us *c:\windows\system32\calc.exe*, which if you simply saved it as is, could overwrite your calculator program. The same goes for Linux systems where, for example, a filename of */bin/sh* could overwrite your shell. A secure system will try and step in to prevent this from happening, but not always. And what if the uploaded filename was a PHP file? Your system could then easily be compromised and taken control of.

The following is a full example of the type of code you might write to make use of the plug-in:

```
echo <<<_END
<form method="post" action="$_SERVER[PHP_SELF]"
    enctype="multipart/form-data">
<input  type="hidden" name="flag" value="1" />
<input  type="file" name="test" />
<input  type="submit" value="Upload" /></form>
_END;

if (isset($_POST['flag']))
{
    $result = PIPHP_UploadFile("test",
        array("image/jpeg", "image/pjpeg"), 100000);

    if ($result[0] == 0)
    {
        file_put_contents("test.jpg", $result[2]);
        echo "File received with the type '$result[1]' and saved ";
        echo "as <a href='test.jpg'>test.jpg</a><br />";
    }
    else
    {
        if ($result[0] == -2) echo "Wrong file type<br />";
        if ($result[0] == -3) echo "Maximum length exceeded<br />";
        if ($result[0] > 0)   echo "Error code: $result<br />";
        echo "File upload failed<br />";
    }
}
```

The first section is a multiline echo that displays an HTML web form for uploading images. After that, the POST variable $_POST['flag'] is checked. This is a hidden form field that will have the value 1 only if the form is submitted. If so, something was uploaded and the rest of the code is executed.

First, $result is assigned the file returned from the call to PIPHP_UploadFile(). Then, if $result[0] has a value of 0, the upload succeeded and the contents of the file are saved as *test.jpg*. A message is then displayed, along with a link to the file.

If $result[0] is non-zero, then there was an error and its value is the error number, as detailed in the *About the Plug-in* section.

The Plug-in

```
function PIPHP_UploadFile($name, $filetypes, $maxlen)
{
    if (!isset($_FILES[$name]['name']))
        return array(-1, NULL, NULL);

    if (!in_array($_FILES[$name]['type'], $filetypes))
        return array(-2, NULL, NULL);

    if ($_FILES[$name]['size'] > $maxlen)
        return array(-3, NULL, NULL);

    if ($_FILES[$name]['error'] > 0)
        return array($_FILES[$name]['error'], NULL, NULL);

    $temp = file_get_contents($_FILES[$name]['tmp_name']);
    return array(0, $_FILES[$name]['type'], $temp);
}
```

PLUG-IN 12 Resize Image

Although you can easily resize an image using HTML by specifying the width and height at which to display it, the way the image will appear depends entirely on the browser being used, and whether the original is resampled rather than simply pixel resized. Also, if you wish an image to be reduced in size, changing its dimensions from within HTML won't reduce the amount of data transferred from the server to the browser.

Instead, try using this plug-in to resize images first. With it you can choose whether to resize an image on the fly before sending it to a browser, or you can save the resized image to the hard disk. Figure 4-2 shows a 313×317 pixel image that has been resized to 500×100 pixels. Although it is now squashed, the resampling used has ensured that the new image remains smooth, and without the jagged edges a pixel resize would create.

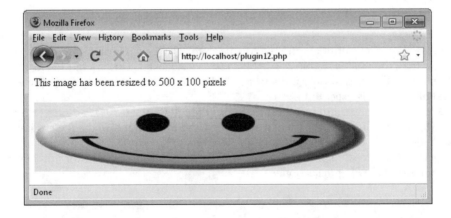

FIGURE 4-2   Using the Resize Image function, you can reduce, enlarge, and change the ratio of image dimensions.

About the Plug-in

This plug-in accepts an image to be resized and the new dimensions required. It takes these arguments:

> **$image**   An image to be transformed, as a GD library object
>
> **$w**   The new required width
>
> **$h**   The new height

Variables, Arrays, and Functions

$oldw	Integer representing the image's current width
$oldh	Integer representing the image's current height
$temp	Temporary copy of the new GD image

How It Works

This plug-in first looks up the image's current width and height and places these values in the variables $oldw and $oldh. It then creates a new GD image object of the new width and height, as supplied in $w and $h.

The imagecopyresampled() function is then called, passing these values to it. It takes the old image, resamples it to the new width and height, and the new image is then placed in the $temp GD image object, which is returned by the function.

How to Use It

The way you use this plug-in is to have an image already created or loaded into a GD image object, which you then pass to the function, along with two arguments stating the new width and height needed. Once the new image has been created, it's returned by the function.

So, for example, the following code loads in the image $image from the file *test.jpg*, resizes it into the new image object $newim using PIPHP_ImageResize(), and saves it as the new image *squashed.jpg* using the imagejpeg() function:

```
$image = imagecreatefromjpeg("test.jpg");
$newim = PIPHP_ImageResize($image, 500, 100);
imagejpeg($newim, "squashed.jpg");
```

If you prefer, you can have your PHP program act as if it were the new image itself by outputting it directly to the browser, like this:

```
$image = imagecreatefromjpeg("test.jpg");
header("Content-type: image/jpeg");
imagejpeg(PIPHP_ImageResize($image, 500, 100));
```

Here, after loading the image into $image, a special header is sent to the browser, "Content-type: image/jpeg", which tells it that the next data to arrive will be a JPEG image. Then, the imagejpeg() function is called using the value returned from the plug-in, but without a filename argument, so the resulting JPEG is sent straight to the browser, rather than saved to disk.

The Plug-in

```
function PIPHP_ImageResize($image, $w, $h)
{
    $oldw = imagesx($image);
    $oldh = imagesy($image);
    $temp = imagecreatetruecolor($w, $h);
    imagecopyresampled($temp, $image, 0, 0, 0, 0,
        $w, $h, $oldw, $oldh);
    return $temp;
}
```

PLUG-IN 13 Make Thumbnail

Many thumbnail programs exist that will take a large image and reduce it to a thumbnail for you, often supporting working in batches. But what about turning user uploaded images into thumbnails? Obviously you don't want to simply send a large image to the browser and have HTML resize it since the quality wouldn't be great, and your bandwidth would go through the roof. So you need something to handle this process on the fly, which is where this plug-in comes in handy.

With it you specify a source image and the maximum dimensions allowed for the new thumbnail. The function will then resize the image, retaining the aspect ratio, so that whichever of the height or width is the larger dimension is then set to the new maximum size, and the other is reduced in proportion. Figure 4-3 shows the smiley face image, from the previous plug-in, used as a thumbnail source for two smaller thumbnail images.

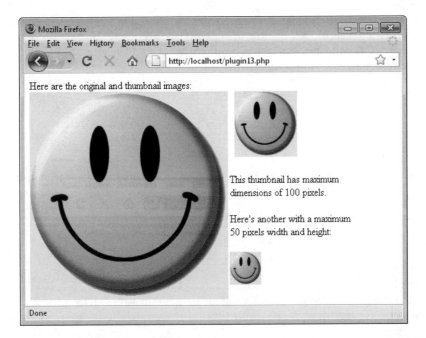

FIGURE 4-3 The Make Thumbnail plug-in has been used to make two different thumbnails of a smiley face.

About the Plug-in

This plug-in accepts an image to be converted into a thumbnail and the new maximum width or height. It takes these arguments:

> $image   A GD image to be transformed

> $max   The new maximum width or height (whichever is the greater dimension)

Variables, Arrays, and Functions

$w	Integer representing the image's current width
$h	Integer representing the image's current height
$thumbw	Integer representing the thumbnail's new width
$thumbh	Integer representing the thumbnail's new height

How It Works

To create the new thumbnail image, this plug-in accepts a GD image object and then sets $w and $thumbw to its width, and $h and $thumbh to its height. Next it looks at these values to find out which dimension is the larger. If $w is greater than $h, then the image is wider than it is high, so the new width will take the value in $max, and thus $thumbh, the smaller thumbnail height, is set to the maximum dimension value of $max divided by the original image's width, in $w, and multiplied by its height, in $h.

So, for example, if the original image's width is 1200 pixels, the height is 1000, and the new maximum dimension size is 100 pixels, the following formula is applied:

```
Thumbnail Height = 100 / 1200 × 1000
```

This becomes:

```
Thumbnail Height = 0.0833 × 1000
```

Which results in:

```
Thumbnail Height = 83.33
```

Therefore, if the new width is to be 100 pixels, then the new height must be 83.33 pixels (which will be rounded down to 83). Similarly, if the height is greater than the width, then the height will be set to the value in $max and the width will be set to a percentage of that height.

In both cases, a test is made to see whether $max is already smaller than the new height or width, because if it's not then the image is already of thumbnail size.

A final test is made for whether the value in $max is less than that in $h. If so this means that the requested new image size is smaller than the original, and that the width and height required are equal, so $thumbw and $thumbh are both set to the value in $max. In this case, the thumbnail will be square and so both $thumbw and $thumbh are assigned the value in $max.

With all the calculations over, the previous plug-in, PIPHP_ImageResize(), is called to perform the resizing. The image that is returned from this plug-in is returned to the calling code.

How to Use It

To create a thumbnail, you pass the function `PIPHP_MakeThumbnail()` a GD image object and the maximum value of the greater dimension for the thumbnail. For example, the following code loads in the image in *test.jpg* using the `imagecreatefromjpeg()` function, and then passes it to the plug-in, along with a maximum dimension of 100. The function then returns the new thumbnail to the string variable `$thumb`, which is then saved to the file *thumb.jpg* using the `imagejpeg()` function.

```
$image = imagecreatefromjpeg("test.jpg");
$thumb = PIPHP_MakeThumbnail($image, 100);
imagejpeg($thumb, "thumb.jpg");
```

You can also output the thumbnail straight to the browser by first sending the correct header, like this:

```
$image = imagecreatefromjpeg("test.jpg");
header("Content-type: image/jpeg");
imagejpeg(PIPHP_MakeThumbnail($image, 100));
```

Because this plug-in also uses the `PIPHP_ImageResize()` function, you will need both of these in (or included by) your program file.

The Plug-in

```
function PIPHP_MakeThumbnail($image, $max)
{
    $thumbw = $w = imagesx($image);
    $thumbh = $h = imagesy($image);

    if ($w > $h && $max < $w)
    {
        $thumbh = $max / $w * $h;
        $thumbw = $max;
    }
    elseif ($h > $w && $max < $h)
    {
        $thumbw = $max / $h * $w;
        $thumbh = $max;
    }
    elseif ($max < $w)
    {
        $thumbw = $thumbh = $max;
    }

    return PIPHP_ImageResize($image, $thumbw, $thumbh);
}
```

PLUG-IN 14

Image Alter

The PHP GD library is so powerful that it can perform a variety of image manipulations you would normally only find in a graphics program. In fact, you could probably build quite an advanced image editor using them. This plug-in goes someway towards that by providing

FIGURE 4-4   This photograph has been modified by passing it through the Image Alter plug-in.

14 different image transformations you can apply to your graphics, and Figure 4-4 shows just one of these, Edge Detect, in use.

About the Plug-in

This plug-in accepts an image to be converted, along with the transformation required. It takes these arguments:

$image   A GD image to be transformed

$effect   The transformation to apply, between 1 and 14:

$effect	Action
1	Sharpen
2	Blur
3	Brighten
4	Darken
5	Increase contrast
6	Decrease contrast
7	Grayscale
8	Invert
9	Increase red
10	Increase green
11	Increase blue
12	Edge detect
13	Emboss
14	Sketchify

Variables, Arrays, and Functions

None

How It Works

To select between the available transformation effects, the plug-in uses a large switch statement that supports 14 different cases to apply to the supplied GD image object. It then calls the relevant function with the required parameters and returns the new image.

How to Use It

To perform an Edge Detect transformation on a file called *photo.jpg*, as shown in Figure 4-4, you could use the following code, which will load a GD image object using the imagecreatefromjpeg() function, and save the transformed image with the function imagejpeg(), using the filename *photo2.jpg*:

```
$image = imagecreatefromjpeg("photo.jpg");
$copy = PIPHP_ImageAlter($image, 12);
imagejpeg($copy, "photo2.jpg");
```

Or to output the transformed image directly to a browser, you could use the following code to output the correct header first:

```
$image = imagecreatefromjpeg("photo.jpg");
header("Content-type: image/jpeg");
imagejpeg(PIPHP_ImageAlter($image, 12));
```

The Plug-in

```
function PIPHP_ImageAlter($image, $effect)
{
    switch($effect)
    {
        case 1:  imageconvolution($image, array(array(-1, -1, -1),
                     array(-1, 16, -1), array(-1, -1, -1)), 8, 0);
                 break;
        case 2:  imagefilter($image,
                     IMG_FILTER_GAUSSIAN_BLUR); break;
        case 3:  imagefilter($image,
                     IMG_FILTER_BRIGHTNESS, 20); break;
        case 4:  imagefilter($image,
                     IMG_FILTER_BRIGHTNESS, -20); break;
        case 5:  imagefilter($image,
                     IMG_FILTER_CONTRAST, -20); break;
        case 6:  imagefilter($image,
                     IMG_FILTER_CONTRAST, 20); break;
        case 7:  imagefilter($image,
                     IMG_FILTER_GRAYSCALE); break;
        case 8:  imagefilter($image,
                     IMG_FILTER_NEGATE); break;
        case 9:  imagefilter($image,
                     IMG_FILTER_COLORIZE, 128, 0, 0, 50); break;
```

```
        case 10: imagefilter($image,
                 IMG_FILTER_COLORIZE, 0, 128, 0, 50); break;
        case 11: imagefilter($image,
                 IMG_FILTER_COLORIZE, 0, 0, 128, 50); break;
        case 12: imagefilter($image,
                 IMG_FILTER_EDGEDETECT); break;
        case 13: imagefilter($image,
                 IMG_FILTER_EMBOSS); break;
        case 14: imagefilter($image,
                 IMG_FILTER_MEAN_REMOVAL); break;
    }

    return $image;
}
```

PLUG-IN 15 · Image Crop

This plug-in lets you crop a portion from an image by passing it as a GD image object, along with the top-left x and y coordinates, and the width and height to crop. Figure 4-5 shows a 285×214 pixel image, which has been cropped starting 100 pixels in from the left and 0 pixels from the top, with dimensions of 110×140 pixels.

About the Plug-in

This plug-in accepts a GD image from which a portion is to be cropped, along with details about the crop offset and dimensions. If any arguments are out of the image bounds, then FALSE is returned. It takes these arguments:

$image   A GD image to be transformed

$x   Offset from the left of the image

FIGURE 4-5   Images are easily cut down to size using the Image Crop plug-in.

$y   Offset from the top of the image

$w   The width to crop

$h   The height to crop

Variables, Arrays, and Functions

$temp	GD image copy of the cropped image
$tw	Integer containing the width of the passed image
$th	Integer containing the height of the passed image

How It Works

This plug-in works by creating a new GD image object of the dimensions supplied in $w and $h using the imagecreatetruecolor() function. This blank image is stored in $temp. Then, the imagecopyresampled() function is called, passing the required arguments to copy a portion of the image supplied in $image, starting at the offset $x pixels in and $y pixels down (and with a width and height of $w by $h), into the image held in $temp, which is then returned.

How to Use It

To crop a section out of an image, you need to first place the image in a GD image object and then call the PIPHP_ImageCrop() function with the required parameters, like this:

```
$image = imagecreatefromjpeg("photo.jpg");
$copy =  PIPHP_ImageCrop($image, 100, 0, 110, 140);
if (!$copy) echo "Crop failed: Argument(s) out of bounds";
else imagejpeg($copy, "photo1.jpg");
```

This code creates a GD image object in $image by loading it in from the file *photo. jpg* using the imagecreatefromjpeg() function. Then, the plug-in is called with the top-left corner of the crop and the dimensions to use, the returned result of which is assigned to $copy. The cropped image is then saved as the file *photo1.jpg* using the imagejpeg() function. Note that arguments passed with values outside the image bounds will result in FALSE being returned so you can check for this and issue an appropriate message.

To output the resulting cropped image to a browser, you can use the following code instead, which as long as there wasn't an error, first sends the correct header:

```
$image = imagecreatefromjpeg("photo.jpg");
$copy = PIPHP_ImageCrop($image, 100, 0, 110, 140);
if ($copy != FALSE)
{
   header("Content-type: image/jpeg");
   imagejpeg();
}
```

The Plug-in

```
function PIPHP_ImageCrop($image, $x, $y, $w, $h)
{
    $tw = imagesx($image);
    $th = imagesy($image);

    if ($x > $tw || $y > $th || $w > $tw || $h > $th)
        return FALSE;

    $temp = imagecreatetruecolor($w, $h);
    imagecopyresampled($temp, $image, 0, 0, $x, $y,
        $w, $h, $w, $h);
    return $temp;
}
```

PLUG-IN 16 Image Enlarge

I've already covered a couple of image resizing plug-ins in this chapter, including *Image Resize* and *Image Thumbnail*. So, you may wonder why the need for yet another? The reason is that a standard enlargement, even if it resamples the original image rather than merely resizing the pixels, will still result in a pixelated blow up. And the more you enlarge an image, the more it will pixelate. For example, imagine increasing the size of an image by a factor of ten in each dimension; this results in the contents of every original pixel now occupying 100 pixels. Even with resampling the pixels nearby, this will still result in an exceedingly blocky enlargement with only the edges of each block of 100 pixels showing any differences.

Now imagine resizing by just doubling each dimension, which results in the data from each original pixel only occupying four pixels. With resampling of the surrounding pixels, this new group of four will contain averaged values from similar pixels, and therefore pixelation will be minimized as the color and brightness information is spread out smoothly.

And that's how this plug-in works. To achieve a smoother enlargement it resamples an original image upwards just a little at a time, spreading the color and brightness smoothly at each enlargement until the desired final dimensions are reached.

If you look closely at Figure 4-6, you'll see that an original thumbnail of 100×75 pixels has been resampled in a single pass to 285×214 pixels, and that this eightfold increase in size has introduced substantial pixelation into the left-hand enlargement. The increase in size is calculated by multiplying each pair of dimensions together and then dividing the larger result by the smaller. Therefore, 100×75 is 7,500, and 285×214 is 60,990, and so 60,990 / 7,500 gives an enlargement amount of 8.132 times.

The image on the right, however, was passed through the Image Enlarge plug-in and, as you can see from the insets, there is almost no pixelation. Instead, the blockiness has been replaced with even transitions of color and brightness. Of course, the image appears a little blurred, but what do you expect from creating picture data out of thin air? The new picture is eight times the size and therefore comprises over 85 percent made up (or interpolated) data. But this plug-in even gives you control over that because you can specify the amount of smoothing to apply to get just the right balance between pixelation and blurring.

FIGURE 4-6   Even with resampling, enlarging a picture causes pixelation—but this plug-in helps reduce it, as shown by the zoomed-in insets.

About the Plug-in

This plug-in accepts a GD image to enlarge, along with details about the new dimensions and amount of smoothing. It takes these arguments:

> **$image**   A GD image to be enlarged
>
> **$w**   The new width
>
> **$h**   The new height
>
> **$smoothing**   The amount of smoothing (0 = minimum, 90 = Maximum)

Variables, Arrays, and Functions

$oldw	Integer representing the image's current width
$oldh	Integer representing the image's current height
$step	Float representing the amount of each enlargement
$max	Integer representing the number of steps to take
$ratio	Float representing the new width relative to the height
$j	Temporary counter to track iterations

How It Works

This plug-in first makes a note of the image's current dimensions, placing them in $oldw and $oldh, and then calculates the step size between each of the enlargements. This is derived by multiplying the value of π (3.1415927) by the amount of smoothing required.

You may ask, "Why this formula?" Well, I have to be honest here. I tried dozens of different step sizes until it occurred to me to enter π, and then the amount of smoothing increased substantially. Without being able to explain why, I suspect it has something to do with sines and cosines and the resampling routines used by the GD library.

Anyway, armed with these values, a for loop then iterates through all the steps, enlarging the original image a little at a time by passing it to plug-in number 12, *Image Resize*. Because each step is a floating point number, the final image will be close to, but rarely exactly, the new dimensions required. Therefore, before returning the final enlargement, PIPHP_ImageResize() is called one last time to ensure the exact size needed is returned.

How to Use It

To enlarge an image with this plug-in, you must already have it stored as a GD image object, which you then pass to PIPHP_ImageEnlarge(), along with the new width and height, and a smoothing level, like this:

```
$image = imagecreatefromjpeg("icon.jpg");
$image = PIPHP_ImageEnlarge($image, 285, 214, 15);
imagejpeg($image, "enlarged.jpg");
```

Here the image *icon.jpg* is loaded into memory using imagecreatefromjpeg() and then passed to the plug-in, with requested new dimensions of 285 × 214 pixels and a smoothing level of 15. The returned enlargement is then saved using the filename *enlarged.jpg* with the imagejpeg() function. The enlargement could equally be output directly to the browser like this:

```
$image = imagecreatefromjpeg("icon.jpg");
header("Content-type: image/jpeg");
imagejpeg(PIPHP_ImageEnlarge($image, 285, 214, 15));
```

Because the plug-in PIPHP_ImageResize() is called by this plug-in, you will need to ensure you have it already copied to, or included by, your program.

CAUTION   *Because this plug-in requires multiple iterations of a time-intensive resampling function, it's not recommended for on-the-fly conversion of images on a production server, and is much better suited for running as part of a background or housekeeping image management process, or for use on a personal PHP installation.*

The Plug-in

```
function PIPHP_ImageEnlarge($image, $w, $h, $smoothing)
{
    $oldw  = imagesx($image);
    $oldh  = imagesy($image);
    $step  = 3.1415927 * ((100 - $smoothing) / 100);
```

```
$max   = $w / $step;
$ratio = $h / $w;

for ($j = $oldw ; $j < $max; $j += $step)
    $image = PIPHP_ImageResize($image, $j * $step,
        $j * $step * $ratio);

return PIPHP_ImageResize($image, $w, $h);
}
```

17 Image Display

I've already shown you how to output a JPEG image directly to a browser by sending the correct header. But here's a plug-in that will output any GIF, JPEG, or PNG image, and if it's a JPEG or PNG, at whatever quality you choose to achieve the optimum balance between bandwidth use and image quality. For example, Figure 4-7 shows a JPEG image displayed by a PHP program at the default quality setting of 75.

About the Plug-in

This plug-in accepts a filename to display, the image type, and the quality required. It takes these arguments:

$filename A string containing the path/filename of an image

$type The file type of the image (either *gif, jpeg,* or *png*)

$quality The display quality if *jpeg* or *png* (0 = lowest, up to 99 = highest quality)

FIGURE 4-7 Using this plug-in, you can display images in a variety of formats and quality settings.

Variables, Arrays, and Functions

`$contents`	Temporary copy of the image loaded from file
`$filetype`	Array containing details about the file
`$mime`	String containing the image's type (such as "image/png")
`$image`	GD image object created from `$contents`

How It Works

The first thing this plug-in does is load the contents of the file pointed to by `$filename` into the string variable `$contents`. Next, if the `$type` parameter hasn't been given a value, the calling code wants the output type to remain unchanged, so it's looked up by calling the `imagegetsize()` function and the result is saved in the array `$filetype`. The third element of this array is a string containing the mime file type, so that is extracted and placed in the variable `$mime`. The correct header is then output followed by the value in `$contents`, which is the unaltered original image. The `die()` function is used to send the image because it combines an `echo` and `exit` statement in one, so it's more efficient.

The rest of the code is only executed if `$type` has a value, specifying the output type. In this case, a GD image is created from the file stored in `$contents` using `imagecreatefromstring()`, and the chosen mime type header is sent to the browser.

Next a `switch` statement tests `$type` to see whether it refers to a GIF, JPEG, or PNG image and calls the correct function to display it using either `imagegif()`, `imagejpeg()`, or `imagepng()`.

If the file is a JPEG or a PNG file, then the quality setting is applied. For a JPEG, the value passed needs to be between 0 and 99, with 0 being worst and 99 the best. This is exactly how the `imagejpeg` function expects to receive this value so the value of `$quality` is passed as-is. But the `imagepng()` function requires a quality value between 0 and 9, where 0 is the best and 9 the worst, which is the inverse of the former and also one tenth of the value. Therefore, a quick formula is applied to `$quality` to conform.

Using a lower quality setting results in the sent image being smaller with a corresponding saving in bandwidth, whereas a higher setting uses more bandwidth but results in better quality.

How to Use It

To display a file directly to a browser, just call the plug-in passing the filename, file type, and quality setting as in the following, which outputs a JPEG image in PNG format at a compression level of 50:

```
PIPHP_ImageDisplay("pic.jpg", "png", 50);
```

To display an image in its native format, you can omit the file type argument, as you can with the quality, by replacing these parameters with NULL:

```
PIPHP_ImageDisplay("pic.jpg", NULL, NULL);
```

The Plug-in

```
function PIPHP_ImageDisplay($filename, $type, $quality)
{
   $contents = file_get_contents($filename);

   if ($type == "")
   {
      $filetype = getimagesize($filename);
      $mime     = image_type_to_mime_type($filetype[2]);
      header("Content-type: $mime");
      die($contents);
   }

   $image = imagecreatefromstring($contents);
   header("Content-type: image/$type");

   switch($type)
   {
      case "gif":  imagegif($image); break;
      case "jpeg": imagejpeg($image, NULL, $quality); break;
      case "png":  imagepng($image,  NULL,
                      round(9 - $quality * .09)); break;
   }
}
```

PLUG-IN 18   Image Convert

This plug-in is similar to the previous one, Image Display, but it saves the new image to disk. Wrapped in suitable code, it's very handy for automatically changing the type (and quality) of images either singly or in batches. Figure 4-8 shows a 42Kb JPEG image that has been converted to another JPEG of only 8Kb by using a quality setting of 25.

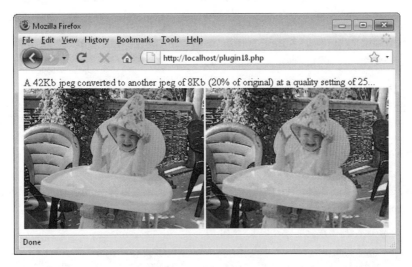

FIGURE 4-8   This plug-in converts images to JPEG, GIF, and PNG, and can change the quality setting, too.

The second image isn't too discernibly degraded, but the conversion achieves an 80 percent saving on bandwidth. You can specify the quality setting yourself. If you increase the quality, the image will use more bandwidth. If the image quality is decreased it will use less bandwidth. But remember that you cannot increase the quality above that of the original image.

About the Plug-in

This plug-in accepts the name of a file to convert, the name of the file it should be saved as, and the quality required. It takes these arguments:

$fromfile   String containing the path/filename of an image

$tofile   String containing the path/filename to save the new image

$type   The file type of the image (either *gif, jpeg,* or *png*)

$quality   The image quality if JPEG or PNG (0 = lowest, up to 99 = highest quality)

Variables, Arrays, and Functions

$contents	Temporary copy of the image loaded from the file
$image	GD image object created from $contents

How It Works

This plug-in loads in the contents of the image referred to by $fromfile into the string variable $contents, from where it creates a GD image object using the imagecreatefromstring() function.

Then, a switch statement is used to check whether the new image type required is GIF, JPEG, or PNG, and accordingly calls the imagegif(), imagejpeg(), or imagepng() function, passing the value of $tofile, which holds the path and name of the file to save, and $quality, which describes the quality setting if the image is a JPEG or PNG.

As with the previous plug-in, *Image Display,* the quality setting must be specially calculated for PNG files since the imagepng() function expects the compression setting in a different format than imagejpeg().

How to Use It

To convert an image type, call PIPHP_ImageConvert() with the source and destination path and/or filenames, along with the type to convert to and the quality setting to use, as in the following line of code, which converts the image in *photo.jpg* to a PNG file, and saves it as *photo.png*, using a compression value of 50:

```
PIPHP_ImageConvert("photo.jpg", "photo.png", "png", 50);
```

The Plug-in

```
function PIPHP_ImageConvert($fromfile, $tofile, $type, $quality)
{
   $contents = file_get_contents($fromfile);
```

```
$image    = imagecreatefromstring($contents);

switch($type)
{
   case "gif":  imagegif($image,  $tofile); break;
   case "jpeg": imagejpeg($image, $tofile, $quality); break;
   case "png":  imagepng($image,  $tofile,
                      round(9 - $quality * .09)); break;
}
}
```

Note that GIF images do not have a quality setting, so this value will make no difference to the resulting image. Also, to see the differences between before and after, make sure you reload any converted images into your browser so that previous unconverted images are not served up from the cache in place of the converted ones.

PLUG-IN 19 Gif Text

Although web browsers come with a reasonable range of default fonts, they don't always provide the look you need for a particular web site. In such cases, you usually must resort to calling up a graphics editor and creating logos or headlines there.

However, with this plug-in, all you have to do is upload the TrueType fonts you wish to use to your web site. You can then display text in these fonts by having the GD library convert it on the fly to GIF images. Figure 4-9 shows the text "Old English Font" displayed at four different sizes using an Old English TrueType font.

FIGURE 4-9   Now you can use any fonts you like on your web pages thanks to this plug-in.

About the Plug-in

This plug-in takes the name of a file to save as a finished GIF, the text and font to use in it, and various details such as color, size, and shadowing. It takes these arguments:

$file   The path/filename to save the image

$text   The text to create

$font   The path/filename of the TrueType font to use

$size   The font size

$fore   The foreground color in hexadecimal (such as "000000")

$back   The background color (such as "FFFFFF")

$shadow   The number of pixels to offset a shadow underneath the text (0 = no shadow)

$shadowcolor   The shadow color (such as "444444")

Variables, Arrays, and Functions

$bound	Array containing the boundaries required to make room for the text
$width	Integer containing the text width in pixels calculated from $bound
$height	Integer containing the text height in pixels calculated from $bound
$image	Temporary copy of the final image
$bgcol	The background color identifier created from $back
$fgcol	The foreground color identifier created from $fore
$shcol	The shadow color identifier created from $shadowcolor
PIPHP_GD_FN1()	Function to create color identifiers

How It Works

To create a GIF image of the correct dimensions to hold the text, the function imagettfbbox() is called with the font, its size, and the text to display as arguments. The result, which contains the x and y coordinates of all four corners, is then stored in the array $bound.

Using these, the variables $width and $height are assigned values sufficiently large to accommodate the text and any shadow, as well as a few pixels space all around. Then, a new GD image is created in $image using this width and height.

Next, three color identifiers are created in $bgcol, $fgcol, and $shcol using the string values supplied in $fore, $back, and $shadowcolor by calling the function PIPHP_GD_FN1(), which takes a six-character hexadecimal string and converts it to a color identifier. These identifiers are unique to the $image object and are used to set colors in it. This function is just a helper function to the main plug-in and is not documented because it's not intended to be called directly by any other code.

With the colors prepared, the image is then filled with the background color using the imagefilledrectangle() function.

Next, if $shadow is greater than 0, then a shadow needs to be displayed so the imagettftext() function is called to display the text at an offset of two pixels along and two pixels down, and in the correct shadow color.

After that, the code for adding the main text itself is called. This is the same as for the shadow text except that no offset is used and the text is created in the foreground color.

Finally, the imagegif() function is called to save the finished image using the path/filename stored in $file.

How to Use It

To use this plug-in, upload the TrueType file(s) you want to the same folder as the PHP program. In this case, it's assumed that you have uploaded a font called *oldenglish.ttf*. You can then create a GIF containing text of your choice like this:

```
PIPHP_GifText("greeting.gif", "Hello there!", "oldenglish.ttf",
    26, "ff0000", "ffffff", 1, "444444");
```

To display the image you then only need to output some HTML code, like this:

```
echo "<img src='greeting.gif' />";
```

However, to ensure the image is only created the first time it is needed, you will probably want to wrap the above code within an if statement, like this:

```
if (!file_exists("greeting.gif"))
{
    PIPHP_GifText("greeting.gif", "Hello there!", "oldenglish.ttf",
        26, "ff0000", "ffffff", 1, "444444");
}
```

The Plug-in

```
function PIPHP_GifText($file, $text, $font, $size, $fore, $back,
    $shadow, $shadowcolor)
{
    $bound   = imagettfbbox($size, 0, $font, $text);
    $width   = $bound[2] + $bound[0] + 6 + $shadow;
    $height  = abs($bound[1]) + abs($bound[7]) + 5 + $shadow;
    $image   = imagecreatetruecolor($width, $height);
    $bgcol   = PIPHP_GD_FN1($image, $back);
    $fgcol   = PIPHP_GD_FN1($image, $fore);
    $shcol   = PIPHP_GD_FN1($image, $shadowcolor);
    imagefilledrectangle($image, 0, 0, $width, $height, $bgcol);

    if ($shadow > 0) imagettftext($image, $size, 0, $shadow + 2,
        abs($bound[5]) + $shadow + 2, $shcol, $font, $text);

    imagettftext($image, $size, 0, 2, abs($bound[5]) + 2, $fgcol,
        $font, $text);
    imagegif($image, $file);
}
```

```
function PIPHP_GD_FN1($image, $color)
{
    return imagecolorallocate($image,
        hexdec(substr($color, 0, 2)),
        hexdec(substr($color, 2, 2)),
        hexdec(substr($color, 4, 2)));
}
```

PLUG-IN 20 | Image Watermark

In a similar way to creating GIF images of text, you can also overlay text on an existing image to create watermarks. With the amount of copying and pasting of images across the web, when you have one you would like to protect, sometimes watermarking is the best way. This plug-in provides a variety of options. For example, Figure 4-10 shows a photograph with the word *Watermark* overlaid in white at a transparency setting of 10 percent.

About the Plug-in

This plug-in takes the name of a file in which to save a finished GIF, the text and font to use, and various details such as color, size, and shadowing. It takes these arguments:

$fromfile   The path/filename of the original image

$tofile   The path/filename to save the image

FIGURE 4-10   Now you don't have to load your images into a graphics editor to add watermarks.

$type   One of *gif*, *jpeg*, or *png*

$quality   Quality setting of final image (0 = worst, up to 99 = best)

$text   The text to create

$font   The path/filename of the TrueType font to use

$size   The font size

$fore   The foreground color in hexadecimal (such as "000000")

$opacity   The opacity of the watermark (0 = transparent, up to 100 = opaque)

Variables, Arrays, and Functions

$contents	The image contents loaded in from $fromfile
$image1	GD image object created from $contents
$bound	Array containing the boundaries required to make room for the text
$width	Integer containing the text width in pixels calculated from $bound
$height	Integer containing the text height in pixels calculated from $bound
$image2	GD image object created to hold watermarking text
$bgcol	The background color identifier, from the string "fedcba" (see the *How It Works* section)
$fgcol	The foreground color identifier created from $fore
PIPHP_GD_FN1()	Function to create color identifiers

How It Works

This plug-in starts by loading the image referred to by $fromfile into $contents, from where it's changed to a GD image object and stored in $image1. Then, the array $bound is populated with the result of calling imagettfbbox() to get the coordinates of all the corners needed to create a space big enough to store the watermark text.

The width and height of this box are then extracted from $bound into $width and $height, with a few pixels leeway being left in all dimensions. Using this width and height, a new GD image object is created in $image2. Then, two color identifiers are created for the background and foreground colors in $bgcol and $fgcol. This is done using the function PIPHP_GD_FN1(), which is designed for use only by these plug-ins and is not intended to be called directly from your programs.

Because the text for watermarking will be transparent, I selected a background color of "fedcba", which is unlikely to be used as the foreground color. If you do need that as a foreground color, I'm sure you could get away with using "fedcb9" or "fedcbb", and so on, instead.

As I said, the background color must be transparent so it's passed to the function imagecolortransparent(), and then the entire $image2 rectangle is filled in that color using imagefilledrectangle(). With the background canvas prepared, the text is then written to it in the foreground color, using the font and size specified.

At this point the function now has two separate images—the original, and the watermark to add—so it calls the imagecopymerge() function to merge the watermark onto the original image, exactly in the middle, and with an opacity of $opacity.

Finally, a switch statement is used to check the image type for being one of GIF, JPEG, or PNG and then calls either imagegif(), imagejpeg(), or imagepng() accordingly to save the image, using the path/filename in $tofile. If the type you wish to save it as is a PNG or JPEG, then the quality setting in $quality is also applied, although a little math is required to manipulate it into the correct form required for the imagepng() function.

How to Use It

To watermark an image, supply the function PIPHP_ImageWatermark() with the names of a source and destination file, the image type, and the parameters required for font, size, color, and transparency, like this:

```
PIPHP_ImageWatermark("pic.jpg", "wmark.png", "png", 75,
    "Watermark", "oldenglish.ttf", 90, "ffffff", 10);
```

Here the file *pic.jpg* is overlaid with a watermark containing the text "Watermark", using the *oldenglish.ttf* font with a size of 90, a color of "ffffff" and an opacity value of 10. The file is saved as a PNG image, at a quality setting of 75, using the filename *wmark.png*.

The Plug-in

```
function PIPHP_ImageWatermark($fromfile, $tofile, $type,
    $quality, $text, $font, $size, $fore, $opacity)
{
    $contents = file_get_contents($fromfile);
    $image1   = imagecreatefromstring($contents);
    $bound    = imagettfbbox($size, 0, $font, $text);
    $width    = $bound[2] + $bound[0] + 6;
    $height   = abs($bound[1]) + abs($bound[7]) + 5;
    $image2   = imagecreatetruecolor($width, $height);
    $bgcol    = PIPHP_GD_FN1($image2, "fedcba");
    $fgcol    = PIPHP_GD_FN1($image2, $fore);

    imagecolortransparent($image2, $bgcol);
    imagefilledrectangle($image2, 0, 0, $width, $height, $bgcol);
    imagettftext($image2, $size, 0, 2, abs($bound[5]) + 2,
        $fgcol, $font, $text);
    imagecopymerge($image1, $image2,
        (imagesx($image1) - $width) / 2,
        (imagesy($image1) - $height) / 2,
        0, 0, $width, $height, $opacity);

    switch($type)
```

```php
    {
        case "gif":  imagegif($image1,  $tofile); break;
        case "jpeg": imagejpeg($image1, $tofile, $quality); break;
        case "png":  imagepng($image1,  $tofile,
                        round(9 - $quality * .09)); break;
    }
}

function PIPHP_GD_FN1($image, $color)
{
    return imagecolorallocate($image,
        hexdec(substr($color, 0, 2)),
        hexdec(substr($color, 2, 2)),
        hexdec(substr($color, 4, 2)));
}
```

CHAPTER 5

Content Management

W hen developing web projects, there are certain content management processes that are so common it can save you a great deal of programming to have ready-made plug-ins available. Some examples include converting relative to absolute URLs, checking for broken links, tracking web visitors, and more.

This chapter explores ten of these types of functions that you can add to your toolbox, and explains how they work so you can further tailor them to your own requirements. Along the way, it covers parsing URLs, extracting information from web pages (even on other servers), reading the contents of local files and directories, accessing query strings that result from search engine referrals, embedding YouTube videos, counting raw and unique web visits, and tracking where users are coming from.

PLUG-IN 21   Relative to Absolute URL

Any project that needs to crawl web pages, whether their own or a third party's, needs a way to convert relative URLs into absolute URLs that can be called up on their own, without reference to the page in which they are located. For example, the URL */sport/index .html* means nothing at all when looked at on its own, and there is no way of knowing that the URL was extracted from the web page *http://server.com/news/*.

Using this plug-in, relative URLs can be combined with the referring page to create stand-alone absolute URLs, such as *http://server.com/sport/index.html*. Figure 5-1 shows a variety of links being converted to absolute.

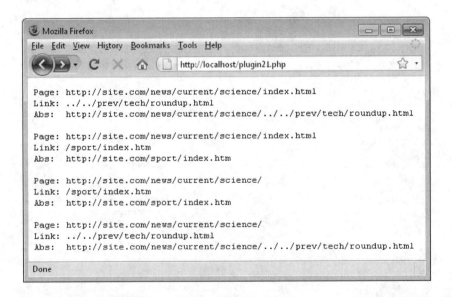

FIGURE 5-1   This plug-in provides the solution to a common problem encountered in web development: converting a relative URL to absolute.

About the Plug-in

This plug-in takes the URL of a web page, along with a link from within that page, and then returns the link in a form that can be accessed without reference to the calling page—in other words, an absolute URL. It takes these arguments:

- **$page**   A web page URL, including the *http://* preface and domain name
- **$url**   A link extracted from $page

Variables, Arrays, and Functions

$parse	Associative array derived from parsing $page
$root	String comprising the first part of $page up to and including the host domain name
$p	Integer pointer to the final / in $page
$base	The current directory where $page is located

How It Works

In order to convert a URL from relative to absolute it's necessary to know *where* the relative URL is relative *to*. This is why the main page URL is passed along with the relative URL. In fact, not all the URLs passed may be relative, and they could even all be absolute, depending on how $page has been written. But what this plug-in does is process a URL anyway, and if it's determined to be relative, then it's turned into an absolute URL.

It does this by first parsing the original URL, passed in $page, and extracting the scheme (for example, *http://* or *ftp://*, and so on) and host (such as *myserver.com*) and combining just these two parts together into the string variable $root to create, for example, the string *http://myserver.com*.

Then, $page is examined to see if there are any / characters after the initial *http://*. If so, the final one is located and its position is placed in $p. If there isn't one, then $p is set to 0. Using this value, $base is assigned either the substring of $page all the way up to and including the final /, or if there wasn't one, $base is assigned the value of $page itself, but with a final / appended to it. Either way, $base now represents the location of the directory containing $page.

Next $url is examined, and if it starts with a /, then it must be a relative URL—referring to an offset from the domain's document root. In which case $url is replaced with a value comprising the concatenation of $root and $url. So, for example, *http://myserver.com* and */news/index.html* would combine to become *http://myserver.com/news/index.html*.

If $url doesn't start with a /, then a test is made to see whether it begins with *http://*. If not, the URL must also be relative, but this time it is relative to the directory location of $page, so $url is replaced with a value comprising the concatenation of $base and $url. So, for example, *http://myserver.com/sport* and *results.html* would combine to become *http://myserver.com/sport/results.html*.

If both these tests fail, then $url commences with *http://* and therefore is an absolute URL and cannot be converted. It is therefore returned unchanged.

> *NOTE   For the sake of speed and simplicity, a complete relative-to-absolute URL conversion is not made. For example, the URL ../news/index.html in the page* http://myserver.com/sport/ *is not converted to* http://myserver.com/news/index.html. *Instead it becomes* http://myserver.com/sport/../news/index.html. *This saves the code having to further parse a URL, locating examples of ../ and then removing the directory immediately previous to it. There's no need because this longer form of absolute URL is perfectly valid and works just fine.*

How to Use It

To use this plug-in, pass it the full URL of a page that contains a relative link, along with the relative link itself, like this:

```
$page = "http://site.com/news/current/science/index.html";
$link = "../../prev/tech/roundup.html";
echo PIPHP_RelToAbsURL($page, $link);
```

The value returned will be an absolute URL that can be used to access the destination page without recourse to the original web page. In the preceding case, the following URL will be returned:

```
http://site.com/news/current/science/../../prev/tech/roundup.html
```

The Plug-in

```
function PIPHP_RelToAbsURL($page, $url)
{
    if (substr($page, 0, 7) != "http://") return $url;

    $parse = parse_url($page);
    $root  = $parse['scheme'] . "://" . $parse['host'];
    $p     = strrpos(substr($page, 7), '/');

    if ($p) $base = substr($page, 0, $p + 8);
    else $base = "$page/";

    if (substr($url, 0, 1) == '/')            $url = $root . $url;
    elseif (substr($url, 0, 7) != "http://")  $url = $base . $url;

    return $url;
}
```

PLUG-IN 22   Get Links from URL

When you first need to extract HTML links from a web page (even your own) it looks almost impossible and seems quite a daunting task. And it's true, parsing HTML is quite complex. But with this plug-in all you need to do is pass it the URL of a web page and all the links found within it will be returned. Figure 5-2 shows links being extracted from a web page.

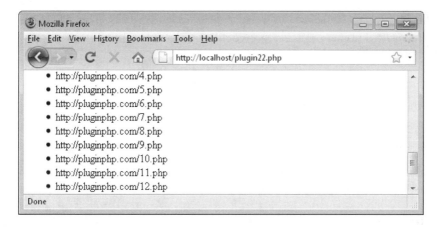

FIGURE 5-2   Using this plug-in you can extract and return all the links in a web page.

About the Plug-in

This plug-in takes the URL of a web page and parses it looking only for <a href links, and returns all that it finds in an array. It takes a single argument:

- **$page**   A web page URL, including the *http://* preface and domain name

Variables, Arrays, and Functions

$contents	String containing the HTML contents of $page
$urls	Array holding the discovered URLs
$dom	Document object of $contents
$xpath	XPath object for traversing $dom
$hrefs	Object containing all href link elements in $dom
$j	Integer loop counter for iterating through $hrefs
PIPHP_RelToAbsURL()	Function to convert relative URLs to absolute

How It Works

This plug-in first reads the contents of $page into the string $contents (returning NULL if there's an error). Then it creates a new Document Object Model (DOM) of $contents in $dom using the loadhtml() method. The statement is prefaced with an @ character to suppress any warning or error messages. Even poorly formatted HTML is generally useable with this method because it finds the URLs easy to extract and parse.

Then a new XPath object is created in $xpath with which to search $dom for all instances of href elements, and all those discovered are then placed in the $hrefs object. Next a for loop is used to iterate through the $hrefs object and extract all the attributes, which in this case are the links we want. Prior to storing the URLs in $urls, each one is passed through the PIPHP_RelToAbsURL() function to ensure they are converted to absolute URLs (if not already).

Once extracted, the links are then returned as an array.

How to Use It

To extract all the URLs from a page and receive them in absolute form, just call PIPHP_ GetLinksFromURL() like this:

```
$result = PIPHP_GetLinksFromURL("http://pluginphp.com");
```

You can then display (or otherwise make use of) the returned array like this:

```
for ($j = 0 ; $j < count($result) ; ++$j)
   echo "$result[$j]<br />";
```

Note that this plug-in makes use of plug-in 21, PIPHP_RelToAbsURL(), and so it must also be pasted into (or included by) your program.

The Plug-in

```
function PIPHP_GetLinksFromURL($page)
{
   $contents = @file_get_contents($page);
   if (!$contents) return NULL;

   $urls  = array();
   $dom   = new domdocument();
   @$dom  ->loadhtml($contents);
   $xpath = new domxpath($dom);
   $hrefs = $xpath->evaluate("/html/body//a");

   for ($j = 0 ; $j < $hrefs->length ; $j++)
      $urls[$j] = PIPHP_RelToAbsURL($page,
         $hrefs->item($j)->getAttribute('href'));

   return $urls;
}
```

PLUG-IN 23   Check Links

The two previous plug-ins provide the foundation for being able to crawl the Internet by:

- Reading in a third-party web page
- Extracting all URLs from the page
- Converting all the URLs to absolute

Armed with these abilities, it's now a simple matter for this plug-in to offer the facility to check all links on a web page and test whether the pages they refer to actually load or not; a great way to alleviate the frustration of your users upon encountering dead links or mistyped URLs. Figure 5-3 shows this plug-in being used to check the links on the *alexa.com* home page.

FIGURE 5-3   The plug-in has been run on the alexa.com home page, with all URLs reported present and correct.

About the Plug-in

This plug-in takes the URL of a web page (yours or a third party's) and then tests all the links found within it to see whether they resolve to valid pages. It takes these three arguments:

- **$page**   A web page URL, including the *http://* preface and domain name
- **$timeout**   The number of seconds to wait for a web page before considering it unavailable
- **$runtime**   The maximum number of seconds your script should run before timing out

Variables, Arrays, and Functions

$contents	String containing the HTML contents of $page
$checked	Array of URLs that have been checked
$failed	Array of URLs that could not be retrieved
$fail	Integer containing the number of failed URLs
$urls	Array of URLs extracted from $page
$context	Stream context to set the URL load timeout
PIPHP_GetLinksFromURL()	Function to retrieve all links from a page
PIPHP_RelToAbsURL()	Function to convert relative URLs to absolute

How It Works

The first thing this plug-in does is set the maximum execution time of the script using the ini_set() function. This is necessary because crawling a set of web pages can take a considerable time. I recommend you may want to experiment with maximums of up to 180 seconds or more. If the script ends without returning anything, try increasing the value.

The contents of $page are then loaded into $contents. After these two arrays are initialized. The first, $checked, will contain all the URLs that have been checked so that, where a page links to another more than once, a second check is not made for that URL.

The second array, $failed, will contain all the URLs that couldn't be loaded. The counter $fail is initially set to 0. When any URL fails to load, $fail will be incremented.

Next the array $urls is populated with all the URLs from $page using the PIPHP_ GetLinksFromURL() plug-in, and $context is assigned the correct values to set the timeout for each checked page to the value that was supplied to the function in the variable $timeout. This will be used shortly by the file_get_contents() function.

With all the variables, objects, and arrays initialized, a for loop is entered in which each URL is tested in turn, but only if it hasn't been already. This is determined by testing whether the current URL already exists in $checked, the array of checked URLs. If it doesn't, the URL is added to the $checked array and the file_get_contents() function is called (with the $context object) to attempt to fetch the first 256 bytes of the web page. If that fails, the URL is added to the $failed array and $fail is incremented.

Once the loop has completed, an array is returned with the first element containing 0 if there were no failed URLs. Otherwise, it contains the number of failures, while the second element contains an array listing all the failed URLs.

How to Use It

To check all the links on a web page, call the function using code such as this:

```
$page = "http://myserver.com";
$result = PIPHP_CheckLinks($page, 2, 180);
```

To then view or otherwise use the returned values, use code such as the following, which either displays a success message or lists the failed URLs:

```
if ($result[0] == 0) echo "All URLs successfully accessed.";
else for ($j = 0 ; $j < $result[0] ; ++$j)
    echo $result[1][$j] . "<br />";
```

Because this plug-in makes use of plug-in 22, PIPHP_GetLinksFromURL(), which itself relies on plug-in 21, PIPHP_RelToAbsURL(), you must ensure you have copied both of them into your program file, or that they are included by it.

TIP *Because crawling like this can take time, when nothing is displayed to the screen you may wonder whether your program is actually working. So, if you wish to view the plug-in's progress, you can uncomment the line shown to have each URL displayed as it's processed.*

The Plug-in

```
function PIPHP_CheckLinks($page, $timeout, $runtime)
{
    ini_set('max_execution_time', $runtime);
    $contents = @file_get_contents($page);
    if (!$contents) return array(1, array($page));

    $checked = array();
    $failed  = array();
    $fail    = 0;
    $urls    = PIPHP_GetLinksFromURL($page);
```

```
$context = stream_context_create(array('http' =>
    array('timeout' => $timeout)));

for ($j = 0 ; $j < count($urls); $j++)
{
    if (!in_array($urls[$j], $checked))
    {
        $checked[] = $urls[$j];

        // Uncomment the following line to view progress
        // echo " $urls[$j]<br />\n"; ob_flush(); flush();

        if (!@file_get_contents($urls[$j], 0, $context, 0, 256))
            $failed[$fail++] = $urls[$j];
    }
}

return array($fail, $failed);
}
```

PLUG-IN 24 — Directory List

When you need to know the contents of a directory on your server—for example, because you support file uploads and need to keep tabs on them—this plug-in returns all the filenames using a single function call. Figure 5-4 shows the plug-in in action.

FIGURE 5-4   Using the Directory List plug-in under Windows to return the contents of Zend Server CE's document root

About the Plug-in

This plug-in takes the location of a directory on your server and returns all the files within it in an array. Upon success, it returns a four-element array, the first of which is the number of directories found. The second is the number of files found, the third is an array of directory names, and the fourth is an array of file names. On failure, it returns a single-element array with the value FALSE. It requires this argument:

- **$path**   The path of a directory on the server

Variables, Arrays, and Functions

$files	Array containing the files encountered
$dirs	Array containing the directories encountered
$fnum	Integer containing the number of files
$dnum	Integer containing the number of directories
$dh	Handle to identify the directory
$item	String containing each encountered item in turn

How It Works

This program initializes the two arrays, $files and $dirs, which will contain the files and directories encountered in $path, and sets the two counters for the numbers of files and directories, $fnum and $dnum, to 0.

Then, $path is checked to ensure it's a valid directory. If it is, the directory is opened using opendir() and a handle to it is placed in $dh. Then, a do loop is entered in which each item in the directory is read in turn into the string $item. If the value of $item is FALSE at any time, the end of the directory listing has been encountered. However, there's a slight problem because a file or subdirectory could have the name "0", which would be interpreted as having the value FALSE by PHP. To avoid this, instead of comparing using the != operator, !== is used instead. This tells PHP not to try to evaluate anything before making the comparison, and only to compare exact values. The file names . and .. are also ignored.

Next the current item is tested to see whether it's a file or a directory. If it's a directory, it is placed in the $dirs array and $dnum is incremented. If it's a file, it is placed in the $files array and $fnum is incremented. The do loop then continues until $item has a value of FALSE, at which point the $dh handle is closed.

At the end of the code the results are returned in an array of four elements as follows:

- Element 0: The number of directories found
- Element 1: The number of files found
- Element 2: Array containing the directory names
- Element 3: Array containing the file names

If $path was not a valid directory, the return statement will simply return zeros and empty array values.

How to Use It

You call up the plug-in using code such as this, setting $directory to the folder whose contents you are interested in:

```
$directory = "c:\windows";
$result = PIPHP_DirectoryList($directory);
```

You can then use the returned values like this to display the directories found:

```
if ($result[0] == 0) echo "No Directories found";
else for ($j=0 ; $j < $result[0] ; ++$j)
   echo $result[2][$j] . "<br />";
```

Or like this to list the files:

```
if ($result[1] == 0) echo "No files found";
else for ($j=0 ; $j < $result[1] ; ++$j)
   echo $result[3][$j] . "<br />";
```

Or you might prefer to use foreach instead of for loops, like this:

```
if ($result[0] == 0) echo "No Directories found";
else foreach($result[2] as $directory)
   echo "$directory<br />";

if ($result[1] == 0) echo "No files found";
else foreach($result[3] as $file)
   echo "$file<br />";
```

The Plug-in

```
function PIPHP_DirectoryList($path)
{
   $files = array();
   $dirs  = array();
   $fnum  = $dnum = 0;

   if (is_dir($path))
   {
      $dh = opendir($path);

      do
      {
         $item = readdir($dh);

         if ($item !== FALSE && $item != "." && $item != "..")
         {
            if (is_dir("$path/$item")) $dirs[$dnum++] = $item;
            else $files[$fnum++] = $item;
         }
      } while($item !== FALSE);

      closedir($dh);
   }

   return array($dnum, $fnum, $dirs, $files);
}
```

25 Query Highlight

When a visitor comes to your web site from a search engine result, you can use this plug-in to be helpful and highlight all the items from their search in your text, deciding whether to highlight these terms with either boldface, italics, or an underline. Figure 5-5 shows some words from a Shakespeare play being highlighted using this plug-in.

About the Plug-in

This plug-in takes the text to display and the type of highlighting required for any search terms encountered. It requires these arguments:

- **$text** The text to highlight
- **$highlight** The type of highlight to use, either b, i, or u for bold, italic, or underline

Variables, Arrays, and Functions

`$refer`	The referring web page, if any
`$parse`	Array containing the parts of `$refer`
`$queries`	String containing queries extracted from `$refer`
`$key`	String containing first half of a key/value pair
`$value`	String containing second half of a key/value pair
`$matches`	Array containing search words
`PIPHP_WordSelector()`	Function used to highlight selected words in text

How It Works

The URL of the referring page is placed in `$refer`, and the array `$parse` is set to the component parts of `$refer`. If there was no referring page, the text supplied in `$text` is returned unmodified. This is also the case if there *was* a referring page but *no* search string query. Otherwise, the array `$queries` is filled with the various queries that can follow a URL, and which are separated by & characters.

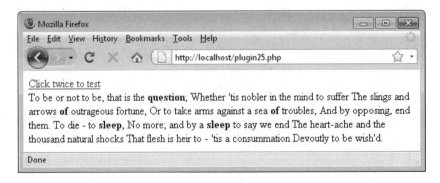

FIGURE 5-5 If a page has been arrived at from a search engine, you can highlight all the words matching the query with this plug-in.

A foreach loop is then entered, which iterates through each of the strings in the $queries array, setting $key and $value to the left and right halves of each. If any of the $key values is either q or p, chances are the code is looking at the result of a search query made with one of the major search engines (Yahoo!, Bing, Google, or Ask Jeeves), and so the contents of $value will be passed to urldecode() to turn any unusual characters into regular ones, and then all words found in this string will be split out into the array $matches.

Provided with this array of search words, PIPHP_WordSelector() is then called to highlight any of these words that appear within the string $text. The result of this is then returned.

How to Use It

To highlight search terms within some text, call the plug-in like this:

```
$text = "To be or not to be, that is the question; " .
        "whether 'tis nobler in the mind to suffer " .
        "the slings and arrows of outrageous fortune, " .
        "or to take arms against a sea of troubles, " .
        "and by opposing, end them. To die - to sleep, " .
        "no more; and by a sleep to say we end " .
        "the heart-ache and the thousand natural shocks " .
        "that flesh is heir to - 'tis a consummation " .
        "devoutly to be wish'd.";

echo PIPHP_QueryHighlight($text, "b");
```

In this example, any words in the string $text, which were used as a search term at a major search engine to discover the current page, will be highlighted in bold face. So, for example, if the user searched for "question of sleep" then the previous text would be highlighted like this:

> To be or not to be, that is the **question**; whether 'tis nobler in the mind to suffer the slings and arrows **of** outrageous fortune, or to take arms against a sea **of** troubles, and by opposing, end them. To die - to **sleep**, no more; and by a **sleep** to say we end the heart-ache and the thousand natural shocks that flesh is heir to - 'tis a consummation devoutly to be wish'd.

You can include any text or HTML you like and the plug-in will still work correctly. Punctuation is also fully supported, so you don't have to ensure spaces exist on either side of keywords for them to be recognized.

On its own, if you just type in the preceding example and call it up in a browser, you will not see any highlighting because there is no referring page; you will have entered the page directly. So to simulate a referred visit from a search engine, you can add the following code to the preceding two commands:

```
echo "<br /><a href=\"" . $_SERVER['PHP_SELF'] .
     "?q=" . rawurlencode("question of sleep") .
     "\">Click twice to test</a><br />";
```

This displays an HTML link that will cause the PHP program to call itself up when the link is clicked, acting as its own referring page. You need to do this twice, though, in order to properly simulate a visit referred from a search engine. The first click adds the referrer information to the tail of the URL (as displayed in the browser address field), and the second passes that tail to the program where it can be processed. After the second click, you'll see that the text has been highlighted.

Because this plug-in makes use of plug-in 5, PIPHP_WordSelector(), you need to also copy it into your program or otherwise include it.

The Plug-in

```
function PIPHP_QueryHighlight($text, $highlight)
{
    $refer = getenv('HTTP_REFERER');
    $parse = parse_url($refer);

    if ($refer == "") return $text;
    elseif (!isset($parse['query'])) return $text;

    $queries = explode('&', $parse['query']);

    foreach($queries as $query)
    {
        list($key, $value) = explode('=', $query);

        if ($key == "q" || $key == "p")
        {
            $matches = explode(' ', preg_replace('/[^\w ]/', '',
                urldecode($value)));
            return PIPHP_WordSelector($text, $matches, $highlight);
        }
    }
}
```

PLUG-IN 26   Rolling Copyright

If you've developed for the Web for more than a couple of years, you're bound to have encountered the problem whereby every January you have to wade in and locate all the copyright statements to bring them up to date with the new year. Well, with this short and sweet plug-in, that never need be a problem again, since it will ensure your web sites always show the current year, as shown in Figure 5-6.

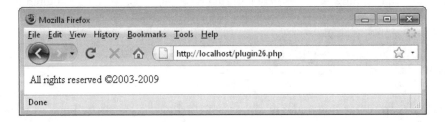

FIGURE 5-6   Ensuring your copyright message is always up-to-date is easy with this plug-in.

About the Plug-in

This plug-in takes a copyright message and the first year the copyright began. It requires these arguments:

- **$message** The copyright message
- **$year** The year the copyright began

Variables, Arrays, and Functions

- None.

How It Works

Although this is a very short plug-in, it's well worth using because it can save you no end of time. What it does is return the message supplied in $message, along with a copyright sign, the start year in $year and the current year, as returned by the date() function.

How to Use It

To add an always up-to-date copyright message to your web site, use code such as this:

```
echo PIPHP_RollingCopyright("All rights reserved", 2003);
```

The Plug-in

```
function PIPHP_RollingCopyright($message, $year)
{
    return "$message &copy;$year-" . date("Y");
}
```

Embed YouTube Video

How often have you grabbed the embed code for a YouTube video only to find you have to tweak it to get the right dimensions for your web site, or select high-quality video, or make it auto start? With this plug-in you can replace all that with a single function call whenever you need to embed a video. Figure 5-7 shows such a video displayed with a single call to this plug-in.

About the Plug-in

This plug-in takes the YouTube ID of a video and the parameters required to display it to your requirements. It accepts these arguments:

- **$id** A YouTube video ID such as "VjnygQ02aW4"
- **$width** The display width
- **$height** The display height
- **$hq** If set to 1, enable high-quality display, if available
- **$full** If set to 1, enable the video to play in full-screen mode
- **$auto** If set to 1, start the video playing automatically on page load

FIGURE **5-7**   This plug-in facilitates embedding a YouTube video with various options such as video quality and auto start.

Variables, Arrays, and Functions

$q	String variable set to the required value to enable high-quality display

How It Works

This plug-in first checks whether $hq has a value of 1, and if so, sets $q to the value &ap=%2526fmt%3D18, which will be tacked onto the YouTube URLs in order to enable high-quality video (where available).

Then, a <<<_END ... _END; construct is entered, which passes all the HTML within these tags to the return keyword *after* substituting any PHP variables encountered with their values. This means that, for example, in the <object> tag $width and $height are substituted by the supplied values, and so on.

The result is that the plug-in returns the HTML required to display a YouTube video exactly to your requirements.

How to Use It

To embed a YouTube video in a web page, call the plug-in like this:

```
echo PIPHP_EmbedYouTubeVideo("VjnygQ02aW4", 370, 300, 1, 1, 0);
```

Here a video showing President Obama's inauguration has been selected to be displayed at a width of 370 and height of 300 pixels, with both the high-quality and full-screen options enabled, but with auto start disabled.

TIP *If you wish to display videos using YouTube's recommended default dimensions, select a width and height of 425 × 344 pixels.*

The Plug-in

```
function PIPHP_EmbedYouTubeVideo($id, $width, $height, $hq,
    $full, $auto)
{
    if ($hq == 1) $q = "&ap=%2526fmt%3D18";
    else $q = "";

    return <<<_END
<object width="$width" height="$height">
<param name="movie"
    value="http://www.youtube.com/v/$id&fs=1&autoplay=$auto$q">
</param>
<param name="allowFullScreen" value="true"></param>
<param name="allowscriptaccess" value="always"></param>
<embed src="http://www.youtube.com/v/$id&fs=1&autoplay=$auto$q"
    type="application/x-shockwave-flash"
    allowscriptaccess="always" allowfullscreen="true"
    width="$width" height="$height"></embed></object>
_END;
}
```

PLUG-IN 28 Create List

Displaying lists is one of the most common elements of a web page. Whether for lists of related blog entry URLs, headlines, navigation, or others, lists provide an instant visual cue and are easy to use. With this plug-in, you can easily create the HTML for eight different types of lists using a single function call. Figure 5-8 shows the types of list this plug-in suports.

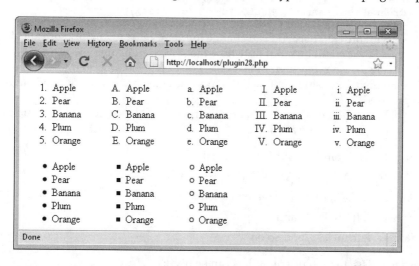

FIGURE 5-8 Using this plug-in, you can automatically create the HTML for eight different types of lists.

About the Plug-in

This plug-in takes an array containing all the items in a list, along with parameters to control the display formatting. It accepts these arguments:

- **$items**   An array containing all the items in the list
- **$start**   The start number for ordered lists
- **$type**   The type of list: ul for unordered and ol for ordered
- **$bullet**   The type of bullet. For unordered lists: square, circle, or disc. For ordered lists: 1, A, a, I, or i

Variables, Arrays, and Functions

$list	String variable containing HTML to be returned

How It Works

This plug-in starts by opening a new HTML list tag, which can be either <ol or <ul, depending on the value in $type. It also sets the start value to $start and the bullet type to $bullet.

A foreach loop is then entered to iterate through every element in the $items array, temporarily placing each in the string variable $item, which is then enclosed by <li> and </li> tags. The result is then appended to the string $list which, once the loop completes, is returned to the calling code, along with a closing </ol> or </ul> tag.

How to Use It

To create the HTML for a list, pass it an array containing the list of elements, along with the formatting arguments required, as in the following, which creates the HTML for an unordered list using the circle character as a bullet:

```
$fruits = array("Apple", "Pear", "Banana", "Plum", "Orange");
echo PIPHP_CreateList($fruits, NULL, "ul", "circle");
```

If you wish, with ordered lists you can change the start value to any numerical value you like, instead of the default of 1. But note how the start argument in the preceding code is set to NULL because it isn't required. In this case, you could actually set it to any value since it will be ignored, but using NULL will remind you when browsing your code that no value is being passed.

The types of bullets you can use depend on the type of list being created. For an ordered list, five different bullet types are available:

- **1**   Numerical: From 1 onwards in decimal
- **A**   Alphabetic: A–Z, then AA–AZ, then BA to BZ, and so on
- **a**   Alphabetic: a–z, then aa–az, then ba to bz, and so on
- **I**   Roman: I, II, III, IV, V, and so on
- **i**   Roman: i, ii, iii, iv, v, and so on

For unordered lists, three types of bullets can be used:

- **square**   A filled-in square

- **circle**   An open circle
- **disc**   A filled-in circle

The Plug-in

```
function PIPHP_CreateList($items, $start, $type, $bullet)
{
    $list = "<$type start='$start' type='$bullet'>";
    foreach ($items as $item) $list .= "<li>$item</li>\n";
    return $list . "</$type>";
}
```

PLUG-IN 29   Hit Counter

For long-term statistical information, you can always use a service such as Google Analytics to keep track of your web visitors. However, when you have a brand new page and need to know instantly whether and how much traffic it is attracting, your normal recourse is to view the server log files. But now you can use this plug-in to add a simple, invisible, counter to your web pages in order to get a quick snapshot of raw and unique hits, as shown in Figure 5-9.

About the Plug-in

This plug-in takes the name of a file to hold the counts for the current page, as well as details on what to do with it. It accepts these arguments:

- **$filename**   A path/filename to use for storing hit count data
- **$action**   What to do with the data: reset = reset all counts, add = add the current visit to the data, get = retrieve hit stats, delete = delete the counter file

Variables, Arrays, and Functions

$data	String containing user's IP address and browser details
$fp	File pointer to the counter file
$file	String containing contents of $filename
$lines	Array containing all lines extracted from $file
$raw	Numeric variable containing the total number of hits saved in the file
$unique	Numeric variable containing the number of hits with unique IP/browser details

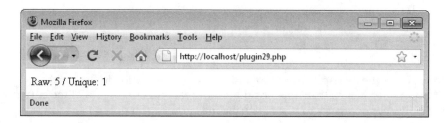

Figure 5-9   When you need instant stats from your web site, this plug-in will provide them.

How It Works

The first thing this plug-in does is make a note of the current visitor's IP address, which is a four-part number that directly identifies that user, and looks something like 208.77.188.166. Then, because IP addresses can be shared, for example across a business or home network, the browser's User Agent string is also noted. This is a string that identifies the type and version of a browser and varies widely in use but may look something like "Mozilla/4.0 (compatible; MSIE 8.0; Windows NT 6.1; Media Center PC 6.0)". These two strings are then combined and placed in the string variable $data, followed by a \n newline character.

Next a switch statement with four sections is entered. The first section is processed if $action is set to reset. It opens the file $filename for writing, using an argument of "w", and then calls the function flock(). This is PHP's file locking mechanism and what this call does is request an exclusive lock on the file by passing the argument LOCK_EX. The function waits until any and all other processes have finished using the file and then releases the lock using flock() with an argument of LOCK_UN, and closes the file. This has the effect of truncating the file to zero bytes. Had a lock not been set (and the program not waited its turn), if two requests came through at the same time, one to append to the file, and this one to truncate it, there would be no way of knowing which process might "win." This way, all accesses to the file are queued up and all processes take their turn.

The second section is executed if $action is set to add. Here the file is opened in a similar way to the previous example, except that the argument "a+" is used, which stands for *append to*. Again the flock() function is called, and when control over the file is gained, the data in $data is appended to the file, the lock is released, and the file closed.

The third section is executed if $action is set to get, in which case the file is opened just for reading using an argument of "r". Then, flock() is called, and after control is gained, the fread() function is called to read the entire contents of $filename into $file, except for the final character which will be a \n newline, and is not needed. The file lock is then released and the file is closed. With the contents of the file now stored in the variable $file, it is extracted into the array $lines by using the explode() function, which splits the contents of $file at every \n linefeed character. Then, the number of elements is counted using count() and assigned to the variable $raw. To obtain the unique counts (the number of hits made by different IP/browser combinations, ignoring multiple hits by the same user), the array_unique() function is called before using count() and passing the result to $unique. Afterward, a two-element array containing these raw and unique values is returned.

The final section is executed when $action is set to delete and simply uses the unlink() function to delete the file pointed to by $filename.

How to Use It

The way you will mostly use this plug-in is as follows:

```
PIPHP_HitCounter("counter.txt", "add");
```

This code passes the filename *counter.txt* and the parameter "add" to the function PIPHP_HitCounter(), which then appends the IP address and User Agent of the current user to the file. It's not necessary to first create the file because, if it doesn't already exist, it will be created.

Should you wish to reset the file data and start over, you can issue the following command, which truncates the data file back to zero bytes in length:

```
PIPHP_HitCounter("counter.txt", "reset");
```

To delete the counter, use this command:

```
PIPHP_HitCounter("counter.txt", "delete");
```

To instead get an instant hit count report, use code such as this:

```
$result = PIPHP_HitCounter("counter.txt", "get");
echo "Raw: $result[0] / Unique: $result[1]";
```

You can give the counter any name you like, but if you use the *.txt* extension, as in these examples, you'll be able to load it into a text editor and browse through it.

The Plug-in

```
function PIPHP_HitCounter($filename, $action)
{
   $data = getenv("REMOTE_ADDR") .
           getenv("HTTP_USER_AGENT") . "\n";

   switch ($action)
   {
      case "reset":
         $fp = fopen($filename, "w");
         if (flock($fp, LOCK_EX))
            ;
         flock($fp, LOCK_UN);
         fclose($fp);
         return;

      case "add":
         $fp = fopen($filename, "a+");
         if (flock($fp, LOCK_EX))
            fwrite($fp, $data);
         flock($fp, LOCK_UN);
         fclose($fp);
         return;

      case "get":
         $fp = fopen($filename, "r");
         if (flock($fp, LOCK_EX))
            $file = fread($fp, filesize($filename) - 1);
         flock($fp, LOCK_UN);
         fclose($fp);
         $lines  = explode("\n", $file);
         $raw    = count($lines);
         $unique = count(array_unique($lines));
         return array($raw, $unique);

      case "delete":
         unlink($filename);
         return;
   }
}
```

30 Referer Log

In a similar way to being able to instantly track visitor hits, this plug-in keeps constant track of the URLs from which your users are being sent. Again, this is something you can track with a service such as Google Analytics, or by processing your log files, but neither of these methods is as quick and easy to use as this plug-in for providing instant data, as shown in Figure 5-10.

About the Plug-in

This plug-in takes the name of a file to hold the referring data for the current page, as well as details on what to do with it. Upon success, it either updates or returns details from the data file. It accepts these arguments:

- **$filename**   A path/file name to use for storing referring page data
- **$action**   What to do with the data: reset = reset all data; add = add the current visit to the data; get = retrieve referrer stats; delete = delete the file

Variables, Arrays, and Functions

$data	String containing the referring page URL
$fp	File pointer to the referrer file
$file	String containing the contents of $filename
$temp	Temporary array containing unique referring URLs

How It Works

The first thing this plug-in does is make a note of the referring page's URL, if there is one, placing it in $date, followed by a \n newline character. If no referring page was passed to the current program, perhaps because the URL was typed in directly, then $data is assigned the string "No Referrer", followed by a \n newline.

Next a switch statement with four sections is entered. The first section is processed if $action is set to reset. It opens the file $filename for writing, using an argument of "w", and then calls the function flock(). The function waits until all other processes have finished using the file and then releases the lock and closes the file, truncating it to zero bytes.

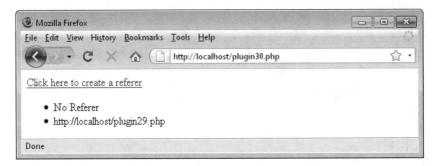

FIGURE 5-10   Keeping track of pages referring to your site is easy using this plug-in.

The second section is executed if $action is set to add. Here the argument "a+" is used to open the file for appending. Again the flock() function is called, and when control over the file is gained, the data in $data is appended to the file, the lock is released, and the file is closed.

The third section is executed if $action is set to get, in which case the file is opened for reading using an argument of "r". Then flock() is called, and after control is gained, the fread() function is called to read the entire contents of $filename into $file, excepting the final character which will be a \n newline character, and is therefore not needed. The file lock is then released and the file is closed. With the contents of the file now stored in the variable $file, the explode() function is used to extract this contents into the array $temp, splitting it at every \n linefeed character. All non-unique entries are then removed from the array, which is sorted to remove the gaps, and the resulting array is returned.

The final section is executed when $action is set to delete and simply uses the unlink() function to delete the file pointed to by $filename.

How to Use It

You will normally call the plug-in with code such as the following, which creates the file *refer.log* if it doesn't already exist, and writes the contents of $data to it. If the file does exist, the data is appended to it:

```
PIPHP_RefererLog("refer.log", "add");
```

To delete this log file, use this command:

```
PIPHP_RefererLog("refer.log", "delete");
```

Or to reset the log file by truncating it back to zero length, use:

```
PIPHP_RefererLog("refer.log", "reset");
```

To display all the entries in the log file, you could use code such as the following, which uses a for loop to iterate through all the entries in the returned array and display them:

```
$result = PIPHP_RefererLog("refer.log", "get");
for ($j = 0 ; $j < count($result) ; ++$j)
   echo "$result[$j]<br />";
```

The Plug-in

```
function PIPHP_RefererLog($filename, $action)
{
   $data = getenv("HTTP_REFERER") . "\n";
   if ($data == "\n") $data = " No Referrer\n";

   switch ($action)
   {
      case "reset":
         $fp = fopen($filename, "w");
         if (flock($fp, LOCK_EX))
            ;
```

```
        flock($fp, LOCK_UN);
        fclose($fp);
        return;

    case "add":
        $fp = fopen($filename, "a+");
        if (flock($fp, LOCK_EX))
            fwrite($fp, $data);
        flock($fp, LOCK_UN);
        fclose($fp);
        return;

    case "get":
        $fp = fopen($filename, "r");
        if (flock($fp, LOCK_EX))
            $file = fread($fp, filesize($filename) -1);
        flock($fp, LOCK_UN);
        fclose($fp);
        $temp = array_unique(explode("\n", $file));
        sort($temp);
        return $temp;

    case "delete":
        unlink($filename);
        return;
    }
}
```

CHAPTER 6

Forms and User Input

E ven with the growth in Web 2.0 Ajax techniques, most people still interact with web
sites using forms. They are a tried and tested means of obtaining user input and are
likely to retain an important position for a long time to come.

Receiving user input is all well and good—that's the easy part. But turning that input
into usable and secure data is another matter. In this chapter, you'll find a collection of
solutions for helping you with expression evaluation, validation of credit card details,
e-mail addresses and text strings, identifying spam, preventing automated input from
"bots," and ways of supporting user-supplied text formatting.

PLUG-IN 31 Evaluate Expression

You might think that offering support for evaluating expressions would be a simple matter
of calling the PHP `eval()` function with a user supplied input. Unfortunately, though,
`eval()` is an extremely powerful function that will interpret any string supplied to it as if it
were a PHP program; using it could completely open up your web site to any intruder with
a minimum of PHP knowledge.

However, with this plug-in the user input is completely sanitized by stripping out any
characters and functions that are not safe, leaving only a selection of 22 mathematical
functions and the basic math operators (plus, minus, multiply, and divide), and only then
is the input passed to `eval()`. Figure 6-1 shows a variety of expressions being calculated.

About the Plug-in

This plug-in accepts a string containing a mathematical expression and returns the result of
evaluating it. It takes this argument:

- **$expr**   A string containing an expression

Variables, Arrays, and Functions

$f1	Array containing the 22 mathematical function names supported
$f2	Array containing tokens that the function names are temporarily converted to

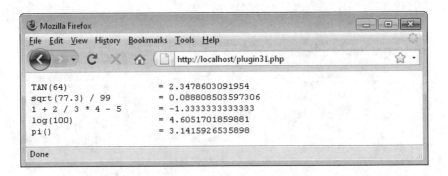

FIGURE 6-1   This plug-in enables powerful calculator functionality on your web site.

How It Works

To allow the use of PHP's build-in `eval()` function, it is necessary to remove any harmful expressions before passing them to the function. To achieve this, the array `$f1` contains 22 function names (out of the hundreds supported by PHP) that are considered safe. Using the `$f2` array, which contains a matching set of tokens, any of the 22 functions found in the argument `$expr` are converted to a corresponding token. This means that any remaining alphabetical characters may form other function names and therefore are stripped out.

The preceding is achieved by first converting the string `$expr` to lowercase using the function `strtolower()` and then employing `str_replace()` to replace all occurrences of the allowed function names with their tokens.

Next `preg_replace()` is called to strip out anything remaining that is not required, using the regular expression `/[^\d\+\*\/\-\.()! ]/`. Okay, I know it looks like I just dropped the keyboard on the floor but this is actually a powerful expression which I'll now break up for you.

The outer / characters denote the start and end of a regular expression.

The square brackets, `[]`, state that a match should be made against any single character enclosed within them.

The `^` symbol, when immediately following a `[` symbol, forces negation, so that the expression will match anything that is *not* one of the characters following.

Next comes a sequence of characters, which are all escaped by prefacing them with a `\` symbol, because otherwise they would be interpreted as special regular expression operators:

- `\d` Any digit (0–9)
- `\+` An addition symbol
- `\*` A multiplication symbol
- `\/` A division symbol
- `\-` A subtraction symbol
- `\.` A decimal point symbol

So, if any symbol is *not* one of these escaped symbols, it will be considered a match and the second argument to `preg_replace()`, `''`, will replace it with nothing—in other words, the symbol will be removed.

Finally, a few other symbols are also allowed through. These are the left and right brackets, the comma, the exclamation mark, and a space.

You might wonder why the exclamation mark is allowed within a mathematical expression. Well, the answer isn't that the exclamation mark is needed for use in expressions, because it isn't. Instead, it's there because it forms part of each of the 22 tokens in the array `$f2`. Once the mathematical functions have been converted to tokens, the `!` symbols remain there so that the tokens can be converted back again after stripping the remaining unwanted characters out, which is done using another call to the `str_replace()` function. I chose the exclamation mark at random and could equally have used any one of many other symbols.

After all this processing, the resulting sanitized string is passed to the `eval()` function, the result of which is returned to the calling statement. If you wish to see what the sanitized expression looks like, you can uncomment the line shown in the source code.

How to Use It

To evaluate a user-supplied expression, just call the function PIPHP_EvaluateExpression(), passing the expression to be calculated, in the following manner, which calculates the area of a circle with a radius of 4:

```
echo PIPHP_EvaluateExpression("pi() * pow(4, 2)");
```

The Plug-in

```
function PIPHP_EvaluateExpression($expr)
{
    $f1 = array ('abs',    'acos',   'acosh', 'asin',  'asinh',
                 'atan',   'atan2', 'atanh', 'cos',   'cosh',
                 'exp',    'expm1', 'log',   'log10', 'log1p',
                 'pi',     'pow',   'sin',   'sinh',  'sqrt',
                 'tan',    'tanh');

    $f2 = array ('!01!',  '!02!',  '!03!',  '!04!',  '!05!',
                 '!06!',  '!07!',  '!08!',  '!09!',  '!10!',
                 '!11!',  '!12!',  '!13!',  '!14!',  '!15!',
                 '!16!',  '!17!',  '!18!',  '!19!',  '!20!',
                 '!21!',  '!22!');

    $expr = strtolower($expr);
    $expr = str_replace($f1, $f2, $expr);
    $expr = preg_replace("/[^\d+\*\/\-\.(),! ]/", '', $expr);
    $expr = str_replace($f2, $f1, $expr);

    // Uncomment the line below to see the sanitized expression
    // echo "$expr<br />\n";

    return eval("return $expr;");
}
```

32 Validate Credit Card

PLUG-IN

Sometimes people make mistakes when entering credit card numbers in web forms, or even just make numbers up to see what will happen. Using this plug-in you can at least ensure that a credit card number and expiration date you have been provided with has an acceptable number sequence, a correct checksum, and a valid expiration date.

This enables you to only pass on sensible-looking details to your card processing organization, and possibly limit any additional fees that may be charged. In Figure 6-2 you can see a made-up card number that has not validated.

About the Plug-in

This plug-in accepts a credit card number and expiration date and returns TRUE if they validate, otherwise it returns FALSE. It takes these arguments:

- **$number** A string containing a credit card number
- **$expiry** A credit card expiration date in the form 07/12 or 0712

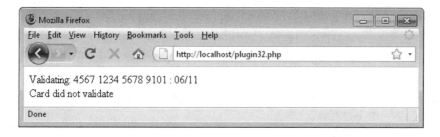

Figure 6-2   Credit card numbers have a built-in checksum that this plug-in will validate.

Variables, Arrays, and Functions

$left	String containing the left four digits of $number
$cclen	Integer containing the number of characters in $number
$chksum	Integer containing the credit card checksum
$j	Loop counter
$d	Character containing individual digits extracted from $number

How It Works

In the 1950s, Hans Peter Luhn, a scientist working at IBM, created the Luhn checksum algorithm, also known as the *modulus 10* or *mod 10* algorithm. It will detect any single-digit error, as well as almost all transpositions of adjacent digits in a string of digits. This makes it very useful for verifying whether a credit card number has been successfully entered by using the simple method of adding a checksum digit at the number's end. All major credit companies use this system, and so can we.

The first thing the plug-in does is remove any non-digit characters from $number; the same is done for the expiration date in $expiry. Then, the contents of the first four digits of $number are placed in the variable $left, the length of $number is placed in $cclen, and $checksum is initialized to 0.

Each card issuer has their own initial sequences of numbers, and card number length can vary between 13 and 16 digits depending on the issuer. So, using the contents of $left, the next main section of code looks up the type of card and, based on the result, returns FALSE if $number does not contain the correct number of digits for that card.

Once all the known sequences of initial digits have been processed, if no card has yet been matched, then FALSE is returned because $number represents the number for a card type the program is unaware of—most likely it's a made-up number.

Otherwise, the card type has been identified and $number has been found to have the right number of digits, so the next portion of code runs the Luhn algorithm to see whether the sequence of numbers appears valid. It does this by checking alternate digits and adding them together in a pre-set manner. If the result is exactly divisible by 10, then the sequence is valid. If not, FALSE is returned.

Lastly, the expiration date is checked against the date of the last day of the current month, and if the card has expired, FALSE is returned.

If all these tests pass, a value of TRUE is returned.

TIP *If you are interested in exactly how the Luhn algorithm works, there's an explanation at* http://en.wikipedia.org/wiki/Luhn_algorithm.

How to Use It

To verify a credit card's details prior to submitting it to a credit card processing organization, you could use code such as this:

```
$card   = "4567 1234 5678 9101";
$exp    = "06/14";
$result = PIPHP_ValidateCC($card, $exp);
if (!$result)
{
    // Ask for details again
}
else
{
    // Debit the card
}
```

In the preceding example, if the card doesn't validate, the details are re-requested, or if it does, the card is processed.

CAUTION *All this plug-in does is check whether the credit card details entered meet the issuer identity, checksum, and date requirements for a valid card. It should only be used as a quick test to ensure that a user has not made a typographical error when entering their details. Also you should keep yourself informed about all the latest card numbers allocated so that you can update this validator and not incorrectly reject any cards. You can keep track of the major credit card issuers at* http://en.wikipedia.org/wiki/Credit_card_numbers.

The Plug-in

```
function PIPHP_ValidateCC($number, $expiry)
{
    $ccnum  = preg_replace('/[^\d]/', '', $number);
    $expiry = preg_replace('/[^\d]/', '', $expiry);
    $left   = substr($ccnum, 0, 4);
    $cclen  = strlen($ccnum);
    $chksum = 0;

    // Diners Club
    if (($left >= 3000) && ($left <= 3059) ||
        ($left >= 3600) && ($left <= 3699) ||
        ($left >= 3800) && ($left <= 3889))
        if ($cclen != 14) return FALSE;

    // JCB
```

```
    if (($left >= 3088) && ($left <= 3094) ||
        ($left >= 3096) && ($left <= 3102) ||
        ($left >= 3112) && ($left <= 3120) ||
        ($left >= 3158) && ($left <= 3159) ||
        ($left >= 3337) && ($left <= 3349) ||
        ($left >= 3528) && ($left <= 3589))
        if ($cclen != 16) return FALSE;

// American Express
elseif (($left >= 3400) && ($left <= 3499) ||
        ($left >= 3700) && ($left <= 3799))
    if ($cclen != 15) return FALSE;

// Carte Blanche
elseif (($left >= 3890) && ($left <= 3899))
    if ($cclen != 14) return FALSE;

// Visa
elseif (($left >= 4000) && ($left <= 4999))
    if ($cclen != 13 && $cclen != 16) return FALSE;

// MasterCard
elseif (($left >= 5100) && ($left <= 5599))
    if ($cclen != 16) return FALSE;

// Australian BankCard
elseif ($left == 5610)
    if ($cclen != 16) return FALSE;

// Discover
elseif ($left == 6011)
    if ($cclen != 16) return FALSE;

// Unknown
else return FALSE;

for ($j = 1 - ($cclen % 2); $j < $cclen; $j += 2)
    $chksum += substr($ccnum, $j, 1);

for ($j = $cclen % 2; $j < $cclen; $j += 2)
{
    $d = substr($ccnum, $j, 1) * 2;
    $chksum += $d < 10 ? $d : $d - 9;
}

if ($chksum % 10 != 0) return FALSE;

if (mktime(0, 0, 0, substr($expiry, 0, 2), date("t"),
    substr($expiry, 2, 2)) < time()) return FALSE;

return TRUE;
}
```

PLUG-IN 33 Create Captcha

Spam is everywhere these days, and not just in our e-mail inboxes. The net is saturated with *bots* (automated programs) trawling web pages in search of web forms that will let them drop their payload into a comment or other field. Usually they try to drop in a link leading to a knock-off product they are trying to sell. But worse than that, many of these bots inject pornographic links, or attempt to get users to visit phishing sites where their bank, credit card, or other personal details may be stolen.

One of the most successful ways to prevent this is the Captcha, a type of challenge-response test used in computing to ensure that the response is not generated by a computer. The word is a highly contrived acronym that stands for Completely Automatic Public Turing Test to Tell Computers and Humans Apart.

With a Captcha you are asked to re-enter some text displayed in a graphic image. If the image is complex enough, a bot will not be able to decipher it and so only human input is able to get through. This still doesn't guarantee you will be spam-free, but with this plug-in you'll prevent the majority of it from getting through. Figure 6-3 shows the plug-in generating a Captcha.

About the Plug-in

This plug-in creates a temporary image containing a word that must be typed in to verify a user is human. It returns a three-element array in which the first element is the Captcha text to be entered, the second is a unique 32-character token, and the third is the location of the Captcha image. It takes these arguments:

- **$size** The font size of a TrueType font
- **$length** The number of characters in the Captcha word
- **$font** The location of a TrueType font to use
- **$folder** The location of a folder to store the Captcha images. This must be web accessible and end with a trailing / character, or to use the current folder use a value of NULL.
- **$salt1** A string to make the Captcha hard to crack
- **$salt2** A string to make cracking even harder

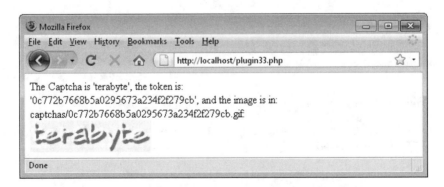

Variables, Arrays, and Functions

$file	String containing the contents of the file *dictionary.txt*
$temps	Array of all words extracted from $file
$temp	String containing each value in turn from $temps
$dict	Array of all correct length words extracted from $temps
$captcha	String containing the Captcha word
$token	String containing an md5() hash based on $captcha, $salt1, and $salt2
$fname	String containing the Captcha image location
$image	GD Library image of the Captcha image
$j	Loop counter
PIPHP_GifText()	Plug-in 19 function: converts text to a GIF image
PIPHP_GD_FN1()	Function used by plug-in 19
PIPHP_ImageAlter()	Plug-in 14 function: modifies an image

How It Works

Rather than simply supplying a selection of random letters for the Captcha, I decided it's much more natural to enter an English word, and so this plug-in requires a file called *dictionary.txt* to be in the same directory. This file should be a list of words with one per line and each line separated by a \r\n carriage return\linefeed pair. On the companion web site to this book at *www.pluginphp.com* there's an 80,000-word *dictionary.txt* file already saved in the same zip file as this plug-in. Or you can choose to use your own list of words.

Either way, the first thing the function does is load the contents of *dictionary.txt* into the variable $temps from where all the words with a length of the value in $length are extracted into the array $dict using a foreach loop, and the Captcha word is then selected from this subset of words.

Next a token is created with which the Captcha can be uniquely connected. This is done by calling the PHP md5() function, which is a one-way function that converts the input into a 32-character string in such a way that the algorithm cannot be reversed. This is why it's called a one-way function. However, instead of simply taking the dictionary word and creating an md5() hash of it, it's necessary to obfuscate things a little. This is because some people have spent a lot of time assembling dictionaries containing the hashes of every single word. Therefore, for example, the md5() hash of the word "hello" is easily looked up and is known to be the following:

```
5d41402abc4b2a76b9719d911017c592
```

Wherever this particular hash is encountered, the chances are very high indeed that it was created from the string "hello", and so it would be a cinch to crack this Captcha system. So, like I said, it's necessary to be a little sneaky by making it impossible for a dictionary crack to work.

We do this by adding additional characters to the Captcha word that only we know. Such strings of characters are called *salts* and this plug-in uses two of them for good measure. When you call the plug-in you will have to provide values for $salt1 and $salt2, which will be inserted on either side of the Captcha word chosen. For example, if you choose the strings 3$a7* and dk%%d, and the Captcha word is hello, then the string that will be passed to md5() is 3$a7*hellodk%%d, which results in the following hash:

```
99ccb37e57e885ac76b0145246ef7e8e
```

As you can see, this is a totally different string and, without knowing the two salt values, it is utterly impossible to crack without attempting brute force (multiple attempts), which would take thousands of years, even using a modern supercomputer.

So, the result of creating the hash token is placed in $token, and $fname is set to point to the location where the resulting Captcha GIF file will be stored. This is based on concatenating the value supplied in $folder, the md5() token in $token, and the file extension *.gif*.

The function then creates the graphic image by calling PIPHP_GifText() (plug-in 19 from Chapter 5) with the correct values to form a shadowed word. This function also saves the image to disk when done.

To complete the Captcha creation, the image is reloaded into memory and PIPHP_ImageAlter() (plug-in 14 from Chapter 5) is called in four different ways (and in a couple of instances multiple times) to blur, emboss, brighten, and increase its contrast. The result is then resaved back into the GIF image and an array containing three elements is returned. These are:

- The Captcha text
- The md5() token
- The location of the Captcha image

How to Use It

To create a Captcha, you call up PHP_CreateCaptcha(), passing it the required values, like this:

```
$result = PIPHP_CreateCaptcha(26, 8, 'captcha.ttf', '',
    '!*a&K', '.fs£!+');
```

In this example, the passed values are 26 for the font size, 8 for the length of the Captcha word required, captcha.ttf for the name of a TrueType file to use, '' for the image folder to use, and !*a&K and .fs£!+ for the two salt values. You should have already uploaded a suitable TrueType font file, named *captcha.ttf*, to your server— preferably a nonstandard or script type font.

The plug-in will return an array of three values with which you can display the Captcha image, and create a form to request the Captcha word as text input. The first of the returned values is the Captcha word itself and you don't actually need it other than for testing purposes. So at this point let's forget it and concentrate on the other two returned values. The first of these is the image that you need to display, like this:

```
<img src="$result[2]" />
```

You also need to embed the image URL in a hidden form field so that it can be passed to the following function where it will be erased from the hard disk when no longer needed. At the same time, you should embed the value of the token in another hidden field, like this:

```
<input type="hidden" name="token" value="$result[1]" />
<input type="hidden" name="image" value="$result[2]" />
```

Taking all this into account, the following example code creates a Captcha, and then displays the Captcha image along with a form for requesting the Captcha word to be entered:

```
<?php
$result = PIPHP_CreateCaptcha(26, 8, 'captcha.ttf', '',
    '!*a&K', '.fs£!+');
echo <<<_END
<img src="$result[2]" /><br />
Please enter the word shown<br />
<form method="post" action="checkcaptcha.php">
<input type="hidden" name="token" value="$result[1]" />
<input type="text" name="captcha" />
<input type="submit" />
</form>
_END;
```

You may wish to save this example (giving it a filename such as *testcaptcha.php*) as you'll be able to test it with an example from the following plug-in. Or you can download the file using the *Download* link at *pluginphp.com*—look in the folder named *6* in the *plug-ins.zip* file.

If you would like to have random length words in your Captchas, you can achieve this by modifying the function call to use the rand() function as in the following, which will generate a Captcha of between four and ten letters in length:

```
$result = PIPHP_CreateCaptcha(26, rand(4,10), 'captcha.ttf', '',
    '!*a&K', '.fs£!+');
```

Note that this plug-in relies on the plug-ins PIPHP_GifText(), PIPHP_GD_FN1(), and PIPHP_ImageAlter(), so they should also appear in the same program file as this one, or be otherwise included in it.

TIP *If you ever find your Captchas are not preventing all bots anymore, perhaps because their image recognition has improved, I suggest you upload a different TrueType font and start using that. You could also modify PIPHP_CreateCaptcha() itself and introduce a few more (or use different) image manipulations.*

The Plug-in

```
function PIPHP_CreateCaptcha($size, $length, $font,
    $folder, $salt1, $salt2)
{
```

```
$file    = file_get_contents('dictionary.txt');
$temps   = explode("\r\n", $file);
$dict    = array();

foreach ($temps as $temp)
    if (strlen($temp) == $length)
        $dict[] = $temp;

$captcha = $dict[rand(0, count($dict) - 1)];
$token   = md5("$salt1$captcha$salt2");
$fname   = $folder . $token . ".gif";
PIPHP_GifText($fname, $captcha, $font, $size, "444444",
    "ffffff", $size / 10, "666666");
$image   = imagecreatefromgif($fname);
$image   = PIPHP_ImageAlter($image, 2);
$image   = PIPHP_ImageAlter($image, 13);

for ($j = 0 ; $j < 3 ; ++$j)
    $image = PIPHP_ImageAlter($image, 3);
for ($j = 0 ; $j < 2 ; ++$j)
    $image = PIPHP_ImageAlter($image, 5);

imagegif($image, $fname);
return array($captcha, $token, $fname);}
```

PLUG-IN 34 Check Captcha

Once you have created a Captcha image and asked a user to type it in you can use this plug-in to verify their input, and determine whether they entered the correct word. Figure 6-4 shows the plug-in being used.

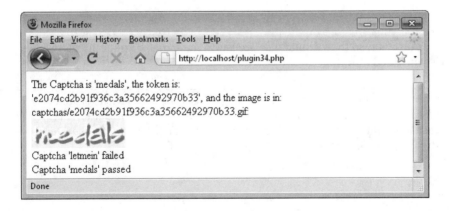

FIGURE 6-4   This plug-in verifies a Captcha word entered by a user.

About the Plug-in

This plug-in verifies the Captcha word input by a user, in response to a request made using a Captcha created with plug-in 33, `PIPHP_CreateCaptcha()`. It takes these arguments:

- **$captcha** The Captcha as typed in by a user
- **$token** The token representing the current Captcha
- **$salt1** The first salt string
- **$salt2** The second salt string

Variables, Arrays, and Functions

- None

How It Works

The first thing this function does is remove the Captcha GIF image from the hard disk, if it still exists, and then returns the result of recreating the md5() hash from plug-in 33, based on the user string provided in $captcha, and the two salts in $salt1 and $salt2.

As long as the salts are the same as when the Captcha was created, if the user has typed in the correct hash word, then the result of concatenating all three and passing them to the md5() function will be the same as the value stored in $token. In which case a value of TRUE is returned. Otherwise, the correct word was not entered and FALSE is returned.

How to Use It

After a Captcha has been created using the previous plug-in, you will have been provided with the location of a GIF image and a token representing the Captcha. Using these you will then have displayed the image and provided a web form requesting that the user type in the word in the Captcha image. This form will now have been posted to your server and the two items of data received will be:

- **$_POST['captcha']** The Captcha text entered by the user
- **$_POST['token']** The token embedded in the hidden form field

Using these values, the following example code will verify the Captcha word as entered by the user.

```
if (PIPHP_CheckCaptcha($_POST['captcha'], $_POST['token'],
   '!*a&K', '.fs£!+')) echo "Captcha verified";
else echo "Captcha failed";
```

Note that the two salts are not passed as arguments because they are a secret and only your code should know them. Just ensure that you use the same salts for both PIPHP_CreateCaptcha() and PIPHP_CheckCaptcha() or the plug-ins won't work.

If you wish to test the example code (*testcaptcha.php*) in the previous plug-in, type in the preceding example and save it as *checkcaptcha.php* and it will verify the result of using the Captcha. Both of these programs can be found in a folder named *6* of *plug-ins.zip* available using the *Download* link at *pluginphp.com*. By the way, the file *plugin34.php*, which is in the same folder of the zip file, simulates creating a Captcha, posting it, and verifying it, all in a single program.

After a while you will find that your folder of Captcha images gets quite full. You may therefore wish to use code, such as the following, to clear these files out every now and then:

```
foreach (glob("*.gif") as $file)
    if (time() - filectime($file) > 300)
        unlink($file);
```

What the code does is use the glob() function to search for all files with a *.gif* extension and then, if they are more than 5 minutes (300 seconds) old, they are removed using the unlink() function. If the files are in a different folder then you should ensure that you have first assigned that name to a variable called $folder, and that it has a trailing /, for example, using a value such as images/ if your folder is called *images*. Then you can use the following code instead:

```
foreach (glob($folder . "*.gif") as $file)
    if (time() - filectime($file) > 300)
        unlink($file);
```

The Plug-in

```
function PIPHP_CheckCaptcha($captcha, $token,
    $salt1, $salt2)
{
    return $token == md5("$salt1$captcha$salt2");
}
```

35 Validate Text

Processing user input takes a lot of work, especially when you need data to be in a certain format or to fit within various constraints. Using this plug-in you can check user input to ensure it is the right length and contains the right types of data, whether alphabetical, numeric, or something else.

It's also highly versatile, allowing you to specify the allowed characters (and therefore those that are disallowed), as well as types of characters that must be used. Figure 6-5 shows two different strings being validated.

About the Plug-in

This plug-in accepts a string to be validated, along with parameters describing what is and isn't allowed in the string. The function returns a two-element array on failure. The first of which is the value FALSE; the second is an array of error messages. On success, it returns a single element with the value TRUE. It takes these arguments:

- **$text** The text to be validated
- **$minlength** The minimum acceptable length
- **$maxlength** The maximum acceptable length

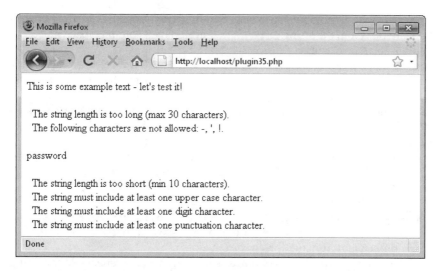

FIGURE 6-5 Processing form input is now easier than ever using this plug-in.

- **$allowed** The characters that are allowed in the text. Any characters can be entered here, including ranges indicated by using a - character, such as a-zA-Z.
- **$required** Types of characters of which at least one of each must be in the text, out of a, l, u, d, w, and p which, in order, stand for any letter, lowercase, uppercase, digit, word (any letter or number), or punctuation.

Variables, Arrays, and Functions

$len	Integer containing the length of $text
$error	Array of all error message strings
$result	Integer result of matching the $allowed characters
$caught	String containing matched characters from $allowed
$plural	String with the value " is", or "s are" if there is more than one match
$j	Loop counter

How It Works

This plug-in sets the value of $len to the length of $text, and after initializing the array $error ready to hold any error messages, it checks whether $len is smaller or larger than the required minimum and maximum lengths. If either is the case, a suitable error message is added to the $error array.

Next the preg_match_all() function is called to check for the existence of any characters *not* in the string $allowed, which contains a list of all allowed characters, including supporting ranges created using the - character. Thus, instead of having to use the string abcde, the equivalent of a-e is allowed; so, for example, to accept all upper- and lowercase letters, the string a-zA-Z could be used.

Those characters that do not match are placed in the array $matches by the function, and from there are placed in the string $caught, separated by a comma/space pair so that they can be added to an error message.

The string variable $plural is then assigned the value " is" if there is a single match, or "s are" if there is more than one. This is then used when constructing the error message so that it reads grammatically, using one or other of the forms (the value of $plural is shown in bold): "The following character **is** not allowed"; "The following characters **are** not allowed".

Then, a for loop is entered for iterating through all the characters in the variable $required, which can contain any or all of the letters a, l, u, d, w, or p, which stand for any letter, lowercase, uppercase, digit, word (any letter or number), or punctuation.

Depending on which letter is being processed, the variable $regex is assigned the correct value to enable the following preg_match() call to ensure that at least one of that character type is included in the string. This feature is very useful in cases where a certain type of input is required such as a number, or maybe a password that must have at least one each of a letter, number, and punctuation character.

As the variable's name indicates, all characters in $required must exist in the string being validated. Therefore if any one of the types of characters described by $required is not encountered, another error message is added to the $error array.

Finally, if $error has no messages in it, then no errors were encountered, so a single-element array containing the value TRUE is returned. Otherwise, a two-element array is returned, the first of which is the value FALSE, and the second is the array of error messages.

How to Use It

To validate a user-supplied string, call the PIPHP_ValidateText() function, giving it the string to validate and various parameters indicating which characters are both allowed and required.

For example, to ensure that a string to be used for a password has one of each type of character—lowercase, uppercase, digit, and punctuation—and is at least 6 and no more than 16 characters long, you could use code such as the following, where $text is extracted from the form input password:

```
echo "<form method='post' action='$_SERVER[PHP_SELF]'>";
echo "<input type='text' name='password' />";
echo "<input type='submit' /></form>";

if (isset($_POST['password']))
{
    $text     = $_POST['password'];
    $allowed  = "a-zA-Z0-9 !&*+=:;@~#";
    $required = "ludp";
    $result = PIPHP_ValidateText($text, 10, 16, $allowed, $required);
    if ($result[0] == FALSE)
        for ($j = 0 ; $j < count($result[1]) ; ++$j)
            echo $result[1][$j] . ".<br>";
    else echo "Password validated";
}
```

You may wish to save this file with a filename such as *validate.php*, then you can call it up in your browser and view the result of entering different values. A copy of this file is also in the *plug-ins.zip* file (in */6/validate.php*), which is downloadable from the companion web site at *pluginphp.com*.

In this code, the string variable $allowed sets the plug-in to accept any of the following: letters of any case, as well as digits, the space character, and any characters out of ! & * + = : ; @ ~ and #. The $required string simultaneously tells the plug-in that there must be at least one lowercase letter, one uppercase letter, one digit, and one punctuation character.

Upon the function's return, if the first element of the array $result is FALSE, then validation failed and so the strings in the array stored in the second element are displayed—they are the error messages returned by the plug-in. But if the first element is TRUE, validation succeeded.

Here's another example. Because $allowed may include regular expression operators such as \w, which means any letter or digit, or the _ character, you could use the plug-in to ensure that a username (determined by you), which should only include letters, digits, underlines, periods, and hyphens (and cannot be comprised only of punctuation), has been correctly entered, like this:

```
$result = PIPHP_ValidateText($username, 4, 20,  "\w\.\-", "a");
```

In this case, the $allowed argument of \w means "allow letters, digits, and the underline," while \. and \- also allow the period and hyphen. The $required parameter of a ensures there is at least one letter, which can be of either case.

The Plug-in

```
function PIPHP_ValidateText($text, $minlength, $maxlength,
   $allowed, $required)
{
   $len   = strlen($text);
   $error = array();

   if ($len < $minlength)
      $error[] = "The string length is too short " .
         "(min $minlength characters)";
   elseif ($len > $maxlength)
      $error[] = "The string length is too long " .
         "(max $maxlength characters)";

   $result = preg_match_all("/([^$allowed])/", $text, $matches);
   $caught = implode(array_unique($matches[1]), ', ');
   $plural = strlen($caught) > 1 ? $plural = "s are" : " is";

   if ($result) $error[] = "The following character$plural " .
      "not allowed: " . $caught;

   for ($j = 0 ; $j < strlen($required) ; ++$j)
   {
      switch(substr(strtolower($required), $j, 1))
```

```
    {
        case "a": $regex = "a-zA-Z"; $str = "letter";
                break;
        case "l": $regex = "a-z";    $str = "lower case";
                break;
        case "u": $regex = "A-Z";    $str = "upper case";
                break;
        case "d": $regex = "0-9";    $str = "digit";
                break;
        case "w": $regex = "\w";     $str = "letter or number";
                break;
        case "p": $regex = "\W";     $str = "punctuation";
                break;
    }

    if (!preg_match("/[$regex]/", $text))
        $error[] = "The string must include at least one " .
            "$str character";
    }

    if (count($error)) return array(FALSE, $error);
    else return array(TRUE);
}
```

PLUG-IN 36 Validate E-mail

Quite often people will make mistakes when entering their e-mail address into a web form. This is also another common area where some users just enter rubbish to see what happens. To catch these things, you can use this plug-in to at least check whether the format of an e-mail address supplied to you is valid, as shown in Figure 6-6.

About the Plug-in

This plug-in accepts an e-mail address whose format requires validating. On success, it returns TRUE, otherwise it returns FALSE. It takes this argument:

- **$email**   The e-mail address to be validated

FIGURE 6-6   Using this plug-in you can ensure that the format of an e-mail address is valid.

Variables, Arrays, and Functions

`$at`	Integer pointing to the position of the @ sign
`$left`	String containing the left half of the e-mail address
`$right`	String containing the right half of the e-mail address
`$res1`	Array result from validating `$left`
`$res2`	Array result from validating `$right`
`PIPHP_ValidateText()`	Plug-in 35: function to validate a string

How It Works

The most obvious required part of an e-mail address is the @ symbol, so the first thing this plug-in does is locate its position and store it in the variable $at. If $at is given the value FALSE, or if the length of $email is less than the minimum of six characters that an e-mail address can have (*a@b.cc*), then the value FALSE is returned, because the address is already found to be invalid.

Next the e-mail address is split into the two halves on either side of the position pointed to by $at using the substr() function. The left portion is assigned to the variable $left and the right to the variable $right.

Then plug-in 35, PIPHP_ValidateText(), is called to evaluate each half. The left half must be between one and 64 characters in length and may comprise any letters, digits, underlines, periods, and + or - symbols. This is enforced using the argument of \w\.\+\-. Also, at least one letter must be included, so the second argument of a checks for that.

The right half of an e-mail address must be between one and 255 characters in length and may be comprised of any mix of letters, digits, hyphens, or periods. This validation is accomplished using the argument \a-zA-Z0-9\.\-. And to ensure at least one letter appears in the domain, a second argument of a is supplied. The results of these two validations are placed in the arrays $res1 and $res2.

Final validation is achieved by ensuring there is at least one period in the right half of the e-mail address and that both the previous two validations were also successful. If so, then TRUE is returned, otherwise FALSE is returned.

How to Use It

To validate an e-mail address, just pass it to PIPHP_ValidateEmail(), which will return TRUE if successful, otherwise it will return FALSE, like this:

```
if (PIPHP_ValidateEmail($email)) echo "Validation succeeded";
```

Note that because this plug-in makes use of plug-in 35, PIPHP_ValidateText(), you must also have a copy of it in the same program file, or otherwise include it.

The Plug-in

```
function PIPHP_ValidateEmail($email)
{
   $at = strrpos($email, '@');

   if (!$at || strlen($email) < 3) return FALSE;
```

```
$left  = substr($email, 0, $at);
$right = substr($email, $at + 1);
$res1  = PIPHP_ValidateText($left,  1, 64,   "\w\.\+\-",

    "a");
$res2  = PIPHP_ValidateText($right, 1, 255, "\a-zA-Z0-9\.\-",

    "a");

if (!strpos($right, '.') || !$res1[0] || !$res2[0])
    return FALSE;
else return TRUE;
}
```

PLUG-IN 37 Spam Catch

Even with a strong Captcha system in place, you will still find users trying to manually spam your web site. They tend to be people who discover your site through a very specific search engine query for which they would like their own site to also rank well, and they hope that by adding a link back to their site from yours this will happen.

Using this plug-in you can specify a set of keywords that will trigger spam detection, and then use the level of spam certainty returned by the function to decide whether to ignore a user post. Figure 6-7 illustrates the plug-in in action.

About the Plug-in

This plug-in accepts a user-supplied string and matches it against a list of keywords to determine the likelihood that the string contains spam. It takes these arguments:

- **$text**   The e-mail address to be validated
- **$words** An array of keywords against which to check

Variables, Arrays, and Functions

- None

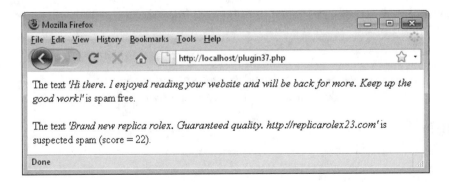

FIGURE 6-7   This plug-in will go a long way towards further reducing spam on your web site.

How It Works

This is another of those extremely short and sweet, yet exceedingly powerful plug-ins. What it does is take the text you supply it with, along with the array of keywords, and then calls plug-in 5, `PIPHP_WordSelector()`, with a blank replace string. This has the effect of removing every matching word from the string.

It's then a simple matter to subtract the length of the new string from the original one and return the difference. The larger this difference, the more words were removed from the string and so the more keywords have matched, and therefore the more likely it is that the string contained spam. If there is no difference, then no words matched and the string is considered spam-free.

How to Use It

To use this plug-in well, you need to first create your array of trigger keywords. You should base this on words unique to user spam that you have already received, with code like the following to filter user posts:

```
$words  = array('rolex', 'replica', 'loan', 'mortgage', 'viagra',
                'cialis', 'acai', 'free', 'stock', 'guaranteed',
                'refinancing', 'cartier', 'manhood', 'drugs');
if (PIPHP_SpamCatch($text, $words) < 15) echo "Probably not spam";
else echo "Probably spam";
```

Of course, this is a very small set of keywords and you will very likely need to come up with your own much larger list. This you will probably compile over time, and will include large numbers of keywords unsuitable for publication in this book.

You may also wish to experiment with the spam score of 15 used earlier to distinguish between spam and non-spam. Set it lower if too much is getting through, or higher if too many non-spams are being rejected.

The Plug-in

```
function PIPHP_SpamCatch($text, $words)
{
    return strlen($text) -
        strlen(PIPHP_WordSelector($text, $words, ''));
}
```

PLUG-IN 38 Send E-mail

Often, after receiving user input you need to send an e-mail, perhaps to yourself, to a colleague, or maybe to the e-mail submitter, thanking them for their input.

Sending an e-mail from your server isn't too hard using PHP's built-in `mail()` function. But if you want to send CCs or BCCs, you have to start assembling headers, which starts getting complicated. Using this plug-in, all that's handled for you. You just supply the message, subject lines, and the e-mail addresses of all recipients and it gets on with sending the e-mail for you. You can even specify a different Reply-To address if needed. Figure 6-8 shows the plug-in in use.

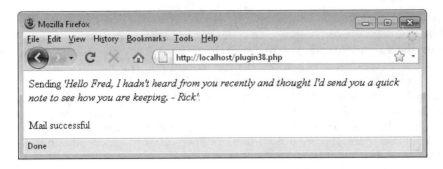

FIGURE 6-8 Sending an e-mail with this plug-in is a single-line function call.

About the Plug-in

This plug-in accepts a string containing the text of an e-mail to send, along with another for a subject line, and various other arguments specifying the e-mail addresses of people to whom it should also be sent. It takes these arguments:

- **$message** The text of the e-mail
- **$subject** The e-mail's subject
- **$priority** The message's priority: 1 (high) – 5 (low), or leave it blank for none
- **$from** The e-mail address of the sender
- **$replyto** The e-mail address to which replies should be addressed
- **$to** The e-mail address of the recipient
- **$cc** An array of e-mail addresses for CC copies
- **$bcc** An array of e-mail addresses for Blind CC copies (no recipient will see any BCC e-mail addresses in the message they receive)
- **$type** If set to "HTML," the e-mail will be sent in HTML format; otherwise, it will be sent as text.

Variables, Arrays, and Functions

$headers	String containing additional headers to be sent

How It Works

A lot of the work is handled by the mail() function built into PHP, but it needs help constructing additional headers because it only supports arguments of *recipient*, *subject*, *message*, and *headers*.

Therefore, this plug-in starts by assigning to the variable $headers the string value "From:", followed by the value in $from and a \r\n carriage return\linefeed pair. If this were not done, the e-mail might be sent as if the sender were the web server itself. Next, if the value of $type is set to "HTML," then the correct headers to send the e-mail using HTML are appended to $headers.

After that, if $priority has a value greater than 0, then an *X-Priority:* header is appended to $headers. Also, if the $replyto variable has a value, then the correct *Reply-To:* header is appended to $headers.

Then, the CC and BCC headers are created by iterating through the arrays of e-mail addresses in $cc and $bcc (if any), appending each to the relevant header line.

Finally, the mail() function is called with the values in $to, $subject, and $message, but now with a properly formatted sequence of headers in $headers to handle the other parameters.

How to Use It

Sending an e-mail with this plug-in is as easy as the following example, in which *me@myserver.com* is the sender's e-mail address, and *rick@otherserver.net* is the recipient's:

```
if (PIPHP_SendEmail($message, $subject, '', 'me@myserver.com', '',
    'rick@otherserver.net', NULL, NULL, ''))
        echo "Mail successful";
```

Or, to add a CC line this might change to the following, noting that the CC and BCC arguments must be passed as arrays of e-mail addresses:

```
if (PIPHP_SendEmail($message, $subject, '', 'me@myserver.com', '',
    'rick@otherserver.net', array('bill@test12.com'), NULL, ''))
        echo "Mail successful";
```

TIP *If, when you use this plug-in, you get an error such as* Warning: mail() [function.mail]: Failed to connect to mailserver at "localhost" port 25… *then you don't have your server properly configured for e-mail. In fact, if you are using Zend Server CE and/or a web development server, you may not actually want to run a mail server on that machine anyway, and should probably test this code on a server already configured for mail.*

The Plug-in

```
function PIPHP_SendEmail($message, $subject, $priority, $from,
    $replyto, $to, $cc, $bcc, $type)
{
    $headers = "From: $from\r\n";

    if (strtolower($type) == "html")
    {
        $headers .= "MIME-Version: 1.0\r\n";
        $headers .= "Content-type: text/html; charset=iso-8859-1\r\n";
    }

    if ($priority > 0)  $headers .= "X-Priority: $priority\r\n";
    if ($replyto != "") $headers .= "Reply-To: $replyto\r\n";

    if (count($cc))
```

```
{
    $headers .= "Cc: ";
        for ($j = 0 ; $j < count($cc) ; ++$j)
            $headers .= $cc[$j] . ",";
    $headers = substr($headers, 0, -1) . "\r\n";
}

if (count($bcc))
{
    $headers .= "Bcc: ";
        for ($j = 0 ; $j < count($bcc) ; ++$j)
            $headers .= $bcc[$j] . ",";
    $headers = substr($headers, 0, -1) . "\r\n";
}

    return mail($to, $subject, $message, $headers);
}
```

PLUG-IN 39   BB Code

Because of the risks involved with allowing users to enter HTML via a web form, alternatives had to be invented that would offer freedom of textual formatting without the risk of server hacking. One of the first and most popular of these systems was BB Code, which stands for Bulletin Board Code.

Because it is used on web forums all over the Internet, your users will be very familiar with BB Code, and using this plug-in you can now fully support it on your web site—including making URLs clickable, as you can see in Figure 6-9.

About the Plug-in

This plug-in accepts a string containing BB Code and returns it translated into safe HTML. It takes this argument:

- **$string**   The string to translate.

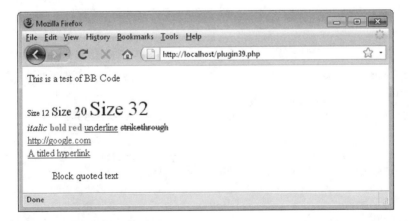

FIGURE 6-9   BB Code is a great way to allow users the ability to control their HTML layout without worrying about getting hacked.

Variables, Arrays, and Functions

`$from`	Array containing the supported BB Codes
`$to`	Array containing the HTML equivalents to BB Code

How It Works

This plug-in starts by replacing all occurrences found in the string `$string` from the array `$from` with those in the array `$to`, using the `str_replace()` function. It then uses the `preg_replace()` function four times to perform slightly more complex translations:

- Converts any [size=??] codes to CSS `font-size:??px` tags
- Converts any [color=??] codes to `<font color='??'>` HTML tags
- Converts any [url]??[/url] codes to `<a href='??>??</a>` HTML tags
- Converts any [url=??] codes to `<a href='??'>` HTML tags

With all translations completed, the modified string is returned. If no modifications were made, then the original string is returned.

How to Use It

To use this plug-in, just pass the function `PIPHP_BBCode()` some text to be translated and it will be returned to the calling code. If there is BB Code in the text, it will be replaced with matching HTML and/or CSS tags, otherwise it will be returned unchanged. The following example populates `$text` with some text, including BB Code, and then calls the plug-in to display it:

```
$text = <<<_END
This is a test of BB Code
[size=12]Size 12[/size]
[size=20]Size 20[/size]
[size=32]Size 32[/size]
[i]italic[/i]
[color=red][b]bold red[/b][/color]
[u]underline[/u]
[s]strikethrough[/s]
[url]http://google.com[/url]
[url=http://yahoo.com]A titled hyperlink[/url]
[quote]Block quoted text[/quote]
_END;

echo PIPHP_BBCode($text);
```

The list of BB Codes supported by this plug-in and the actions they perform are shown in Table 6-1.

I should mention that I believe BB Code's support for images and URLs represents a potential security risk and I would recommend using Pound Code (the next plug-in) instead. Or, on a site that makes use of GET requests, if you must support BB Code, you should consider removing or commenting out the sections supporting images and URLs. I have more to say on this matter in the "How to Use It" section of the Pound Code plug-in, following.

Opening BB Code	Closing BB Code	Action
[b]	[/b]	Bold face on and off
[i]	[/i]	Italics on and off
[u]	[/u]	Underline on and off
[s]	[/s]	Strikethrough on and off
[quote]	[/quote]	Blockquote on and off
[code]	[/code]	*Preformatted* text on and off
[img] *url*	[/img]	Start and end of an image URL
[url] *url*	[/url]	Start and end of a hyperlink
[url=*url*] *text*	[/url]	Start and end of a hyperlink (display *text* not *url*)
[size=??]	[/size]	Font size = ?? and End font size
[color=??]	[/size]	Font color = ?? and End font color

TABLE 6-1   List of BB Codes Supported by plug-in 39

You must also remember that this plug-in provides support for BB Code but *does not* reject HTML code. For that, you need to first run inputted text through functions to strip out HTML and JavaScript, which would probably look like this:

```
$text = htmlentities(strip_tags($text));
```

The strip_tags() function removes all HTML tags from a string, and htmlentities() turns all quotation marks and other punctuation into harmless entities that will be displayed and not acted upon.

The Plug-in

```
function PIPHP_BBCode($string)
{
    $from   = array('[b]', '[/b]',    '[i]', '[/i]',
                    '[u]', '[/u]',    '[s]', '[/s]',
                    '[quote]',        '[/quote]',
                    '[code]',         '[/code]',
                    '[img]',          '[/img]',
                    '[/size]',        '[/color]',
                    '[/url]');
    $to     = array('<b>', '</b>',    '<i>', '</i>',
                    '<u>', '</u>',    '<s>', '</s>',
                    '<blockquote>', '</blockquote>',
                    '<pre>',          '</pre>',
                    '<img src="',     '" />',
                    '</span>',        '</font>',
                    '</a>');
    $string = str_replace($from, $to, $string);
    $string = preg_replace("/\[size=([\d]+)\]/",
        "<span style=\"font-size:$1px\">", $string);
```

```
$string = preg_replace("/\[color=([^\]]+)\]/",
    "<font color='$1'>", $string);
$string = preg_replace("/\[url\]([^\[]*)<\/a>/",
    "<a href='$1'>$1</a>", $string);
$string = preg_replace("/\[url=([^\]]*)]/",
    "<a href='$1'>", $string);
return $string;
}
```

PLUG-IN 40 Pound Code

BB Code is all well and good but in my opinion it makes for a lot of typing of square brackets. So I invented a sleeker and simpler code called Pound Code (or Hash Code outside of the USA). With it you don't need to surround a code with brackets. Instead, you just type a # symbol followed by the action you want to achieve, and the plug-in works out the rest for you. Figure 6-10 shows the result.

About the Plug-in

This plug-in accepts a string containing Pound Code and returns it translated into safe HTML. It takes this argument:

- **$text**   The string to translate

Variables, Arrays, and Functions

$names	Array containing the supported short font names
$fonts	Array containing the HTML long names of $names
$to	Array containing the strings required to translate the short font codes to HTML

How It Works

This plug-in performs in a similar way to the BB Code plug-in but starts off by offering nine different font styles. It takes the short codes in $names and, using the long names of each stored in $fonts, creates <font face='fontname'> strings for all of them using

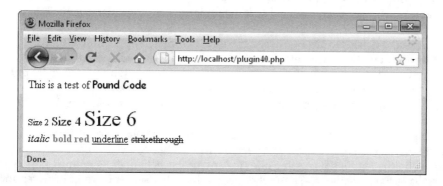

FIGURE 6-10   Pound Code is easier than BB Code and offers more flexibility.

a `for` loop to iterate through them, placing the results in the array `$to`. Then the function `str_ireplace()` is called to replace all occurrences found, regardless of whether they are in upper- or lowercase.

Afterward, it uses the `preg_replace()` function four times to perform the more complex translations:

- Converts any `#b-`, `#i-`, `#u-` or `#s-` codes into `</b>`, `</i>`, `</u>`, or `</s>`
- Converts any `#b`, `#i`, `#u` or `#s` codes into `<b>`, `<i>`, `<u>`, or `<s>`
- Converts any of `#1` to `#7` into `<font size='1'>` through `<font size='7'>`
- Converts any other `#code` into `<font color='code'>`

Finally, any instances of `#-` are translated into `</font>`.

Then, with all translations completed, the modified string is returned. If no modifications were made, the original string is returned.

How to Use It

To use this plug-in, just pass it the code that needs to be translated. If it includes any Pound Code, the returned result will be modified accordingly, otherwise it will be the same as the original. In the following example, `$string` is populated with some text and Pound Code, and then passed to the plug-in:

```
$string = <<<_END
This is a test of #comicPound Code#-
#2Size 2#-
#4Size 4#-
#6Size 6#-
#iitalic#i-
#red#bbold red#b-#-
#uunderline#u-
#sstrikethrough#s-
_END;

echo PIPHP_PoundCode($string);
```

The list of Pound Codes supported by this plug-in and the actions they perform are shown in Table 6-2. If your users are new to it, you might wish to copy this table to your web site.

Note that I have deliberately not offered the facility for users to include either image or hyperlink URLs, and that's for very good security reasons. Based on many years of experience in writing chat room software, you'd be amazed how often programmers put things in GET requests (tails of posted data appended to URLs, also known as a *query string*) thinking only the user can see them. This can sometimes even include password or other login details!

The problem with this is that if you allow an image to be displayed on that web site from a third-party server, then the current page's URL will be sent to the other server where it can be saved in the log files. The same goes for any users clicking links to third-party sites: The full details of the page they are on will be sent to the other server by their browser and

Opening # Code	Closing # Code	Action
#b	#b-	Bold face on and off.
#i	#i-	Italics on and off.
#u	#u-	Underline on and off.
#s	#s-	Strikethrough on and off.
#*font*	#-	Change to the *font* name provided (out of #arial, #chicago, #comic, #courier, #georgia, #impact, #script, #times and #verdana). The #- code reverts to the previous font.
#*color*	#-	Change to any legitimate HTML *color* name (such as #red or #purple, etc.). The #- code reverts to the previous font color.
#1 - #7	#-	Change to an HTML font size between 1 and 7. The #- code reverts to the previous font size.

TABLE 6-2　List of Pound Codes Supported by plug-in 40

if either of these includes login details or a session ID embedded in a GET query string, the other server will gain access to it.

So, if your site uses GET requests, the proper way to do this is to write a routine to retrieve the image from the other server and then display it from a local cache on your own server without any GET query string appended to the URL. While for URLs, you should create a redirection link on your web site and send your users off via that, also ensuring there is no GET query string. This is one reason why (apart from the fact that I wrote it and think it's easier to use) I would generally recommend Pound Code over BB code.

In a similar way to the previous one, this plug-in *does not* reject HTML code, and so you will probably first want to run inputted text through functions to strip out HTML and JavaScript such as these:

```
$string = htmlentities(strip_tags($string));
```

The strip_tags() function removes all HTML tags from a string, and htmlentities() turns all quotation marks and other punctuation into harmless entities that will be displayed and not acted upon.

The Plug-in

```
function PIPHP_PoundCode($text)
{
   $names = array('#georgia', '#arial',   '#courier',
                  '#script',  '#impact',  '#comic',
                  '#chicago', '#verdana', '#times');
   $fonts = array('Georgia',  'Arial',    'Courier New',
                  'Script',   'Impact',   'Comic Sans MS',
                  'Chicago',  'Verdana',  'Times New Roman');
   $to    = array();
```

```php
      for ($j = 0 ; $j < count($names) ; ++$j)
        $to[] = "<font face='$fonts[$j]'>";

    $text = str_ireplace($names, $to, $text);

    $text = preg_replace('/#([bius])-/i', "</$1>",
      $text);
    $text = preg_replace('/#([bius])/i',  "<$1>",
      $text);
    $text = preg_replace('/#([1-7])/',    "<font size='$1'>",
      $text);
    $text = preg_replace('/#([a-z]+)/i',  "<font color='$1'>",
      $text);
    $text = str_replace('#-', "</font>", $text);

    return $text;
}
```

CHAPTER 7

The Internet

Whatever you create a web site, rather than existing on its own, it becomes part of the wider Internet as a whole. This means people will interact with it in many ways, from bookmarking pages they like, to subscribing to RSS feeds. While other web sites may wish to exchange links with you to help pool and build traffic, Twitter users may want to tweet about something on your site and so on.

This chapter provides a range of plug-ins to help integrate your new property into the Internet community at large, including link management, creating short URLs, converting between HTML and RSS, adapting a site to mobile browsers and more.

Check Links

When building up a web site, and especially if the marketing budget is tight, you often have to embark on a campaign of link exchanges with other sites. But tracking all those link exchanges to ensure the other sites keep their end of the deal is time-consuming. However, with this plug-in you simply pass an array of one or more links which should be present on a particular web page and you will be informed whether those links are all in place. Figure 7-1 shows the plug-in in action; two of the links have passed, but a link to *http://doesnotexist.com/index.html* is not found on the *www.pluginphp.com* index page.

About the Plug-in

This plug-in accepts the URL of a web page to check, along with a set of links that ought to be present on it. If all the links are present, it returns an array with the single value TRUE, otherwise it returns a two-element array, of which the first element is FALSE. The second is an array containing all the links that were not present. It takes these arguments:

- **$url**   A string containing the URL of a page to check
- **$links**   An array of links to look for on the page at $url

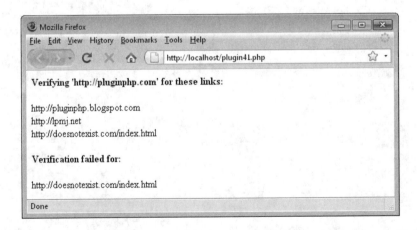

FIGURE 7-1   This plug-in tests whether certain links are present on a particular web page.

Variables, Arrays, and Functions

`$results`	Array containing all the links found at `$url`
`$missing`	Array containing any links passed in `$links` that are not present in `$results`
`$failed`	Integer counter that indexes into `$missing`, incrementing on each failed match
`$link`	String containing the current link being processed, as extracted from `$links`
`PIPHP_GetLinksFromURL()`	Plug-in 22: This function returns all the links at a given URL.
`PIPHP_RelToAbsURL()`	Plug-in 21: This function converts a relative-to-absolute URL and is used by plug-in 22.

How It Works

The first thing this plug-in does is call plug-in 22, `PIPHP_GetLinksFromURL()`, to fetch all the links within the page supplied in the variable `$url`. All links found are then placed in the array `$results`. Next, a couple of variables are initialized, ready for checking whether these links include the ones being looked for. These are the array `$missing`, which will hold any links not found, and the integer `$failed`, which is set to zero and will be incremented when any link is determined to not be present.

Then a `foreach` loop iterates through all the returned links, temporarily placing each in the string variable `$link`, where it is then checked against the array of all links in `$results`, using the function `in_array()`. Any that are not found are placed in `$missing` and the array pointer `$failed` is incremented.

After the checking is complete, if any links are not found, then a two-element array is returned, the first element of which is FALSE, and the second is an array containing all the links that failed the check. Otherwise, a single-element array is returned, containing the value TRUE.

How to Use It

To use this plug-in, you should supply a URL to be checked and a list of links that should be included within the page at that URL, like this:

```
$url   = "http://pluginphp.com";
$links = array("http://pluginphp.blogspot.com",
               "http://lpmj.net",
               "http://doesnotexist.com/index.html");
$result = PIPHP_CheckLinks($url, $links);
```

If the value in `$result[0]` is TRUE, then all the links are present and correct. But if `$result[0]` is FALSE, then `$result[1]` will contain an array of all failed links. You can check for these conditions using code such as the following, which employs a `for` loop to iterate through the failed links:

```
if ($result[0]) echo "All links verified";
else
{
   echo "<br /><b>Verification failed for:<br />";
   for ($j = 0 ; $j < count($result[1]) ; ++$j)
      echo $result[1][$j] . "<br />";
}
```

Remember that because this plug-in also uses plug-ins 21 and 22, `PIPHP_RelToAbsURL()` and `PIPHP_GetLinksFromURL()`, you should also copy and paste them into your program, or otherwise include them.

The Plug-in

```
function PIPHP_CheckLinks($url, $links)
{
    $results = PIPHP_GetLinksFromURL($url);
    $missing = array();
    $failed  = 0;

    foreach($links as $link)
        if (!in_array($link, $results))
            $missing[$failed++] = $link;

    if ($failed == 0) return array(TRUE);
    else return array(FALSE, $missing);
}
```

PLUG-IN 42 Get Title from URL

Sometimes you want to know what the title of a web page is. Using this plug-in in combination with the following one (plug-in 43), it's possible to link back to a referring web page using its title. Figure 7-2 shows the title being fetched from the Yahoo! News home page.

About the Plug-in

This plug-in accepts the URL of a web page whose title is to be extracted and returns the title. It takes this argument:

- **$page**   A string containing the URL of a page to check

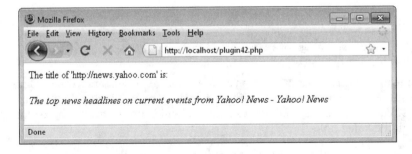

FIGURE 7-2   When you need to know the title of a web page, you can call this plug-in.

Variables, Arrays, and Functions

$contents	String containing the contents of $page

How It Works

This simple plug-in calls get_file_contents() to load the contents of $page into the string variable $contents. If for any reason the page could not be read in, then FALSE is returned. Otherwise preg_match() is called to extract the contents between the page's <title> and </title> tags. This is denoted by the (.*) in the expression passed to the function.

Of course, some pages may not include a title and this plug-in may fail. So, before returning it checks whether a title has been successfully extracted, and if so, the information needed as a result of calling the function is placed in the second element of the array $matches, and this is then returned. Otherwise, FALSE is returned.

How to Use It

To extract the title from a page, you can call this plug-in in the following way:

```
$page   = "http://news.yahoo.com";
$result = PIPHP_GetTitleFromURL($page);
```

Then, to act on the value returned, use code such as this:

```
if (!$result) echo "The URL could not be accessed";
else echo "The title is: $result";
```

The Plug-in

```
function PIPHP_GetTitleFromURL($page)
{
    $contents = @file_get_contents($page);
    if (!$contents) return FALSE;

    preg_match("/<title>(.*)<\/title>/i", $contents, $matches);

    if (count($matches)) return $matches[1];
    else return FALSE;
}
```

PLUG-IN 43 Auto Back Links

A traffic-building technique that is known to work is to offer automatic back links to sites that link to yours. Using this program, providing that facility is extremely easy and will help you build more traffic with a minimum of extra work. Figure 7-3 shows example output from this plug-in.

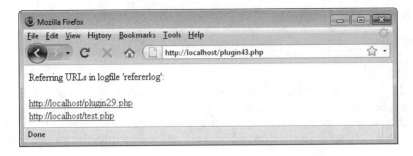

FIGURE 7-3   With this plug-in you can automatically link back to sites that link to yours.

About the Plug-in

This plug-in accepts the name of a file used as a datafile for storing details about sites linking to the current web page. This will be the file created by plug-in 30, PIPHP_ RefererLog(). It takes this argument:

- **$filename**   The file and/or path name to read

Variables, Arrays, and Functions

$inbound	Array containing all the inbound links in the log file
$logfile	String containing the contents of $filename
$links	Array of data extracted from $logfile
$key	String containing a link extracted from $links
$val	String containing the number of visitors who came from $key

How It Works

This plug-in assumes you are already using plug-in 30, PIPHP_RefererLog(), to track inbound links to a web page, and that you've already specified a datafile where the data is being stored, which you have also passed to this function in $filename.

What it does is then read the datafile into the string variable $logfile. If the file is unreadable (perhaps because it doesn't yet exist), then a single-element array is returned with the value FALSE.

Otherwise $logfile is split into lines at the line feed characters, \n, using the explode() function, and then the lines are placed in the array $links. At this point, many of the links in $links will be repeated due to multiple visitors coming from a referring page, so the array_ count_values() function is called, which returns an array using the values of $links as keys, and each unique key's frequency as values.

This has the effect of determining the popularity of each referring page by counting the number of occurrences of each. The result is placed back in the array $links and then arsort() is called to sort the array numerically in *reverse* order, so that those referring URLs with the most counts come first.

Next, a `foreach` loop is initiated to iterate through all the elements of $links, which are placed in $key and $val ($key for the link and $val for its count, although the latter is no longer needed and is ignored), removing all the entries listed as " No Referer" since they must also be ignored. All other links are added to the array $inbound.

At this point the $inbound array now contains a list of all the referring URLs in order of numbers of visitors sent by each, so a two-element array is returned. The first element of this is TRUE, while the second is the array $inbound.

How to Use It

To extract all referring pages from the log file, use code such as this:

```
$logfile = "refer.log";
$results = PIPHP_AutoBackLinks($logfile);
```

$results will now be an array with either one element, FALSE, in which case no referring links were found, or it will be a two-element array, the first value of which will be TRUE, while the second element will be an array of referring URLs in order of number of visitors referred. You can act on this data like this:

```
if (!$results[0]) echo "No referring URLs";
else foreach ($results[1] as $result) echo "$result<br />";
```

This provides you with useful data, but you can also provide automatic back link for your users to follow by using this code instead:

```
echo "The following sites kindly link to us:<br />";
foreach ($results[1] as $result)
    echo "<a href='$result'>$result</a><br />";
```

However, we can do better than that because plug-in 42, `PIPHP_GetTitleFromURL()`, can also be brought into the equation to link back to the referring site by name, like this:

```
foreach ($results[1] as $result)
{
    $title = PIPHP_GetTitleFromURL($result);
    echo "<a href='$result'>";
    echo $title ? $title : $result;
    echo "</a><br />";
}
```

If a referring page has a title, it will be used in the link back, otherwise the page URL will be used. Of course, for this trick to work you must make sure plug-in 42, PIPHP_GetTitleFromURL(), is also copied into the program file, or otherwise included. You are likely to be using plug-in 30, PIPHP_RefererLog(), within this program, too.

The Plug-in

```
function PIPHP_AutoBackLinks($filename)
{
    if (!file_exists($filename)) return array(FALSE);
```

```
$inbound = array();
$logfile = file_get_contents($filename);
$links   = explode("\n", rtrim($logfile));
$links   = array_count_values($links);
arsort($links, SORT_NUMERIC);

foreach ($links as $key => $val)
    if ($key != " No Referer")
        $inbound[] = $key;

return array(TRUE, $inbound);
}
```

PLUG-IN 44 Create Short URL

With the rapid growth of Twitter and its short message lengths, many services have sprung up offering short URL services. These are all well and good except that they tend to also be used by spammers to disguise links that might reveal their destination. Consequently, some of these services are slow, while others disappear overnight. What's more, users can be wary of entering a short URL, even from an established service, because they are never sure where the URL may lead.

To help diminish all these negatives, this plug-in lets you offer your own short URLs using your own domain name, not a third party's, which should mean it is more trusted. For example, which URL would you rather follow, *microsoft.com/go.php?u=12345* or *somesite. net/go.php?u=12345*? I would be far less worried about visiting the former. Figure 7-4 shows a long URL being shortened with this plug-in.

About the Plug-in

This plug-in accepts a URL to be shortened, along with some other data, and returns a short URL. It takes these arguments:

- **$url** The URL to be shortened
- **$redirect** The name of a php file on your server that will make the redirects from short URLs to their original destinations

FIGURE 7-4   Use this plug-in to create short aliases for long URLs on your web site.

- **$len**   The number of characters to use in the token part of a short URL. The more you use, the more URLs are supported. For example, three characters will support 4,096 URLs since this plug-in uses the hexadecimal digits 0–9 and a–f.
- **$file**   The name of a file in which to store the short URL data

Variables, Arrays, and Functions

`$contents`	String variable containing the contents of `$file`
`$lines`	Array containing all the separate lines from `$contents`
`$shorts`	Array of short token versions of `$longs`
`$longs`	Array of full URL versions of `$shorts`
`$line`	String containing a single line extracted from `$lines`
`$j`	Integer counter for iterating through `$longs`
`$str`	String containing a newly created short token

How It Works

This plug-in reads the contents of `$file` into the variable `$contents`, from where all the individual lines are extracted into the array `$lines`. Then two arrays (`$shorts` and `$longs`) are initialized to hold the short tokens and their long URL equivalents, as extracted from `$lines`.

Then, if `$contents` actually contains anything—in other words, there was data in `$file` and it was successfully loaded—an `if` statement is entered. In this case, a `foreach` loop iterates through all the lines in `$lines` and assigns the left and right items of data on either side of the `|` symbol, which divides them into the `$shorts` and `$longs` arrays. The function `list()` is used to neatly extract both halves at once. When complete, for example, `$shorts[1]` will contain a token that represents the URL in `$longs[1]`.

Next the `in_array()` function is called to see whether `$url` already exists in the datafile. If so, the `$longs` array, which contains the list of URLs, is stepped through, incrementing the pointer `$j` until the matching URL is found, at which point `$j` is used to index into `$shorts` and extract the equivalent token from there. This token is then returned, along with some other details, as follows:

The variable `$redirect` is passed to the function and represents the name of a PHP program you will use to handle the short URL redirects. Suppose this is called `go.php`. Therefore, when the function returns it will pass back the string `go.php?u=nnnn`, where `nnnn` is the short token equivalent to the URL in `$url`.

If `$url` is not already in the datafile, a `do` loop is entered to randomly construct a new token `$len` characters in length, which is stored in `$str`. The loop repeats until the value of `$str` is unique to the datafile, so that no two URLs can have the same short token.

With a short token now created in `$str`, the `file_put_contents()` function is called to save the new details into the datafile. It does this by saving `$contents` (the data previously read from the file), followed by `$str`, a `|` symbol, and `$url`. It is terminated with a `\n` (newline character). So an example line from this file would look like this:

```
f8c52|http://pluginphp.com/longfoldername/index.html
```

Finally a redirect URL is returned comprising the values of $redirect, ?u=, and $str, such as go.php?u=xxxx.

How to Use It

To create a short URL, use this plug-in. The following one, plug-in 45, is for using the short URLs you create. To create a short URL, you need to pass four arguments to the function, like this:

```
$long     = "http://pluginphp.com/longfoldername/index.html";
$redirect = "go.php";
$len      = 5;
$file     = "shorturls.txt";
$result   = PIPHP_CreateShortURL($long, $redirect, $len, $file);
```

Now you can display the link to this shortened URL using code such as this:

```
echo " http://mysite.com/$result";
```

In the preceding case, this will display a link looking like the following:

```
http://mysite.com/go.php?u=abcde
```

This is much shorter than the original of:

```
http://pluginphp.com/longfoldername/index.html
```

You will use the following plug-in, plug-in 45, to create go.php. You'll also see how you can use the *mod rewrite* facility in an *.htaccess* file to make the shortened URL even smaller, like the following, which is half the length of the original:

```
http://mysite.com/abcde
```

The Plug-in

```php
function PIPHP_CreateShortURL($url, $redirect, $len, $file)
{
   $contents = @file_get_contents($file);
   $lines    = explode("\n", $contents);
   $shorts   = array();
   $longs    = array();

   if (strlen($contents))
      foreach ($lines as $line)
         if (strlen($line))
            list($shorts[], $longs[]) = explode('|', $line);

   if (in_array($url, $longs))
      for ($j = 0 ; $j < count($longs) ; ++$j)
         if ($longs[$j] == $url) return $redirect .
            "?u=" . $shorts[$j];
```

```
    do $str = substr(md5(rand(0, 1000000)), 0, $len);
    while (in_array($str, $shorts));

    file_put_contents($file, $contents . $str . '|' . $url .
        "\n");
    return $redirect . "?u=$str";
}
```

45 Use Short URL

Once you've created a short URL, you need a means to access it. You do this via a plug-in that accepts a short token in a GET tail, known as a query string, and then redirects the user to the equivalent longer URL. Figure 7-5 shows the function being used just to decode a short token, without redirecting.

About the Plug-in

This plug-in accepts a short token and returns its longer URL equivalent. It takes these arguments:

- **$token** A short token with which to look up the equivalent URL
- **$file** The datafile for this plug-in

Variables, Arrays, and Functions

$contents	String variable containing the contents of $file
$lines	Array containing all the separate lines from $contents
$shorts	Array of short token versions of $longs
$longs	Array of full URL versions of $shorts
$line	String containing a single line extracted from $lines
$j	Integer counter for iterating through $longs

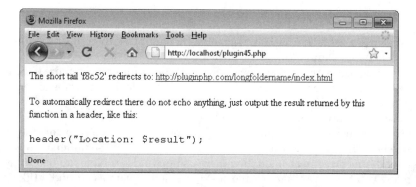

FIGURE 7-5 Creating short URLs using your own domain is easy with this plug-in.

How It Works

This plug-in must be passed a short token as created by the previous plug-in, PIPHP_ CreateShortURL(). It then returns the associated URL. It does this by reading the contents of $file into the variable $contents, from where all the individual lines are extracted into the array $lines. Then two arrays ($shorts and $longs) are initialized to hold the short tokens and their long URL equivalents, as extracted from $lines.

Then, if the data in $file was successfully loaded into $contents, an if statement is entered. In this case, a foreach loop iterates through all the lines in $lines and assigns the left and right items of data on either side of the | symbol, which divides them into the $shorts and $longs arrays. The function list() is called to extract both halves at once.

Next the in_array() function is called to see whether $token already exists in the datafile. If so, the $shorts array, which contains the list of tokens, is stepped through, incrementing the pointer $j until the matching URL is found, at which point $j is used to index into $longs and extract the equivalent URL from there. This URL is then returned. If the token is not found in the datafile, FALSE is returned.

How to Use It

In the previous section I discussed a program called *go.php*. This is what we will write here. It's very short and simple:

```
$file   = "shorturls.txt";
$result = PIPHP_UseShortURL($_GET['u'], $file);
if ($result) header("Location: $result");
else echo "That short URL is unrecognized";
```

What this code does is fetch the argument passed to it in the GET variable 'u' and run it through PIPHP_UseShortURL(), which then looks up the associated URL and returns it to the string variable $result. The header() function is then called to issue a Location: header, informing the browser where the contents it is requesting can be found.

All you need to do is save these four lines of code (along with the PIPHP_UseShortURL() plug-in, to your server's document root as *go.php* (remembering to add the surrounding <?php and ?> tags), and it can be called up as follows (assuming your server has the domain name *myserver.com*):

```
http://myserver.com/go.php?u=nnnn
```

As long as nnnn is a valid short token, as created by plug-in 44, then this program will look up the associated URL and redirect the browser to it.

But there's a very neat trick you can employ to make this plug-in even more effective, and that's to use *mod rewrite* to further modify the short URL, making it even shorter. You do this by creating (or editing) a file called *.htaccess* in the same directory as *go.php*.

If you are using Windows, you will not be able to create the *.htaccess* file by right-clicking and selecting New because Windows will tell you that you need a file name before the period. Instead you must use a program editor to save the file, as most of these understand what a *.htaccess* file is, and can correctly create it. If you are using Windows Notepad or a program that doesn't allow you to save an *.htaccess* file, just place double quotes around it (like this: ".htaccess") when saving, which tells Windows to save it as is.

Once you have the *.htaccess* file, add the following two lines of code to it:

```
RewriteEngine On
RewriteRule ^([a-zA-Z0-9]+)$ go.php?u=$1 [L]
```

What this does is tell the Apache web server that when it can't find a file or folder on your server it should translate the filename requested (which can be any combination of letters and numbers) into the following form, where *request* is the original location requested:

```
go.php?u=request
```

So, for example, assume your web domain is *myserver.com*, you already have the short token 12345 which redirects to a valid URL, and you have entered the following short URL into your browser:

```
http://myserver.com/12345
```

The mod rewrite module in the Apache web server will notice there is no file or folder named 12345 and therefore translate the request into the following:

```
http://myserver.com/go.php?u=12345
```

And, hey presto, this is a valid URL pointing to the *go.php* program, which has been arrived at using the smallest possible short URL for your domain.

If you find using mod rewrite and *.htaccess* don't work for you, it may be because your *httpd.conf* configuration file doesn't have AllowOverride enabled. In which case you'll need to modify the relevant line and restart Apache. Under Windows, using Zend Server CE, you will find *httpd.conf* at *c:\program files\zend\apache2\conf\httpd.conf*. On Linux/Mac, you should find the file at */usr/local/zend/apache2/conf/httpd.conf*. On other Apache installations the file may be elsewhere and you should consult the relevant documentation.

You can open *httpd.conf* with any text editor and at (or somewhere near) line 211 you should see AllowOverride None, which should be changed to AllowOverride All. Then resave the file. If you are not allowed to save the file, you may need to adjust the file and/or folder permissions first.

You should now restart Apache by clicking the Apache icon in your system tray and selecting Restart. Or, on Linux/Mac, using Zend Server CE, you would type /usr/local/zend/bin/zendctl.sh restart into a Terminal window.

For more about the mod rewrite program and *.htaccess* files on the Apache web server, please visit *httpd.apache.org/docs/2.0/misc/rewriteguide.html*.

The Plug-in

```
function PIPHP_UseShortURL($token, $file)
{
   $contents = @file_get_contents($file);
   $lines    = explode("\n", $contents);
   $shorts   = array();
   $longs    = array();
```

```
    if (strlen($contents))
        foreach ($lines as $line)
            if (strlen($line))
                list($shorts[], $longs[]) = explode('|', $line);

    if (in_array($token, $shorts))
        for ($j = 0 ; $j < count($longs) ; ++$j)
            if ($shorts[$j] == $token)
                return $longs[$j];

    return FALSE;
}
```

PLUG-IN 46 Simple Web Proxy

There are times when you are unable to browse to a site from one location but you can ping it from a server at another location. You know the site should be up and running, but your connection to it from the original location is probably temporarily blocked. When this happens you can use this plug-in to act as a simple web proxy to browse right through to that site from your web server. Or, if you wish, you can use this code as a basis for your own web proxy service. You could provide this for free, or you could even drop in a small advertisement to cover bandwidth costs—although you'd have to add that code yourself.

Figure 7-6 shows the *www.news.com* web site as browsed to using this plug-in. You can see from the status bar that all URLs in the page have been updated to call up linked pages through the proxy, too. And, yes, even the images have been served via the proxy.

FIGURE 7-6 This small plug-in provides powerful web proxy functionality, including web images.

About the Plug-in

This plug-in accepts a URL to fetch, and returns it with all URLs and links to images altered to run through the proxy. It takes these arguments:

- **$url** The URL to fetch
- **$redirect** The filename of a PHP program to act as the web proxy

Variables, Arrays, and Functions

`$contents`	String containing the contents of `$url`
`$dom`	Document object of `$contents`
`$xpath`	XPath object for traversing `$dom`
`$hrefs`	Object containing all `a href=` link elements in `$dom`
`$sources`	Object containing all `img src=` link elements in `$dom`
`$iframes`	Object containing all `iframe src=` link elements in `$dom`
`$scripts`	Object containing all `script src=` link elements in `$dom`
`$css`	Object containing all `link href=` link elements in `$dom`
`$links`	Array of all the links discovered in `$contents`
`$to`	Array containing the version of what each `$link` should be changed to in order to ensure it is absolute
`$count`	Integer containing the number of elements in `$to`
`$link`	Each link in turn extracted from `$links`
`$j`	Integer counter for iterating through `$to`
`PIPHP_RelToAbsURL()`	Plug-in 21: This function converts a relative URL to absolute.

How It Works

This plug-in fetches the contents of `$url` and places it in `$contents`. If it cannot load the page at `$url`, FALSE is returned. Next, if `$url` refers to any image file such as *.jpg*, *.gif*, *.png*, or *.ico*, or any of a *.css*, *.js*, or *.xml* file, then the contents of the file are returned unaltered, as there is no need to attempt to convert relative links to absolute in these types of file because they are not HTML. However, any file that is not one of those mentioned here is assumed to be HTML. If you wish to improve on this plug-in, here's one area where you could add support for many other file types. HTML will be assumed from here on, however.

So the next thing that happens is all instances of & (the XML and XHTML required form of the & symbol) are converted to just the & symbol, and then all & symbols are changed to a special token with the value !!**1**!!. You may wonder what on earth is going on here. Well, I can report that after a huge amount of time testing the str_replace() function built into PHP, I believe it has an obscure, and hard to catch, bug when it comes to processing the & symbol. In the end I gave up trying to find out why and simply chose to convert all occurrences of & to a sequence of characters I could be pretty sure would not appear in any HTML document, hence the string !!**1**!!.

So, having got the & problem out of the way, a new document object is created in $dom and the document in $contents is loaded into it. This makes the whole HTML page easily searchable using the $xpath object, which is created from $dom.

Next, five types of tags are searched for using the $xpath object; a href=, img src=, iframe src=, script src=, and link src=. All the associated strings for each tag are then placed in the objects $hrefs, $sources, $iframes, $scripts, and $css. The reason for this is that it is necessary to ensure that all links within a page are of the absolute type so that the page this plug-in returns can be served up from any server and, by grabbing all the links, it will be possible to perform a relative-to-absolute conversion on each.

To facilitate this, all the separate objects are then traversed, and the links found in each extracted into the array $links. Then, to ensure there is no duplication of conversions, the array_unique() function is called to remove all duplicates, and the resulting set of unique URLs is then saved back into the $links array.

Now that the entire set of links from the document are in the $links array, a foreach loop is used to iterate through each. The first part of the loop ensures there was actually a URL supplied in a link before continuing, and if so, the string variable $temp is assigned the contents of each link, but with the & symbols replaced. This is so that the array $to can be assigned an untokenized URL in the next step, in which the value /$redirect?u= is assigned to the current element of $to, as indexed by $count, which is incremented after each insertion.

After the /$redirect?u=, the URL itself is attached to the end of the element, after first running it through the PIPHP_RelToAbsURL() function to ensure it is absolute. So, if the value in $redirect is webproxy.php, and the link to add is http://google.com, then $to[$count] will be assigned the string /webproxy.php?u=http://google.com.

Now it's time to make the link replacements within the document itself, which, as you'll recall, is stored in $contents. This is done by two sets of str_replace() calls to cover the three types of links allowed in an HTML document: (1) single quoted, (2) double quoted, and (3) without quotes. To do this, all href="link", href='link' and href=link statements are replaced with a unique token comprising the value of $count surrounded by two pairs of exclamation marks. The first link is replaced with !!0!!, the second with !!1!!, and so on. Again, I chose this as being unlikely to appear within an HTML document. This process is then repeated with all occurrences of src="link", src='link', and src=link.

At the end of the loop there will be no URLs remaining in the document, only the exclamation mark tokens representing them. And there's a very good reason for all these shenanigans, which is that the final part of this plug-in needs to convert all the links to absolute, but if it tried to do this with all the links still in place it would seriously mess up.

To explain why, imagine that the server being proxied is http://server.com and therefore all occurrences of /news/index.html must be replaced with http://server .com/news/index.html. This is all fine and dandy, but what if all occurrences of /news/ need changing too? When this happens it will also impact the previous change because the newly converted http://server.com/news/index.html strings will get changed to http://server.com/http://server.com/news/index.html. Do you see the problem? The changes will get changed.

This is why all the links that need converting are first pre-processed into tokens. Then all the tokens can be safely processed into the absolute URLs, without new changes modifying previous ones. And that's what the next bit of code does. It's a for loop that iterates through all the entries in $to (the absolute URLs) and changes each of the tokens in turn to each of the values in $to.

Once all that has been achieved, then all the links in the document will now be in absolute format, so it's safe to make a final conversion, changing any remaining !!**1**!! tokens back into & symbols, the result of which is then returned by the plug-in.

How to Use It

At it's simplest, all you need to use this plug-in is to create a program, perhaps called *webproxy.php*, looking like this, but also including the functions: PIPHP_SimpleWebProxy() and PIPHP_RelToAbsURL():

```
$url = urldecode($_GET['u']);
echo PIPHP_SimpleWebProxy($url, "webproxy.php");
```

This program should be saved in the document root of your server.

The first line simply extracts the contents following the ?u= part of a GET request (the query string) into the variable $url, and the second makes the call to the plug-in.

You can call up the web proxy by typing a command such as the following into your browser's address bar (making sure you always enter the http:// part of the URL or the program won't work):

```
webproxy.php?u=http://google.com
```

Or, more likely, if your server domain is *myserver.com*:

```
http://myserver.com/webproxy.php?u=http://google.com
```

Your new web proxy will now work, including sending images, because each link in a document has been converted to run through the web proxy, and therefore all images do so, too.

However, to make the program work as well as possible, you will probably want to support all the content types checked for near the start of the plug-in, and send the correct headers for each prior to sending the data. Therefore your program should probably look more like this (not forgetting to also add the two plug-ins it relies on):

```
$url    = urldecode($_GET['u']);
$result = PIPHP_SimpleWebProxy($url, "webproxy.php");

switch(strtolower(substr($url, -4)))
{
   case ".jpg": header("Content-type: image/jpeg");   die($result);
   case ".gif": header("Content-type: image/gif");    die($result);
   case ".png": header("Content-type: image/png");    die($result);
   case ".ico": header("Content-type: image/x-icon"); die($result);
   case ".css": header("Content-type: text/css");     die($result);
   case ".xml": header("Content-type: text/xml");     die($result);
   case ".htm": case "html": case ".php":
      header("Content-type: text/html"); die($result);
   default:
      if (strtolower(substr($url, -3)) == ".js")
         header("Content-type: application/x-javascript");
      die($result);
}
```

In the preceding code a `switch` statement is used to determine the current file type. Then, the appropriate header for each is sent to the browser, followed by the contents, as returned in `$result`. This is sent using the `die()` function since it combines both an `echo` and an `exit` statement in one. In the case of HTML files, the extensions *.htm* and *.php*, as well as *.html* are allowed.

Under the `default` section, *.js* JavaScript files are caught. They are handled separately as their extensions are only two characters long, instead of three. Finally, if nothing else matches, `$contents` is simply sent without a header, and it is hoped this will be good enough (generally it is).

Not including whitespace and comments, you will now have a web proxy program in under 100 lines of code that will work quite well, but you should realize that it only likes properly formed pages and is not forgiving of badly formatted HTML. Therefore some pages will display strangely, if at all. But now that you know how it all works, you can easily tweak the code to your preferences.

Remember that plug-in 21, `PIPHP_RelToAbsURL()`, also needs to be copied into, or otherwise included in, your program.

The Plug-in

```php
function PIPHP_SimpleWebProxy($url, $redirect)
{
    $contents = @file_get_contents($url);
    if (!$contents) return NULL;

    switch(strtolower(substr($url, -4)))
    {
        case ".jpg": case ".gif": case ".png": case ".ico":
        case ".css": case ".js": case ".xml":
            return $contents;
    }

    $contents = str_replace('&amp;', '&',          $contents);
    $contents = str_replace('&',     '!!**1**!!', $contents);

    $dom      = new domdocument();
    @$dom     ->loadhtml($contents);
    $xpath    = new domxpath($dom);
    $hrefs    = $xpath->evaluate("/html/body//a");
    $sources  = $xpath->evaluate("/html/body//img");
    $iframes  = $xpath->evaluate("/html/body//iframe");
    $scripts  = $xpath->evaluate("/html//script");
    $css      = $xpath->evaluate("/html/head/link");
    $links    = array();

    for ($j = 0 ; $j < $hrefs->length ; ++$j)
        $links[] = $hrefs->item($j)->getAttribute('href');

    for ($j = 0 ; $j < $sources->length ; ++$j)
        $links[] = $sources->item($j)->getAttribute('src');

    for ($j = 0 ; $j < $iframes->length ; ++$j)
        $links[] = $iframes->item($j)->getAttribute('src');
```

```
    for ($j = 0 ; $j < $scripts->length ; ++$j)
        $links[] = $scripts->item($j)->getAttribute('src');

    for ($j = 0 ; $j < $css->length ; ++$j)
        $links[] = $css->item($j)->getAttribute('href');

$links = array_unique($links);
$to    = array();
$count = 0;
sort($links);

foreach ($links as $link)
{
    if ($link != "")
    {
        $temp = str_replace('!!**1**!!', '&', $link);

        $to[$count] = "/$redirect?u=" .
          urlencode(PIPHP_RelToAbsURL($url, $temp));
        $contents = str_replace("href=\"$link\"",
            "href=\"!!$count!!\"", $contents);
        $contents = str_replace("href='$link'",
            "href='!!$count!!'",    $contents);
        $contents = str_replace("href=$link",
            "href=!!$count!!",      $contents);
        $contents = str_replace("src=\"$link\"",
            "src=\"!!$count!!\"",   $contents);
        $contents = str_replace("src='$link'",
            "src='!!$count!!'",     $contents);
        $contents = str_replace("src=$link",
            "src=!!$count!!",       $contents);
        ++$count;
    }

}

    for ($j = 0 ; $j < $count ; ++$j)
        $contents = str_replace("!!$j!!", $to[$j],
            $contents);

    return str_replace('!!**1**!!', '&', $contents);
}
```

47 Page Updated?

If you want to allow your users to be notified whenever one of your pages is updated, or perhaps you would like to be informed when a web page that interests you has been changed, all you need is this plug-in. For example, Figure 7-7 shows the index page at *www.pluginphp.com* being monitored for changes.

About the Plug-in

This plug-in accepts the URL of a web page to monitor and lets you know whether it has been changed. It returns 1 if the page has changed, 0 if it is unchanged, -1 if the page is a new one not yet in the datafile, or -2 if the page was inaccessible. It takes these arguments:

- **$url** The URL to check
- **$datafile** The filename of a file containing the datafile

Variables, Arrays, and Functions

$contents	String containing the contents of $url
$checksum	String containing the result of passing $contents through the md5() function
$rawfile	String containing the contents of $datafile
$data	Array containing the lines extracted from $rawfile
$left	Array of all the left halves of $data
$right	Array of all the right halves of $data
$exists	Integer pointer to the location in $left of $page if it is already in the datafile
$j	Integer counter for iterating through $left
PIPHP_PU_F1()	Function to extract the left half of a supplied string
PIPHP_PU_F2()	Function to extract the right half of a supplied string

How It Works

This plug-in loads the contents of $page into $contents, returning the value FALSE if it could not be fetched. Otherwise, an md5() checksum is made of the page's contents. This is a one-way function that creates a 32-character unique string. Should even one letter change on a web page, the resulting md5() string will be substantially different, so it's the perfect way to detect changes in a web page.

Next a check is made to see whether $datafile already exists. If it does, then its contents are loaded into $rawfile, which is then split line by line into the array $data by using the explode() function based around the \n linefeeds in the file. Then, instead of using a loop to iterate through each element of $data, the much faster and more efficient array_map() function is called. This does the same thing, only requiring the name of a function to call for each element. In the case of populating the $left array, which will be assigned all the left halves of each line, the function PIPHP_PU_F1() is called. For the $right array, PIPHP_PU_F2() is called.

The reason for the split is that the checksum and URL are stored side by side on a line, separated only by the token !1!, which is unlikely to appear in any URL.

A for loop is then started to iterate through the $left array and check whether $page already exists in the datafile. If so, $exists is set to point to the element number within the array where it is located. Using this pointer, the matching element in $right is compared with the value of $checksum and, if it is the same, zero is returned to indicate that the page is still the same as last time the program checked.

If, on the other hand, $page exists in the datafile but $checksum does not match the saved value, then the page contents must have changed. In this case, the old checksum value in the datafile is overwritten with the new value in $checksum using the str_replace() function, the datafile is saved back to disk, and a value of 1 is returned to indicate that the web page has changed.

At the end of the if (file_exists($datafile)) set of statements, if the file does not already exist, then the string $rawfile is assigned the empty string.

Finally, whether or not the file exists, the contents of $rawfile are saved to disk, along with the values of $page and $checksum, separated by the token !1!. This has the effect of either creating the datafile if it doesn't exist, or if it does, a new line of data is appended to it, followed by a \n newline character. Either way, a value of -1 is returned to indicate that the URL in $page was new to the datafile and has now been saved.

Note that the two functions PIPHP_PU_F1() and PIPHP_PU_F2() are for the exclusive use of the main plug-in and are not intended to be called elsewhere.

How to Use It

To use this plug-in, call it like this:

```
$page     = "http://pluginphp.com";
$datafile = "urldata.txt";
$result   = PIPHP_PageUpdated($page, $datafile);
```

Then, to act on the value in $result, you might use code such as this:

```
echo    "<pre>(1st call) The URL '$page' is ";
if      ($result == -1) echo "New";
elseif  ($result == 1)  echo "Changed";
elseif  ($result == 0)  echo "Unchanged";
else                    echo "Inaccessible";
```

This will tell you (or your users) whether the index page at *www.pluginphp.com* has changed since the last time it was checked, or whether it is new to the datafile or even inaccessible. The first time you make the call regarding a new page it will always report that the page is new. If you try an additional call (such as via the following code) immediately after on a site that is not dynamically generated, you will then be informed that the page is unchanged, otherwise you'll be told it has changed:

```
$result   = PIPHP_PageUpdated($page, $datafile);
echo        "<br />(2nd call) The URL '$page' is ";
if      ($result == -1) echo "New";
elseif  ($result == 1)  echo "Changed";
elseif  ($result == 0)  echo "Unchanged";
else                    echo "Inaccessible";
```

You might prefer to send an e-mail instead of displaying this information to a browser, in which case just replace the echo statements with a call to plug-in 38, PIPHP_SendEmail(), sending the contents of the echo statements in the $message argument.

The Plug-in

```
function PIPHP_PageUpdated($page, $datafile)
{
   $contents = @file_get_contents($page);
   if (!$contents) return FALSE;

   $checksum = md5($contents);

   if (file_exists($datafile))
   {
      $rawfile  = file_get_contents($datafile);
      $data     = explode("\n", rtrim($rawfile));
      $left     = array_map("PIPHP_PU_F1", $data);
      $right    = array_map("PIPHP_PU_F2", $data);
      $exists   = -1;

      for ($j = 0 ; $j < count($left) ; ++$j)
      {
         if ($left[$j] == $page)
         {
            $exists = $j;
            if ($right[$j] == $checksum) return 0;
         }
      }

      if ($exists > -1)
      {
         $rawfile = str_replace($right[$exists],
            $checksum, $rawfile);
         file_put_contents($datafile, $rawfile);
         return 1;
      }
   }
   else $rawfile = "";

   file_put_contents($datafile, $rawfile .
      "$page!1!$checksum\n");
```

```
    return -1;
}

function PIPHP_PU_F1($s)
{
    list($a, $b) = explode("!1!", $s);
    return $a;
}

function PIPHP_PU_F2($s)
{
    list($a, $b) = explode("!1!", $s);
    return $b;
}
```

PLUG-IN 48   HTML To RSS

The popularity of RSS (Really Simple Syndication) feeds is still growing due to the ease with which you can subscribe to a feed and have updates automatically sent to the feed reader. In fact, most decent browsers also offer RSS reading facilities. But what if you're too busy developing the HTML portion of your site to start building RSS feeds? Or what if you'd like to be able to view other web sites in RSS?

The solution comes with this plug-in, which will fetch a web page, analyze it, strip out non-essential and formatting items, and reformat it into RSS (see Figure 7-8 for an example).

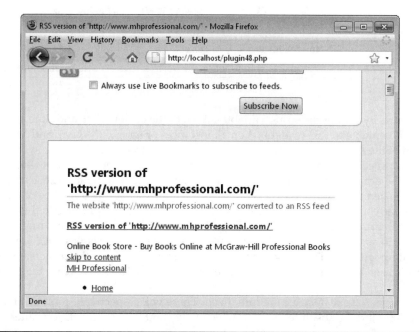

Figure 7-8   The plug-in is used to output the McGraw-Hill web site as an RSS feed.

About the Plug-in

This plug-in accepts a string containing the HTML to be converted, along with other required arguments, and returns a properly formatted RSS document. It takes these arguments:

- **$html**   The HTML to convert
- **$title**   The RSS feed title to use
- **$description**   The RSS description to use
- **$url**   The URL to which the feed should link
- **$webmaster**   The e-mail address of the responsible webmaster
- **$copyright**   The copyright details

Variables, Arrays, and Functions

$date	String containing the date in RSS-compatible form
$dom	Document object of $contents
$xpath	XPath object for traversing $dom
$hrefs	Object containing all a href= link elements in $dom
$links	Array of all the links discovered in $url
$to	Array containing the version of what each $link should be changed to in order to ensure it is absolute
$count	Integer containing the number of elements in $to
$j	Integer counter for iterating through $hrefs and $to
$link	Each link in turn extracted from $links
$temp	Non-tokenized copy of $link
PIPHP_RelToAbsURL()	Plug-in 21: This function converts a relative URL to absolute.

How It Works

This plug-in starts by setting the string variable $date to the current date and time, in a format that is acceptable to RSS readers. Then all instances of & (the XML and XHTML required form of the & symbol) are converted to just the & symbol, and then all & symbols are changed to a special token with the value !!**1**!!. As described in plug-in 46, this is done because the str_replace() function seems to have a bug relating to the use of the & symbol, so the token is substituted to avoid it. The & symbols will be swapped back later.

After that, the code has much in common with many of the other plug-ins in this chapter in that it must traverse an HTML DOM (Document Object Model), ensuring all a href= links are in absolute format. It does this by creating a new DOM object in $dom and then loading it up with the HTML tags from $html. Then a new XPath object is created in $xpath. This is used by $xpath->evaluate to extract all the a href= tags into the $hrefs array.

Next the arrays $links and $to are initialized. These will respectively contain all the encountered links and the absolute forms to which they should be changed. A counter that will index into these arrays, $count, is also initialized.

A `for` loop is then used to extract the links from each `a href=` tag into the array `$links`, which then has all duplicates removed using the `array_unique()` function. This simply removes duplicates in place so the array can be sorted so that all elements are stored contiguously.

A `foreach` loop is then used to iterate through each link, first checking that a link actually has been assigned a value. If it has, the string variable `$temp` is assigned a version of `$link` *without* any `!!**1**!!` tokens that may have replaced any `&` symbols. This ensures a properly formed URL is ready for converting to absolute format using the `PIPHP_RelToAbsURL()` function, and for assigning to an element in the `$to` array.

Again, as in plug-in 46, tokens are substituted for all links within the main document to prevent potential clashes during multiple replace operations. Every form of allowable link is substituted, whether single, double, or unquoted: `href="link"`, `href='link'`, and `href=link`. The tokens take the form `!!$count!!` and therefore start at `!!0!!` and proceed on through `!!1!!` and so on each time a new link is substituted.

Once all the tokens are in place in the document, and there is no chance of clashes during string substitutions, a `for` loop is used to convert them into the absolute URLs held in the `$to` array.

Next, any encoded URLs in which `http://` has been turned into `http%3A%2F%2F` are restored back to `http://`, any `&` symbols are restored back from the token `!!**1**!!`, and all whitespace is removed from the document using the `preg_replace()` function with a parameter of `/[\s]+/`, which forces all consecutive strings of one or more whitespace characters to be replaced with a single space.

The next lines strip out any `<script>` and `<style>` tags and their contents, followed by ensuring that all `<h>` tags have their contents removed. This is done so a conversion can easily be made later into RSS headers.

With those tags removed, all remaining tags are also stripped out, with the exception of those listed in the string `$ok`. This process is handled by the function `strip_tags()`. In case you're wondering, I tried to also remove the `<script>` and `<style>` tags using `strip_tags()`, but the function seems buggy and would not always remove them, so that's why these are handled separately.

After that, all remaining HTML characters are replaced with their RSS equivalents; so, for example, the `<` symbol becomes `&lt;`, the `>` becomes `&gt;`, and so on.

The final two `preg_replace()` calls substitute the two opening and closing forms of the `<h>` tag, which previously had any contents stripped out, into the XML required for properly formatted RSS headers. In other words, this plug-in assumes that anything between `<h>` and `</h>` tags should be treated as RSS headers.

Finally, the RSS itself is returned within a `return <<<_END ... _END` construct, where you can see `$title`, `$url`, `$description`, and all the other variables in their correct places, all the way down to `$html`, the main contents of the feed on which this plug-in has performed all the processing.

How to Use It

When you want to convert HTML to RSS, you can use code such as the following, in which your web site domain is assumed to be *myserver.com*:

```
$html       = "Your HTML content goes here";
$title      = "RSS version of my webpage";
```

```
$description = "This feed was converted from HTML";
$url         = "http://myserver.com";
$webmaster   = "webmaster@myserver.com";
$copyright   = "Copyright 2010 myserver.com";
header('Content-Type: text/xml');
echo PIPHP_HTMLToRSS($html, $title, $description, $url,
   $webmaster, $copyright);
```

Or, you can convert almost any HTML page on the Web by using code such as this:

```
$url         = "http://www.mhprofessional.com/";
$html        = file_get_contents($url);
$title       = "RSS version of '$url'";
$description  = "The website '$url' converted to an RSS feed";
$webmaster   = "nobody@nowhere.com";
$copyright   = "Copyright $url";
header('Content-Type: text/xml');
echo PIPHP_HTMLToRSS($html, $title, $description, $url,
   $webmaster, $copyright);
```

Remember that because this plug-in relies on plug-in 21, PIPHP_RelToAbsURL(), you must make sure you have also copied it into your program, or otherwise included it.

The Plug-in

```
function PIPHP_HTMLToRSS($html, $title, $description, $url,
   $webmaster, $copyright)
{
   $date  = date("D, d M Y H:i:s e");
   $html  = str_replace('&amp;', '&',           $html);
   $html  = str_replace('&',     '!!**1**!!', $html);
   $dom   = new domdocument();
   @$dom  ->loadhtml($html);
   $xpath = new domxpath($dom);
   $hrefs = $xpath->evaluate("/html/body//a");
   $links = array();
   $to    = array();
   $count = 0;

   for ($j = 0 ; $j < $hrefs->length ; ++$j)
      $links[] = $hrefs->item($j)->getAttribute('href');

   $links = array_unique($links);
   sort($links);

   foreach ($links as $link)
   {
      if ($link != "")
      {
         $temp = str_replace('!!**1**!!', '&', $link);
         $to[$count] = urlencode(PIPHP_RelToAbsURL($url, $temp));
```

```php
        $html = str_replace("href=\"$link\"",
            "href=\"!!$count!!\"", $html);
        $html = str_replace("href='$link'",
            "href='!!$count!!'",    $html);
        $html = str_replace("href=$link",
            "href=!!$count!!",      $html);
        ++$count;
    }
  }

  for ($j = 0 ; $j < $count ; ++$j)
    $html = str_replace("!!$j!!", $to[$j],
        $html);

  $html = str_replace('http%3A%2F%2F', 'http://', $html);
  $html = str_replace('!!**1**!!', '&', $html);

  $html = preg_replace('/[\s]+/', ' ', $html);
  $html = preg_replace('/<script[^>]*>.*?<\/script>/i', '',
      $html);
  $html = preg_replace('/<style[^>]*>.*?<\/style>/i', '',
      $html);
  $ok   = '<a><i><b><u><s><h><img><div><span><table><tr>';
  $ok  .= '<th><tr><td><br><p><ul><ol><li>';
  $html = strip_tags($html, $ok);
  $html = preg_replace('/<h[1-7][^>]*?>/i', '<h>',
      $html);
  $html = htmlentities($html);
  $html = preg_replace("/&lt;h&gt;/si",
      "</description></item>\n<item><title>", $html);
  $html = preg_replace("/&lt;\/h[1-7]&gt;/si",
      "</title><guid>$url</guid><description>", $html);

  return <<<_END
<?xml version="1.0" encoding="UTF-8"?>
<rss version="2.0"><channel>
<generator>Pluginphp.com: plug-in 48</generator>
<title>$title</title><link>$url</link>
<description>$description</description>
<language>en</language>
<webMaster>$webmaster</webMaster>
<copyright>$copyright</copyright>
<pubDate>$date</pubDate>
<lastBuildDate>$date</lastBuildDate>
<item><title>$title</title>
<guid>$url</guid>
<description>$html</description></item></channel></rss>
_END;
}
```

RSS to HTML

This plug-in provides the inverse functionality of plug-in 48—it converts an RSS feed into standard HTML format. It's perfect for when you don't have a feed reader on hand or wish to grab some syndicated content and put it in one of your own web pages (if you do though, make sure you have any required permissions).

Figure 7-9 shows the NASA Image of the Day RSS feed after converting it to HTML. You can access this feed at *www.nasa.gov/rss/image_of_the_day.rss*.

About the Plug-in

This plug-in accepts a string containing the contents of an RSS feed to be converted and returns that string transformed into HTML. It takes this argument:

- **$rss**   The contents of an RSS feed to convert

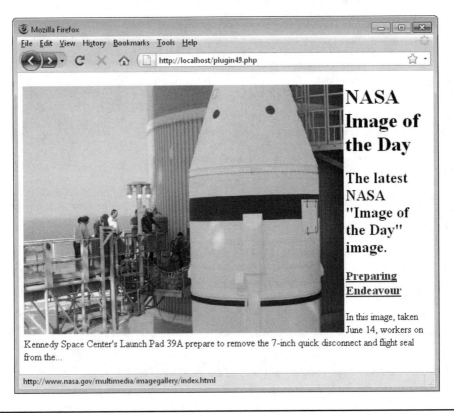

FIGURE 7-9   This plug-in will convert RSS feeds into regular HTML web pages.

Variables, Arrays, and Functions

$xml	XML object created from $rss
$title	String extracted from the RSS title tag
$link	String extracted from the RSS link tag
$desc	String extracted from the RSS description tag
$copyr	String extracted from the RSS copyright tag
$ilink	String extracted from the RSS image link tag
$ititle	String extracted from the RSS image title tag
$iurl	String extracted from the RSS image url tag
$out	String containing converted HTML
$tlink	String containing link of current item
$tdate	String containing publication date of current item
$ttitle	String containing title of current item
$tdesc	String containing description of current item

How It Works

This plug-in uses the `simplexml_load_string()` function to create an XML object in `$xml`, from the RSS feed in `$rss`. From there the string variables `$title`, `$link`, `$desc`, `$copyr`, `$ilink`, `$ititle`, and `$iurl` are easily assigned by extracting the various items from `$xml->channel`. In case any items do not exist in the RSS feed, each of these extractions is prefaced by an @ symbol which will suppress any error messages.

Next, the string variable `$out` is initialized with the opening tags for a standard HTML document and then, if an image was specified in the feed, the image and its associated title and description are also added. I have decided to align the image to the left and allow the description to butt up to the right of it because the main image in an RSS feed is generally a logo. This seems to work well with most other main images, too.

After that, `<h1>` and `<h2>` headings containing the main RSS feed title and description are added to `$out`.

Then a `foreach` loop is used to iterate through every item within the feed. As each is extracted, its details are placed in the variables `$tlink`, `$tdate`, `$ttitle`, and `$tdesc`, from where they are appended to `$out`, within suitable HTML heading and paragraph tags.

And that's it. All that remains is to return `$out`, along with the copyright string in `$copyr` and the closing HTML tags.

How to Use It

To convert an RSS feed to HTML, just pass it to the plug-in, like this:

```
$url = "http://www.nasa.gov/rss/image_of_the_day.rss";
$rss = file_get_contents($url);
echo   PIPHP_RSSToHTML($rss);
```

As you can see, the feed can be pulled in from anywhere on the Web, or it can be a feed from your own site. All you need to do is pass the feed itself (not the URL it came from) to the plug-in and display the result returned.

Alternatively, to insert the HTML version of the feed into your own web pages, just use the string returned by the plug-in, like this:

```
$result = PIPHP_RSSToHTML($rss);
echo "<h1>Here's NASA's image of the day</h1>$result";
```

The Plug-in

```
function PIPHP_RSSToHTML($rss)
{
    $xml     = simplexml_load_string($rss);
    $title   = @$xml->channel->title;
    $link    = @$xml->channel->link;
    $desc    = @$xml->channel->description;
    $copyr   = @$xml->channel->copyright;
    $ilink   = @$xml->channel->image->link;
    $ititle  = @$xml->channel->image->title;
    $iurl    = @$xml->channel->image->url;

    $out = "<html><head><style> img {border: 1px solid " .
           "#444444}</style>\n<body>";

    if ($ilink != "")
        $out    .= "<a href='$ilink'><img src='$iurl' title=" .
                   "'$ititle' alt='$ititle' border='0' style=" .
                   "'border: 0px' align='left' /></a>\n";

    $out .= "<h1>$title</h1>\n<h2>$desc</h2>\n";

    foreach($xml->channel->item as $item)
    {
        $tlink  = @$item->link;
        $tdate  = @$item->pubDate;
        $ttitle = @$item->title;
        $tdesc  = @$item->description;

        $out    .= "<h3><a href='$tlink' title='$tdate'>" .
                   "$ttitle</a></h3>\n<p>$tdesc</p>\n";
    }

    return "$out<a href='$link'>$copyr</a></body></html>";
}
```

50 HTML to Mobile

The final plug-in in this chapter will take an HTML page and format it in such a way that it will load faster on a mobile browser that may have limited download speeds, and also display better due to removing a lot of style and formatting information.

Figure 7-10 shows the *www.yahoo.com* web page after being processed by this plug-in.

As you can see in Figure 7-11, the plug-in has substantially reduced the original web page.

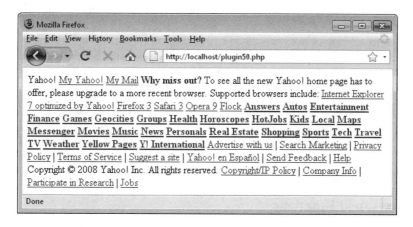

FIGURE 7-10   With this plug-in you can make the busiest of web pages load quickly on a mobile browser.

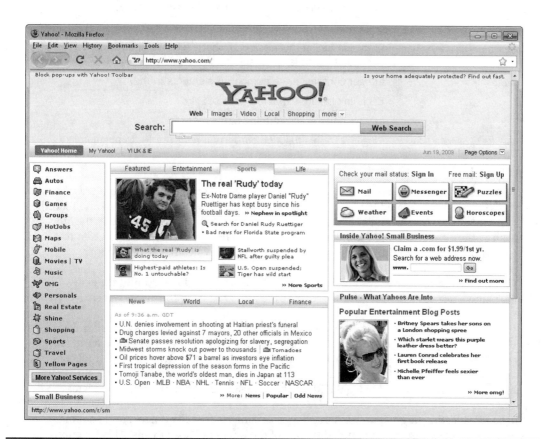

FIGURE 7-11   This is the original Yahoo! home page before the plug-in is applied.

About the Plug-in

This plug-in accepts a string containing the HTML to be converted, along with other required arguments, and returns a properly formatted HTML document with various formatting elements removed. It takes these arguments:

- **$html**   The HTML to convert
- **$url**   The URL of the page being converted
- **$style**   If "yes", style and JavaScript elements are retained, otherwise they are stripped out
- **$images**   If "yes", images are kept, otherwise they are removed

Variables, Arrays, and Functions

$dom	Document object of $contents
$xpath	XPath object for traversing $dom
$hrefs	Object containing all a href= link elements in $dom
$links	Array of all the links discovered in $url
$to	Array containing the version of what each $link should be changed to in order to ensure it is absolute
$count	Integer containing the number of elements in $to
$link	Each link in turn extracted from $links
$j	Integer counter for iterating through $to
PIPHP_RelToAbsURL()	Plug-in 21: This function converts a relative URL to absolute.

How It Works

This function starts off by creating a DOM object that is loaded with the HTML from $html. Then an XPath object is created from this, with which all a href= tags are extracted and placed in the object $hrefs. After initializing the arrays $links and $to, which will contain the links before and after converting to absolute format, all occurrences of & are converted to & symbols, and then all & symbols to the token !!**1**!!, to avoid the suspected str_replace() bug that doesn't handle & symbols well.

Next the link parts of the tags are pulled out from $hrefs and placed into the array $links using a for loop, and all duplicate links are removed from the array, which is then sorted.

After this, the technique used in plug-ins 46 and 48 is implemented to swap all links in $html with numbered tokens. This ensures that multiple replaces don't interfere with each other. First the $to array is loaded with a proper URL which has had any !!**1**!! tokens changed back to & symbols after running them through PIPHP_RelToAbsURL() to ensure they are absolute. This makes sure that legal URLs will be substituted when the tokens are later changed back.

To be flexible, the plug-in supports three types of links—double quoted, single quoted, and unquoted—each case being handled by one of the str_replace() calls. This function substitutes links within $html for the token !!$count!!. This means that the first link becomes !!0!!, the second !!1!!, and so on, as $count is incremented at each pass.

With all the tokens having been substituted they can now be swapped with their associated links from the $to array. This is achieved using the following for loop.

Then, any remaining occurrences of the URL encoded format http%3A%2F%2F are rectified to http://, and any !!**1**!! tokens are returned to being & symbols.

Next, if $style does not have the value "yes", then whitespace, styling, and JavaScript are removed from $html.

After this, $images is also tested and if it's equal to "yes", then images are allowed to remain in place. This is achieved, along with removing all remaining tags, by appending the tag <img> to the list of allowed tags in $allowed, which is then passed to the strip_tags() function, along with $html. If $images is not equal to "yes", then the <img> tag will not be appended to $allowed, and consequently all image tags will also be removed by this function.

Upon completing all the processing, the result (in $html) is returned.

How to Use It

To convert HTML to a format more suitable for mobile browsers, use the plug-in like this:

```
$url     = "http://yahoo.com";
$html    = file_get_contents($url);
$style   = "no";
$images  = "no";
echo     PIPHP_HTMLToMobile($html, $url, $style, $images);
```

This loads in the HTML from the index page at *www.yahoo.com* and then passes it to the plug-in with both $style and $images set to "no". This means that neither styling nor JavaScript will be allowed in the converted HTML, and neither will images.

If $style is set to "yes", then style tags and JavaScript are retained in the HTML. If $images is also equal to "yes", then some images will be retained—but not all, due to a lot of the page's content being removed.

If you play with this plug-in you'll find that often you can set both $style and $images to "yes" and many web pages will still return a lot less information because the strip_tags() function removes plenty of HTML not strictly needed to use a web page.

Remember that this plug-in relies on plug-in 21, PIPHP_RelToAbsURL(). Therefore, you must also copy it into your program or otherwise include it.

The Plug-in

```
function PIPHP_HTMLToMobile($html, $url, $style, $images)
{
    $dom    = new domdocument();
    @$dom   ->loadhtml($html);
    $xpath  = new domxpath($dom);
    $hrefs  = $xpath->evaluate("/html/body//a");
    $links  = array();
    $to     = array();
    $count  = 0;
    $html   = str_replace('&amp;', '&',          $html);
    $html   = str_replace('&',     '!!**1**!!',  $html);
```

```php
    for ($j = 0 ; $j < $hrefs->length ; ++$j)
        $links[] = $hrefs->item($j)->getAttribute('href');

    $links = array_unique($links);
    sort($links);

    foreach ($links as $link)
    {
        if ($link != "")
        {
            $temp = str_replace('!!**1**!!', '&', $link);
            $to[$count] = urlencode(PIPHP_RelToAbsURL($url, $temp));
            $html = str_replace("href=\"$link\"",
                "href=\"!!$count!!\"", $html);
            $html = str_replace("href='$link'",
                "href='!!$count!!'",   $html);
            $html = str_replace("href=$link",
                "href=!!$count!!",        $html);
            ++$count;
        }
    }

    for ($j = 0 ; $j < $count ; ++$j)
        $html = str_replace("!!$j!!", $to[$j],
            $html);

    $html = str_replace('http%3A%2F%2F', 'http://', $html);
    $html = str_replace('!!**1**!!', '&', $html);

    if (strtolower($style) != "yes")
    {
        $html = preg_replace('/[\s]+/', ' ', $html);
        $html = preg_replace('/<script[^>]*>.*?<\/script>/i', '',
            $html);
        $html = preg_replace('/<style[^>]*>.*?<\/style>/i', '',
            $html);
    }

    $allowed = "<a><p><h><i><b><u><s>";
    if (strtolower($images) == "yes") $allowed .= "<img>";
    return strip_tags($html, $allowed);
}
```

CHAPTER 8

Chat and Messaging

Offering chat, messaging, and user interaction features are fundamental ways to create addictive content and build up traffic to a site. The phenomenal growth of sites such as MySpace, Facebook, and Twitter (as well as the huge increase in use of instant messaging software) all serve to show that what Internet users love to do more than anything else is communicate with other users.

Whether leaving messages, commenting on blogs or web sites, e-mailing, or Tweeting, if you provide the right services, your users will not only take to them, they'll invite their friends along, too. And presto, you'll now have free compelling content, as long as you treat your users well and make your web site easy to use.

And that's the aim of this batch of plug-ins: to provide a collection of ready-made functions you can draw on to add the user interaction features your web site needs.

Users Online

One of the things that drives webmasters crazy is the fact that getting the ball rolling and building up a user base is very hard, but the more users you have the easier it is to get more. Why? One answer has to be that people don't want to feel alone on a web site. So what better way to reassure them than to display the number of users currently using your web site? And that's what this plug-in will do for you: It lists the total number of people who have used your web site within a recent period decided by you.

Of course, at times when you don't have many active users you may want to disable this plug-in, or maybe increase the time span during which a visitor is considered recent. But if you do have a few visitors online, discretely displaying the number in a sensible place will reassure them that your web site has something going on. Figure 8-1 shows a web page with five active users.

About the Plug-in

This plug-in reports the number of users who have recently been active. It takes these arguments:

- **$datafile** A string containing the location of a file for storing the data
- **$seconds** The period of time, in seconds, during which a recent user is considered active

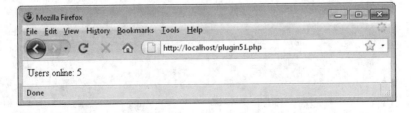

FIGURE 8-1   This plug-in provides a quick snapshot of your site's usage and popularity.

Variables, Arrays, and Functions

`$ip`	String containing the IP address and the User Agent of the current user
`$out`	String containing the contents of the datafile to be written back to the server
`$online`	Integer counter containing the number of users online
`$users`	Array containing unique user details
`$usertime`	String containing time the user being processed last accessed the web site
`$userip`	String containing the IP and User Agent string of the user being processed

How It Works

This plug-in starts by determining the current user's IP address and User Agent string, as provided by their browser, and then assigning the result to the string `$ip`. Then a couple of variables are initialized: `$out`, the contents of the datafile that will be written back, is set to the empty string; and `$online`, the number of users online is set to 1 (since the program knows that at least the current user is active).

If the file `$datafile` already exists, then there may be previous users who have been active within the last number of seconds specified by `$seconds`. In which case the contents of `$datafile` are loaded in, with the last character (a \n linefeed) being removed by the `rtrim()` function since it is not needed. The result is then split at each remaining \n linefeed into the array `$users`, so that `$users` will now have one entry for each user.

A `foreach` loop is then used to iterate through `$users`, with the details of each one being processed stored in `$user`. Then the `list()` function is used to assign `$usertime` and `$userip` the time and IP/User Agent details for the user being processed. These are split out of `$user` using the `explode()` function with an argument of | (the | symbol being the separator I chose for this plug-in's data).

Then, the current time is looked up using the `time()` function. If that value, less the value stored in `$usertime`, is less than the number of seconds stored in `$seconds`, then that user is considered to still be active, and so their details are appended to the string `$out`, and the count of active users in `$online` is incremented.

However, if more seconds than the value in `$seconds` have elapsed since their last access, then they are assumed to no longer be active and their details are forgotten by not appending them to `$out`.

Note how a test is made to ensure the current user's details are always ignored using the code `&& $userip != $ip`, so that the IP/User Agent details of the user being processed are not the same as the current user's. This is to ensure those details are removed so they will not be duplicated when the datafile is written back to disk.

After completing, the loop `$out` has the current time and IP/User Agent details appended to it from the function `time()` and the variable `$ip`, separated by a | character and terminated with a \n newline. The contents of `$out` are then saved to the file `$datafile`, and the number of active users in `$online` is returned.

How to Use It

When you want to keep a count of the active users on your web site you should include a call to this plug-in on all your pages where the count is wanted. Doing so is as simple as ensuring the plug-in has been included or pasted, and then using the following code:

```
PIPHP_UsersOnline('users.txt', 300);
```

Here the 300 represents 300 seconds or five minutes, which is probably a reasonable time window to start with. Whenever you want to know the number of active users, you assign the result returned by the function to a variable, or simply echo it, like this:

```
echo "Users online: " . PIPHP_UsersOnline('users.txt', 300);
```

You can replace the datafile name *users.txt* with whatever name you prefer.

The Plug-in

```
function PIPHP_UsersOnline($datafile, $seconds)
{
    $ip     = getenv("REMOTE_ADDR") .
              getenv("HTTP_USER_AGENT");
    $out    = "";
    $online = 1;

    if (file_exists($datafile))
    {
        $users  = explode("\n",
            rtrim(file_get_contents($datafile)));

        foreach($users as $user)
        {
            list($usertime, $userip) = explode('|', $user);

            if ((time() - $usertime) < $seconds &&
                $userip != $ip)
            {
                $out .= $usertime . '|' . $userip . "\n";
                ++$online;
            }
        }
    }

    $out .= time() . '|' . $ip . "\n";
    file_put_contents($datafile, $out);
    return $online;
}
```

PLUG-IN 52 Post to Guestbook

No self-respecting web site is complete without some means of providing feedback, so here's a simple plug-in to enable you to offer a Guestbook feature in just a few lines of PHP code. Figure 8-2 shows the same information posted twice, but because flooding control is enabled, the second post is not added to the Guestbook.

About the Plug-in

This plug-in posts a message to a Guestbook. It takes these arguments:

- **$datafile** A string containing the location of a file for storing the data
- **$name** The name of the poster

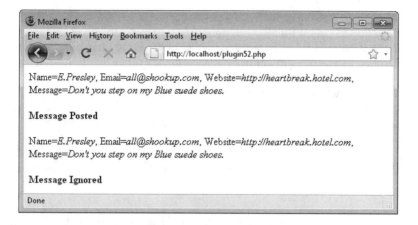

FIGURE 8-2 This plug-in provides easy posting to a Guestbook with flood control.

- **$email**   The poster's email address
- **$website**   The poster's website
- **$message**   The message to be posted

Variables, Arrays, and Functions

$data	String containing a concatenation of $name, $email, $website, and $message, separated by the token !1!
$lines	Array containing the messages extracted from $datafile
$fh	File handle into the file $datafile

How It Works

This plug-in takes all the data supplied to it, and if it's not a duplicate of an existing entry, adds it to the datafile. It begins by first creating the line of data to add to $datafile by concatenating the values of $name, $email, $website, and $message, separating them all by the token !1!, which I chose as being unlikely to be ever used in a message or name, and so on. It then places the result in the string $data.

Then, if the file $datafile already exists, it is opened and its contents are extracted into the array $lines after the final character, a \n newline character, is removed. The extraction is performed using the explode() function with an argument of \n, newline, the points at which to perform the splitting.

Using the function in_array(), each element of $lines is then checked to see whether it already contains the contents of $data. If so, then this would be a duplicate entry and so a value of 0 is returned to indicate the fact, and the post is therefore not added.

Otherwise the entry is not a duplicate, so the file handle $fh is assigned the value returned upon opening $datafile for appending, with the fopen() function and an argument of 'a'. If $fh is set to FALSE, then the file could not be opened and so -1 is returned to indicate that fact.

Then the flock() function is called with a parameter of LOCK_EX (for EXclusive lock). This forces the function to wait until all other processes have finished accessing the file. This is done because other users could be posting to the file at the same time and could end up corrupting it. So, once flock() gains control over the file, all other functions that access $datafile using the flock() method will now have to wait their turn.

Once the flock() function allows execution to proceed, the fwrite() function is called to write the data in $data to $datafile, followed by a \n newline. This is to separate each line from the next. Because the parameter of 'a' was used with fopen(), this data is appended to the end of the file's existing contents.

Finally, the lock is released using flock() with a parameter of LOCK_UN (for UNlock) and the file is closed. At this point, the write has been made successfully and so a value of 1 is returned.

CAUTION *The flock() function will not work on NFS and many other networked file systems, or on FAT and its derivatives. Also, when using a multithreaded server API like ISAPI, you may not be able to rely on flock() to protect files against other PHP scripts running in parallel threads of the same server instance.*

How to Use It

To add a post to your Guestbook, you just have to decide on the name of a file in which to store the data and then pass that and the post details to the function PIPHP_PostToGuestBook(), like this:

```
$name    = 'F. Gump';
$email   = 'run@forestrun.com';
$website = 'http://www.mymommaalwayssaid.com';
$message = 'Life is like a box of chocolates';
$result  = PIPHP_PostToGuestBook('guestbook.txt', $name, $email,
   $website, $message);
```

Of course, when handling user submitted data you will probably also want to sanitize the input using other plug-ins from this book, such as *Caps Control* or *Spell Check* from Chapter 3, or some of the Form and User Input plug-ins from Chapter 6, before saving data to the Guestbook.

The Plug-in

```
function PIPHP_PostToGuestBook($datafile, $name, $email,
   $website, $message)
{
   $data = $name . '!1!' . $email . '!1!' . $website .
      '!1!' . $message;
   if (file_exists($datafile))
   {
      $lines = explode("\n",
         rtrim(file_get_contents($datafile)));

      if (in_array($data, $lines)) return 0;
   }
```

```
    $fh = fopen($datafile, 'a');
    if (!$fh) return -1;

    if (flock($fh, LOCK_EX)) fwrite($fh, $data . "\n");
    flock($fh, LOCK_UN);
    fclose($fh);
    return 1;
}
```

PLUG-IN 53 Get Guestbook

Once you have a Guestbook and the facility to post messages to it, you'll also want to be able to display the messages. This function goes most of the way towards that by fetching all the messages from the datafile and returning them in an array.

It does this (rather than display them directly) to leave you in complete control over how you want the output to appear. Figure 8-3 shows posts from a Guestbook simply being displayed as regular text with no special formatting.

About the Plug-in

This plug-in accepts the name of a datafile containing Guestbook data and returns all the messages from that file. Upon success it returns a two-element array, the first of which contains the number of posts. The second element is a further array containing all the posts. Or, upon failure, it returns a single-element array with the value FALSE. It takes these arguments:

- **$datafile** A string containing the location of a Guestbook datafile.
- **$order** The order in which to return the messages. If its value is "r", then posts are returned in reverse order, with newest posts first, otherwise posts are returned in order from oldest to newest.

Variables, Arrays, and Functions

$data	Array containing sub-arrays, each with all the items extracted from a post
$posts	Array containing the messages extracted from $datafile
$post	The current post being processed

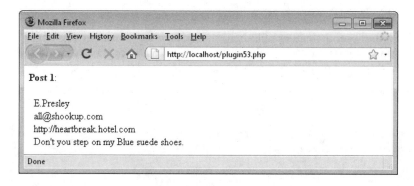

FIGURE 8-3   Using this plug-in it's easy to list all your Guestbook posts.

How It Works

This plug-in reads in a previously created and posted-to-Guestbook datafile and returns all the messages it contains. If the file cannot be read, it returns a single-element array with the value FALSE.

Once read in, the array $posts is populated with the contents of $datafile, which is split into separate entries using the explode() function with an argument of \n, making the newline character the split boundary. The rtrim() function is also used to remove the final character, which is a \n newline and is not required.

Next, the argument $order is tested. If it contains the value "r", then the order of messages returned needs to be reversed so the function array_reverse() is applied to $posts.

With $posts now in the order required, a foreach loop then steps through the array, placing each element in turn into the variable $post. From here the array $data (which was previously initialized as an empty array) then has another element added to it comprising an array extracted from the data in $post. This is done using the explode() function with an argument of !1!, which is the token I chose to use to split fields in a record. This separates out all the parts (name, e-mail, web site, and message) and returns an array, which is assigned to the current element of the $data array.

Finally a two-element array is returned, of which the first element contains the number of messages returned, and the second contains an array of arrays, each sub-array containing the parts of a single message.

How to Use It

To use this plug-in you only need to pass it the name of a datafile containing Guestbook data and an argument telling it which order to use when returning the messages, like this:

```
$result = PIPHP_GetGuestBook('guestbook.txt', 'f');
```

Then, you test $result[0] to see whether it contains the value FALSE. If it does, the function call failed and there are no messages to display. You can check for it like this:

```
if (!$result[0]) echo "Could not read file";
```

Otherwise, it contains a value representing the number of messages returned by the function. You can display this number like this:

```
echo "There are $result[0] posts";
```

If posts exist, the second element will then contain an array of arrays, each main array element containing a sub-array of four elements representing, in order, the name, e-mail, web site, and message of a post. You can therefore act on this data like this:

```
for ($j = 0 ; $j < $result[0] ; ++$j)
{
   for ($k = 0 ; $k < 4 ; ++$k)
      echo $result[1][$j][$k] . "<br />";
   echo "<br />";
}
```

This code loops through all main elements in the array $result[1], with $result[1][0] being the first element of this array, and itself being an array with the following elements:

```
$result[1][0][0]
$result[1][0][1]
$result[1][0][2]
$result[1][0][3]
```

These four values represent the name, e-mail, web site, and message of the first post. The second post (if there is one) is returned in these four array elements (and so on):

```
$result[1][1][0]
$result[1][1][1]
$result[1][1][2]
$result[1][1][3]
```

Using these values it's now up to you to create the styling and layout needed to make your Guestbook look just how you want it. Displaying them is as easy as placing them after echo statements, like this:

```
echo $result[1][1][0];
echo $result[1][1][1];
echo $result[1][1][2];
echo $result[1][1][3];
```

The Plug-in

```
function PIPHP_GetGuestBook($datafile, $order)
{
    if (!file_exists($datafile)) return array(0);

    $data  = array();
    $posts = explode("\n",
        rtrim(file_get_contents($datafile)));

    if (strtolower($order) == 'r')
        $posts = array_reverse($posts);

    foreach ($posts as $post)
        $data[] = explode('!1!', $post);

    return array(count($posts), $data);
}
```

PLUG-IN 54 Post to Chat

Some of the more popular features of a web site are messaging and chat facilities, particularly if they are fast and easy to use, which this plug-in is—even though it's only about 30 lines of actual code, without a sign of Java or Flash in sight.

I first wrote the predecessor of this chat in 1996 using Perl scripts and later transported it to compiled C code and then, with the advent of PHP, due to its tremendous speed (even though it's not compiled) I rewrote it again. But the code's format has remained pretty much the same: a simple text file that is continuously read from and written to, using file locking to prevent file corruption.

It also uses a feature that predates Ajax (the sending of background requests to a server to exchange data), but provides similar functionality in that messages appear in the browser when posted, without having to refresh the page. Figure 8-4 shows this Post part of the chat engine being used to post a message, with and without flood control.

About the Plug-in

This plug-in posts a message to a live chatroom and supports a number of parameters. Upon success, the plug-in returns a value of 1. If the file could not be written to, then -1 is returned, or if flooding control is on and a duplicate post has been prevented, then 0 is returned. If $message is empty or there are illegal | symbols in either $to or $from, then -2 is returned. The plug-in takes these arguments:

- **$datafile**   A string containing the location of a chatroom datafile
- **$maxposts**   The maximum number of messages to retain at a time
- **$maxlength**   The maximum message length in characters
- **$from**   The username of the message poster
- **$to**   The message recipient's username—leave blank if the message is public
- **$message**   The contents of the message
- **$floodctrl**   If this has the value "on", the same message cannot be reposted by the same user within $maxposts messages

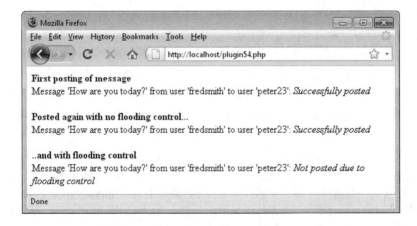

FIGURE 8-4   You can operate your own chatroom using this plug-in.

Variables, Arrays, and Functions

$data	Array used to populate $datafile with blank messages
$fh	File handle used to reference $datafile
$text	String containing all but the first message in $datafile
$lines	Array containing posts extracted from $text
$temp	String containing the post number of the final post in the file

How It Works

The object of this plug-in is to remove the oldest message from the datafile and add the new message—if, that is, the new message is not a repeat, or flood control has not been enabled.

The first thing it does if the datafile doesn't exist is create it by putting together a collection of dummy blank posts in $data. Each post is of the form: number|recipient| sender|message. The | symbols serving to separate the parts. Therefore if, for example, the value in $maxposts is 20, then $data will be populated with 20 | | |\n strings. This ensures that, for an initial chat file, all fields in each post are blank and that each is terminated with a \n newline to separate records from each other. This whole string is then saved to $datafile using the file_put_contents() function.

At this point there is definitely a datafile of posts, either one just created or one that was preexisting. So now the arguments passed to the plug-in are checked. If $message is blank, or either of $from or $to contains a banned | symbol, then there was a problem. In the former case, there is nothing to post, and in the latter the | symbols would corrupt the datafile and therefore are not allowed. Ideally, when users enter your chatroom you will already have weeded out any such occurrences, but if not, this check will catch them. A value of -2 is returned in either case.

The | symbol can actually be useful in messages, so if any are encountered in $message they are converted to their HTML entity equivalent of |. Also, if $message has more characters than the value specified in $maxlength, then $message is passed through the substr() function to truncate it to the maximum length allowed.

With all the fields now prepared, the datafile is opened using the fopen() function and the file handle for manipulating it is assigned to $fh. If $fh is FALSE, the file couldn't be opened and so -1 is returned.

Otherwise, the flock() function is called (see plug-in 52, *Post to Guestbook* for further details) to ensure the program has exclusive access to the file so there will be no clashes of concurrent writes. With the file lock obtained, the very first line of the file is returned using fgets(). This is the oldest post and therefore it will be discarded—so the value returned is not used and is simply ignored.

Next, the string variable $text is assigned the remaining contents of the file using the fread() function, with an argument of 100000. This tells the function to read in at most 100,000 characters from the file, up to the file's end. This should be more than you are likely to need because, for example, 20 messages of 1,000 characters each would only occupy 20,000 bytes. But you can easily change this value if you need to.

Next, the argument $floodctrl is checked, and if it has the value "on", then no repeated posts are allowed. To check for this, the function strpos() is called, which returns a value of 0 or greater if a match is found, or FALSE if not. The string being checked for is |$to|$from|$message\n, which will ensure that only repeated posts from the same poster, to the same recipient, with the same message will be ignored.

If the post is a duplicate and flood control is on, then the file lock is released, the file is closed, and a value of 0 is returned. Otherwise, the posts in the string variable $text are extracted into the array $lines using the explode() function to split them all out at \n newlines.

Next, the counter at the start of the last line of chat is extracted into the array $temp. This is done by referencing the correct element of $lines and then using explode() to pull all the parts into $temp. The plug-in is only interested in the first element of $temp, so that value is looked up and the number 1 is added to increment it. This gives the value to use for the message number of the new post being appended—the next in sequence. Therefore, $text (which contains the remaining chat posts, after ignoring the first one) has the message number appended to it, followed by the contents of $to, $from, and $message, separated by | symbols, and terminated with a \n newline character.

To update the file's contents, the fseek() command is called to move the read and write pointer into $datafile to the very start. You remember that the first post was discarded? Well, now all the following posts must be moved back accordingly, so after seeking, the contents of $text are then written to the file starting at position 0.

Lastly, because the file is readable and writeable and we have been treating it like random access memory, if the size of the new set of posts is smaller than the previous set, then the file will have some spurious text remaining at its end. This has to be discarded by issuing a call to the truncate() function, passing it the exact size of $text. The file lock is then released, the file closed, and a value of 1, representing success, is returned.

How to Use It

Generally, you will use this plug-in as part of an HTML form submission and processing program. To allow the chat to be viewed without interruption, you will also probably place the program within an <iframe> tag so it takes up just a portion of the screen and works independently from the rest of the chat.

A good way to do this is to create a simple web form like the following, but embedded within your PHP code:

```
echo <<<_END
<form method=post action="$_SERVER[PHP_SELF]"><pre>
   From: <input type=text name='from' />
     To: <input type=text name='to' />
Message: <input type=text name='message' />
         <input type=submit value='Post Message' />
</pre></form>
_END;
```

Instead of using a program name for the action of the form, this script uses the PHP system variable $_SERVER[PHP_SELF], which simply refers to the program currently running, whatever name it may have. This means you can call the program anything you like.

For simplicity of layout, I have used a <pre> tag here to force a monospaced font. You will probably want a much more interesting layout for your own program. Also, you will most likely have already asked for the user's name and, if so, could use the following From: input line instead:

```
<input type=hidden name='from' value='$from' />
```

This means that the only two items you will ask your users for are the recipient's name and the message to post. To simplify things even further for your users, you might even replace the To: input line with a <select> tag and a drop-down list of all current users—but with the default name being blank for public posts.

In other words, you should think about how your users will initially enter their usernames, which you will then store if you are going to offer pull-down lists of names for private messaging. So, when about to call this plug-in, your program should be armed with three pieces of information:

1. The poster's username

2. The recipient's name (or blank if a post is public)

3. The message to post

If these have been posted to your program, they will appear in the $_POST array and can be referenced like this (not forgetting that you may wish to also use some other plug-ins in this book to sanitize user input):

```
$from    = $_POST['from'];
$to      = $_POST['to'];
$message = $_POST['message'];
```

You can then add the post to the chat by calling the plug-in like this:

```
$result = PIPHP_PostToChat('chatroom.txt', 20, 1000, $from, $to,
    $message, 'off');
```

Here the chatroom datafile is *chatroom.txt*, the maximum number of posts to keep stored is 20, the maximum length allowed for each post is 1000 characters, and flood control is set to "off".

If $result contains the value 1, then the message has been successfully posted. Otherwise, see the preceding section, *About the Plug-in*, for the list of error codes and their meanings.

Bringing this all together, a program to display a single line input, residing in an iframe, that continually allows posting of public messages to the chat might look like this:

```
<?php
if (isset($_POST['message']))
{
    $from    = $_POST['from'];
    $to      = $_POST['to'];
    $message = $_POST['message'];
    PIPHP_PostToChat('chatroom.txt', 20, 1000, $from, $to,
        $message, 'off');
}
else $from = 'username'; // Enter the poster's username here
```

```
echo <<<_END
<form method=post action="$_SERVER[PHP_SELF]">
<input type=hidden name='from' value='$from' />
<input type=hidden name='to' value='' />
Message: <input type=text name='message' />
<input type=submit value='Post Message' />
</form>
_END;
?>
```

This code will keep displaying a prompt similar to the following, and whenever a message is entered it will post it to the chat datafile and redisplay the prompt:

Message: _____ [Post Message]

As discussed previously, posting private messages to other users is a little more complicated, but *only* a little, in that you simply have to set $to to the recipient's username. To do this, you would probably change the input form display to look something like the following, in which the first entry of a drop-down list is *ALL*, and then, if the variable $to ever has the value *ALL*, you would simply set it to the empty string before calling the plug-in.

Message: _____ To: [*All*] [Post Message]

Or you may wish to offer other ways of sending private messages such as listing all current users in a side panel and making them clickable to pull up a private messaging input prompt. That's why I have left the plug-in fully flexible, so you can choose exactly how your chat should look and work.

The following plug-in, *View Chat*, will be used to display the messages in real time with auto scrolling.

The Plug-in

```
function PIPHP_PostToChat($datafile, $maxposts, $maxlength,
    $from, $to, $message, $floodctrl)
{
    if (!file_exists($datafile))
    {
        $data = "";
        for ($j = 0 ; $j < $maxposts ; ++$j) $data .= "$j|||\n";
        file_put_contents($datafile, $data);
    }

    if ($message == "" || strpos($from, '|') ||
        strpos($to, '|')) return -2;

    $message = str_replace('|',  '&#124;', $message);
    $message = substr($message, 0, $maxlength);
    $fh      = fopen($datafile, 'r+');
    if (!$fh) return -1;
```

```
    flock($fh, LOCK_EX);
    fgets($fh);
    $text = fread($fh, 100000);

    if (strtolower($floodctrl) == 'on' &&
        strpos($text, "|$to|$from|$message\n"))
    {
        flock($fh, LOCK_UN);
        fclose($fh);
        return 0;
    }

    $lines = explode("\n", $text);
    $temp  = explode('|', $lines[$maxposts - 2]);
    $text .= ($temp[0] + 1) . "|$to|$from|$message\n";
    fseek($fh, 0);
    fwrite($fh, $text);
    ftruncate($fh, strlen($text));
    flock($fh, LOCK_UN);
    fclose($fh);
    return 1;
}
```

View Chat

This plug-in is surprisingly small considering the power it packs, providing a continuously open connection to a chat server using just HTML, so that new messages appear as posted, without having to refresh the page. With some nifty JavaScript, it also auto scrolls the page when new messages display at the page bottom, and it can distinguish between a private and a public message, displaying each to the correct people.

Figure 8-5 shows four users chatting, as viewed from the user *fredsmith*'s perspective. You can see all the public messages in regular typeface, while the private ones from and to *fredsmith* are shown in italic font and prefaced by the string (PM to *username*).

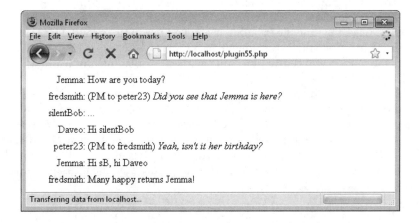

FIGURE 8-5   This plug-in handles viewing of public and private messages and includes auto scrolling.

About the Plug-in

This plug-in takes a chatroom datafile and displays all the messages the current user is allowed to see: either public or private ones to or from that user. It takes these arguments:

- **$datafile** A string containing the location of a chatroom datafile
- **$username** The username of the current user viewing the chat
- **$maxtime** The maximum time in seconds a connection will stay open to the server. This needs to be a large value to prevent the chat reloading too often. About 300 seconds (5 minutes) is a good start point.

Variables, Arrays, and Functions

$tn	String containing the current time as a timestamp
$tstart	String containing the HTML table start tags
$tmiddle	String containing the HTML table middle tags
$tend	String containing the HTML table end tags
$oldpnum	Integer containing the value of the highest read post number
$lines	Array containing the posts extracted from $datafile
$line	String containing a single line of data from $lines
$thisline	Array containing all the elements extracted from $line
$postnum	Integer containing the number of the current post being read
$to	String containing the recipient name of the current post being read
$from	String containing the sender name of the current post being read
$message	String containing the message of the current post being read

How It Works

This plug-in is really one big loop that goes round and round checking the contents of $datafile and displaying any new posts it finds that the user is authorized to view.

It starts by trying to load in the chatroom datafile $datafile, and returns FALSE if it can't be read. Otherwise, the time the program is allowed to run (in seconds) is set using the set_time_limit() function and the argument $maxtime + 5. The extra 5 seconds are added to ensure the plug-in will return gracefully, without displaying any warning message about the program having timed out.

Tables are used to isolate the messages from each other so the next three string variables are initialized: $tstart, $tmiddle, and $tend. These contain HTML tags suitable for building a table in which to place each displayed message. This is a particularly useful trick, for example, when you offer the use of BB Code or Pound Code (plug-ins 39 and 40) and the user doesn't properly close tags. By placing the strings in a table, all tags will be fully closed regardless of which ones are left open and the formatting from any one message won't affect any other.

The final variable to initialize is $oldpnum. This is set to 0 to start with but will be increased to the value of the highest numbered post read so far. This way the program can tell when a new post comes in by noting whether it has a higher post number.

Now the main while loop begins. It is set to loop forever by being passed an argument of 1. Each time around the loop the contents of $datafile are read in; the final character, an unwanted \n newline is removed using rtrim(); and the posts are extracted into the array $lines using the explode() function, with an argument of \n to split all lines at the newline characters.

Next, a foreach loop is entered in which each post in the $lines array is placed into $line and then the parts of that post's details are extracted into the array $thisline using the explode() function, with the argument |, the separator I chose to signify field boundaries. These four items of information are then saved in $postnum, $to, $from, and $message.

Next, a test is made to see whether the number of the current post being processed is greater than the value stored in $oldpnum. If it is, then a post that has not been read yet has been encountered, and so it must be examined to see if it should be displayed.

If the contents of $to is an empty string, then the post is public, in which case it is displayed using the echo command, by being placed into the correct position between the table-building strings $tstart, $tmiddle, and $tend. The $from string is also inserted to show who posted the message. The output will look something like the following (taken from the movie *Home Alone*):

```
Kevin: You guys give up, or are you thirsty for more?
```

If $to is not empty, then the message is private and tests are made to determine whether the post is either *to* or *from* the current user. If either is the case, then the message is displayed in the correct place within the array strings, along with the $from string. In addition, the string (PM to *username*) is inserted to make it clear that the message is private, and the message itself is displayed in italics as a further indication. It will look something like this:

```
Marv: (PM to Harry) He's only a kid, Harry. We can take him.
```

Once the post has been processed, $oldpnum is set to the value of the post's number so it won't be looked at again. Then two functions are called, ob_flush() and flush(), to ensure that all the text is sent to the browser. If they were not called, PHP would try to be helpful and hold back on sending all the posts until the script ended. Generally, this is the behavior you want from a web page—all the data in one block. But for chat, where you want to see messages in real time, and particularly in this case where a program could run for some minutes, the output needs to be flushed out after each post is displayed.

After processing all the posts in $datafile, the sleep() function is called with a parameter of 2. This makes the PHP program sit and do nothing for two seconds. It's necessary to do this because a delay of up to two seconds (and therefore an average of only one second) before seeing a new post is not very noticeable; it does wonders, however, for ensuring that the server runs smoothly. Without this delay, $datafile would be constantly called by all the chat view processes, when most of the time there would be no new posts to display, while the server's processor and hard disk would be getting thrashed.

Finally, a check is made to see whether the current time, as returned by the function time(), less the time stored in $tn when the program was started, is greater than the value of $maxtime. If it is, then the program has exceeded the maximum number of seconds it is allowed to run for and the function returns with the value TRUE.

Now you may ask why I don't simply allow the program to run for as long as the user is chatting. Well, the answer is that many chatters leave the chat running when they go off to make cups of coffee or do the shopping or even when they go to bed. Unfortunately, leaving a program running in such cases can very soon tie up even a powerful server.

One solution to this is to use an Ajax call to fetch all new posts instead of retaining an open connection to the server, This way the server would only be polled every now and then. But the solution I have used here, as you'll see in the following section, is to exit from displaying the chat after a given length of time and then ask the user to click a link to reload the chat—it's a really simple way of ensuring the user is still active.

How to Use It

Using this plug-in can be as simple as the following code, which restarts the script when the user clicks a link:

```
if (!PIPHP_ViewChat('chatroom.txt', 'fredsmith', 300))
    echo "Error. Could not open the chat data file";
else echo "<a href='" . $_SERVER['PHP_SELF'] .
    "'>Click here to continue</a>";
```

It requires just three arguments: the name of the chatroom datafile; the username of the person viewing the chat; and the timeout in seconds of the program. By using the PHP variable $_SERVER['PHP_SELF'], it doesn't matter what your program is called because this variable will refer to it correctly.

If you know that the current user is still active—for example, because they have recently posted a message—you could restart the script automatically for them. In this case, you needn't impose a Click here message on them. One way to do this would be to load in the $datafile file and process it looking for any *From* fields with the user's username. If you find one, then the user posted recently and you could auto renew the chat using a bit of JavaScript, like this:

```
die("<script>self.location='" . $_SERVER['PHP_SELF'] . "'</script>");
```

The die() function acts as a combined echo and exit statement and the JavaScript in it will cause the current page to be reloaded.

Of course, when you run your own chat server you'll soon see the kinds of loads it is under and the amount of time you can afford to leave the plug-in running in order to get the best uninterrupted user experience. For example, you may find that 15 minutes is more appropriate, particularly when fewer users are active.

The main thing, though, is that you can quickly and easily offer a fast and flexible chat service with a few lines of PHP code, without having to install large programs, or rely on Java or Flash programs, and you don't need to be stuck with a look and feel someone else has designed. The fact that this chat is only a few lines of code means you can tailor it exactly to your requirements, without delving through hundreds or thousands of lines of code.

TIP *Of course, going the Ajax route (where background calls are made behind the scenes to send and retrieve data to and from the server) is an even better solution to providing a smooth and flexible chat service, and you wouldn't need to change a lot to implement it. However, it can be tricky to get just right and would be too large a project for this book. That said, in Chapter 11 I do show you the principles of making Ajax calls and provide you with the plug-ins you will need.*

The Plug-in

```php
function PIPHP_ViewChat($datafile, $username, $maxtime)
{
   if (!file_exists($datafile)) return FALSE;

   set_time_limit($maxtime + 5);
   $tn       = time();
   $tstart   = "<table width='100%' border='0'><tr><td " .
               "width='15%' align='right'>";
   $tmiddle  = "</td><td width='85%'>";
   $tend     = "</td></tr></table><script>scrollBy(0,1000);" .
               "</script>\n";
   $oldpnum  = 0;

   while (1)
   {
      $lines = explode("\n",
         rtrim(file_get_contents($datafile)));

      foreach ($lines as $line)
      {
         $thisline = explode("|", $line);
         $postnum  = $thisline[0];
         $to       = $thisline[1];
         $from     = $thisline[2];
         $message  = $thisline[3];

         if ($postnum > $oldpnum)
         {
            if ($to == "")
            {
               echo $tstart . "$from:" . $tmiddle .
                  $message . $tend;
            }
            elseif ($to == $username || $from == $username)
            {
               echo $tstart . "$from:" . $tmiddle .
                  "(PM to $to) <i>$message</i>" . $tend;
            }

            $oldpnum = $postnum;
            ob_flush();
            flush();
         }
      }

      sleep(2);
      if ((time() - $tn) > $maxtime) return TRUE;
   }
}
```

Send Tweet

I have to admit that Twitter baffled me when it first came out. I asked myself what good was a micro blogging service supporting only 140 characters? And what kind of people would use it?

The message length restriction was obviously based around the constraints of the mobile text messaging system, which is also limited to 140 characters, so if there was going to be a huge crossover between the two then that would make sense.

On the other hand, it soon became obvious to me when one day Google Mail went down for a few hours that Twitter was valuable because I could perform a search at *search .twitter.com* to instantly see whether it was just me, or if others were affected. Pretty soon I got into the habit of checking Twitter for updates on major news stories—and that, as they say, was the start of that.

So now I believe Twitter to be an amazingly powerful tool for performing almost real-time research, interacting with colleagues and customers, and generally keeping up-to-date on the world in general. Therefore, it was a given that I would write a plug-in for it. In fact, this is the first of three plug-ins for Twitter in this book.

Using this one you can send a Tweet to your own account, which Figure 8-6 shows the result of doing.

About the Plug-in

This plug-in accepts the name and password for a Twitter account, along with a message to be Tweeted, and then sends the message to that user's account. Upon success, it returns TRUE. On failure, FALSE is returned. It takes these arguments:

- **$user**   A Twitter username
- **$pass**   The matching password for $user
- **$text**   Up to 140 characters of text to Tweet

Variables, Arrays, and Functions

$url	String containing the URL of Twitter's status update API
$curl_handle	Handle returned by curl_init()
$result	XML result of calling curl_exec()
$xml	XML object created from $result

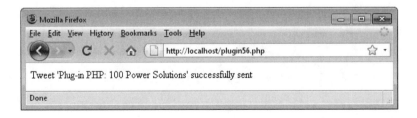

Figure 8-6   Posting a Tweet to Twitter is easy with this plug-in.

How It Works

Sometimes you can fetch web pages from other servers quite easily using the `file_get_contents()` function, but it only works for pages that can be fetched with a GET request. When a POST request is required, you either have to use a web form and submit it to the page in question, or, more simply, you can use *mod curl*, as in this plug-in.

This plug-in starts off by using the `substr()` function to truncate the string `$text` to 140 characters (the maximum number of characters supported by Twitter) if it's longer than that. It does this to ensure that the string won't be truncated by Twitter, because later the code will check to see whether the status string of the user's most recent message is the same as `$text`. If so, then a status update has occurred. If `$text` was ever greater than 140 characters in length, then Twitter would truncate it before posting the Tweet, and so the returned status message would not be the same as the original `$text`. Therefore, the plug-in ensures that Twitter never has to truncate any `$text`.

Next, the variable `$url` is set to the Twitter status update API page. Then, all the parameters required for the call to `curl_exec()` are assigned their correct values, starting with setting the CURLOPT_URL option to `$url` and the CURLOP_CONNECTTIMEOUT option to 2.

The CURLOPT_RETURNTRANSFER option is then set to 1 to prevent `curl_exec()` from directly outputting the result of making the POST request. Instead, the result is returned by the function, in place of the normal success value of TRUE.

Then the CURLOP_POST option is set to 1, indicating that a POST request is to be made, and the CURLOPT_POSTFIELDS option is given the string `"status=$text"`, while CURLOPT_USERPWD is given the value `"$user:$pass"` to set up the login details.

Finally, `curl_exec()` is called, passing the handle `$curl_handle`, which was created at the start, and then `curl_close()` is called to close the connection. The result of the call is now in `$result`. This will be FALSE for failure, or on success it will be a string of XML data containing the result returned by the called URL. If the Tweet was successful, there will be various elements in the XML, but notably the `<text>` field will contain the contents of the most recent status update (or Tweet).

To examine this field, a new XML object is created from `$result` in `$xml` using the `simplexml_load_string()` function. If it cannot be created, then the value FALSE is returned, otherwise the object property `$xml->text` is compared with the value of `$text`, and if they are the same, the Tweet was successful and a value of TRUE is returned. Otherwise, FALSE is returned to indicate failure.

How to Use It

To send a Tweet to your Twitter account, just call the plug-in like this:

```
$user   = 'twitteruser';
$pass   = 'twitterpass';
$text   = 'Hello world';
$result = PIPHP_SendTweet($user, $pass, $text);
```

The variables `$user` and `$pass` must be a valid Twitter username and password pair, and `$text` the text to Tweet. If the Tweet was successfully sent, `$result` will be TRUE, otherwise it will have a value of FALSE, and you can use this variable to display a message, like this:

```
if ($result) echo "Tweet '$text' sent";
else echo "Tweet '$text' failed";
```

The Plug-in

```
function PIPHP_SendTweet($user, $pass, $text)
{
    $url = 'http://twitter.com/statuses/update.xml';
    $curl_handle = curl_init();
    curl_setopt($curl_handle, CURLOPT_URL, "$url");
    curl_setopt($curl_handle, CURLOPT_CONNECTTIMEOUT, 2);
    curl_setopt($curl_handle, CURLOPT_RETURNTRANSFER, 1);
    curl_setopt($curl_handle, CURLOPT_POST, 1);
    curl_setopt($curl_handle, CURLOPT_POSTFIELDS, "status=$text");
    curl_setopt($curl_handle, CURLOPT_USERPWD, "$user:$pass");
    $result = curl_exec($curl_handle);
    curl_close($curl_handle);

    $xml  = simplexml_load_string($result);
    if ($xml == FALSE) return FALSE;
    elseif ($xml->text == $text) return TRUE;
    else return FALSE;
}
```

PLUG-IN 57 Send Direct Tweet

You can also send direct messages to other Twitter users as long as you are both following each other. This is an invaluable way to chat with other Twitter users without clogging up your public Twitter feed. Figure 8-7 shows the result of sending a direct message to the Twitter user *otheruser*.

About the Plug-in

This plug-in accepts the name and password for a Twitter account, along with the name of the Twitter user being sent the direct message and the message to Tweet. It then sends the message to that user's account. Upon success it returns TRUE, otherwise FALSE. It takes these arguments:

- **$user**   A Twitter username
- **$pass**   The matching password for $user
- **$to**   The direct Tweet's recipient
- **$text**   Up to 140 characters of text to Tweet

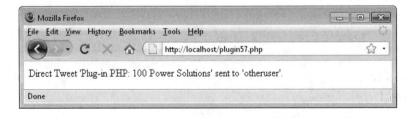

FIGURE 8-7   You can also send direct Tweets to other Twitter users.

Variables, Arrays, and Functions

$url	String containing the URL of Twitter's status update API
$curl_handle	Handle returned by curl_init()
$result	XML result of calling curl_exec()
$xml	XML object created from $result

How It Works

This plug-in is substantially similar to the previous one, with just a few minor differences. So, rather than explain its workings in full, I'll just cover the differences. These are that an additional argument, $to, is required by the plug-in, which then gets appended to the CURLOPT_POSTFIELDS option as &user=$to, and the message now takes the different format of text=$text instead of status=$text. So the full string passed to CURLOPT_POSTFIELDS now becomes user=$to&text=$text.

Also the API URL is different for sending a direct message and is now /direct_messages/new.xml instead of /statuses/update.xml. Apart from that, it's essentially the same code.

It's true, you *can* send a direct Tweet to another Twitter user by starting it with the letter d, followed by a space and then the person's username, but the data returned by curl_exec() would then only be that of the most recent Tweet because of using the /statuses/update.xml API URL.

However, by using the API URL of /direct_messages/new.xml, and passing the recipient to it as well as the message, Twitter will return the most recent direct message data when the Tweet is sent. You can then check this to see if the value in $test was actually posted, and whether the direct message was successfully sent.

How to Use It

To send a direct Tweet, ensure that both the sending and recipient Twitter accounts follow each other, and then call the plug-in, like this:

```
$user    = 'twitteruser';
$pass    = 'twitterpass';
$to      = 'otheruser';
$text    = 'This is a direct Tweet';
$result  = PIPHP_SendDirectTweet($user, $pass, $to, $text);
```

If all is well, $result will be set to a value of TRUE, otherwise it will be FALSE upon failure. You can use this value as follows to display a success or failure message:

```
if ($result) echo "Direct Tweet '$text' sent";
else echo "Direct Tweet '$text' failed";
```

The Plug-in

```
function PIPHP_SendDirectTweet($user, $pass, $to, $text)
{
   $text = substr($text, 0, 140);
   $url  = 'http://twitter.com/direct_messages/new.xml';
```

```
$curl_handle = curl_init();
curl_setopt($curl_handle, CURLOPT_URL, "$url");
curl_setopt($curl_handle, CURLOPT_CONNECTTIMEOUT, 2);
curl_setopt($curl_handle, CURLOPT_RETURNTRANSFER, 1);
curl_setopt($curl_handle, CURLOPT_POST, 1);
curl_setopt($curl_handle, CURLOPT_POSTFIELDS,
    "user=$to&text=$text");
curl_setopt($curl_handle, CURLOPT_USERPWD, "$user:$pass");
$result = curl_exec($curl_handle);
curl_close($curl_handle);

$xml = simplexml_load_string($result);
if ($xml == FALSE) return FALSE;
elseif ($xml->text == $text) return TRUE;
else return FALSE;
}
```

58 Get Tweets

Here's the last of the triumvirate of Twitter treats. It's a plug-in to fetch up to the last 20 posts of any Twitter user who's profile isn't private. Figure 8-8 shows the result of pointing the plug-in at Eminem's Twitter feed.

About the Plug-in

This plug-in accepts the username of a Twitter account, and as long as it's not private, it returns the most recent Tweets. Upon success, it returns a two-element array, the first of which is the number of Tweets found, and the second is an array containing the Tweets. On failure, it returns a single-element array with the value FALSE. It takes this argument:

- **$user**   A Twitter username

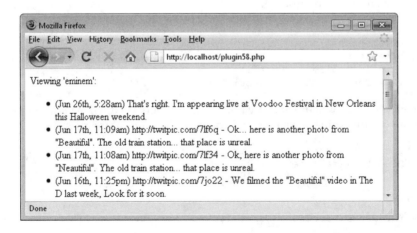

FIGURE 8-8   With this plug-in, you can fetch the most recent posts (up to 20) of a Twitter user.

Variables, Arrays, and Functions

`$url`	String containing the URL of Twitter's user timeline API
`$file`	String containing the data returned by `$url`
`$xml`	XML object created from `$file`
`$tweets`	Array of the most recent Tweets (up to 20) from `$user`
`$tweet`	String containing each property of `$xml->status` as it is processed
`$timestamp`	Unix timestamp extracted from the date and time of a Tweet

How It Works

This plug-in fetches a Twitter user's timeline feed from the following URL, where *username* is the name of the user:

```
http://twitter.com/statuses/user_timeline/username.xml
```

If the account is not set to private, then the feed is returned in XML format. This is achieved by setting `$url` to the URL to be retrieved and then passing it to the `file_get_contents()` function, from where the XML is loaded into the string `$file`. If `$file` is zero characters in length, then a single-element array with the value FALSE is returned because the feed could not be retrieved, or the username was invalid.

Otherwise, a new XML object called `$xml` is created from the contents of `$file` using the `simplexml_load_string()` function. If the object's value is FALSE, then the XML was invalid or otherwise unusable so, again, an array with the value FALSE is returned.

Now the plug-in is ready to extract the Tweets from a feed, so the array `$tweets` is initialized and then a `foreach` loop steps through each `$xml->status` property in the object, passing it into the object `$tweet`.

From here the `strtotime()` function is used to convert the time stored in the property `$tweet->created_at` into a standard Unix timestamp value, which is then stored in `$timestamp`. This allows the plug-in to replace the very awkward and overly precise dates and times used by Twitter, such as `Thu Jun 25 21:28:18 +0000 2009`, with much more friendly and readable strings, like `Jun 25th, 9:28pm`. This is done using the `date()` function with a formatting argument of `"M jS, g:ia"`.

This new version of the date and time is then surrounded by brackets and followed by the Tweet itself, as retrieved from the property `$tweet->text`, and the resulting string is assigned to the next available element of the array `$tweets`.

Once all the Tweets have been processed, a two-element array is returned, the first element of which contains the number of Tweets returned, while the second is an array containing all the Tweets.

Incidentally, the @ symbols are in the code to suppress any warning error messages that might otherwise be displayed.

How to Use It

To use the plug-in, just call it, passing the name of a Twitter user with a public account, like this:

```
$user   = 'stephenhawking';
$result = PIPHP_GetTweets($user);
```

You can then test the value(s) returned by checking $result[0], like this:

```
if (!$result[0]) echo 'Failed';
```

If $result[0] doesn't contain the value FALSE, then $result[1] will contain an array of all the Tweets, which can be displayed like this:

```
for ($j = 0 ; $j < $result[0] ; ++$j)
    echo $result[1][$j] . "<br />";
```

As with most of the plug-ins in this book, this one handles the task of manipulating the data and returning it to you in a sensible format. It's then up to you how you choose to display the result, but the preceding code will, at the very least, provide the information you want.

The Plug-in

```
function PIPHP_GetTweets($user)
{
    $url  = "http://twitter.com/statuses/user_timeline/$user.xml";
    $file = @file_get_contents($url);
    if (!strlen($file)) return array(FALSE);

    $xml  = @simplexml_load_string($file);
    if ($xml == FALSE) return array(FALSE);

    $tweets = array();

    foreach ($xml->status as $tweet)
    {
        $timestamp = strtotime($tweet->created_at);
        $tweets[] = "(" . date("M jS, g:ia", $timestamp) . ") " .
            $tweet->text;
    }

    return array(count($tweets), $tweets);
}
```

59 Replace Smileys

In the early days of bulletin boards, emoticons were invented as a means of expressing emotions not quickly conveyable in brief messages. These included the familiar :) and :(happy and unhappy faces, as well as dozens more. Nowadays you still see them, but they are more often replaced with icons such as smileys.

In fact, many e-mail programs and other applications such as Microsoft Word will substitute emoticons for smileys automatically for you. And that's exactly the functionality that this plug-in offers. Figure 8-9 shows the set of 20 smileys provided by the plug-in, a few of which (such as the kiss smiley) are animated to better convey their meaning.

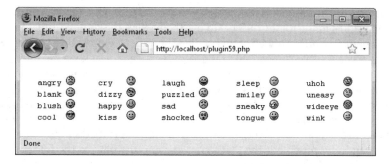

FIGURE 8-9   Use this plug-in to replace text emoticons with smiley GIF images.

About the Plug-in

This plug-in accepts a string of text to search for emoticons to replace with smiley GIF images. It takes these arguments:

- **$text**   The text to process for emoticons
- **$folder**   The folder in which you have saved the smiley GIFs

Variables, Arrays, and Functions

$chars	Array of emoticons to search for
$gifs	Array of GIF filenames without the .gif extensions
$j	Integer index for iterating through the arrays

How It Works

This plug-in supports 20 different types of emoticons and their associated GIF smileys. The emoticons are stored in the array $chars, and the GIF filenames (minus the *.gif* extensions) are housed in the array $gifs. They are all in groups to make the plug-in easy to modify. For example, the first four elements of each array are the *angry* emoticons and smileys.

The emoticons need to be replaced with the correct HTML with which to display an associated GIF image, so the argument $folder is used to provide the correct path to the images. To ensure that paths are accepted either with or without trailing slashes, the plug-in first removes any such slashes, adding it back later where required.

Then a for loop is entered to iterate through all of the names in $gifs, replacing each element with the HTML that will reference each GIF, and providing its *width*, *height*, *alt*, and *title* attributes.

With the $gifs array now suitably processed, both arrays are passed to the str_ireplace() function, which then replaces all occurrences of any emoticons in the $chars array with the replacement code in the $gifs array. It does this while ignoring the case of each character so that, for example, both :S and :s will be replaced with the HTML for displaying the *puzzled.gif* smiley.

How to Use It

Before you call this plug-in, you must download the folder of GIFs from the companion web site at *www.pluginphp.com*. When you click the *Download* link, all the plug-ins will be downloaded in a Zip file called *plug-ins.zip*, which you'll need to extract. Once extracted, you'll immediately see the GIFs in the folder *smileys*. To use them, copy the smileys into a folder within your document root on your web server so that they are accessible by a web browser.

If you wish, you can replace some or all of the icons, as long as you keep the same filenames for the same smiley type. But remember, you may need to alter the *width* and *height* attributes in the code if your new smileys have different dimensions (or just leave those attributes out if the dimensions vary). The provided set of GIFs are all 15×15 pixels in size. Also, make sure you don't rename or delete any of the files, otherwise the plug-in will not work correctly because it assumes all the files have the names specified in the array $gifs.

You use the plug-in by passing it the text to process and the path to the folder of GIFs, like this (where *smileys* is the name of the folder):

```
echo PIPHP_ReplaceSmileys($text, 'smileys');
```

To test it, make sure $text contains a few emoticons, like ':) :] :D XD', and so on.

If you prefer, you can also assign the result of calling the plug-in to a string variable, where it can then be used elsewhere in your program, like this:

```
$html = PIPHP_ReplaceSmileys($text, 'smileys');
```

The Plug-in

```
function PIPHP_ReplaceSmileys($text, $folder)
{
    $chars = array('>:-(', '>:(', 'X-(',   'X(',
                   ':-)*', ':)*', ':-*',   ':*', '=*',
                   ':)',   ':]',
                   ':-)',  ':-]',
                   ':(',   ':C',    ':[',
                   ':-(',  ':\'(', ':_(',
                   ':O',   ':-O',
                   ':P',   ':b',    ':-P', ':-b',
                   ':D',   'XD',
                   ';)',   ';-)',
                   ':/',   ':\\',   ':-/', ':-\\',
                   ':|',
                   'B-)',  'B)',
                   'I-)',  'I)',
                   ':->',  ':>',
                   ':X',   ':-X',
                   '8)',   '8-)',
                   '=-O',  '=O',
                   'O.o',  ':S',    ':-S',
                   '*-*',  '*_*');

    $gifs = array( 'angry',   'angry',   'angry',  'angry',
                   'kiss',    'kiss',    'kiss',   'kiss',    'kiss',
                   'smiley',  'smiley',
                   'happy',   'happy',
                   'sad',     'sad',     'sad',
                   'cry',     'cry',     'cry',
                   'shocked', 'shocked',
                   'tongue',  'tongue',  'tongue', 'tongue',
                   'laugh',   'laugh',
```

```
                   'wink',     'wink',
                   'uneasy',   'uneasy',   'uneasy', 'uneasy',
                   'blank',
                   'cool',     'cool',
                   'sleep',    'sleep',
                   'sneaky',   'sneaky',
                   'blush',    'blush',
                   'wideeye',  'wideeye',
                   'uhoh',     'uhoh',
                   'puzzled',  'puzzled', 'puzzled',
                   'dizzy',    'dizzy');

   if (substr($folder, -1) == '/')
      $folder = substr($folder, 0, -1);

   for ($j = 0 ; $j < count($gifs) ; ++$j)
      $gifs[$j] = "<image src='$folder/$gifs[$j].gif' " .
         "width='15' height='15' border='0' alt='$gifs[$j]' " .
         "title='$gifs[$j]' />";

   return str_ireplace($chars, $gifs, $text);
}
```

PLUG-IN 60 Replace SMS Talk

Sometimes your users will use *text speak* in their posts, so-called because it evolved through the use of texting messages on mobile phones. It's a more compact and less time consuming way of communicating that's also often used on Twitter due to its similar restriction on message length.

But one thing it isn't is pretty. So if you would like to clean up posts a little before adding them to your site, this plug-in will do the trick. Figure 8-10 shows the result of passing a string containing several text speak acronyms to the plug-in, which it suitably corrects.

About the Plug-in

This plug-in accepts a string which, if it contains recognized text speak acronyms, is converted to standard English and returned. It takes this argument:

- **$text** The text to be processed

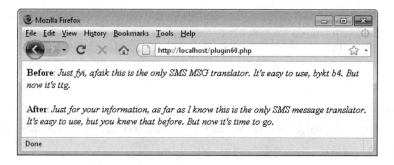

Figure 8-10   Want to translate your users' text speak? Do it with this plug-in.

Variables, Arrays, and Functions

`$sms`	Array of text speak acronyms to be replaced and their equivalents in standard English
`$from1`	Array based on the `$sms` array with regular expression operators for processing uppercase
`$to1`	Array containing the standard English replacements for `$from1`
`$from2`	Array based on the `$sms` array with regular expression operators for processing lowercase
`$to2`	Array containing the standard English replacements for `$from2`
`$j`	Integer index for iterating through the arrays

How It Works

This function is based around the array `$sms`, which contains pairs of data: a text speak SMS acronym and its equivalent in standard English. I built the plug-in this way to make it very easy for you to change any pairs or add more of your own. Just remember to precede any apostrophes with a \ escape character (like this \ ') to avoid getting an error message.

Because of the way these pairs are stored, they do need a little massaging to get them into a state with which `$text` can be processed. This is done by first initializing two pairs of *from* and *to* arrays: `$from1` / `$to1` and `$from2` / `$to2`. Then a `for` loop iterates through the `$sms` array, extracting the *from* and *to* halves of each pair.

This is done twice so all the uppercase text speak acronyms can have an effect different from the lowercase ones. For example, the acronym BTW should be replaced with By the way (note the initial capital letter), but the acronym btw should be replaced with by the way (with no initial capital letter).

To achieve this, the `$from1` array is populated with the correct regular expression to match only the uppercase acronyms. It does this using the \b operator, which marks the boundary between a word and a non-word character, so that only acronyms are matched and not groups of the same letters that may occur within words.

Next, `$to1` has each replacement string passed through the `ucfirst()` function, which forces the initial letter of a string to uppercase, before being assigned the resulting value.

On the other hand, `$from2` uses the same regular expression as `$from1`, except that a letter i is added after the closing / of the expression. This tells the `preg_replace()` function that matching should take place regardless of the whether acronyms are upper- or lowercase (or even a combination). The `$to2` array doesn't get passed through the `ucfirst()` function, so those replacements remain unchanged.

When the loop has completed, the arrays will all be correctly populated, and the `preg_replace()` function will have been called twice to perform the replacements. The first time, `$from1` acronyms are replaced with `$to1` standard English and have their first letters capitalized. The second time, `$from2` acronyms are replaced with `$to2` standard English equivalents. The result of all these translations is then returned.

How to Use It

To use this plug-in, pass a string of text that you think may contain text speak to it, like this:

```
$text = "FYI, afaik imho this is a cool plug-in. LOL.";
echo PIPHP_ReplaceSMSTalk($text);
```

The plug-in will then make any required substitutions and return the result, which in the preceding case would be: "For your information, as far as I know in my humble opinion this is a cool plug-in. Laughing out loud".

The Plug-in

```
function PIPHP_ReplaceSMSTalk($text)
{
    $sms = array('ABT2', 'about to',
                 'AFAIC', 'as far as I\'m concerned',
                 'AFAIK', 'as far as I know',
                 'AML', 'all my love',
                 'ATST', 'at the same time',
                 'AWOL', 'absent without leave',
                 'AYK', 'as you know',
                 'AYTMTB', 'and you\'re telling me this because?',
                 'B4', 'before',
                 'B4N', 'bye for now',
                 'BBT', 'be back tomorrow',
                 'BRB', 'be right back',
                 'BTW', 'by the way',
                 'BW', 'best wishes',
                 'BYKT', 'but you knew that',
                 'CID', 'consider it done',
                 'CSL', 'can\'t stop laughing',
                 'CYL', 'see you later',
                 'CYT', 'see you tomorrow',
                 'DGA ', 'don\'t go anywhere',
                 'DIKU', 'do I know you?',
                 'DLTM', 'don\'t lie to me',
                 'FF', 'friends forever',
                 'FYI', 'for your information',
                 'GBH', 'great big hug',
                 'GG', 'good game',
                 'GL', 'good luck',
                 'GR8', 'great',
                 'GTG', 'got to go',
                 'HAK', 'hugs and kisses',
                 'ILU', 'I love you',
                 'IM', 'instant message',
                 'IMHO', 'in my humble opinion',
                 'IMO', 'in my opinion',
                 'IMS', 'I\'m sorry',
                 'IOH', 'I\'m outta here',
                 'JK', 'just kidding',
                 'KISS', 'Keep it simple silly',
                 'L8R', 'later',
                 'LOL', 'laughing out loud',
                 'M8 ', 'mate',
                 'MSG', 'message',
                 'N1', 'nice one',
                 'NE1', 'anyone?',
                 'NMP', 'not my problem',
                 'NOYB', 'none of your business',
```

```
                        'NP', 'no problem',
                        'OMDB', 'over my dead body',
                        'OMG', 'oh my gosh',
                        'ONNA', 'oh no, not again',
                        'OOTO', 'out of the office',
                        'OT', 'off topic',
                        'OTT', 'over the top',
                        'PLS', 'please',
                        'PM', 'personal message',
                        'POOF', 'goodbye',
                        'QL', 'quit laughing',
                        'QT', 'cutie',
                        'RBTL ', 'reading between the lines',
                        'ROLF', 'rolling on the floor laughing',
                        'SMEM', 'send me an email',
                        'SMIM', 'send me an instant message',
                        'SO', 'significant other',
                        'SOHF', 'sense of humor failure',
                        'STR8', 'straight',
                        'SYS', 'see you soon',
                        'TAH', 'take a hike',
                        'TBC', 'to be continued',
                        'TFH', 'thread from hell',
                        'TGIF', 'thank goodness it\'s Friday',
                        'THX', 'thanks',
                        'TM', 'trust me',
                        'TOM', 'tomorrow',
                        'TTG', 'time to go',
                        'TVM', 'thank you very much',
                        'VM', 'voice mail',
                        'WC', 'who cares?',
                        'WFM', 'Works for me',
                        'WTG', 'way to go',
                        'WYP', 'what\'s your problem?',
                        'WYWH', 'wish you were here',
                        'XOXO', 'hugs and kisses',
                        'ZZZ', 'sleeping, bored');

    $from1 = array(); $from2 = array();
    $to1   = array(); $to2   = array();

    for ($j = 0 ; $j < count($sms) ; $j += 2)
    {
        $from1[$j] = "/\b$sms[$j]\b/";
        $to1[$j]   = ucfirst($sms[$j + 1]);

        $from2[$j] = "/\b$sms[$j]\b/i";
        $to2[$j]   = $sms[$j + 1];
    }

    $text = preg_replace($from1, $to1, $text);
    return  preg_replace($from2, $to2, $text);
}
```

CHAPTER 9

MySQL, Sessions, and Cookies

T his chapter covers a lot of different topics, ranging from using MySQL to working with PHP sessions, and from basic security measures to handling cookies. Although at first sight these topics may not seem too closely related, they actually are because they're mostly to do with the processing, storage, and recall of data.

The three MySQL plug-ins provide a means of creating a database to hold various details about a user, the facility to add new users, and a plug-in to verify a user against their username and password; while the PHP session plug-ins provide the ability to hold a user's details across multiple instances of the same or different web pages or PHP programs. Finally, the cookie plug-ins provide similar functionality to the session variables, except that you can set cookies to live for a shorter or longer time than the current session.

Along the way you'll also learn how to roll your own variations of these plug-ins, or how to extract the basic functionality from them to create totally new functions.

PLUG-IN 61 Add User to DB

This plug-in saves a user's details in a MySQL database. If the data table used doesn't already exist, it even creates it for you so there's minimum setup required.

So why MySQL? Well, so far in this book I've concentrated on using "flat" text files for storing data on the server. This is a quite adequate solution for small applications and utilities, and it saves on having to configure and maintain a database such as MySQL. Indeed, had I gone the database route (or if you've been experimenting with the plug-ins), you'd probably have dozens of databases residing within MySQL. Instead, you should only have a collection of text files, which you can simply delete when you don't want them any more.

However, the time comes when the benefits of using a database begin to outweigh those of not doing so, and this plug-in, which allows thousands of users and several fields per user, is such a case. Yes, I could have used a text file and split all records at line breaks, separating out the fields with a special token. But the code required to support such a system would never run as fast or be as flexible as using a database.

Figure 9-1 shows this plug-in in action with a user being added twice to the database, the duplicate checking ensuring that the second insertion is ignored.

FIGURE 9-1 This plug-in creates a user database and adds users to it.

About the Plug-in

This plug-in inserts a record into a MySQL database. If the database table does not already exist, it creates it first. Upon success, a value of 1 is returned. Otherwise, -1 is returned if the insert failed, or -2 if the handle already exists. It requires these arguments:

- **$table**   The name of the data table
- **$nmax**   The maximum length allowed for $name
- **$hmax**   The maximum length allowed for $handle
- **$salt1**   Semi-random string to help secure the password
- **$salt2**   A second string to go with $salt1
- **$name**   The user's full name to add to the database
- **$handle**   The user's username
- **$pass**   The user's password
- **$email**   The user's e-mail address

Variables, Arrays, and Functions

$query	String containing the query to pass to the MySQL database

How It Works

At the start of this plug-in, the query required to create the table named by $table is put together. For example, assuming that names are allowed 32 characters and handles 16, then the command-line MySQL statements in the query would be as follows:

```
CREATE TABLE IF NOT EXISTS Users
(
    name VARCHAR(32),
    handle VARCHAR(16),
    pass CHAR(32),
    email VARCHAR(256),
    INDEX(name(6)),
    INDEX(handle(6)),
    INDEX(email(6))
);
```

As you may know, when the command-line interface is used, MySQL allows you to input a line at a time, and only sends the completed instructions when a final semicolon is encountered. So the preceding is valid MySQL syntax that you could type in. If you were to then enter:

```
DESCRIBE Users;
```

MySQL would show you the format of the table by displaying the following, which shows that the table *Users* has four fields (also known as columns), with *name, handle,* and *email* being variable length character fields of up to 32, 16, or 256 characters respectively, and *pass* being a fixed length field of exactly 32 characters:

```
+---------+---------------+------+-----+---------+-------+
| Field   | Type          | Null | Key | Default | Extra |
+---------+---------------+------+-----+---------+-------+
| name    | varchar(32)   | YES  | MUL | NULL    |       |
| handle  | varchar(16)   | YES  | MUL | NULL    |       |
| pass    | char(32)      | YES  |     | NULL    |       |
| email   | varchar(256)  | YES  | MUL | NULL    |       |
+---------+---------------+------+-----+---------+-------+
```

This output also shows another thing worth pointing out, which is that all of *name*, *handle*, and *email* have been given indexes by the MySQL INDEX() statement, as shown by the word MUL under the Key heading. This means that, just like using a card index in a library, they will be quick to search.

Back to the PHP, though. No semicolon is required (or even allowed) when using the mysql_query() function, so all the preceding commands are run together into a single string stored in $query, which is then passed onto the mysql_query() function. If the call fails, then something has gone very wrong and so the code exits, returning an error message. This will enable you to properly debug your program, but on a production server you may wish to replace the die() function call with error handling of your own.

By the way, did you notice the IF NOT EXISTS clause at the start of the query? Using this means that the CREATE TABLE instruction will only ever be called once. Thereafter, the table will already exist and the command will be ignored. It's a neat way of avoiding having to issue an additional MySQL call to see whether a table exists before creating it. Note that this code assumes you have already created a suitable database and a user to access it (there's more on this in the following section).

So, having ensured that the table named by $table exists, a new query is placed in $query with which to check whether the user already exists in the table. We need to do this to avoid filling it up with duplicates. The query takes the following form (although *tablename* and *handle* would be replaced by the actual values):

```
SELECT * FROM tablename WHERE handle='handle';
```

Again, the preceding is a MySQL command as you would type it into the command line—just leaving off the final semicolon makes it work with mysql_query(), to which the query is passed. Upon success, the mysql_query() function always returns a resource after a SELECT command, which can be used to examine the result of the query. In this case the resource is returned directly to the mysql_num_rows() function, which returns a count representing the number of times the search is found in the database.

In this case only a single entry of any handle is allowed, so this value will be either 0 or 1. If the returned value is 1, then an entry already exists and so the function returns with a value of -2 to indicate the fact. Otherwise, it is all right to proceed with inserting the data into the database.

First, however, the password needs to be obfuscated to protect all the users should the database get into the wrong hands. This is done by converting the password into a special string called a *hash* using the md5() function. This is a type of function that only goes one way, and so the input cannot be derived from the output. In addition, to prevent attempts at dictionary hash cracking, a semi-random sequence of characters called a *salt* is added to both ends of the password before passing it to md5(). There's more on passwords and salting in the *Create Captcha* plug-in section of Chapter 6, but suffice it to say that you must decide on the values of $salt1 and $salt2 and stick to them for as long as you use your database. These two values will be used for all stored password hashes.

The hash, created by concatenating the password and two salts, and passing them to md5(), is then assigned back to the variable $pass, which means that from this point onwards even the program doesn't know the user's password.

A final query string is then assembled in $query along the lines of this MySQL command-line statement:

```
INSERT INTO tablename VALUES
(
    name,
    handle,
    pass,
    email
);
```

Of course these values are replaced with the actual contents of the variables $table, $name, $handle, $pass, and $email, and the semicolon is omitted. The string is then passed to mysql_query(), and if the result of the call is TRUE, a value of 1 is returned; otherwise, -1 is returned to indicate failure.

More experienced MySQL users may wonder why I didn't make the *handle* field UNIQUE and simply try to apply the INSERT INTO regardless, which would automatically fail if a handle of the same name already exists. The answer is that mysql_query() only returns either TRUE or FALSE for an INSERT command. Therefore it would not be possible to distinguish between a call that failed due to a record already existing, or one that failed from a syntax or other error. As well as being perfect for preventing duplicate entries, the former case is important to check for so that a user can be told whether or not the handle they have chosen has already been taken.

TIP *MySQL doesn't mind whether you enter commands in upper- or lowercase. Neither does it worry about the case of database, table, or field names. It is case-insensitive. However, the convention for SQL queries is to use uppercase for commands and lowercase (or mixed upper and lower) for everything else, but it's up to you whether or not to follow this suggested style. Note that this does not affect the contents of fields which are usually stored exactly as provided.*

How to Use It

Before using this plug-in, you will need to have created a MySQL database and a MySQL user that has access to that database. If you are using Zend Server CE, as described in Chapter 1, you should log in to the Command Line Client, which you can do as follows, according to the operating system upon which you installed it:

- *Windows*
  Select Start | All Programs | Zend Server Community Edition | MySQL Server 5.1 | MySQL Command Line Client. When the terminal window appears, as long as you haven't yet set up a password, just press Return.

- *Linux*
  Open up a terminal window and enter the following, followed by your MySQL root
  password (which should be the same as your Linux root password):
  ```
  mysql -uroot -p
  ```
- *Mac OS X*
  Open up a terminal window and enter the following (assuming you have not yet
  created a root password for MySQL):
  ```
  /usr/local/zend/mysql/bin/mysql -uroot
  ```

If you aren't using Zend Server CE or have a different installation of MySQL, you will
need to refer to the documentation that came with your version to see how to enter the
MySQL command-line prompt as user *root*.

Whatever setup you have, you should now be able to create a new database. So let's
create one called `piphp` by entering the following MySQL command:

```
CREATE DATABASE piphp;
```

Now you need to create a user that has access to this new database. So, for example, to
create the user *testing* with the password *testing* you would enter the following:

```
GRANT ALL ON piphp.* TO testing@localhost IDENTIFIED BY 'testing';
```

The GRANT command is the standard way to create a MySQL user and the qualifier ALL
tells MySQL to allow the user to do anything with the database `piphp` and any of its objects
(such as tables) denoted by the `.*` part. The user is given the `@localhost` suffix because
that is where the PHP program that will access MySQL will reside. The IDENTIFIED BY
`'testing'` portion sets the password for the user.

Some of the examples on the *www.pluginphp.com* web site use a user/password pair of
testing/testing by default, so you may want to issue the preceding command exactly as you
see it, as well as creating any other users you think you will need. When you've finished
with the *testing* user account, you can always delete it by entering:

```
DROP USER testing@localhost;
```

With the database and a user now created, let's get onto using the plug-in. The first
thing you must do before using it is establish a connection to the MySQL database. To do
this, you need to provide the details given in the following code:

```
$dbhost = 'localhost';
$dbname = 'piphp';
$dbuser = 'testing';
$dbpass = 'testing';
```

Because the web server will generally be running on the same computer as the MySQL
database, the $dbhost will usually require the value *localhost*. If you were using a different
server for your database, you would replace this with its domain name or IP address.

The name of the database to use is placed in $dbname—if you followed the earlier
instructions, you will have created a database called `piphp` that you can use. You will also
have created a MySQL user called *testing* with a password of *testing*, so $dbuser and

$dbpass can be set to those values. Otherwise, assign values for another user you have created with access to the database referred to by $dbname.

You are now ready to establish a connection to MySQL by issuing a mysql_connect() call, like this:

```
mysql_connect($dbhost, $dbuser, $dbpass) or die(mysql_error());
```

Because success of this call is fundamental to the plug-in, if it fails an error is instantly output and the program quits. This will enable you to fully debug your code before using it on a production server. However, you will probably want to replace the call to die() with your own error management when you do so.

Once the connection has been made, you can then select the database to be used by the program by employing the mysql_select_db() function like this:

```
mysql_select_db($dbname) or die(mysql_error());
```

Again, failure will generate an error and cause the program to exit. But, all being well, execution will then move on to the remainder of your program which, for illustration of the use of this plug-in, needs to prepare a selection of variables, as follows:

```
$table  = 'Users';
$nmax   = 32;
$hmax   = 16;
$name   = "George Washington";
$handle = "firstprez";
$pass   = "GW022232";
$email  = "george@washington.com";
$salt1  = "F^&fg";
$salt2  = "9*hz!";
```

The string value of *Users* in $table is the name of the MySQL table to create and use within the database piphp (or whatever you called it). Although I have shown it with an initial capital letter to differentiate it from a field name, it could have the value *users* or *USERS* and so on, as table names are case-insensitive.

The numeric variables $nmax and $hmax respectively represent the maximum number of characters allowed in the strings $name and $handle. You will very likely decide to use different values in your own programs.

The $name, $handle, $pass, and $email string variables contain the name, username, password, and e-mail details for the current user, while $salt1 and $salt2 are semi-random strings you should create to help make it next to impossible to deduce a password from the md5() hash, which will be created from the concatenation of the password with these strings.

We are now ready to insert a new record into the database using code such as this:

```
$result = PIPHP_AddUserToDB($table, $nmax, $hmax, $salt1, $salt2,
    $name, $handle, $pass, $email);
```

If this is the first record to add, then a table with the name in $table will be created before the record is inserted. If the insert was successful, $result will now contain a value of 1; otherwise, it will be -1 if the insert failed, or -2 if a record containing the string in

$handle already exists in the database. You can therefore test this value as follows to decide what to do next.

```
if ($result == -2) echo "The handle '$handle' already exists." .
    "Please choose a different handle.";
elseif ($result == 1) echo "User '$name' successfully added.";
else echo "Failed to add user '$name'.";
```

The Plug-in

```
function PIPHP_AddUserToDB($table, $nmax, $hmax, $salt1, $salt2,
    $name, $handle, $pass, $email)
{
    $query = "CREATE TABLE IF NOT EXISTS $table(" .
             "name VARCHAR($nmax), handle VARCHAR($hmax), " .
             "pass CHAR(32), email VARCHAR(256), " .
             "INDEX(name(6)), INDEX(handle(6)), " .
             "INDEX(email(6)))";
    mysql_query($query) or die(mysql_error());

    $query = "SELECT * FROM $table WHERE handle='$handle'";
    if (mysql_num_rows(mysql_query($query)) == 1) return -2;

    $pass  = md5($salt1 . $pass . $salt2);
    $query = "INSERT INTO $table VALUES('$name', '$handle', " .
             "'$pass', '$email')";
    if (mysql_query($query)) return 1;
    else return -1;
}
```

PLUG-IN 62 Get User from DB

Using this plug-in, you can look up a user's details as entered using the previous plug-in, *Add User to DB*, by passing just their handle (username) and the name of the table in which the database details are stored. Figure 9-2 shows the items returned, including the obfuscated password, which cannot be used to determine the original password.

Name   = George Washington
Handle   = firstprez
Pass(salted) = 7f5cf80f9e1e4941b19755aeb0a6be5f
Email   = george@washington.com

FIGURE 9-2   Four items of information are stored for each user.

About the Plug-in

Provided with a table name and handle, this plug-in retrieves a user's details and returns them. Upon success, it returns a two-element array with the first element having the value TRUE and the second being an array containing the user's details (in turn: *name, handle, pass,* and *email*). On failure, it returns a single-element array with the value FALSE. It requires these arguments:

- **$table**   The name of the data table
- **$handle**   The user's username

Variables, Arrays, and Functions

$query	String containing the query to pass to the MySQL database
$result	Integer result of performing the query in $query

How It Works

This plug-in expects a database and associated table to have already been created and to contain the details for the user being looked up. Because a connection to MySQL should already be open and the database selected, it takes just the arguments $table and $handle, from which it constructs a MySQL query, which it assigns to $query. In standard command-line MySQL syntax, the query looks like this:

```
SELECT * FROM tablename WHERE handle='username';
```

This tells MySQL to search through the table *tablename* and make a note of every record in which the field (also known as the column) called *handle* contains the string *username*. When sent to the mysql_query() function, the semicolon is omitted and the variables $table and $handle are substituted with their contents. The result of making the function call is then assigned to $result.

---

*TIP   The * symbol tells MySQL to fetch all the fields in a record and is shorthand for providing all the field names individually, separated with commas. However, when you only want some of the fields to be returned, using a * would be wasteful of both memory and CPU cycles, and therefore in such a case naming each one would be the more efficient method.*

Then the mysql_num_rows() function is called using $result as its argument. Because no handle is allowed to be duplicated, this function can only ever return 0 if the handle doesn't already exist, or 1 if it does. So, if a value of 0 is returned, then the plug-in returns FALSE to indicate no matching record exists in the database.

Otherwise, a matching record has been found and the plug-in returns a two-element array, the first of which contains the value TRUE to indicate success, and the second holds a four-element array containing all the fields in the record.

How to Use It

To use this plug-in it is assumed you have already created a MySQL database and a MySQL user that has been allowed access to it (as in the previous plug-in, *Add User to DB*). You will therefore have to provide these details to your program so it can connect to MySQL and select the database. You can do this with the following code:

```
$dbhost = 'localhost';
$dbname = 'piphp';
$dbuser = 'testing';
$dbpass = 'testing';
mysql_connect($dbhost, $dbuser, $dbpass) or die(mysql_error());
mysql_select_db($dbname) or die(mysql_error());
```

These six lines define the database host and name, as well as a MySQL username and password, connect to MySQL, and select the database. If any errors occur in this process, program execution is terminated and an error message is displayed. On a production server, you may wish to replace the calls to the die() function with your own more user-friendly error handling.

Next you need to define the table name and the handle of the user whose details you wish to look up, and then call the plug-in, like this:

```
$table  = 'Users';
$handle = 'firstprez';
$result = PIPHP_GetUserFromDB($table, $handle);
```

After the call, if $result[0] is FALSE, then the lookup failed and no matching user was found, otherwise $result[0] will have a value of TRUE and $result[1] will contain a sub-array with the user's details, which you can access using code such as this:

```
if ($result[0] == FALSE) echo "Lookup failed.";
else echo "Name         = " . $result[1][0] . "<br />" .
          "Handle       = " . $result[1][1] . "<br />" .
          "Pass(salted) = " . $result[1][2] . "<br />" .
          "Email        = " . $result[1][3];
```

The Plug-in

```
function PIPHP_GetUserFromDB($table, $handle)
{
    $query  = "SELECT * FROM $table WHERE handle='$handle'";
    $result = mysql_query($query);
    if (mysql_num_rows($result) == 0) return array(FALSE);
    else return array(TRUE, mysql_fetch_array($result, MYSQL_NUM));
}
```

PLUG-IN 63 Verify User in DB

Using this plug-in, you can pass a username (handle) and password, as entered by a user and, without needing to look up any details, just pass these on to the plug-in, which will then report whether they verify or not. In Figure 9-3 the handle *firstprez* is checked against two similar but different passwords. Only the correct one of *GW022232* verifies.

Incidentally, *GW022232* is not a very secure password, and the user would be well advised *not* to use his birthday of February 22nd '32 in future passwords.

FIGURE 9-3   A username (handle) and password must match exactly to be verified.

About the Plug-in

This plug-in compares a supplied handle (username) and password to those stored in the database. If they match, it returns TRUE; otherwise, it returns FALSE. It requires these arguments:

- **$table**   The name of the data table
- **$salt1**   The first salt as supplied to PIPHP_AddUserToDB()
- **$salt2**   The second salt value
- **$handle**   The user's username as entered by them
- **$pass**   The user's password

Variables, Arrays, and Functions

$result	Array result of calling PIPHP_GetUserFromDB()

How It Works

This function takes the handle supplied to it, which will in turn have been provided by a user, and passes it to the PIPHP_GetUserFromDB() plug-in to retrieve the accompanying user details from the database.

If the call fails, signified by the return value $result[0] having a value of FALSE, then the handle in $handle was not found in the database. Otherwise, the value in $result[1][2], which is the stored salted and md5() processed password, is compared with the result of performing the identical salting and md5() transformation on the supplied password.

If the results are the same, then the password supplied is the same as the one originally used to create the account, and so a value of TRUE is returned. Otherwise, FALSE is returned.

How to Use It

To use this plug-in you need to have opened a connection to MySQL and selected the database to use, with code such as this:

```
$dbhost = 'localhost';
$dbname = 'piphp';
$dbuser = 'testing';
```

```
$dbpass = 'testing';
mysql_connect($dbhost, $dbuser, $dbpass) or die(mysql_error());
mysql_select_db($dbname) or die(mysql_error());
```

In the preceding, $dbhost is likely to remain with a value of *localhost* since the web server and PHP processor will be running on the same computer as the MySQL database. The variable $dbname is the database you should have created, as advised in plug-in 61, *Add User to DB*. The variables $dbuser and $dbpass should be the username and password of a MySQL user that has been granted access to the database.

The remaining two lines connect to MySQL and select the database. If either action fails, an error message is displayed and program execution stops. Therefore, on a production server, you may wish to replace the die() call with an error handling function of your own.

Next you need to assign values for the table and two salts used, as well as the handle and password to be verified, like this:

```
$table   = 'Users';
$salt1   = "F^&£g";
$salt2   = "9*hz!";
$handle  = 'firstprez';
$pass    = 'GW022231';
```

The two salts, $salt1 and $salt2, must be the same semi-random strings you assigned when using PIPHP_AddUSerToDB().

You are now ready to verify the user's details in the following way:

```
$result = PIPHP_VerifyUserInDB($table, $salt1, $salt2,
   $handle, $pass);
```

Upon success, $result will have the value TRUE, otherwise it will be FALSE. You can use this return value in the following manner:

```
if ($result) echo "Login details $handle/$pass verified.";
else echo "Login details $handle/$pass could not be verified.";
```

Other than for testing the plug-in, this code isn't actually useful. Instead, your code will likely re-present a form to the user if verification failed; otherwise, it will probably log a user in, possibly using PHP sessions, described a little later on in this chapter, starting with plug-in 65, *Create Session*.

Incidentally, if you entered the details for this sample user earlier on in this chapter, this example will not verify unless you change the password from *GW022231* to *GW022232*.

The Plug-in

```
function PIPHP_VerifyUserInDB($table, $salt1, $salt2,
   $handle, $pass)
{
   $result = PIPHP_GetUserFromDB($table, $handle);
   if ($result[0] == FALSE) return FALSE;
   elseif ($result[1][2] == md5($salt1 . $pass . $salt2))
      return TRUE;
   else return FALSE;
}
```

64 Sanitize String and MySQL Sanitize String

When accepting user input for redisplay, and particularly if it will be inserted into a database, it's important that you sanitize the input to remove any malicious attempts at hijacking your server, or otherwise injecting unwanted MySQL commands, HTML, or JavaScript. Figure 9-4 shows each of the plug-ins in this section being used to sanitize a string. The function `PIPHP_SanitizeString()` has removed the HTML `<b>` and `</b>` tags from the string and converted the & symbol to the `&amp;` HTML entity, while `PIPHP_MySQLSanitizeString()` has also added escape characters before the single quotation marks, so that they will be inserted into a field by MySQL rather than possibly being interpreted.

About the Plug-ins

These plug-ins take a string and sanitize it for reuse on your web site and/or in a MySQL database. They require this argument:

- `$string`   A string to be sanitized

Variables, Arrays, and Functions

`PIPHP_SanitizeString()`	The function `PIPHP_MySQLSanitizeString` calls the function `PIPHP_SanitizeString()` to prevent code duplication

How They Work

Let's start with the `PIPHP_SanitizeString()` function, which calls two PHP functions: `strip_tags()` and `htmlentities()`. The former removes all HTML tags from a string, while the latter converts all instances of characters such as < and > to `&lt;` and `&gt;`, & to `&amp;`, and so on.

Between them they will remove any attempts at inserting any HTML tags into your web site, whether they are simple tags such as `<b>` for bold or more dangerous `<script>` tags. They also see to it that no special characters are allowed by replacing them with HTML entities that will not perform an action, but only display in a browser as the characters they represent.

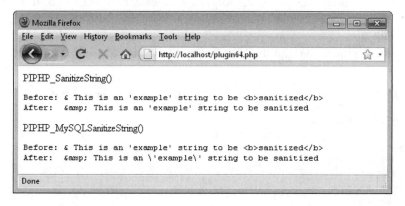

FIGURE 9-4   This pair of plug-ins will protect your web site from hacking attempts.

Calling the `PIPHP_MySQLSanitizeString()` function does the same as calling the `PIPHP_SanitizeString()` function, but in addition it deals with potential problems relating to MySQL.

First, it checks whether the *Magic Quotes* setting of PHP is enabled, which is a method of dealing with quotation marks supplied by the user. When Magic Quotes is on, all single- and double-quote characters, as well as backslashes and NULL characters are escaped automatically by preceding them with a backslash. However, the feature is now deprecated and should not be used as there are better ways of sanitizing data (such as using the two plug-ins presented in this section).

Therefore, if Magic Quotes is enabled, then the first thing this plug-in does is call the `stripslashes()` function to remove any that may have been added. Next it calls the `PIPHP_SanitizeString()` function, and finally it calls the `mysql_real_escape_string()` function, which renders a string totally harmless to MySQL injection attacks. These attacks occur when a malicious user enters a quotation mark in the hope that it will close a MySQL statement, enabling MySQL commands they add after the quote to be executed.

For example, the following MySQL command, resulting from a user having entered the handle `jjones`, looks quite safe:

```
SELECT * FROM Users WHERE handle='jjones' AND pass='secret';
```

But what if, when asked for their handle, a user were to input a value of `Admin'#` and it wasn't sanitized? Well, if this string were allowed through to MySQL, the complete command would become:

```
SELECT * FROM Users WHERE handle='Admin'#' AND pass='secret';
```

What has happened here is that the user closed the quotation mark and then supplied a # symbol, which is treated by MySQL as the start of a comment. Therefore everything from the # onwards (highlighted in the preceding code in italics) gets ignored and so users find themselves logged in as the user *Admin*. Obviously this is not good, to say the least.

However, a simple call to `mysql_real_escape_string()` replaces all such possible hacks with escaped versions of the characters, so that the string can only ever be used as data and never treated as a command to be executed. Combining all these security measures into these new functions ensures you never forget any when coding your web sites.

How to Use Them

To use either of these functions, simply call them up by passing a string to be sanitized, like this:

```
$string = "& This is an 'example' string to be <b>sanitized</b>";
echo "Using Sanitize String<xmp>";
echo "Before: " . $string . "\n";
echo "After:  " . PIPHP_SanitizeString($string);
echo "</xmp>";
$dbhost = 'localhost';
$dbname = 'piphp';
$dbuser = 'testing';
$dbpass = 'testing';
mysql_connect($dbhost, $dbuser, $dbpass) or die(mysql_error());
```

```
echo "Using MySQL Sanitize String<xmp>";
echo "Before: " . $string . "\n";
echo "After:  " . PIPHP_MySQLSanitizeString($string);
echo "</xmp>";
```

The <xmp> tag sets the typeface to a form that indicates example text. The PIPHP_
SanitizeString() function is quite straightforward, but there are two important things to
note about the PIPHP_MySQLSanitizeString() function. These are that the function will
generate an error if it is called when a connection to a database is not already open (which is
why the preceding example creates a database connection before calling it): and you must
make sure that PIPHP_SanitizeString() is also pasted into your program, or otherwise
included by it, because it is referenced.

The Plug-ins

```
function PIPHP_SanitizeString($string)
{
   $string = strip_tags($string);
   return htmlentities($string);
}

function PIPHP_MySQLSanitizeString($string)
{
   if (get_magic_quotes_gpc())
      $string = stripslashes($string);
   $string = PIPHP_SanitizeString($string);
   return mysql_real_escape_string($string);
}
```

PLUG-IN 65 Create Session

If you have a web site that a user can join, then you need a way to keep track of that person
as they navigate through the site. Not for reasons of spying on them or anything like that,
but purely in order to keep them logged in and to offer them all the benefits that membership
provides. Figure 9-5 shows this plug-in being used to create a session and read back one of
the session variables.

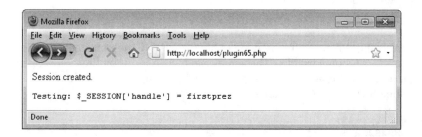

FIGURE 9-5   Creating a PHP session allows you to maintain a user's details across multiple pages.

About the Plug-in

This plug-in takes all the same details about a user we have previously been storing in a MySQL database and saves them in PHP session variables. It requires these arguments:

- `$handle`   A username
- `$pass`   A matching password
- `$name`   The user's real name
- `$email`   The user's e-mail address

Variables, Arrays, and Functions

`$_SESSION['handle']`	The user's handle stored in a session variable
`$_SESSION['pass']`	The user's password stored in a session variable
`$_SESSION['name']`	The user's name stored in a session variable
`$_SESSION['email']`	The user's e-mail address stored in a session variable
`$_SESSION['ipnum']`	The user's IP number stored in a session variable
`$_SESSION['agent']`	The user's web browser User Agent string stored in a session variable

How It Works

This is a plug-in that provides convenience more than anything else because it simply starts a new PHP session using the `session_start()` function and then assigns the values passed to the plug-in to the various session variables. If the session can't be started, then FALSE is returned; otherwise, TRUE.

One reason the call may fail is if any text has already been output by your program. This is because session details are often stored in cookies (unless the user has cookies disabled, in which case they are stored in the query string), and therefore they must be exchanged between the server and browser before any other data.

You should note how the user's IP address and the User Agent string supplied by their browser are also saved as session variables. You will see how they will be used later in plug-in 68, *Secure Session*.

Don't worry about this method possibly storing private details, such as a username and password, anywhere unsafe because it doesn't. PHP stores these details internally and they are never sent to the browser. Instead, an identifying token is all that is ever passed back and forth between the server and browser.

How to Use It

In order to use this plug-in, you already need to have available the four items of data about a user to store in the session variables. These may have been input by the user or retrieved from a MySQL database, but in the following example they are simply assigned to some variables and then the `PIPHP_CreateSession()` function is called:

```
$handle = "firstprez";
$pass   = "GW022232";
$name   = "George Washington";
$email  = "george@washington.com";
$result = PIPHP_CreateSession($handle, $pass, $name, $email);
```

Upon success, $result will have the value TRUE; otherwise, it will be FALSE. You can act on this value in the following manner, which displays the contents of one of the session variables to demonstrate that the call succeeded:

```
if (!$result) echo "Could not create session.";
else
{
    echo 'Session created.<br /><pre>';
    echo 'Testing: $_SESSION[\'handle\'] = ' .
        $_SESSION['handle'];
}
```

For correct results make sure that you only call this plug-in before you output any text, otherwise session creation and variable assignment may fail.

The Plug-in

```
function PIPHP_CreateSession($handle, $pass, $name, $email)
{
    if (!session_start()) return FALSE;

    $_SESSION['handle'] = $handle;
    $_SESSION['pass']   = $pass;
    $_SESSION['name']   = $name;
    $_SESSION['email']  = $email;
    $_SESSION['ipnum']  = getenv("REMOTE_ADDR");
    $_SESSION['agent']  = getenv("HTTP_USER_AGENT");

    return TRUE;
}
```

PLUG-IN 66 Open Session

Once you have used PIPHP_CreateSession() to store a user's details, any other pages (or even the same one if called up separately) can easily retrieve these values using this plug-in. Figure 9-6 shows data that has been saved in a session using the PHP program file *plugin65.php*, being fully recalled by calling up *plugin66.php*.

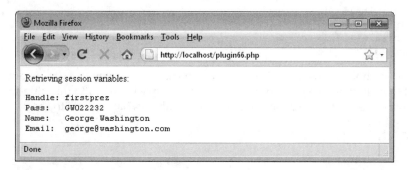

FIGURE 9-6 With this plug-in, a single function call will retrieve a range of user details, even across different web pages.

About the Plug-in

This plug-in opens a previously created PHP session and returns the session variables stored in it. It does not require any arguments.

Variables, Arrays, and Functions

$vars	Array containing the various session variables' values

How It Works

This plug-in first attempts to start a session using the session_start() function. If that fails for any reason, a single-element array with the value FALSE is returned. One reason it could fail is if a session is already open, which is why the @ symbol prefaces the function call; it is there to suppress any error messages.

If a session is successfully opened, a check is then made for one of the session variables that ought to be set, namely $_SESSION['handle']. If it's not set, an error has occurred and a single-element array with the value FALSE is returned.

Otherwise, everything seems to be in order so the array $vars is initialized and then the four main user session variables are inserted in to this array and a two-element array is returned, the first of which has the value TRUE, while the second contains the $vars array.

How to Use It

Using this plug-in is as easy as making a short function call, like this:

```
$result = PIPHP_OpenSession();
```

If $result[0] has the value FALSE, an error occurred; otherwise, $result[1] contains a sub-array that will itself contain the four main items of user details. You can use code such as the following to act on the value of $result[0] and retrieve the details:

```
if (!$result[0]) echo "Could not open session.";
else list($handle, $pass, $name, $email) = $result[1];
```

Here, use has been made of the list() function, which takes an array and assigns its elements to the variables passed to it, providing an excellent means of quickly retrieving the four values. It could be considered shorthand code for the following:

```
$handle = $result[1][0];
$pass   = $result[1][1];
$name   = $result[1][2];
$email  = $result[1][3];
```

Whichever method you use, you will now have retrieved four items of data about the user without them having to enter those details again; by placing a call to this plug-in on each page where these details may be needed, you will always have access to them.

The Plug-in

```
function PIPHP_OpenSession()
{
   if (!@session_start()) return array(FALSE);
   if (!isset($_SESSION['handle'])) return array(FALSE);
```

```
    $vars = array();
    $vars[] = $_SESSION['handle'];
    $vars[] = $_SESSION['pass'];
    $vars[] = $_SESSION['name'];
    $vars[] = $_SESSION['email'];
    return array(TRUE, $vars);
}
```

Close Session

When a user has finished with your web site, it's a good idea to provide them with a logout button or link with which they can close the current session in order to prevent another user on their PC from coming back to it. With this plug-in you can not only close the session, but all associated data is also destroyed, leaving no potential security risk behind. Figure 9-7 shows the result of first opening a session with `PIPHP_OpenSession()`, and then closing it again.

After closing it, you will not be able to open the session again since all its data was destroyed. Your only option is to create a new one.

About the Plug-in

This plug-in closes a previously created and/or opened PHP session and destroys any associated data. It does not require any arguments.

Variables, Arrays, and Functions

$_SESSION	The PHP main session array which is reinitialized to an empty array to delete its data

How It Works

This plug-in ensures that any data stored in the PHP $_SESSION array is destroyed by reinitializing the array, which it does by assigning it the value `array()`.

FIGURE 9-7   Closing a session will completely log a user out of your web site.

Next, a couple of tests are made. These check whether the value returned by session_ id() is not FALSE, in which case a session does exist (and that value will be the session ID), and whether a cookie exists with the name returned by session_name(). If either of these cases is TRUE, then it's necessary to destroy any session cookie that may exist on the user's computer. This is done by issuing a setcookie() call with the same details that will have been used to create it, but with an expiry date of 30 days in the past. Being a month ago, the browser will automatically delete the cookie as having expired already. Any time in the past will do. I chose a month just to be sure.

Finally, the session_destroy() function is called and the value returned by it is returned by the plug-in. The @ symbol prefacing the call is there to suppress any error messages that might occur, particularly if the call fails due to the session already having been destroyed, or the plug-in having been called with no session in existence.

How to Use It

To terminate a session, place a call to this plug-in before any text is output, like this:

```
$result = PIPHP_CloseSession();
```

The variable $result will have the value TRUE if the call succeeded, otherwise it will be FALSE. You generally don't need to worry if the call fails as it usually only happens if there is no session to close, which is the situation you wanted anyway.

The Plug-in

```
function PIPHP_CloseSession()
{
  $_SESSION = array();

  if (session_id() != "" ||
      isset($_COOKIE[session_name()]))
    setcookie(session_name(), '', time() - 2592000, '/');

  return @session_destroy();
}
```

PLUG-IN 68   Secure Session

If there's a way a hacker can break into your web site, you can bet they'll try. One trick they use is to hijack PHP sessions. This might be achieved in different ways, but the main security hole is when a hacker locates a site that passes the session ID in a GET URL tail.

Given this information, a hacker could start a session and then pass on the URL (including the session ID) in spam or other links. They could then go back and look for evidence of any of these links having being followed and, if the user hasn't logged out, they may be able to hijack the session and assume the user's identity.

But by using this simple plug-in, tricks of that nature are rendered completely useless. Figure 9-8 shows a session that is opened with PIPHP_OpenSession() and then tested for security with this plug-in.

FIGURE 9-8   This plug-in helps secure against hackers hijacking a user's session.

About the Plug-in

This plug-in checks whether a session appears to not be secure, and if not, it closes the session. It does not require any arguments.

Variables, Arrays, and Functions

$ipnum	String variable containing the IP number of the current user
$agent	String variable containing the browser User Agent string of the current user

How It Works

In plug-in 65, *Create Session*, I mentioned the session variables containing the IP number and browser User Agent string which are set up when a session is created using the PIPHP_CreateSession() plug-in. Well, this plug-in is where they come into use.

What it does is check the current browser's User Agent and IP number against those saved in the session variables. If either is different, the session is closed using PIPHP_CloseSession() and a value of FALSE is returned. This is done to ensure that only the user who was online and present when the session was created can continue to use it, neatly avoiding any attempts by hackers to either poison a new session or take over an existing one.

If the strings do match, it is assumed the user is the same person, and so TRUE is returned. Oh, and if there appears to be no session active (tested by seeing whether $_SESSION['ipnum'] has a value), then FALSE is returned.

How to Use It

To use the function, you would probably call it immediately after a call to PIPHP_OpenSession(), like this:

```
if (!PIPHP_SecureSession())
{
   // Login code goes here to log the
   // user back into a secure session
}
```

It may be extra work but it's worth implementing this feature for your users' protection.

The Plug-in

```
function PIPHP_SecureSession()
{
    $ipnum = getenv("REMOTE_ADDR");
    $agent = getenv("HTTP_USER_AGENT");

    if (isset($_SESSION['ipnum']))
    {
        if ($ipnum != $_SESSION['ipnum'] ||
            $agent != $_SESSION['agent'])
        {
            PIPHP_CloseSession();
            return FALSE;
        }
        else return TRUE;
    }
    else return FALSE;
}
```

PLUG-IN 69 Manage Cookie

Cookies are a great way to provide additional functionality to your users, and contrary to the impression that some news reports might give, they have other more beneficial functions besides tracking users for advertising purposes. For example, you can save a token representing a person's username and password in a cookie to keep them logged in to a site, something PHP sessions do unless cookies are disabled, in which case the query string is used for this.

Cookies are also great for associating variables directly with a user via the browser they use. You could use them, for example, to note that a user has already completed a questionnaire on your site and should not be asked again.

Figure 9-9 shows the cookie *Test* being given the value *3.1415927* by this plug-in. The cookie is sent to the browser but has not been returned by it because cookies are only transferred in the header exchange that takes place before the contents of a web page are transferred. After reloading the page, the cookie is passed back to the web server by the browser, and so the cookie returns the assigned value, as the figure inset shows.

FIGURE 9-9   This plug-in lets you set, read, and delete cookies in a user's browser.

About the Plug-in

This plug-in sets, reads, and deletes cookies. It requires the following arguments:

- **$action**   The action to take: set, read, or delete
- **$cookie**   The name to use for the cookie
- **$value**   The value to give the cookie
- **$expire**   The number of seconds after which the cookie will expire
- **$path**   The path to the cookie on the server

Variables, Arrays, and Functions

- None

How It Works

This plug-in comprises three parts, separated by the case qualifiers of a switch statement, based on the value of $action after converting it to lowercase.

If the value is set, then the number of seconds passed in $expire is added to the value returned by time() to create a timestamp $expire seconds into the future. Or, if $expire is NULL, it is left alone. When this value is passed to the setcookie() function, the expiry date of that cookie will either be $expire seconds in the future, or if $expire is NULL, the cookie will expire when the browser is closed.

Next, the setcookie() call is made, passing the name of the cookie in $cookie, the value to assign to it in $value, the value in $expire, and the path to the server in $path. The latter defines the scope over which a cookie is valid. For example, if $path has the value /news/, then only that folder (and its subfolders) can access the cookie. But if it is /, then the cookie can be accessed by all folders on that web domain.

If $action has the value read, then, using the function isset(), a test is made to see whether a cookie of the name stored in $cookie exists. If so, that value is returned, otherwise FALSE is returned.

If $action contains the word delete, then, using isset(), if the cookie with the name in $cookie is found to exist, the cookie is resent to the browser using its current name and an expiry date of a month in the past, as calculated by subtracting 30 days' worth of seconds from the value returned by a call to time(). This has the effect of making the cookie instantly expire.

If $action contains none of the preceding words, then FALSE is returned.

How to Use It

To set a browser cookie, you could use code such as this:

```
$cookie = 'Test';
$val    = '3.1415927';
$exp    = 300;
$path   = '/';
$result = PIPHP_ManageCookie('set', $cookie, $val, $exp, $path);
```

If $result has a value of TRUE, then the cookie was successfully set. To then read back the value of a cookie (which would have to occur the subsequent time the page loads), you would then use code like this:

```
$result = PIPHP_ManageCookie('read', $cookie, NULL, NULL, NULL);
```

Upon success, $result will contain the contents of the cookie; otherwise, it will have the value FALSE.

To delete the cookie, issue the following command:

```
$result = PIPHP_ManageCookie('delete', $cookie, NULL, NULL, NULL);
```

Successful deletion will give $result a value of TRUE, otherwise it will be FALSE. Possible reasons for the call failing are if the cookie is already deleted or it doesn't exist.

The Plug-in

```
function PIPHP_ManageCookie($action, $cookie, $value, $expire,
    $path)
{
    switch(strtolower($action))
    {
        case 'set':
            if ($expire) $expire += time();
            return setcookie($cookie, $value, $expire, $path);

        case 'read':
            if (isset($_COOKIE[$cookie]))
                return $_COOKIE[$cookie];
            else return FALSE;

        case 'delete':
            if (isset($_COOKIE[$cookie]))
                return setcookie($cookie, NULL,
                    time() - 60 * 60 * 24 * 30, NULL);
            else return FALSE;
    }

    return FALSE;
}
```

PLUG-IN 70 Block User by Cookie

If you've ever done any chat-related programming, you'll have come across *trolls*: downright nasty individuals who you don't want on your site. You may even have banned them via their IP address. If you have, you may also have encountered the problem of these individuals restarting their web connections to obtain new IP addresses with which to harass you and your users. You will also possibly have noticed that some "bad" users share their IP address with "good" ones, generally because they work in the same building and share a DSL or similar Internet connection. So blocking a "bad" user by IP would also block "good" ones.

But there is a way you can ban unwanted users more permanently and precisely, and that's to leave a cookie on their computer, as this plug-in does. For example, Figure 9-10 shows

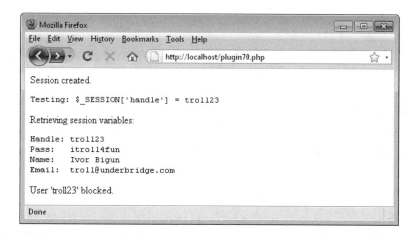

FIGURE 9-10   Some users can be pests, but this plug-in can help you block them.

a session being opened with the PIPHP_OpenSession() plug-in, and then this plug-in, PIPHP_BlockUserByCookie(), being called to send a blocking cookie to the user's browser.

About the Plug-in

This plug-in sets a cookie in a user's browser with which you can tell whether or not they have been blocked from using your site. It requires the following arguments:

- **$action**   The action to take
- **$handle**   The handle of the user to block
- **$expire**   The number of seconds after which the cookie will expire

Variables, Arrays, and Functions

PIPHP_ManageCookie()	The plug-in for setting, reading, and deleting cookies

How It Works

This function checks the value of the argument $action after converting it to lowercase. If it is block, then a special cookie is saved on the user's web browser. Because we don't want to alert the user to the fact that they have a blocking cookie, I chose to call it simply *user*. To make it even more innocuous, I give it the value of their handle (or username) so that, at a brief rummage through their cookies, most users will assume this is a simple username cookie for your web site. The cookie is set to expire after $expire seconds, so you can choose how long to lock a user out for.

If $action doesn't have the value block, then the value of the cookie named *user* is looked up. If it has a value, then that is returned; otherwise, FALSE is returned. Figure 9-11 shows the cookie *user* with the value *troll23* as sent to a Firefox browser.

Note how the cookie's details such as the Host, Path, and Expires fields are all available for the user to look up, hence the deviousness. You can call up this window on Firefox versions prior to 3.5 using the Tools menu followed by Options | Privacy | Show Cookies.

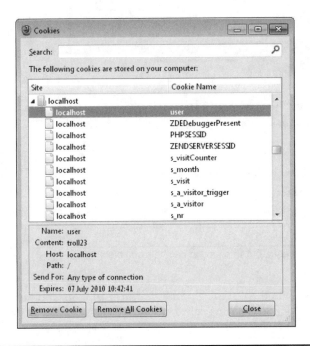

FIGURE **9-11**   The cookie "user" with the value "troll23" as sent to a Firefox browser

On Firefox 3.5 and later, you need to select Tools | Page Info | Security | View Cookies. Other major browsers also allow you to view their cookies.

How to Use It
The beauty of this plug-in (as long as the user has cookies enabled, which most do) is that it doesn't matter what handle (or username) you ban someone under, because the cookie will still work. So even if they manage to sign up for another account, a quick call of this plug-in will still tell you whether the person has already been blocked. What's more, it will reveal to you the handle of the original account which got them blocked in the first place. The only downside is that all users on the same computer account using the same web browser will be denied access.

To use the plug-in, you will likely already have a PHP session running and will pass a few arguments to the plug-in taken from the session variables. So here are some lines of example code to set up a session with which the plug-in can be tested:

```
$handle = "troll23";
$pass   = "itroll4fun";
$name   = "Ivor Bigun";
$email  = "troll@underbridge.com";
$result = PIPHP_CreateSession($handle, $pass, $name, $email);
```

If you run this code and there are no errors, you should now have a session created with the various values assigned to session variables, so you can now simulate being a user to be blocked like this:

```
$result = PIPHP_BlockUserByCookie('block', $handle, 60*60*24*365);
```

This line of code will set the block cookie on the computer belonging to the owner of $handle, which, in this case, will only expire after one year. If you now use the following line of code in a new program (or after reloading the same one) to ensure the cookie has been passed back from the user's web browser, you will see that the user has been blocked:

```
$result = PIPHP_BlockUserByCookie(NULL, $handle, NULL);
```

By passing a value of NULL instead of block as the first parameter, this tells the plug-in to return either the value of the block cookie (which will be the user's original handle), or the value FALSE if the user has not been blocked. Thus, if $result is not FALSE, then the user has been blocked. You can therefore use the value of $result like this:

```
if ($result)
{
    // User is blocked so place code here
    // to provide limited or zero functionality
}
else
{
    // User is not blocked so place code here
    // to provide full functionality
}
```

Rather than letting a user know they are blocked, I have found it a good idea *not* to tell them, as they will then try everything in their power to circumvent the block. Instead I tend to resort to tactics such as blocking a user for an hour or a day and then unblocking and re-blocking them randomly. And, in place of telling them about this, I will do things such as continuing to display their own posts to the screen but not to any other user, so they will assume they are simply being ignored.

They will never be able to work out exactly what is going on. Sometimes their trolling will work; other times it won't. Eventually, in most cases the user will drift away from your site and find another one to bother. Sneaky? Yes. Effective? Also yes. But now you have the means to deal with unwanted users, I leave it up to you to devise your own methods of blocking or banning them.

By the way, when using this plug-in, make sure you have also copied PIPHP_ManageCookie() into your program, or otherwise included it, as it is called by the code.

The Plug-in

```
function PIPHP_BlockUserByCookie($action, $handle, $expire)
{
    if (strtolower($action) == 'block')
    {
        if ($_SESSION['handle'] != $handle) return FALSE;
        else return PIPHP_manageCookie('set', 'user', $handle,
            $expire, '/');
    }

    return PIPHP_manageCookie('read', 'user', NULL, NULL, NULL);
}
```

CHAPTER 10

APIs, RSS, and XML

O ne of the most interesting recent developments on the Web is the trend of providing Application Programming Interfaces (APIs) to web sites, with which you can integrate content from other sites into your own. Generally such APIs accept standard POST or GET requests as might be sent from an HTML form or hyperlink, and then return data in the form of XML (Extensible Markup Language), JSON (JavaScript Object Notation), or other easy-to-process formats.

For example, both Google and Yahoo! provide a range of APIs for many of their web properties, such as Google Book Search and Charts or Yahoo! Search, Answers, and Stocks. There are plug-ins for all of these in this chapter. There are also plug-ins for handling Wikipedia entries, Flickr photo streams, and currency conversion from the European Central Bank.

However, although these plug-ins provide the functionality to process the information supplied by those companies, it's your responsibility to ensure you follow each service's rules and guidelines and have sufficient permission to reuse or republish data extracted from their sites.

PLUG-IN 71 Create Google Chart

Google Charts is a great API that not too many people seem to know about yet. With it you can create a huge variety of charts to display on your web site, incorporate in your documents, and so on. However, it is quite complex and requires using a number of different command strings, which is where this plug-in comes in.

Using the plug-in, you only have to supply the data to be charted and (optionally) various widths, heights, colors, and other details. The plug-in then interfaces with Google Charts and returns a ready-made image (as a GD object) containing the chart. You can then display the image straightaway or save it to disk for future use. Figure 10-1 shows a 3D pie chart created from seven items of data, representing types of cheese.

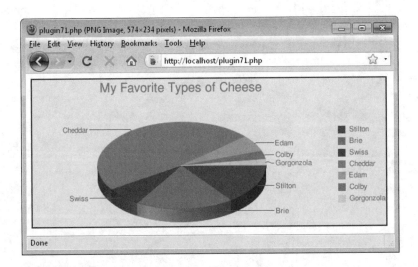

Figure 10-1   Leverage the power of the Google Charts API with this plug-in.

About the Plug-in

This plug-in returns a GD image containing a chart created using the supplied data. Upon failure, it returns FALSE. It requires the following arguments, all of which (except for $width, $height, and $data) may be passed as NULL or the empty string to use default values:

- **$title**   The chart's title
- **$tcolor**   The title's color
- **$tsize**   The title's font size
- **$type**   The chart type to create out of:
   line   A line chart
   vbar   A vertical bar chart
   hbar   A horizontal bar chart
   gometer   A Google-O-Meter chart
   pie   A pie chart (the default)
   pie3d   A 3D pie chart
   venn   A venn chart
   radar   A radar chart
- **$bwidth**   Bar width (only applies for bar charts)
- **$labels**   The data labels, separated by | symbols
- **$legends**   The data legends, separated by | symbols
- **$colors**   The data colors, separated by commas
- **$bgfill**   The background fill color (six hex digits)
- **$border**   The border width in pixels
- **$bcolor**   The border color (six hex digits)
- **$width**   The chart width in pixels
- **$height**   The chart height in pixels
- **$data**   The chart data, separated by commas

Variables, Arrays, and Functions

$types	Associative array containing the chart type names and Google Chart command equivalents
$tail	String containing the command tail to add to the Google Charts URL
$url	String containing the Google charts URL
$image	GD image containing the returned Google chart
$w	The width of $image in pixels
$h	The height of $image in pixels
$image2	GD image containing the final image to return after adding any border
$clr	GD color object created from the $bcolor border color

How It Works

This plug-in starts by populating the $types associative array so that the chart types passed in the argument $type can be quickly converted to the types Google Charts requires. For example, a 3D pie chart is represented by a $type of pie3d, which must be translated to p3 for Google. To facilitate this, the array element $types['pie3d'] has been given the value p3 so that simply looking up the value of $types[$type] will return p3 when $type is pie3d. All the other types will also be similarly translated.

So next the value of $types[$type] is tested with the isset() function to see whether it has a value. If not, then an unknown value was passed in $type, and $type is then set to pie, the default value.

Next, $tail is built up using the various parameters passed to the plug-in such as the title, type, width, height, and so on. The contents of $tail will be appended to the base API URL for Google Charts to make a query string, which is sent as a GET request to the server.

After the main values have been placed in $tail, if they were passed in the function call, the next five if statements add further values. For example, in the fourth of these statements, if $colors is NULL or the empty string, then no color information will be appended to $tail. Otherwise, the Google Charts command &chco= will be appended to $tail, followed by the colors supplied.

Next, the tail is appended to the Google Charts API URL and the result is placed in $url, which is then passed to the imagecreatefrompng() function to call up the API which (on success) returns a chart as a PNG image. This image is then placed in the GD image object $image.

Now that an image has been created, the width and height of it are placed in the variables $w and $h so that a new image can be created by passing these values to imagecreatetruecolor(). If $border has a value, it will define the width of a border to be added to the image, and the new image is made slightly larger than the original to allow for the borders.

The new image is then stored in $image2, and a GD color object is created in $clr from the color in $bcolor. This color is then passed to the imagefilledrectangle() function to fill in the new image with the specified color.

Finally, the original image is copied to the exact center of the new image so that, if the new image is larger, the image will now be a bordered version of the original. If no border width was specified, then the copy will simply overwrite the fill color and the new image will be identical to the original.

Now that it is no-longer required, the original image object is removed from memory using the imagedestroy() function, returning the memory back to the system, and the new image is then returned by the plug-in.

TIP *The Google Charts API actually includes many more features than there is room to include in this plug-in. If you visit http://code.google.com/apis/chart/, you will see more options you may wish to add to the plug-in for your own use. You should be able to slot them in without too much difficulty.*

How to Use It

To obtain a Google Chart using this plug-in, you should prepare all the parameters you want in it and then pass them to the plug-in, like this:

```
$title    = 'My Favorite Types of Cheese';
$tcolor   = 'FF0000';
$tsize    = '20';
$type     = 'pie3d';
$width    = '570';
$height   = '230';
$bwidth   = NULL;
$labels   = 'Stilton|Brie|Swiss|Cheddar|Edam|Colby|Gorgonzola';
$legends = $labels;
$colors   =
    'BD0000,DE6B00,284B89,008951,9D9D9D,A5AB4B,8C70A4,FFD200';
$bgfill   = 'EEEEFF';
$border   = '2';
$bcolor   = '444444';
$data     = '14.9,18.7,7.1,47.3,6.0,3.1,2.1';
$result   = PIPHP_CreateGoogleChart($title, $tcolor, $tsize,
    $type, $bwidth, $labels, $legends, $colors, $bgfill,
    $border, $bcolor, $width, $height, $data);
```

The preceding lines of code will re-create the chart shown in Figure 10-1, which is returned in $result as a GD image object, and which you can then output to a browser by first sending the correct PNG image header, followed by the image data, like this:

```
header('Content-type: image/png');
imagepng($result);
```

According to the Google Charts Usage Policy at *http://code.google.com/apis/chart/*: "There's no limit to the number of calls per day you can make to the Google Chart API. However, we reserve the right to block any use that we regard as abusive. If you think your service will make more than 250,000 API calls per day, please let us know." Therefore, you may prefer to employ caching techniques by saving the chart to disk (if it hasn't already been saved), and then serving it from there. You can save the image using one of these commands where path/filename.ext is the filename, including path and extension:

```
imagepng($result,   'path/filename.png');
imagegif($result,   'path/filename.gif');
imagejpeg($result,  'path/filename.jpg');
```

Just choose the type of file you wish to save the image as, and select one of these three commands accordingly.

On the other hand, if your usage will not be high enough to get your program blocked, you may wish to save on your own bandwidth and use Google's by uncommenting the return $url; command, about two-thirds of the way into the plug-in. You will now only need code such as the following to display the chart directly from Google's servers:

```
echo "<img src='$result' />";
```

However, the border options will be ignored and you'll therefore have to use CSS (Cascading Style Sheets) if you need borders.

The Plug-in

```php
function PIPHP_CreateGoogleChart($title, $tcolor, $tsize,
    $type, $bwidth, $labels, $legends, $colors, $bgfill,
    $border, $bcolor, $width, $height, $data)
{
    $types = array('line'    => 'lc',
                   'vbar'    => 'bvg',
                   'hbar'    => 'bhg',
                   'gometer' => 'gom',
                   'pie'     => 'p',
                   'pie3d'   => 'p3',
                   'venn'    => 'v',
                   'radar'   => 'r');

    if (!isset($types[$type])) $type = 'pie';

    $tail  = "chtt=" . urlencode($title);
    $tail .= "&cht=$types[$type]";
    $tail .= "&chs=$width" . "x" . "$height";
    $tail .= "&chbh=$bwidth";
    $tail .= "&chxt=x,y";
    $tail .= "&chd=t:$data";

    if ($tcolor)
        if ($tsize)  $tail .= "&chts=$tcolor,$tsize";
    if ($labels)     $tail .= "&chl=$labels";
    if ($legends)    $tail .= "&chdl=$legends";
    if ($colors)     $tail .= "&chco=$colors";
    if ($bgfill)     $tail .= "&chf=bg,s,$bgfill";

    $url = "http://chart.apis.google.com/chart?$tail";

    // Uncomment the line below to return a URL to
    // the chart image instead of the image itself
    // return $url;

    $image = imagecreatefrompng($url);

    $w = imagesx($image);
    $h = imagesy($image);
    $image2 = imagecreatetruecolor($w + $border * 2,
        $h + $border * 2);
    $clr = imagecolorallocate($image,
        hexdec(substr($bcolor, 0, 2)),
        hexdec(substr($bcolor, 2, 2)),
        hexdec(substr($bcolor, 4, 2)));
    imagefilledrectangle($image2, 0, 0, $w + $border * 2,
        $h + $border * 2, $clr);
    imagecopy($image2, $image, $border, $border, 0, 0, $w, $h);
    imagedestroy($image);
    return $image2;
}
```

Curl Get Contents

Some web sites don't like to be accessed by anything other than a web browser, which can make it difficult to fetch data from them with a PHP program using a function such as file_get_contents(). Such sites generally block your program by checking for a User Agent string, which is something all browsers send to web sites they visit and which can vary widely. They look something like this:

```
Mozilla/5.0 (Windows; U; Windows NT 6.1; en-GB; rv:1.9.1)
Gecko/20090624 Firefox/3.5 (.NET CLR 3.5.30729)
```

Therefore, to access these sites it is necessary to simulate being a browser, which, as shown in Figure 10-2, this plug-in will do for you.

About the Plug-in

This plug-in is intended to replace the PHP file_get_contents() function when used to fetch a web page. It accepts the URL of a page and a browser User Agent to emulate, and on success it returns the contents of the page at the given URL. On failure, it returns FALSE. It requires these arguments:

- **$url**   The URL to fetch
- **$agent**   The User Agent string of a browser

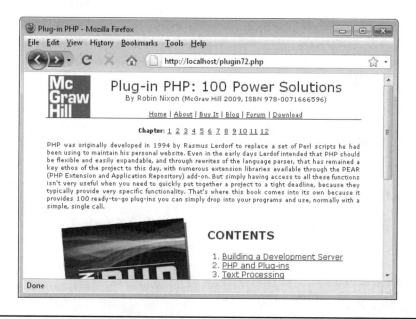

Figure 10-2   This plug-in is used to fetch and display the *www.pluginphp.com* home page.

Variables, Arrays, and Functions

$ch	CURL handle to an opened curl_init() session
$result	The returned result from the curl_exec() call

How It Works

This plug-in uses the Mod CURL (Client URL) library extension to PHP. If it fails, then you need to read your server and/or PHP installation instructions or consult your server administrator about enabling Mod CURL. What it does is open a session with curl_init(), passing a handle for the session to $ch. Such a session can perform a wide range of URL related tasks.

But first the plug-in uses curl_setopt() to set up the various options required prior to making the curl_exec() call. These include setting CURLOPT_URL to the value of $url and CURLOPT_USERAGENT to the value of $agent. Additionally, a number of other options are set to sensible values.

The curl_exec() function is then called, with the result of the call being placed in $result. The session is then closed with a call to curl_close(), and the value in $result is returned.

How to Use It

Using this plug-in is as easy as replacing calls to file_get_contents() with PIPHP_CurlGetContents(). As long as you have also passed a sensible-looking User Agent string, the plug-in will then be able to return some pages that could not be retrieved using the former function call. For example, you can load in and display the contents of a web page like this:

```
$agent = 'Mozilla/5.0 (Windows; U; Windows NT 6.1; en-GB; ' .
         'rv:1.9.1) Gecko/20090624 Firefox/3.5 (.NET CLR ' .
         '3.5.30729)';
$url   = 'http://pluginphp.com';
echo PIPHP_CurlGetContents($url, $agent);
```

This will display the main page of the *www.pluginphp.com* web site, which should look like Figure 10-2. There's a comprehensive explanation (and collection) of User Agent strings at *www.useragentstring.com*.

Caution *Sometimes the reason a web site only allows a browser access to a web page is because other programs are not permitted to access it. So please check how you are allowed to access information from such a web site, and what you are allowed to do with it, before using this plug-in.*

The Plug-in

```
function PIPHP_CurlGetContents($url, $agent)
{
    $ch = curl_init();
    curl_setopt($ch, CURLOPT_URL,        $url);
    curl_setopt($ch, CURLOPT_USERAGENT,  $agent);
    curl_setopt($ch, CURLOPT_HEADER,     0);
```

```
curl_setopt($ch, CURLOPT_ENCODING,       "gzip");
curl_setopt($ch, CURLOPT_RETURNTRANSFER, 1);
curl_setopt($ch, CURLOPT_FOLLOWLOCATION, 1);
curl_setopt($ch, CURLOPT_FAILONERROR,    1);
curl_setopt($ch, CURLOPT_CONNECTTIMEOUT, 8);
curl_setopt($ch, CURLOPT_TIMEOUT,        8);
$result = curl_exec($ch);
curl_close($ch);
return $result;
}
```

PLUG-IN 73 | Fetch Wiki Page

Wikipedia is an excellent resource with several million articles. Even if you take into account that some of the information may not always be correct due to any user being able to edit a page, on the whole, most of the web site is factual and it contains a summary of almost the whole depth and breadth of human knowledge.

What's even better is that Wikipedia is published under the GNU Free Documentation License—see *www.gnu.org/copyleft/fdl.html*. Essentially this means that you can use any text from it as long you give full attribution of the source, and also offer the text (with any amendments) under the same license. As a consequence, I now have the entire Wikipedia database stored in my iPhone so that I can instantly look up any entry, even when mobile connectivity is limited. By using data compression techniques, and keeping only the main article text, it takes up just 2GB of space.

The GFDL license used also means you can use programs such as this plug-in to reformat and reuse articles from Wikipedia, as shown in Figure 10-3, in which just the text has been extracted from its article on PHP.

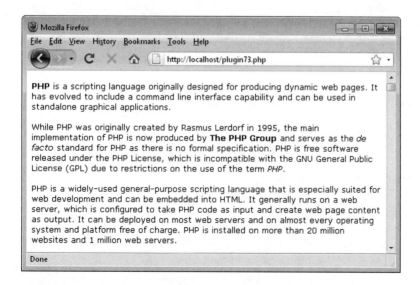

FIGURE 10-3   Using this plug-in, you can extract just the text from a Wikipedia entry.

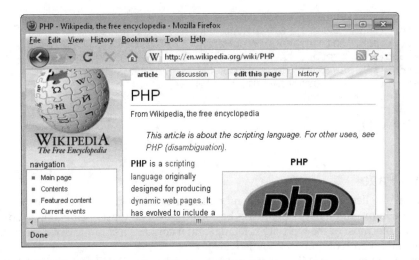

FIGURE 10-4   The original article about PHP on the Wikipedia web site

If you also take a look at Figure 10-4, you'll see the original article at Wikipedia and, comparing the two, you'll notice that the plug-in has completely ignored all the formatting, graphics, tables, and other extras, leaving behind just the text of the article.

Using it you could create your own reduced size local copy of Wikipedia, or perhaps use it to add hyperlinks to words or terms you may wish to explain to your readers. I have used this code to add short encyclopedia entries to searches returned by a customized Google search engine I wrote.

Combined with other plug-ins from this book, you could reformat articles into RSS feeds, translate them into "friendly" text, or, well, once you have access to the Wikipedia text, it's really only up to your imagination what you choose to do with it.

About the Plug-in

This plug-in takes the title of a Wikipedia entry and returns just the text of the article, or on failure it returns FALSE. It requires this argument:

- **$entry**   A Wikipedia article title

Variables, Arrays, and Functions

$agent	String containing a browser User Agent string
$url	String containing the URL of Wikipedia's XML export API
$page	String containing the result of fetching the Wikipedia entry
$xml	SimpleXML object created from $page
$title	String containing the article title as returned by Wikipedia

$text	String containing the article text
$sections	Array of four section headings at which to truncate the text
$section	String containing each element of $sections in turn
$ptr	Integer offset into $text indicating start of $section
$data	Array of search and replace strings for converting raw Wikipedia data
$j	Integer loop counter for processing search and replace actions
$url	String containing the URL of the original Wikipedia article

How It Works

Wikipedia has kindly created an API with which you can export selected articles from their database. You can access it at:

```
http://en.wikipedia.org/wiki/Special:Export
```

Unfortunately, they have set this API to deny access to programs that do not present it with a browser User Agent string. Luckily, the previous plug-in provides just that functionality, so using it, along with this plug-in, it's possible to export any Wikipedia page as XML, which can then be transformed into just the raw text.

This is done by setting up a browser User Agent string and then calling the Export API using `PIPHP_CurlGetContents()`, passing the Export API URL, along with the article title and the browser agent. Before making the call, though, $entry is passed though the `rawurlencode()` function to convert non URL-compatible characters into acceptable equivalents, such as spaces into %20 codes.

The XML page returned from this call is then parsed into an XML object using the `simplexml_load_string()` function, the result being placed in $xml.

Next, the only two items of information that are required, the article title and its text, are extracted from `$xml->page->title` and `$xml->page->text`, into $title and $text.

Notice that all of this occurs inside a `while` loop. This is because by far the majority of Wikipedia articles are redirects from misspellings or different capitalizations. What the loop does is look for the string #REDIRECT in a response and, if one is discovered, the loop goes around again using the redirected article title, which is placed in $entry by using `preg_match()` to extract it from between a pair of double square parentheses. The loop can handle multiple redirects, which are not as infrequent as you might think with the age of Wikipedia, and the amount of times many articles have been moved by now.

So, with the raw Wikipedia text now loaded into $text, the next section truncates the string at whichever of five headings out of *References, See Also, External Links, Notes*, or *Further Reading* (if any) appears first, because those entries are not part of the main article and are to be ignored. This is done by using a `foreach` loop to iterate through the headings, which are enclosed by pairs of = symbols, Wikipedia's markup to indicate an <h2> heading. Because some Wikipedia authors use spaces inside the ==, both cases (with and without spaces) are tested. Each heading in turn is searched for using the `stripos()` function and, if a heading is found in $text, $ptr will point to its start so that $text is then truncated to end at that position.

Now that `$text` has the raw article we want, it's time to convert Wikipedia's special markup into the text and basic HTML this plug-in supports. Before writing this plug-in, I performed hours of searching to try and find other code already doing the job. And while there were a few examples, they were all quite long-winded and seemed overly complicated, which is why I chose to write my own code.

In the end, it turned out that less than a couple of dozen rules were enough to make sense of most of Wikipedia's markup. For example, you've already seen how `==Heading==` stands for `<h2>Heading</h2>`. Similarly, `===Subheading===` stands for `<h3>Subheading</h3>`, and so on. While `'''word'''` (three single quotes on either side of some text) stands for `<i>word</i>` and `''word''` (two single quotes on either side of some text) stands for `<b>word</b>`. Ordered and unordered lists are also indicated by starting a new line with a # or a * symbol for each item, so for simplicity, I chose to convert both into the HTML bullet entity, `&#x25cf;`, and treat nested lists as if they are on the same level.

Tables begin by starting a newline with a { symbol, so the code ignores everything from `\n{` up to a closing } symbol, and double newlines, `\n\n`, are converted into `<p>` tags.

There's also some more complicated markup such as `[[Article]]`, meaning "Place a hyperlink here to Wikipedia's article entitled *Article*," or `[[Article|Look at this]]`, which means "Add a hyperlink to Wikipedia's article entitled *Article* here, but display the hyperlink text *Look at this*." A few more variations on a theme exist here, plus there are several types of markup I chose to ignore such as `[[Image...]]`, `[[File...]]`, and `[[Category...]]`, which contain material supplemental to the main text, and `[http...]` which contains hyperlinks I didn't want to use.

What's more, there are also sections such as `<gallery>` and `<ref>`, which I decided should also be ignored, and some major sections appearing within the `{{` and `}}` pairs of symbols, which are often nested with sub, and sub-sub sections. Again, all of these provide more rich content to a standard Wikipedia article, but are not necessary when we simply want the main text.

Therefore, the `$data` array contains a sequence of regular expressions to be searched for, accompanied by strings with which to replace the matches. Using a `for` loop, the array is iterated through a pair at a time, passing each pair of strings to the `preg_replace()` function. If you want to learn more about the regular expressions used, there's a lot of information at *http://en.wikipedia.org/wiki/Regular_expression*.

Anyway, having massaged the text into almost plain text (with the exception of `<h1>` through `<h7>` headings, and the `<p>`, `<br>`, `<b>`, and `<i>` tags), the `strip_tags()` function is called to remove any other tags (except those just mentioned) that remain.

Finally, before returning the article text, a notice and hyperlink are appended to it showing the original Wikipedia article from which the text was derived.

In all, I think you'll find that these rules handle the vast majority of Wikipedia pages very well, although you will encounter the odd page that doesn't come out quite right. In such cases, you should be able to spot the markup responsible and add a translation for it into the `$data` array.

If you use this plug-in on a production server, you'll also need to comply with Wikipedia's licensing requirements by adding a link to the GNU Free Documentation License, and indicating that your version of the article is also released under this license. For details, please see *http://en.wikipedia.org/wiki/Wikipedia_Copyright*.

How to Use It

To use this plug-in, just pass it a Wikipedia article title and you can display the result returned, like this:

```
$result = PIPHP_FetchWikiPage('Climate Change');
if (!$result) echo "Could not fetch article.";
else echo $result;
```

Incidentally, I chose this article because it is one of those that returns the previously mentioned #REDIRECT string. In this case, Climate Change is redirected to Climate change (with a lowercase c in the second word), and serves to show that the code correctly handles redirects.

Because Wikipedia makes use of the UTF-8 character set to enable all the different languages it supports, you may also need to ensure you include the following HTML <meta> tag in the <head> section of your HTML output, to ensure that all characters display correctly:

```
<meta http-equiv="Content-Type" content="text/html; charset=utf-8"/>
```

To save on thrashing Wikipedia's servers and to also cut down on the programming power required on your own, you should definitely consider saving the result from each call to this plug-in, either as a text file or, preferably, in a MySQL database, and then serve up the cached copy whenever future requests are made for the same article.

If you wish to compile your own database of Wikipedia articles using this plug-in, you can find all the various indexes at *http://en.wikipedia.org/wiki/Portal:Contents*.

Remember, when you use this plug-in you must also copy and paste the PIPHP_CurlGetContents() plug-in into your program, or otherwise include it, due to it being called by this plug-in.

The Plug-in

```
function PIPHP_FetchWikiPage($entry)
{
    $agent = 'Mozilla/5.0 (Windows; U; Windows NT 6.1; en-GB; ' .
             'rv:1.9.1) Gecko/20090624 Firefox/3.5 (.NET CLR ' .
             '3.5.30729)';
    $text = '';

    while ($text == '' || substr($text, 0, 9) == '#REDIRECT')
    {
        $entry = rawurlencode($entry);
        $url   = "http://en.wikipedia.org/wiki/Special:Export/$entry";
        $page  = PIPHP_CurlGetContents($url, $agent);
        $xml   = simplexml_load_string($page);
        $title = $xml->page->title;
        $text  = $xml->page->revision->text;
```

```php
        if (substr($text, 0, 9) == '#REDIRECT')
        {
            preg_match('/\[\[(.+)\]\]/', $text, $matches);
            $entry = $matches[1];
        }
    }

    $sections = array('References', 'See also', 'External links',
        'Notes', 'Further reading');

    foreach($sections as $section)
    {
        $ptr = stripos($text, "==$section==");
        if ($ptr) $text = substr($text, 0, $ptr);
        $ptr = stripos($text, "== $section ==");
        if ($ptr) $text = substr($text, 0, $ptr);
    }

    $data = array('\[{2}Imag(\[{2})*.*(\]{2})*\]{2}', '',
                  '\[{2}File(\[{2})*.*(\]{2})*\]{2}', '',
                  '\[{2}Cate(\[{2})*.*(\]{2})*\]{2}', '',
                  '\{{2}([^\{\}]+|(?R))*\}{2}',          '',
                  '\'{3}(.*?)\'{3}',             '<b>$1</b>',
                  '\'{2}(.*?)\'{2}',             '<i>$1</i>',
                  '\[{2}[^\|\]]+\|(([^\]]*)\]{2}', '$1',
                  '\[{2}(.*?)\]{2}',                '$1',
                  '\[(http[^\]]+)\]',               ' ',
                  '\n(\*|#)+',    '<br /> &#x25cf; ',
                  '\n:.*?\n',                        '',
                  '\n\{[^\}]+\}',                    '',
                  '\n={7}([^=]+)={7}',       '<h7>$1</h7>',
                  '\n={6}([^=]+)={6}',       '<h6>$1</h6>',
                  '\n={5}([^=]+)={5}',       '<h5>$1</h5>',
                  '\n={4}([^=]+)={4}',       '<h4>$1</h4>',
                  '\n={3}([^=]+)={3}',       '<h3>$1</h3>',
                  '\n={2}([^=]+)={2}',       '<h2>$1</h2>',
                  '\n={1}([^=]+)={1}',       '<h1>$1</h1>',
                  '\n{2}',                          '<p>',
                  '<gallery>([^<]+?)<\/gallery>',    '',
                  '<ref>([^<]+?)<\/ref>',            '',
                  '<ref [^>]+>',                     '');

    for ($j = 0 ; $j < count($data) ; $j += 2)
        $text = preg_replace("/$data[$j]/", $data[$j+1], $text);

    $text  = strip_tags($text, '<h1><h2><h3><h4><h5><h6><h7>' .
                            '<p><br><b><i>');
    $url   = "http://en.wikipedia.org/wiki/$title";
    $text .= "<p>Source: <a href='$url'>Wikipedia ($title)</a>";
    return trim($text);
}
```

Fetch Flickr Stream

If you enjoy looking at photographs, chances are you have used the Flickr photo sharing service and may also have discovered a few photographers whose Flickr streams you like to follow. Well, now you can offer the same facility to your users with this plug-in.

Using it you can look up any public Flickr stream and return the (up to) 20 most recent photographs from it. Figure 10-5 shows the result of pointing the plug-in at a new account I created at Flickr. In this instance, I chose to display links to the photos, but you can also embed them in your web pages if you wish.

About the Plug-in

This plug-in takes the name of a public Flickr account and returns the most recent photos. Upon success, it returns a two-element array, the first of which is the number of photos returned, and the second is an array containing URLs for each photo. On failure, it returns a single-element array with the value FALSE. It requires this argument:

- **$account** A Flickr account name such as *xxxxxxxx@Nxx* (where the *x* symbols represent digits), or the more friendly Flickr usernames such as mine, which is *robinfnixon*

Variables, Arrays, and Functions

`$url`	String containing the Flickr photo stream base URL
`$page`	String containing the Flickr stream HTML page contents
`$rss`	String containing the location of the RSS feed for `$page`
`$xml`	String containing the contents of `$rss`
`$sxml`	SimpleXML object created from `$xml`
`$pics`	Array containing the image URLs
`$item`	SimpleXML object extracted from item in `$sxml`
`$j`	Integer loop variable for iterating through image URLs
`$t`	String used for transforming URLs into the form required

FIGURE 10-5   With this plug-in you can view the stream of a public Flickr user.

How It Works

This plug-in takes the base Flickr stream URL and appends the account name in $account to it. This HTML page is then returned using the file_get_contents() function and its contents are stored in $page. The @ symbol prefacing the function suppresses any error messages should the call fail. And, if it does fail, a value of FALSE is returned in a single-element array.

Next, the array that will hold the image URLs, $pics, is initialized and the program *screen scrapes* the HTML page to locate the position of the RSS link within it. Screen scraping is the term given to the process of extracting information from HTML pages that hasn't been explicitly provided to you in an API or via another method. Actually, there are Flickr APIs to do this, but these three lines of code are simpler and represent all the coding required to find the RSS feed on the page and return its URL to the variable $rss.

Using this URL, the RSS feed is fetched and placed in the string $xml, from where it is transformed into a SimpleXML object in $sxml. This is a DOM (Document Object Model) object that can be easily traversed. To do this, a foreach loop iterates through the items in $sxml->entry, placing each in a new object called $item.

Then a for loop is used to iterate though all the items in $item->link, which contains the URLs we are interested in. If $item->link[$j]['type'] has the value image, then $item->link[$j]['href'] will contain a URL, so this is extracted into the variable $t, first removing any _t or _m sequences from the URL, since they represent different sizes of the photo that we are not interested in. Once $t contains the URL wanted, its value is assigned to the next available element of the $pics array and the foreach loop continues.

The plug-in returns a two-element array with the first element containing the number of photos found, calculated using the count() function, and the second containing an array of the photo URLs.

Figure 10-6 shows a photo taken at random from the list returned and entered into a browser. In this case, it has the following Flickr URL:

```
http://farm3.static.flickr.com/2522/3708788611_5a9964f24d_o.jpg
```

FIGURE 10-6 The plug-in determines the exact URL required for each photo.

How to Use It

To return the most recent photos in a public Flickr stream, just pass the Flickr account name to the plug-in, like this:

```
$result = PIPHP_FetchFlickrStream('robinfnixon');
```

You can then choose how to proceed depending on the value of $result, like this:

```
if (!$result[0]) echo 'No photos found.';
else foreach($result[1] as $photo)
    echo "<a href='$photo'>Photo</a> ";
```

Or to display the images, you could use code such as this:

```
foreach($result[1] as $photo)
    echo "<img src='$photo' /><br />";
```

Users of Flickr's API are requested to make polling requests such as this no more than once per hour, so you are recommended to save the stream to a file or database and serve it from the cache in the future, only looking for new photos if 60 minutes has expired.

The Plug-in

```
function PIPHP_FetchFlickrStream($account)
{
    $url  = 'http://flickr.com/photos';
    $rss  = @file_get_contents("$url/$account/");
    if (!$rss) return array(FALSE);

    $rss  = strstr($rss, 'rss+xml');
    $rss  = strstr($rss, 'http://');
    $rss  = substr($rss, 0, strpos($rss, '"'));
    $xml  = file_get_contents($rss);
    $sxml = simplexml_load_string($xml);
    $pics = array();

    foreach($sxml->entry as $item)
    {
        for ($j=0 ; $j < sizeof($item->link) ; ++$j)
        {
            if (strstr($item->link[$j]['type'], 'image'))
            {
                $t=str_replace('_m', '', $item->link[$j]['href']);
                $t=str_replace('_t', '', $t);
                $pics[]=$t;
            }
        }
    }

    return array(count($pics), $pics);
}
```

75 Get Yahoo! Answers

The Yahoo! Answers web site contains questions and answers on just about any subject you can imagine, all supplied by users of the service. Sometimes this means that both the questions and the answers can be foolish or humorous, but equally they can also provide just the answer you are looking for to a problem or question you have.

That makes them ideal to drop in alongside informational web pages, in much the same way as you might link to or display dictionary definitions or encyclopedia entries. Figure 10-7 shows one of the Q&As returned by this plug-in in response to a search for the term *gardening*.

About the Plug-in

This plug-in takes a search term and returns any matches for it found at Yahoo! Answers. Upon success, it returns a two-element array with the first value being the number of question/answer pairs returned, and the second an array of the Q&As, containing a sub-array in each element, with the following five values:

- The subject
- A Unix timestamp representing the date the question was posted
- The question
- The answer
- A URL pointing to the original Q&A

On failure, it returns a single-element array with the value FALSE. It requires this argument:

- **$search** A search string

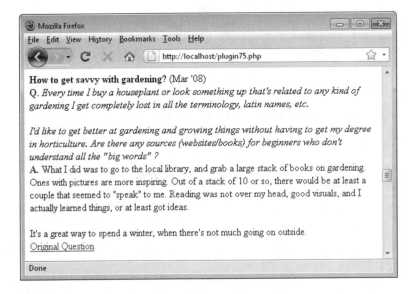

FIGURE 10-7 With this plug-in you can add the wealth of knowledge from Yahoo! Answers to your web site.

Variables, Arrays, and Functions

`$id`	String containing a Yahoo! Answers API key
`$url`	String containing the API URL with the `$id` and `$search` appended
`$xml`	String containing the contents of `$url`
`$sxml`	SimpleXML object created from `$xml`
`$qandas`	Array containing the questions and answers returned
`$question`	SimpleXML object extracted from `$sxml->Question`
`$s`	String containing the current subject
`$t`	String containing the current timestamp
`$q`	String containing the current question
`$a`	String containing the current answer
`$l`	String containing the current link

How It Works

This plug-in calls the Yahoo! Answers API URL in `$url`, which has been preconfigured with the search query in `$search` (after ensuring it is suitably encoded for using in a URL by passing it through the `rawurlencode()` function), and a valid Yahoo! Answers API key, taken from `$id`. In the code provided, you will see that the API key shown is *YahooDemo*, and you may find that it works, although there's no guarantee it will continue to do so.

To ensure your use of this plug-in is uninterrupted, you will need to apply for a free API key of your own at *http://developer.yahoo.com/wsregapp*. Check the box that says *Generic, No user authentication required*, enter your details, and click the Continue button to be provided with your new API key. Or, if you already have any Yahoo! API keys, you can view them at *http://developer.yahoo.com/wsregapp/?view*. If you see generic IDs, then any of those will work.

Once the API has been successfully called with the required arguments using the `file_get_contents()` function (prefaced by an @ symbol to suppress any error messages if it fails), the result is returned to the string `$xml`. If `$xml` is empty or has the value FALSE, then FALSE is returned. Otherwise, the contents of `$xml` is converted into a SimpleXML object and placed in `$sxml`. An array to hold the questions and answers returned, `$qandas`, is also initialized.

Now all the Q&As are extracted from `$sxml` using a `foreach` loop, with each element of `$sxml->Question` being assigned to the object `$question`. From there, the actual parts of each Q&A—the subject, timestamp, question, answer, and link—are retrieved and placed in the variables `$s`, `$t`, `$q`, `$a`, and `$l`. The link in `$l` is a URL pointing to the original question and answer at Yahoo! Answers, as shown in Figure 10-8.

The variables `$s`, `$q`, and `$a` then have any HTML tag symbols such as <, >, or & replaced with their entity equivalents of `&lt;`, `&gt;`, and `&amp;`, and so on. At the same time, any `\n` newline characters are replaced with `<br />` tags. If those strings weren't converted to use HTML entities, then any tags posted in those fields would be treated as HTML markup, rather than displayed. We want to keep the tags viewable as sometimes they are needed to help provide HTML or other programming and web development–related answers.

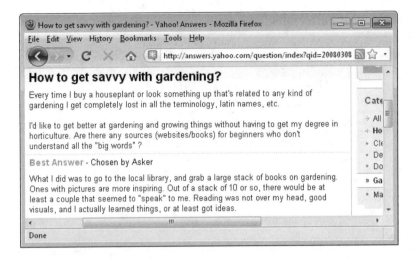

FIGURE 10-8   The question about savvy gardening as displayed on the Yahoo! Answers web site

The five short variables are then grouped into an array and assigned to the next available element of $qandas. Once all have been processed, a two-element array is returned, the first of which is the number of Q&As returned, and the second is an array of sub-arrays, containing all the details.

How to Use It

Using this plug-in is as easy as ensuring you have created and set up an API key for it (as described in the previous section) and then simply calling the plug-in, passing it a search query, like this:

```
$search = 'gardening';
$result = PIPHP_GetYahooAnswers($search);
if (!$result[0]) echo "No matching questions found for $search.";
```

An error message is displayed if $result[0] has the value FALSE. Otherwise, the returned results are all contained in sub-arrays, each within an element of $result[1], and which you could access like this for the first Q&A:

```
$subject   = $result[1][0][0];
$timestamp = $result[1][0][1];
$question  = $result[1][0][2];
$answer    = $result[1][0][3];
$link      = $result[1][0][4];
```

The second Q&A is then accessible like this (and so on):

```
$subject   = $result[1][1][0];
$timestamp = $result[1][1][1];
```

```
$question   = $result[1][1][2];
$answer     = $result[1][1][3];
$link       = $result[1][1][4];
```

However, it's much better to use a `foreach` loop to iterate through all the elements of `$result[1]`, placing each one in another variable such as `$qa`. From there, the various values are easily retrieved, like this:

```
foreach($result[1] as $qa)
    echo "<b>$qa[0]</b> (" . date('M \'y', $qa[1]) . ')<br />'.
        "<b>Q.</b> <i>$qa[2]</i><br />" .
        "<b>A.</b> $qa[3]<br />" .
        "<a href='$qa[4]'>Original Question</a><br /><br />";
```

The only unusual thing of note here is the use of the `date()` function on `$qa[1]`. Because this value is a Unix timestamp, you can reformat it any way you like using `date()`. So, by passing `date()` the argument `'M \'y'`, the three-letter month abbreviation and the shorthand for the year appear next to each message.

The Plug-in

```
function PIPHP_GetYahooAnswers($search)
{
    $search = rawurlencode($search);
    $id     = 'YahooDemo'; // Use your own API key here
    $url    = 'http://answers.yahooapis.com' .
              '/AnswersService/V1/questionSearch' .
              "?appid=$id&query=$search";
    $xml    = @file_get_contents($url);
    if (!$xml) return array(FALSE);

    $sxml   = simplexml_load_string($xml);
    $qandas = array();

    foreach($sxml->Question as $question)
    {
        $s = trim($question->Subject);
        $t = $question->Timestamp + 0;
        $q = trim($question->Content);
        $a = trim($question->ChosenAnswer);
        $l = $question->Link;

        $s = str_replace("\n", '<br />', htmlentities($s));
        $q = str_replace("\n", '<br />', htmlentities($q));
        $a = str_replace("\n", '<br />', htmlentities($a));

        if (strlen($a)) $qandas[] = array($s, $t, $q, $a, $l);
    }

    return array(count($qandas), $qandas);
}
```

PLUG-IN 76   Search Yahoo!

Both Yahoo! and Google provide excellent search results, and Microsoft's Bing search isn't bad either. But because the quality of Yahoo!'s results is, in my opinion, equal to Google's, I thought I would root for the underdog and provide a plug-in for Yahoo!'s search API, particularly considering that their API allows unlimited uses per day (although they reserve the right to limit this and/or charge in the future), plus you are permitted to reorder and blend the results with other content.

Obviously, with the merger of certain Bing and Yahoo! search assets, the results at Yahoo! seem likely to improve even further, since Microsoft is very keen to catch up on Google's search engine lead. It also means this plug-in may require updating if the API is changed. So, for the latest details please see *http://developer.yahoo.com/search/boss*.

Anyway, using this plug-in you can provide three arguments to have up to 50 results returned at a time, and can page through the remaining results as deeply as you like. Figure 10-9 shows it being used to find web sites relating to the query *yahoo search api*.

About the Plug-in

This plug-in takes a search term and returns results from the Yahoo! search engine. Upon success, it returns a two-element array with the first value being the number of results returned, and the second an array of result details, containing a sub-array in each element, with the following values:

- The title
- The abstract
- The URL to be displayed
- The URL for clicking through to

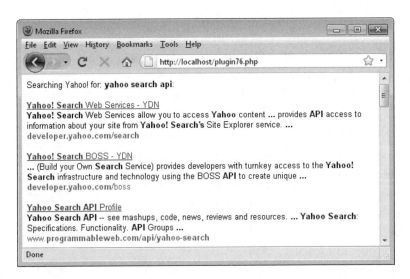

FIGURE 10-9   Use this plug-in to add Yahoo! search results to your web site.

On failure it returns a single-element array with the value FALSE. It requires these arguments:

- **$search**   A search string
- **$start**   The first result to return
- **$count**   The maximum number of results to return

Variables, Arrays, and Functions

$id	String containing a Yahoo! Search API key
$url	String containing the API URL with $id and $search appended
$xml	String containing the contents of $url
$sxml	SimpleXML object created from $xml
$data	Array containing the results returned
$result	SimpleXML object extracted from $sxml->resultset_web->result
$t	String containing the current title
$a	String containing the current abstract
$d	String containing the current display URL
$c	String containing the current click-through URL

How It Works

Because the search query in $search will be passed to the API as part of a URL, it is first encoded using the rawurlencode() function. Then $search, along with a valid Yahoo! Search API key, in $id, is incorporated with the API URL to create the string $url, which is then passed to the file_get_contents() function to retrieve the results into the variable $xml.

The string $id must contain your own unique Yahoo! Search API key; you cannot use the key *YahooDemo* as you can with some other of the company's APIs. If you already have such a key, you can locate it by visiting *http://developer.yahoo.com/wsregapp/?view* and copying the Search API key into your program. If you don't, you can get one free by visiting *http://developer.yahoo.com/wsregapp*. Check the box that says *Browser Based Authentication*, fill in your details, select the *Boss Search Service* checkbox, and click the Continue button.

Once these details have been sent to the API it will return its result in $xml. If it contains the empty string or the value FALSE, then FALSE is returned. An @ symbol is also placed in front of the file_get_contents() call to suppress any error messages.

A bit of work then needs to be done to transform the contents of $xml because the function that will be used to process the XML data, simplexml_load_string(), doesn't seem to like the CDATA that Yahoo! sometimes returns. In XML, a CDATA section is a piece of content that is marked for the parser to interpret as only character data, not markup. So the next few lines of code remove the <![CDATA[and]]> tags, leaving behind just the contents.

The contents are then made XML-safe by saving all examples of & by converting them to the string [ampersand], and then changing any & symbols that remain into & entities. The [ampersand] strings are then changed back to & entities. After that, all

\, \, and \<wbr> tags (the only ones Yahoo! Search seems to employ) are changed into their HTML entity equivalents.

At this point, the XML data should be in a format acceptable to SimpleXML, so the contents of $xml are then processed into a SimpleXML object and placed in the object $sxml, and the array that will be used to store all the result details, $data, is also initialized.

Now, to retrieve all the results, a foreach loop is used to iterate through $sxml->resultset_web->result, placing each element into the object $result. From here the title, abstract, display URL, and click-through URL are retrieved into the variables $t, $a, $d, and $c. If $a, the abstract, has a value, then these four variables are grouped into an array and inserted into the next available element of $data. This check is made because sometimes Yahoo! Search results don't have an abstract, and I choose to ignore such results.

Once $data has been populated, a two-element array is returned, with the first element being the number of results returned, and the second an array, each element of which is a sub-array containing the parts of each result.

How to Use It

As long as you have assigned a valid Yahoo! Search key to $id in the plug-in, you can call it by passing a query string, the number of the first result to return, and the maximum number of results to return, like this:

```
$search  = "yahoo search api";
$results = PIPHP_SearchYahoo($search, 1, 10);
if (!$results[0]) echo "No matching results found for $search.";
```

In this case, the first result requested is 1, and up to ten results are wanted. If $results[0] is FALSE or has the value 0, then no results were retrieved. Otherwise, the first result is accessible in the following way:

```
$title    = $results[1][0][0];
$abstract = $results[1][0][1];
$dispurl  = $results[1][0][2];
$clickurl = $results[1][0][3];
```

And the second result, like this (and so on):

```
$title    = $results[1][1][0];
$abstract = $results[1][1][1];
$dispurl  = $results[1][1][2];
$clickurl = $results[1][1][3];
```

The best way to process these results, though, is with a foreach loop, placing each array of results temporarily in a new array such as $result, and then accessing them from there, like this:

```
foreach($results[1] as $result)
    echo "<a href='$result[3]'>$result[0]<a/><br />".
        "$result[1]<br />" .
        "<font color='green'>$result[2]</font><br /><br />";
```

Yahoo! requires that you observe their terms and only ever offer the click-through URL to your users so that their click tracking will be applied. Make sure you don't use the Display URL in an `<a href='...'>` tag.

If you wish to allow your users to page through the results, you can change the value of the start argument and re-call the plug-in.

The Plug-in

```
function PIPHP_SearchYahoo($search, $start, $count)
{
    $search = rawurlencode($search);
    $id     = 'YourAPIKeyMustGoInThisStringOrItMayFail';
    $url    = 'http://boss.yahooapis.com/ysearch/web/v1/' .
              "$search?appid=$id&format=xml&start=$start" .
              "&count=$count";

    $xml  = @file_get_contents($url);
    if (!$xml) return array(FALSE);

    $xml  = str_replace('<![CDATA[',             '', $xml);
    $xml  = str_replace(']]>',                   '', $xml);
    $xml  = str_replace('&amp;', '[ampersand]', $xml);
    $xml  = str_replace('&',             '&amp;', $xml);
    $xml  = str_replace('[ampersand]', '&amp;', $xml);
    $xml  = str_replace('<b>',       '&lt;b&gt;', $xml);
    $xml  = str_replace('</b>',      '&lt;/b&gt;', $xml);
    $xml  = str_replace('<wbr>', '&lt;wbr&gt;', $xml);
    $sxml = simplexml_load_string($xml);
    $data = array();

    foreach($sxml->resultset_web->result as $result)
    {
        $t = html_entity_decode($result->title);
        $a = html_entity_decode($result->abstract);
        $d = html_entity_decode($result->dispurl);
        $c = $result->clickurl;

        if (strlen($a)) $data[] = array($t, $a, $d, $c);
    }

    return array(count($data), $data);
}
```

PLUG-IN 77 | ## Get Yahoo! Stock News

If you offer any finance-related services, you can add some great content to your site by using this plug-in to retrieve stock information from the Yahoo! Finance web site. With it you can fetch the latest chart for a ticker symbol, along with all the latest news about

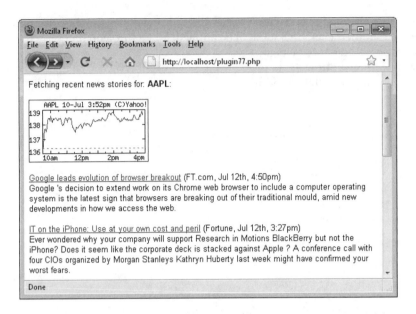

FIGURE 10-10   Add the latest stock news and charts to your web site with this plug-in.

that stock. Figure 10-10 shows it being used to display information for Apple Computer, Ticker Symbol: AAPL.

About the Plug-in

This plug-in takes a stock ticker such as AAPL or MSFT, and returns news and information about the stock. Upon success, it returns a three-element array, the first of which is the number of news items returned; the second is a sub-array of two URLs, the first of which is a small and the second a large intraday chart for the stock; while the third element is a sub-array containing the following report details:

- Title
- Publishing site
- Date
- Story summary/description
- URL to the original story

On failure, a single-element array with the value FALSE is returned. The plug-in requires this argument:

- **$stock**   A valid stock ticker symbol such as YHOO or JPM

Variables, Arrays, and Functions

$url	String containing the Yahoo! Stocks URL
$check	String containing the result of checking whether a ticker symbol exists
$reports	Array containing returned news reports
$xml	String containing news reports in RSS format
$sxml	SimpleXML object created from $xml
$flag	Boolean value set if a story title is too similar to another
$title	String containing the current title
$temp	Array used to extract the publishing site from the title
$site	String containing the current publisher of the story
$desc	String containing the current description/summary
$date	String containing the current story date
$percent	Integer representing how similar one title is to another
$url1	String containing the URL of a small stock chart
$url2	String containing the URL of a large stock chart

How It Works

This plug-in starts by ensuring the value entered for the stock ticker symbol in $stock is in uppercase using the strtoupper() function. Then file_get_contents() is called, passing the values in $url (the main Yahoo! Finance URL), and $stock, to see whether any information is returned. If the string *Invalid Ticker Symbol* appears anywhere in the returned text, saved in $check, then there is no such stock and so a single-element array with the value FALSE is returned.

Otherwise, the array $reports, which will hold the news reports returned later, is initialized, and $xml is loaded with the XML string returned from calling the RSS feed for the ticker in $stock.

Next, because the SimpleXML routines that will be used to process the XML don't seem to like CDATA (character data; see plug-in 76, *Search Yahoo!* for more details), the next few lines of code massage the data into a format it will accept by removing or translating certain tags, replacing them with entities it understands.

After this, $xml is passed to simplexml_load_string() and the resulting object created from it is placed in $sxml. From here, a foreach loop iterates through all the elements in $sxml->channel->item, each time storing them in the object $item to make them easier to access.

Inside the loop, the Boolean variable $flag is set to FALSE at the start of each iteration. Later on, if a story title appears too similar to a previously returned title, this flag will be changed to the value TRUE.

Next, the URL of the original story is extracted into $url and the title is also retrieved in $title. However, because the title also contains the name of the publishing web site in brackets, the explode() function is used to split the title into two elements of an array in $temp. The first now contains just the title so that is saved back to the variable $title.

The second then has the brackets and the word at removed, and the resulting publishing site name is placed in $site.

The description, or summary, is then placed in $desc and the date, which is returned as a timestamp, is converted to a friendly string using the strtotime() and date() functions, and saved in $date.

Next a for loop checks through all the news reports so far saved in the $reports array. Using the similar_text() function, each title is compared to the current one (first converting both to lowercase using the strtolower() function), with a score of between 0 and 100 percent being allocated to the variable $percent, depending on how similar the strings are to each other. A score of 0 means totally different, and 100 means identical.

After some testing, I chose a value of 70 percent or greater to mean that the same or a similar story has already been saved in the array and, if so, the variable $flag is set to TRUE and a break command is issued to exit the loop.

Finally, in the foreach loop, the value of $flag is checked. If it's not TRUE, the story summary doesn't relate to an item on a paid-for subscription site (indicated by the string [$$] in the title), and the value in $desc isn't the empty string, then the story details are grouped together into an array that is inserted into the next available element in the $reports array.

Lastly, the two variables $url1 and $url2 are assigned the URLs of a small (192 × 96 pixels) and a large (512 × 288 pixels) chart of the most recent (or current) day's trading of $stock.

A three-element array is then returned by the plug-in, the first of which is the number of news items returned, the second is a sub-array of two elements containing the small and large chart URLs, and the third element is the $reports array containing all the news stories.

How to Use It

To retrieve stock data using this plug-in, all you have to do is pass the name of a valid stock ticker symbol to it, like this:

```
$stock   = "AAPL";
$results = PIPHP_GetYahooStockNews($stock);
if (!$results[0]) echo "No stories found for $stock.";
```

If $results[0] is FALSE, then an error message is displayed. Otherwise, it contains the number of news stories returned and the value of $results[1] will be an array containing a pair of URLs for a small and a large chart of the stock, which you can display using one or the other of the following lines of code:

```
echo "<img src='" . $results[1][0] . "' />"; // Small chart
echo "<img src='" . $results[1][1] . "' />"; // Large chart
```

Each of the news stories will be supplied in separate details, which can be accessed like this for the first story:

```
$title = $results[2][0][0];
$site  = $results[2][0][1];
$date  = $results[2][0][2];
```

```
$story = $results[2][0][3];
$url   = $results[2][0][4];
```

And the second story's details can be accessed like this (and so on):

```
$title = $results[2][1][0];
$site  = $results[2][1][1];
$date  = $results[2][1][2];
$story = $results[2][1][3];
$url   = $results[2][1][4];
```

But the best way to iterate through the array of stories is to use a `foreach` loop, assigning the value of each element of `$results[2]` to another array such as `$result` (singular as opposed to plural), like this:

```
foreach($results[2] as $result)
    echo "<a href='$result[4]'>$result[0]</a> " .
        "($result[1], $result[2])<br />$result[3]<br /><br />';
```

Because all the individual parts of the story are returned separately, you can rearrange and display each story exactly the way you want. In the preceding code, each title in `$result[0]` is displayed as part of a link to the original story in `$result[4]`, then the originating site in `$result[1]` and the date in `$result[2]` are placed inside brackets, and a `<br />` tag is displayed. Finally, the story in `$result[3]` is displayed followed by a couple more `<br />` tags.

As with some of the other plug-ins similar to this, please be aware that you are using servers and data belonging to other organizations, so make sure you have the relevant permissions required to republish any data. Please also respect the bandwidth and CPU cycles of these companies by caching the results returned, and only requesting updates when necessary.

The Plug-in

```
function PIPHP_GetYahooStockNews($stock)
{
    $stock = strtoupper($stock);
    $url   = 'http://finance.yahoo.com';
    $check = @file_get_contents("$url/q?s=$stock");

    if (stristr($check, 'Invalid Ticker Symbol') || $check == '')
        return FALSE;

    $reports = array();
    $xml     = file_get_contents("$url/rss/headline?s=$stock");
    $xml     = preg_replace('/&lt;\/?summary&gt;/',   '', $xml);
    $xml     = preg_replace('/&lt;\/?image&gt;/',     '', $xml);
    $xml     = preg_replace('/&lt;\/?guid&gt;/',      '', $xml);
    $xml     = preg_replace('/&lt;\/?p?link&gt;/',    '', $xml);
    $xml     = str_replace('&lt;![CDATA[',            '', $xml);
    $xml     = str_replace(']]&gt;',                  '', $xml);
    $xml     = str_replace('&amp;',      '[ampersand]', $xml);
```

```
$xml       = str_replace('&',                    '&amp;', $xml);
$xml       = str_replace('[ampersand]',          '&amp;', $xml);
$xml       = str_replace('<b>',              '&lt;b&gt;', $xml);
$xml       = str_replace('</b>',            '&lt;/b&gt;', $xml);
$xml       = str_replace('<wbr>',         '&lt;wbr&gt;', $xml);
$sxml      = simplexml_load_string($xml);

foreach($sxml->channel->item as $item)
{
    $flag  = FALSE;
    $url   = $item->link;
    $title = $item->title;
    $temp  = explode(' (', $title);
    $title = $temp[0];
    $site  = str_replace(')', '', $temp[1]);
    $site  = str_replace('at ', '', $site);
    $desc  = $item->description;
    $date  = date("M jS, g:ia",
        strtotime(substr($item->pubDate, 0, 25)));

    for ($j = 0 ; $j < count($reports) ; ++$j)
    {
        similar_text(strtolower($reports[$j][0]),
            strtolower($title), $percent);

        if ($percent > 70)
        {
            $flag = TRUE;
            break;
        }
    }

    if (!$flag && !strstr($title, '[$$]') && strlen($desc))
        $reports[] = array($title, $site, $date, $desc, $url);
}

$url1 = "http://ichart.finance.yahoo.com/t?s=$stock";
$url2 = "http://ichart.finance.yahoo.com/b?s=$stock";
return array(count($reports), array($url1, $url2), $reports);
}
```

Get Yahoo! News

PLUG-IN 78

In the last of this chapter's Yahoo! related plug-ins, you can request the latest news results for a given search query. What this plug-in does is load in the Yahoo! News RSS feed for a query and extract the various elements into arrays which are then returned to your program. Figure 10-11 shows it being used to retrieve all the latest news for the query *climate change*.

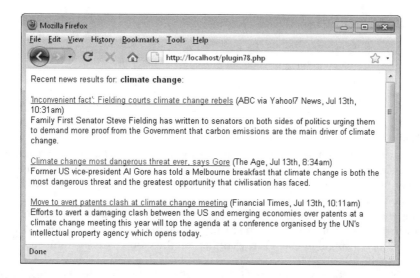

FIGURE 10-11   With this plug-in you can fetch the news headlines for any search query.

About the Plug-in

This plug-in takes a search query and returns news items from *http://news.yahoo.com* based on it. Upon success, it returns a two-element array, the first of which is the number of news items returned, and the second is a sub-array containing the following details:

- Title
- Publishing site
- Date
- Story summary/description
- URL to the original story

On failure it returns a single element array with the value FALSE. It requires this argument:

- **$search**   A standard search query

Variables, Arrays, and Functions

$reports	Array containing returned news reports
$url	String containing the Yahoo! News URL
$xml	String containing news reports in RSS format
$sxml	SimpleXML object created from $xml
$flag	Boolean value set if a story title is too similar to another
$date	String containing the current date

`$title`	String containing the current title
`$temp`	Array used to extract the publishing site from the title
`$site`	String containing the current publisher of the story
`$desc`	String containing the current description/summary
`$percent`	Integer representing how similar one title is to another

How It Works

This program starts by initializing `$reports`, the array that will hold all the news reports. Then `$url` is assigned the location of the Yahoo! News RSS feed for the search term in `$search`—after `$search` has been converted to a form that can be passed in a URL using the `rawurlencode()` function.

The feed is then called up using the `file_get_contents()` function, preceded by an @ symbol to suppress any error messages. The result is then placed in `$xml`. If it is FALSE or an empty string, then a single-element array containing the value FALSE is returned.

Then, because the SimpleXML routines to be used later don't appear to work with CDATA (XML character data; see plug-in 76, *Search Yahoo!*, for details), the next few lines remove the CDATA tags and convert characters that might clash with SimpleXML into entities it understands. Finally, `$xml` is converted into a SimpleXML object using the `simplexml_load_string()` function and the result is stored in `$sxml`.

Next, a `foreach` loop is used to iterate through all the elements of `$sxml->channel->item`, assigning each in turn to the object `$item`. Inside the loop, the first thing that happens is the variable `$flag` is set to FALSE. If it is later set to TRUE, then a title was found that was too similar to a previous one.

The variable `$url` is then extracted and the string `$date` is created from a timestamp by using the `strtotime()` and `date()` functions. After that, the title and publishing site name are extracted into `$title` and `$site`, after exploding the title into the array `$temp` to split `$site` out of the title, where it was stored inside a pair of brackets. The news story is then saved into the variable `$desc`.

To prevent similar stories being returned, a `for` loop is then used to iterate through all the saved stories in the `$reports` array. Using the `similar_text()` function, each previous title is compared to the current one and, if it is more than 70 percent similar, the variable `$flag` is set to TRUE and a `break` command is issued to break out of the loop, as no further duplication checking is necessary.

At the tail end of the loop, as long as `$flag` doesn't have a value of TRUE and `$desc` actually contains some text, the story parts are grouped into an array that is then assigned to the next available element of `$reports`.

The plug-in returns a two-element array in which the first element is the number of news stories returned and the second is the `$reports` array.

How to Use It

To use this plug-in, you pass it a search term, like this:

```
$search = "climate change";
$results = PIPHP_GetYahooNews($search);
if (!$results[0]) echo "No news found for $search.";
```

If $results[0] has the value FALSE or zero, then no stories were returned. Otherwise, you can access the stories in the following manner, which retrieves all the parts of the first story:

```
$title = $results[1][0][0];
$site  = $results[1][0][1];
$date  = $results[1][0][2];
$story = $results[1][0][3];
$url   = $results[1][0][4];
```

And the second result, like this (and so on):

```
$title = $results[1][1][0];
$site  = $results[1][1][1];
$date  = $results[1][1][2];
$story = $results[1][1][3];
$url   = $results[1][1][4];
```

The best way to display the results, though, is to use a foreach loop to iterate through each element of $results[1], placing each in another array such as $result (using the singular version of the variable name for single items extracted from the array), like this:

```
foreach($results[1] as $result)
    echo "<a href='$result[4]'>$result[0]</a> ($result[1], " .
        "$result[2])<br />$result[3]<br /><br />";
```

In this example, each title in $result[0] is made the text of a hyperlink to the story's original URL in $result[4], and the site and date in the variables $result[1] and $result[2] are displayed next to it in brackets. After a <br /> tag, the story in $result[3] is then displayed, followed by a couple more <br /> tags.

To display Yahoo! News results to their best effect, you will probably also want to first echo or print a UTF-8 <meta> tag in the <head> section of your web page, so that any unusual characters display correctly. The correct meta tag looks like this:

```
<meta http-equiv="Content-Type" content="text/html; charset=utf-8"/>
```

The Plug-in

```
function PIPHP_GetYahooNews($search)
{
    $reports = array();
    $url     = 'http://news.search.yahoo.com/news/rss?' .
               'ei=UTF-8&fl=0&x=wrt&p=' . urlencode($search);
    $xml     = @file_get_contents($url);
    if (!strlen($xml)) return array(FALSE);

    $xml     = str_replace('<![CDATA[',          '', $xml);
    $xml     = str_replace(']]>',                '', $xml);
    $xml     = str_replace('&amp;', '[ampersand]', $xml);
```

```
$xml  = str_replace('&',              '&amp;', $xml);
$xml  = str_replace('[ampersand]', '&amp;', $xml);
$xml  = str_replace('<b>',            '&lt;b&gt;', $xml);
$xml  = str_replace('</b>',         '&lt;/b&gt;', $xml);
$xml  = str_replace('<wbr>', '&lt;wbr&gt;', $xml);
$sxml = simplexml_load_string($xml);

foreach($sxml->channel->item as $item)
{
    $flag  = FALSE;
    $url   = $item->link;
    $date  = date('M jS, g:ia', strtotime($item->pubDate));
    $title = $item->title;
    $temp  = explode(' (', $title);
    $title = $temp[0];
    $site  = str_replace(')', '', $temp[1]);
    $desc  = $item->description;

    for ($j = 0 ; $j < count($reports) ; ++$j)
    {
        similar_text(strtolower($reports[$j][0]),
            strtolower($title), $percent);

        if ($percent > 70)
        {
            $flag = TRUE;
            break;
        }
    }

    if (!$flag && strlen($desc))
        $reports[] = array($title, $site, $date, $desc, $url);
}

return array(count($reports), $reports);
}
```

79 Search Google Books

As I write, as well as having already scanned in hundreds of thousands of out-of-copyright books, Google is in the process of making agreements with several book publishers over digitizing their in-copyright publications. This means that Google Books is likely to become an ever more useful research source that we can add to our toolkit. Figure 10-12 shows this plug-in being used to query the database for the term *Mark Twain*.

About the Plug-in

This plug-in takes a search query and returns matching books found in the Google Books database. Upon success it returns a two element array, the first of which is the number of

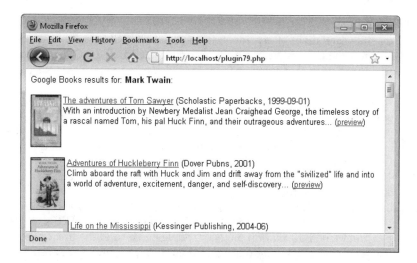

FIGURE 10-12   Add the vast resource of Google Book Search to your web site with this plug-in.

books returned and the second is an array containing details about those books. On failure it returns a single element array with the value FALSE. It requires these arguments:

- **$search**   A standard search query
- **$start**   The first result to return
- **$count**   The maximum number of results to return
- **$type**   The type of result to return. If this is 'none', then all books are returned; if 'partial', then books with partial previews are returned; or if 'full', then only books with full previews are returned.

Variables, Arrays, and Functions

$results	Array containing returned book details
$url	String containing the Google Books API URL
$xml	String containing the result of loading in $url
$sxml	SimpleXML object created from $xml
$title	String containing the current book's title
$author	String containing the current book's author
$pub	String containing the current book's publisher
$date	String containing the current book's publication date
$desc	String containing the current book's description/summary
$thumb	String containing the URL of the current book's cover thumbnail
$info	String containing the URL of the current book's information
$preview	String containing the URL for previewing the current book

How It Works

This plug-in starts off by initializing the array $results, which will be used to store the details of any books returned. Then $url is built up from the URL of the Google Books API, $search, converted into a form that can be passed in a URL using rawurlencode(), and the values of $start, $count, and $type.

The result of calling this URL using file_get_contents(), prefaced by an @ symbol to suppress error messages, is placed in the string variable $xml, which is then passed to simplexml_load_string() to be converted into the object $sxml. But, just before this, all occurrences of the string dc: in $xml have the colon removed for the benefit of the SimpleXML routines, which don't seem to like colons in XML field names.

The $sxml object is then iterated through using a foreach loop, with each element in $sxml->entry being assigned to the object $item for ease of access.

The title, author, publisher, date, and description are then all retrieved and placed in the variables $title, $author, $pub, $date, and $desc. There are then three URLs to fetch: the thumbnail image, a link to the information page at Google Books, and the link to the preview page at Google Books. These are placed in $thumb, $info, and $preview.

Next a few bits of sorting out need to occur. First, if $pub doesn't have a value, then the value in $author is given to it. Similarly, if $preview is found to not link to an actual preview of the book, then it is set to FALSE. If the description in $desc is missing, it is assigned the value (No description), and if it is determined that there is no thumbnail image specific to this book, a link to a generic cover image at Google Books is assigned to $thumb.

At the tail end of the loop, all these items of information are grouped together into an array, which is then assigned to the next available element in $results.

The plug-in returns a two-element array in which the first element is the number of books returned and the second is the $results array.

How to Use It

To use this plug-in, pass it a search query and arguments telling it which number result to start returning details from, the maximum number of results, and the type of results. For example, to return up to 20 books relating to the search *Mark Twain*, starting at the first result, and where any or no summary is available, you would use code such as this:

```
$search = "Mark Twain";
$result = PIPHP_SearchGoogleBooks($search, 1, 20, 'none');
if (!$result[0]) echo "No books found for $search.";
```

If $result[0] is FALSE or zero, then no results were returned. Otherwise, the details returned for the first book will be in the array $result[1] and can be accessed like this:

```
$title       = $result[1][0][0];
$author      = $result[1][0][1];
$publisher   = $result[1][0][2];
$date        = $result[1][0][3];
$description  = $result[1][0][4];
$thumbnail   = $result[1][0][5];
$information = $result[1][0][6];
$preview     = $result[1][0][7];
```

The second book's details can therefore be accessed like this (and so on):

```
$title       = $result[1][1][0];
$author      = $result[1][1][1];
$publisher   = $result[1][1][2];
$date        = $result[1][1][3];
$description = $result[1][1][4];
$thumbnail   = $result[1][1][5];
$information = $result[1][1][6];
$preview     = $result[1][1][7];
```

However, you will probably want to use a foreach loop to iterate through the $result[1] array, passing each element to another array with a name such as $book, like this:

```
foreach($result[1] as $book)
{
    echo "<img src='$book[5]' align='left' border='1'>";
    echo "<a href='$book[6]'>$book[0]</a> ($book[2], " .
        "$book[3])<br />$book[4]";
    if ($book[7]) echo " (<a href='$book[7]'>preview</a>)";
    echo "<br clear='left' /><br />";
}
```

Because all eight items are provided separately, you can choose exactly how you wish to lay out a book's details. In the preceding code, the thumbnail image in $book[5] is displayed aligned to the left and with a 1-pixel border. Then the book title in $book[0] is used as a text hyperlink for the book's information page in $book[6]. Alongside this, the book's publisher and publication date in $book[2] and $book[3] are added within brackets, followed by a <br /> tag and the book's description in $book[4].

After this, if the book has a preview, identified by $book[7] having a value, then a link is provided to it, enclosed in brackets. Finally, the book thumbnail's left alignment is cleared using the tag <br clear='left' />, and then another <br /> tag is used to separate book details from each other.

If you want to only return results for books where the whole text is available in the summary, generally because they are out of copyright control or because their authors have allowed the entire contents to be released, just replace the preceding call to the plug-in with this one:

```
$result = PIPHP_SearchGoogleBooks($search, 1, 20, 'full');
```

Or, to allow results with either partial or full previews, you could use:

```
$result = PIPHP_SearchGoogleBooks($search, 1, 20, 'partial');
```

You can also support paging through the search results by changing the start argument for the book number at which returned results should begin, and re-calling the plug-in.

The Plug-in

```php
function PIPHP_SearchGoogleBooks($search, $start, $count, $type)
{
    $results = array();
    $url     = 'http://books.google.com/books/feeds/volumes?' .
               'q=' . rawurlencode($search) . '&start-index=' .
               "$start&max-results=$count&min-viewability=" .
               "$type";
    $xml     = @file_get_contents($url);
    if (!strlen($xml)) return array(FALSE);

    $xml  = str_replace('dc:', 'dc', $xml);
    $sxml = simplexml_load_string($xml);

    foreach($sxml->entry as $item)
    {
        $title   = $item->title;
        $author  = $item->dccreator;
        $pub     = $item->dcpublisher;
        $date    = $item->dcdate;
        $desc    = $item->dcdescription;
        $thumb   = $item->link[0]['href'];
        $info    = $item->link[1]['href'];
        $preview = $item->link[2]['href'];

        if (!strlen($pub))
            $pub = $author;
        if ($preview ==
            'http://www.google.com/books/feeds/users/me/volumes')
            $preview = FALSE;
        if (!strlen($desc))
            $desc = '(No description)';
        if (!strstr($thumb, '&sig='))
            $thumb = 'http://books.google.com/googlebooks/' .
                'images/no_cover_thumb.gif';

        $results[] = array($title, $author, $pub, $date, $desc,
            $thumb, $info, $preview);
    }

    return array(count($results), $results);
}
```

PLUG-IN 80 Convert Currency

The final plug-in in this chapter allows you to produce up-to-date currency conversions between 34 major currencies. The data used is supplied by the European Central Bank and is based on the prices of each currency relative to the euro at the previous trading session's

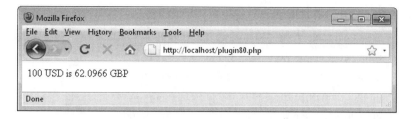

FIGURE 10-13   Using this plug-in, you can instantly convert between 34 currencies.

close of business. Figure 10-13 shows the plug-in being used to convert 100 U.S. dollars into UK pounds.

About the Plug-in

This plug-in takes a value and currencies to convert it from and to. Upon success, it returns a floating point number, accurate to two decimal places, representing the value of the amount given when converted to the new currency. On failure, it returns the value FALSE. It requires these arguments:

- **$amount**   The amount of money to convert
- **$from**   The abbreviation for the source currency
- **$to**   The abbreviation for the destination currency

The available currencies and their abbreviations are:

AUD = Australian Dollar	HRK = Croatian Kuna	PHP = Philippine Peso
BGN = Bulgarian Lev	HUF = Hungarian Forint	PLN = Polish Zloty
BRL = Brazilian Real	IDR = Indonesian Rupiah	RON = Romanian Lei
CAD = Canadian Dollar	INR = Indian Rupee	RUB = Russian Ruble
CHF = Swiss Frank	JPY = Japanese Yen	SEK = Swedish Krona
CNY = Chinese Yuan	KRW = South Korean Won	SGD = Singapore Dollar
CZK = Czech Koruna	LTL = Lithuanian Litas	THB = Thai Baht
DKK = Danish Krone	LVL = Latvian Lats	TRY = Turkish Lira
EEK = Estonian Kroon	MXN = Mexican Peso	USD = U.S. Dollar
EUR = European Euro	MYR = Malaysian Ringgit	ZAR = South African Rand
GBP = British Pound	NOK = Norwegian Krone	
HKD = Hong Kong Dollar	NZD = New Zealand Dollar	

Variables, Arrays, and Functions

$url	String containing the URL for the European Central Bank exchange rates page
$data	String containing the result of loading in $url
$ptr1	Integer pointer to the start of the currency data
$ptr2	Integer pointer to the end of the currency data
$main	Array in which the currencies and prices are stored
$lines	Array of data lines extracted from $data
$line	String containing a line of data from $lines
$l	String containing the left half of a currency/value pair
$r	String containing the right half of a currency/value pair

How It Works

This plug-in loads the XML page that the European Central Bank maintains of currency rates compared to the euro into the variable $data. If no data is returned, then there was an error and FALSE is returned.

Otherwise, instead of converting the XML data into an object as some of the other plug-ins do, the information needed is easily extracted with just a few PHP commands. First, the start and end of the section of XML of interest are put in the variables $ptr1 and $ptr2. This is done using the strpos() function to search for certain strings in the file. The contents of $data are then cropped down to just that section using the substr() function, then a few keywords, tags, and other pieces of XML are replaced with values of more use to the plug-in, and whitespace is also removed.

This leaves $data containing just 33 lines, each of which is a currency/value pair in relation to the euro at the time of closing of the previous day's trading session. Each line is separated from the others with an @ symbol, and the currency abbreviations are separated from their values by | symbols.

Using these as separators, the contents of $data are split into the array $lines at each of the @ symbols using the explode() function. Then, using a foreach loop, each individual line is processed into the associative array $main by using explode() to separate the currencies from their values at the | symbol. The parts are placed in $l and $r using the list() function, and from there the values are assigned to the $main array.

At this point, the $main array has 33 currencies, each one accessible by its abbreviation. For example, $main['DKK'] will return the value of the Danish krone against the euro. But there is one currency missing because all the other values are set against it, and that's the euro, with an abbreviation of EUR. Therefore that gets added to the $main array with a value of 1, because that is its value in relation to itself.

Next, both the values of $from and $to are set to uppercase (if they aren't already) using the strtoupper() function, and then they are also checked to ensure they both have an associated value in the $main array. If either of them doesn't, then an unknown abbreviation was used and so the value FALSE is returned.

Otherwise, a quick calculation converts one currency to another using the formula *New value = Original value / From value * To value*. The result is then passed through the sprintf() function to ensure it has exactly two decimal places and the final result is then returned.

If you need more decimal places in your returned values, you can change the `%.02f` to another string such as `%.04f` for four decimal places, and so on.

How to Use It

To use the plug-in, you pass it a value to convert, along with abbreviations representing currencies from and to which the value should be converted, like this:

```
$amount = 100;
$from   = 'USD';
$to     = 'GBP';
$result = PIPHP_ConvertCurrency(100, $from, $to);
if (!$result) echo "Conversion failed.";
else echo "$amount $from is $result $to";
```

If you plan to call this function a lot, you would be well advised to save the contents of `$data` once per day, and return conversions based on the saved values. This will stop your program excessively calling the ECB server, which is not necessary anyway, because the data there is only updated daily.

The Plug-in

```
function PIPHP_ConvertCurrency($amount, $from, $to)
{
   $url   = 'http://www.ecb.europa.eu/stats/eurofxref/' .
            'eurofxref-daily.xml';
   $data  = file_get_contents($url);
   if (!strlen($data)) return FALSE;

   $ptr1  = strpos($data, '<Cube currency');
   $ptr2  = strpos($data, '</Cube>');
   $data  = substr($data, $ptr1, $ptr2 - $ptr1);
   $data  = str_replace("<Cube currency='", '', $data);
   $data  = str_replace("' rate='",         '|', $data);
   $data  = str_replace("'/>",              '@', $data);
   $data  = preg_replace("/\s/",            '', $data);
   $main  = array();
   $lines = explode('@', substr($data, 0, -1));

   foreach($lines as $line)
   {
      list($l, $r) = explode('|', $line);
      $main[$l]    = $r;
   }

   $main['EUR'] = 1;
   $from        = strtoupper($from);
   $to          = strtoupper($to);

   if (!isset($main[$from]) || !isset($main[$to])) return FALSE;
   return sprintf('%.04f', $amount / $main[$from] * $main[$to]);
}
```

CHAPTER 11

Incorporating JavaScript

JavaScript is a powerful programming language in its own right. Most of the things you can do with other languages like Java, C, and PHP can also be done with JavaScript (although, obviously, you can't create compiled programs such as device drivers and the like). Its great utility lies in the fact that it runs inside a web browser, and therefore, if you interact with it, you can substantially increase the dynamic features of your web site by adding Web 2.0 functionality such as Ajax calls, the manipulating of elements within a web page, assisting user input, and a whole lot more.

Because this is a book on PHP, I have kept the JavaScript code used as basic as possible while still remaining fully featured, so that even if you have never used JavaScript before, you should at least understand what is going on, and see how to modify the plug-ins to your own purposes.

PLUG-IN 81   Ajax Request

Some PHP programmers would argue that the most important use of JavaScript is to provide Ajax functionality to your programs. Whether or not you agree, Ajax is certainly a central part of today's Internet. Standing for Asynchronous JavaScript and XML, Ajax is really a misnomer because it often has little to do with XML as it can handle all manner of file types. However, when Microsoft first introduced the feature in Internet Explorer 5 (back in 1999), they named the new ActiveX object XMLHttpRequest, and the name has stuck ever since.

This plug-in is the pure JavaScript side of the Ajax equation, which requires two programs, one on the client computer and one on the server, to interact with each other. Figure 11-1 shows it being used (along with the following JavaScript plug-in, *Post Request*) to load the main *http://pluginphp.com* web page inside a pair of <div>...</div> tags.

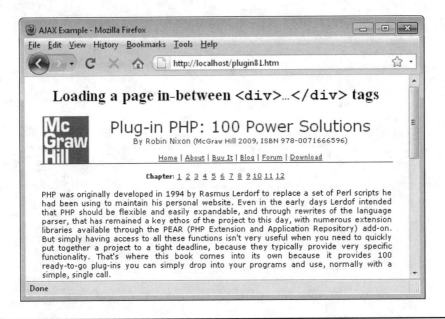

FIGURE 11-1   Using Ajax techniques, you can load new elements into a page in the background.

About the Plug-in

This plug-in doesn't take any arguments but returns an XMLHttpRequest object upon success; otherwise, it returns false.

Variables, Arrays, and Functions

request	XMLHttpRequest object or the value false on failure

How It Works

This and the next two plug-ins in this chapter are comprised entirely of JavaScript code, rather than the amalgam of JavaScript and PHP used by the rest of the plug-ins.

The plug-in is a little more complicated than it ought to be due to the different methods various browser creators have chosen to implement Ajax. For example, although Microsoft came up with the XMLHttpRequest object in Internet Explorer 5, it then decided to use an entirely different approach for IE6. And then other browser developers chose yet another away of doing things.

This means that there are three types of Ajax methods to take into account, according to which browser is in use. Thankfully, there's an easy way to apply these in turn without creating errors, and that's to use JavaScript's try ... catch syntax. With it you can try a command using a try statement, and if it fails, program execution will continue at the matching catch statement. Furthermore, you can nest these inside each other, so you can place another try statement inside a catch statement.

This is exactly the technique employed in this plug-in, except that I choose to test for non-Microsoft browsers first by assigning the variable request the object returned by calling up a new XMLHttpRequest() object. This will usually succeed on Firefox, Chrome, Safari, and Opera (as well as other browsers), but will fail on all versions of Internet Explorer. If this happens, an attempt is then made to assign request the value returned from creating the new ActiveX object Msxml2.XMLHTTP by attempting to use the command new ActiveXObject() with that argument. If the browser is Internet Explorer 6, then it will succeed; otherwise, it will fail.

Again, on failure an attempt is made to assign request the result of creating the new ActiveX object Microsoft.XMLHTTP by attempting to use the command new ActiveXObject() with that argument. If the browser is Internet Explorer 7 or later, this call will succeed. Otherwise, if it fails, the browser has no identifiable means of creating an XMLHttpRequest object and so false is returned to indicate failure.

Upon success, a new XMLHttpRequest object will have been created and assigned to request, which is then returned by the plug-in.

How to Use It

To use this plug-in, you need to incorporate it within the HTML of a web page in between a pair of <script> ... </script> tags. If you want to be properly W3C-standards compliant, you should use <script type="text/JavaScript"> to start a section of JavaScript, but you can normally ignore that parameter if you choose.

You can then call the plug-in from within the same (or another) section of JavaScript, like this:

```
request = new PIPHP_JS_AjaxRequest()
```

As long as `false` wasn't returned, the variable `request` will now contain an `XMLHttpRequest` object which you can use to perform Ajax calls. However, on its own you won't get very far because you also need another JavaScript plug-in to use this request to send either a `POST` or a `GET` request back to the web server. The first of these plug-ins, *Post Ajax Request*, comes next.

The Plug-in

```
function PIPHP_JS_AjaxRequest()
{
    try
    {
        var request = new XMLHttpRequest()
    }
    catch(e1)
    {
        try
        {
            request = new ActiveXObject("Msxml2.XMLHTTP")
        }
        catch(e2)
        {
            try
            {
                request = new ActiveXObject("Microsoft.XMLHTTP")
            }
            catch(e3)
            {
                request = false
            }
        }
    }
    return request
}
```

PLUG-IN 82 Post Ajax Request

The previous plug-in provides a means of creating an `XMLHttpRequest` object, with which this plug-in makes a `POST` request to the server to request some data to be transferred back to the browser. Both of these requests happen seamlessly in the background with the user generally unaware that such things are taking place. A `POST` request is where data is sent to the server within header messages, rather than as part of a URL tail (or query string), as is the case with `GET` requests.

Figure 11-2 shows this plug-in being used to load Facebook's mobile web site main page at *http://m.facebook.com*, replacing the contents of a <div> … </div> pair of tags.

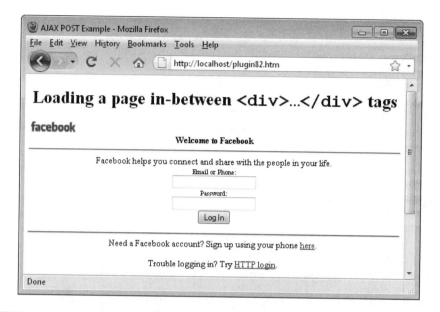

FIGURE 11-2   A one-line PHP program interfaces with a browser via Ajax to insert a web page into an HTML element.

About the Plug-in

This plug-in takes the URL of a web page, any parameters to pass to it and a Document Object Model (DOM) target for inserting the result. It doesn't return any parameters, but upon success the contents of `target` are populated with the result returned from the web server. Upon failure, an alert box will appear to aid with debugging. You may wish to disable this behavior on a production web site. It requires the following arguments:

- `url`   A web page/program to call
- `params`   Any POST parameters to pass, separated by & characters, like this: `var1=val1&var2=val2`
- `target`   A DOM element in which to place the result of the call

Variables, Arrays, and Functions

request	XMLHttpRequest object, or the value `false` on failure

How It Works

This is the second plug-in that is entirely written in JavaScript. It first calls `PIPHP_JS_ AjaxRequest()` to create a new `XMLHttpRequest` object in `request`. Next the `onreadystatechange` event of `request` is assigned to an inline anonymous function. When this state changes, which means a step in the Ajax process has completed, the function is called. There is only one state of interest to this function and that's the value 4, which indicates a completed Ajax call. This value is in `this.readyState`.

In JavaScript the keyword this applies to the current object being processed. Here it could equally be replaced with the word request to directly access the object. Next the function only wants to know if the call completed successfully, which is indicated by this. status having a value of 200.

With both of those cases being true this.responseText is tested to ensure a value of null hasn't been returned, and if not, the innerHTML contents of the target argument is assigned the value returned by the Ajax call in this.responseText.

So, if target is being used to assign the Ajax result to, for example, a <div> with the id 'info', then target will have been give the value:

```
document.getElementById('info')
```

This means that the statement:

```
target.innerHTML = this.responseText
```

is equivalent to:

```
document.getElementById('info').innerHTML = this.responseText
```

Therefore the text within the two following <div> tags would be replaced with the new text from the Ajax call:

```
<div id='info'>The contents of this DIV will be replaced</div>
```

If the value of this.responseText is null, an alert message appears, as also happens if this.status doesn't have the value 200. These alert commands are useful while you are debugging code but you may want to remove them when using this plug-in on a production server.

After assigning the function to request.onreadystatechange, request.open() is called and passed three parameters: "POST", for a POST request; the URL to access in url; and the value true, indicating that the request should take place asynchronously.

Next, three headers have to be sent to the server. These are to tell the server to expect URL encoded form data, to pass the length of the data the server should expect to receive, and to then close the header connection.

Finally, the Ajax request is initiated using a call to request.send() with an argument of params.

How to Use It

The following example shows how you would use this function. To help you see what is going on I have included both the *Ajax Request* and the *Post Ajax Request* plug-ins within the example, which is totally complete except for the PHP component (which comes afterwards):

```
<html><head><title>AJAX POST Example</title>
</head><body><center />
<h1>Loading a page in DIV tags</h1>
<div id='info'>The contents of this DIV will be replaced</div>

<script type="text/javascript">
```

```
PIPHP_JS_PostAjaxRequest('ajaxpost.php',
    'url=http://m.facebook.com/',
    document.getElementById('info'))

function PIPHP_JS_PostAjaxRequest(url, params, target)
{
    request = new PIPHP_JS_AjaxRequest()

    request.onreadystatechange = function()
    {
        if (this.readyState == 4)
            if (this.status == 200)
                if (this.responseText != null)
                    target.innerHTML = this.responseText
// You can remove these two alerts after debugging
                else alert("Ajax error: No data received")
            else alert( "Ajax error: " + this.statusText)
    }

    request.open("POST", url, true)
    request.setRequestHeader("Content-type",
        "application/x-www-form-urlencoded")
    request.setRequestHeader("Content-length",
        params.length)
    request.setRequestHeader("Connection", "close")
    request.send(params)
}

function PIPHP_JS_AjaxRequest()
{
    try
    {
        var request = new XMLHttpRequest()
    }
    catch(e1)
    {
        try
        {
            request = new ActiveXObject("Msxml2.XMLHTTP")
        }
        catch(e2)
        {
            try
            {
                request = new ActiveXObject("Microsoft.XMLHTTP")
            }
            catch(e3)
            {
                request = false
            }
        }
    }
    return request
}
</script>
```

Note that the entire Facebook page is being loaded into the <div>, in the same way as if you had included it within an <iframe> element. This is purely an example of how to incorporate such a page, and you do not gain access to the Facebook API using this method. Instead a surfer using such an embedded page to log in will be directed straight to the Facebook servers for the remainder of the process.

To try this example for yourself, type it in and save it as *ajaxpost.html*. You can also download it from the Download link at *www.pluginphp.com*. After extracting the file *plug-ins. zip*, you will find the example in the location *11/ajaxpost.html*.

However, don't run the file until you also have the PHP part of the equation on the server. It's not a large program but it's very important because it's the part of the process that receives requests from the browser and responds to them. In this case, it returns a requested web page:

```php
<?php // ajaxpost.php
if (isset($_POST['url'])) echo file_get_contents($_POST['url']);
?>
```

What this program does is check whether the variable url has been posted to it, and if so, it loads the page pointed to by the value of url into memory using the function file_get_contents(). It then uses the echo command to return the URL to the calling program—in this case, the Ajax call made by the browser. This file should be typed in and saved as *ajaxpost .php*, or you can find it in the same folder as the *ajaxpost.html* program if you download it from the companion web site.

Of course, your PHP programs are likely to be far more complex than this one, and may return all manner of items to the browser, such as information on available usernames when signing up to a site, or new messages on a social networking site, and so on.

The Plug-in

```
function PIPHP_JS_PostAjaxRequest(url, params, target)
{
   request = new PIPHP_JS_AjaxRequest()

   request.onreadystatechange = function()
   {
      if (this.readyState == 4)
         if (this.status == 200)
            if (this.responseText != null)
               target.innerHTML = this.responseText
// You can remove these two alerts after debugging
            else alert("Ajax error: No data received")
         else alert( "Ajax error: " + this.statusText)
   }

   request.open("POST", url, true)
   request.setRequestHeader("Content-type",
      "application/x-www-form-urlencoded")
   request.setRequestHeader("Content-length",
      params.length)
   request.setRequestHeader("Connection", "close")
   request.send(params)
}
```

83 Get Ajax Request

GET requests are also supported via Ajax and they can achieve the same results as POST requests. The only main difference is that the data sent back to the server is passed in the tail of a URL, known as the query string, rather than in HTML headers. Figure 11-3 shows the Amazon mobile home page being loaded into a `<div> ... </div>` pair of tags using this plug-in.

About the Plug-in

This plug-in takes the URL of a web page, any parameters to pass to it, and a Document Object Model (DOM) target for inserting the result. It doesn't return any parameters, but upon success, the contents of `target` are populated with the result returned from the web server. Upon failure, an alert box will appear to aid with debugging. You may wish to disable this behavior on a production web site. It requires the following arguments:

- **url**   A web page or program to call
- **params**   Any GET parameters to pass, separated by & characters, like this: `var1=val1&var2=val2`
- **target**   A DOM element in which to place the result of the call

Variables, Arrays, and Functions

nocache	String randomly assigned a value to overcome caching
request	XMLHttpRequest object, or the value false on failure

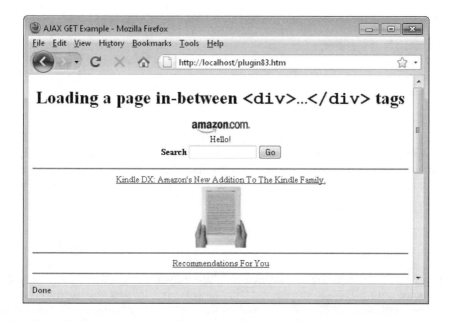

FIGURE 11-3   Ajax works equally well with either POST or (as shown here) GET requests.

How It Works

This is the last of the JavaScript-only plug-ins and it is fairly similar to the previous one, *Post Ajax Request*, except that it handles the passing of arguments back to the server in a slightly different manner, using a GET request.

The first thing to remember when making a GET request is that most browsers will cache them if the URL is the same as a previous call, and pull the previously returned result out of memory. To prevent this, the string nocache is given a random value that will be later appended to the request to make the call different each time.

The next few lines of code are identical to the previous plug-in and set the variable request up with an XMLHttpRequest object and then set request.onreadystatechange to call the inline function whenever the ready state changes. As before, this function will assign the result returned from the Ajax call to the HTML element indicated by the target parameter.

The end of the function is different, though, in that no special headers need sending as this is not a POST request, instead there is just a call to request.open(), passing it three arguments: the command "GET"; the url with a GET query string appended after a ? character, comprising the parameters in params and the nocache anti-caching string; and the value true to force asynchronous requests.

How to Use It

I wrote this plug-in in such a way that you can call it up in the same manner as *Post Ajax Request*. Therefore you can use identical code to that shown in the previous plug-in. Make sure you have an element to which you have assigned an id name, and pass that name, along with the name of a PHP program to handle the GET request, and the required parameters, to the plug-in, like this:

```
<div id='info'>This text will be replaced</div>
<script>
PIPHP_JS_GetAjaxRequest('ajaxget.php',
    'url=http://amazon.com/mobile',
    document.getElementById('info'))

// The plug-ins go here
</script>
```

As long as you have this code and both the plug-ins PIPHP_JS_GetAjaxRequest() and PIPHP_JS_AjaxRequest() within <script> and </script> tags, in the same web page, then the contents of the <div> will be replaced with that of the Amazon Mobile home page.

Note that in this case a slightly different PHP program is used to fetch the requested web page:

```
<?php // ajaxget.php
if (isset($_GET['url'])) echo file_get_contents($_GET['url']);
?>
```

It's pretty much the same as the ajaxpost.php program, except that the array $_POST has been replaced with $_GET. To use the example for this plug-in, you will need to type it in and save the program as *ajaxget.php*. If you download *plug-ins.zip* using the Download link at *www.pluginphp.com*, once extracted you will also find the two files *ajaxget.html* and *ajaxget.php* in the folder called *11*.

Remembering that the *x* in Ajax stands for XML, you can also handle XML data in exactly the same way (or using the *Post Ajax Request* plug-in); just ensure that your PHP program outputs data in XML format and then use JavaScript to access the data. Or if you prefer, you can use the JSON (JavaScript Object Notation) format which, as you might imagine, is particularly suited to handling JavaScript. However, this is a book on PHP and explaining how to parse either of these formats is beyond its scope, but I do recommend *Ajax: The Complete Reference* by Thomas Powell (ISBN 978-0071492164), for further reading.

The Plug-in

```
function PIPHP_JS_GetAjaxRequest(url, params, target)
{
   nocache = "&nocache=" + Math.random() * 1000000
   request = new PIPHP_JS_AjaxRequest()

   request.onreadystatechange = function()
   {
      if (this.readyState == 4)
         if (this.status == 200)
            if (this.responseText != null)
               target.innerHTML = this.responseText
// You can remove these two alerts after debugging
            else alert("Ajax error: No data received")
         else alert( "Ajax error: " + this.statusText)
   }

   request.open("GET", url + "?" + params + nocache, true)
   request.send(null)
}
```

PLUG-IN 84   Protect E-mail

You know the dilemma; you need to get your e-mail address out there so that people can contact you, but doing so leaves you open to being added to spam lists by automatic e-mail address harvesting programs. Well, this plug-in has the solution by obfuscating your e-mail address using JavaScript code.

Figure 11-4 shows an e-mail address that has been displayed making it both copyable and clickable, but as the inset source view shows, the e-mail address itself doesn't appear as a whole within the page, because it has been split into three JavaScript variables and then reassembled, meaning that only a sophisticated harvesting "bot," capable of parsing and running JavaScript, could make sense of it.

About the Plug-in

This plug-in takes an e-mail address and returns JavaScript code that will display it as a hyperlink without leaving the full e-mail address in the HTML. Upon success, it returns the JavaScript or, on failure (for example, if the e-mail address doesn't validate), it returns FALSE. It requires the following argument:

- **$email**   The e-mail address to obfuscate

Figure 11-4 Using this plug-in you can display your e-mail address while preventing access to most "bots."

Variables, Arrays, and Functions

$t1	PHP integer pointer to the @ in $email
$t2	PHP integer pointer to the first period after the @ in $email
$e1	PHP string containing the pre @ part of $email
$e2	PHP string containing part of $email between @ and the first period
$e3	PHP string containing the remainder of $email after the first period
e1	JavaScript string copy of PHP variable $e1
e2	JavaScript string copy of PHP variable $e2
e3	JavaScript string copy of PHP variable $e3

How It Works

This plug-in only requires that e-mail addresses have at least one character before an @ sign and at least one period somewhere after the @. The remaining characters can be anything, including more periods, and even disallowed characters, since no serious validation is made on the e-mail address.

The code uses the PHP strpos() function to locate the position of the @ character in $email, followed by the first period after the @. The values returned are assigned to $t1 and $t2, respectively. If either of these values is zero, then that character is missing and so FALSE is returned because the e-mail address is invalid. This is the only validation performed.

Then three variables representing the start, middle, and end portions of $email are assigned to $e1, $e2, and $e3 using the substr() function to extract the parts.

Finally, some JavaScript within `<script>` and `</script>` tags is returned, which makes use of $e1, $e2, and $e3 by first assigning their values to the JavaScript variables e1, e2, and e3. Then a `document.write()` command is added to the string (this is similar to a PHP echo command) in which an HTML `mailto:` link is displayed by recombining the parts.

How to Use It

To use this function, pass it a valid e-mail address and the returned value can then be output to a browser, like this:

```
$email  = 'billgates@microsoft.com';
$pemail = PIPHP_ProtectEmail($email);
echo "My email address is $pemail";
```

Or more concisely:

```
echo "My email address is " .
    PIPHP_ProtectEmail('billgates@microsoft.com');
```

So, assuming the e-mail address used is *me@mysever.com*, the plug-in will create the JavaScript required to turn the e-mail address into the following format when viewed in a browser with JavaScript enabled:

```
<a href='mailto:me@myserver.com'>me@myserver.com</a>
```

But all an e-mail harvesting program will see is the following:

```
<script>e1='me'; e2='@myserver'; e3='.com'; document.write('<a
href=\'mailto:' + e1 + e2 + e3 + '\'>' + e1 + e2 + e3 + '</a>');
</script>
```

Of course, there is a downside, and that is that people without JavaScript or who have it disabled will not see anything, although that's likely to be very few people—nevertheless it's something you should bear in mind when using this plug-in.

The Plug-in

```
function PIPHP_ProtectEmail($email)
{
   $t1 = strpos($email, '@');
   $t2 = strpos($email, '.', $t1);
   if (!$t1 || !$t2) return FALSE;

   $e1 = substr($email, 0, $t1);
   $e2 = substr($email, $t1, $t2 - $t1);
   $e3 = substr($email, $t2);

   return "<script>e1='$e1';e2='$e2';e3='$e3';document.write" .
          "('<a href=\'mailto:' + e1 + e2 + e3 + '\'>' + e1 " .
          "+ e2 + e3 + '</a>');</script>";
}
```

85 Toggle Text

A great use for JavaScript is to manipulate the contents of a web page without having to reload it. An effect I always feel is quite professional is the use of toggling to switch elements in and out. For example, Figure 11-5 shows this plug-in being used to display a short explanation of photosynthesis, along with a link to a longer definition.

When the link is clicked, instead of a new request being made to the server, JavaScript steps in and hides the current text and link, replacing it with an alternative pair, as you can see in Figure 11-6, where the new text has pushed down the heading on Pollination. If the new link is clicked, the previous text and link will be restored.

About the Plug-in

This plug-in toggles between two sets of text (or HTML) with accompanying links to cause the toggling when they are clicked. It requires the following arguments:

- `$text1`   The main text to display
- `$link1`   The main link text to display
- `$text2`   The alternate text
- `$link2`   The alternate link text

Variables, Arrays, and Functions

$token	Random integer between 0 and 1,000,000
$out	String containing the JavaScript to be returned

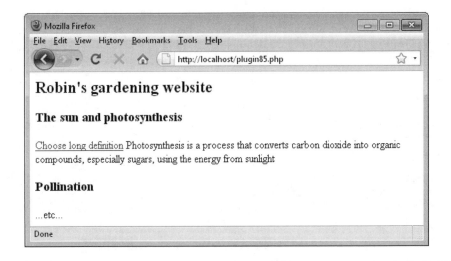

FIGURE 11-6   After clicking the toggle link, an alternative text and link are displayed.

How It Works

This program creates two `<div>` elements and then displays the contents of `$text1` and `$link1` in one of them and `$text2` and `$link2` in the other. The first `<div>` is made visible and the second invisible.

Using JavaScript and the `display` property, the links in each `<div>` are then set to make the other `<div>` visible and their own one invisible, having the effect of toggling between the two.

The links are created by setting the `<a href=` targets to `JavaScript://` and their `onClick` methods to change the display properties of the `<div>` contents. In order to allow you to use this plug-in multiple times within a document, the values assigned to the `id` property of each `<div>` also incorporate a random number between 0 and 1,000,000, created in `$tok` using the `rand()` function, which is appended to the `id` strings `PIPHP_TT1_` and `PIPHP_TT2_`.

All of this JavaScript is assembled into the string `$out`, which is then returned by the plug-in.

How to Use It

To use this plug-in, pass the two sets of texts and links to it and the string returned will be JavaScript that you can output to your document at the current location. For example, if you are writing about photosynthesis, you might like to create the following strings:

```
$text1 = " Photosynthesis is a process that converts carbon " .
         "dioxide into organic compounds, especially sugars, " .
         "using the energy from sunlight.";
$link1 = "Choose long definition";
```

```
$text2 = $text1 .
             " Photosynthesis occurs in plants, algae, and many " .
             "species of Bacteria, but not in Archaea. " .
             "Photosynthetic organisms are called photoautotrophs, " .
             "since it allows them to create their own food.";
$link2 = "Choose short definition";
```

You can then allow for the toggling between each of them by calling up the plug-in like this:

```
echo PIPHP_ToggleText($text1, $link1, $text2, $link2);
```

I have deliberately kept this all very simple so that you can replace the link text with any other text you like, or even a button or other image if you prefer, as you are also not restricted to only text in the $text1 and $text2 variables, and can include any HTML you like, including graphics and other tags.

If you would like to have your toggle link appear after (rather than before) the text, you'll have to modify the plug-in, moving the variables $text1 and $text2 to before the <a href= sections. In fact, now that you see how this works, you should be able to come up with a range of plug-ins for your own purposes to handle multiple <div> sections, not just two.

The Plug-in

```
function PIPHP_ToggleText($text1, $link1, $text2, $link2)
{
   $tok = rand(0, 1000000);
   $out  = "<div id='PIPHP_TT1_$tok' style='display:block;'>" .
           "<a href=\"javascript://\" onClick=\"document." .
           "getElementById('PIPHP_TT1_$tok').style.display=" .
           "'none'; document.getElementById('PIPHP_TT2_$tok')" .
           ".style.display='block';\">$link1</a>$text1</div>\n";

   $out  .= "<div id='PIPHP_TT2_$tok' style='display:none;'>" .
           "<a href=\"javascript://\" onClick=\"document." .
           "getElementById('PIPHP_TT1_$tok').style.display=" .
           "'block'; document.getElementById('PIPHP_TT2_$tok')" .
           ".style.display='none';\">$link2</a>$text2</div>\n";
   return $out;
}
```

Status Message

Sometimes it's useful to be able to change one element in an HTML page when the mouse passes over another one. A typical use for such a facility is offering a status message, or some additional informational text. This technique can also be used to good effect by replacing an image with some HTML as the mouse passes over different items. Figure 11-7 shows this plug-in used to provide a simple status message feature.

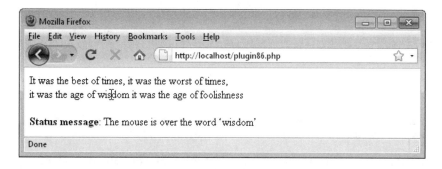

FIGURE 11-7 The opening words of Dickens' *A Tale of Two Cities* with the mouse over the hotspot word "wisdom"

About the Plug-in

This plug-in takes some text to display, for which an onMouseOver event will be created, the ID of an HTML element into which a status is to be inserted, and the status message itself. Both the $text and $status can include text and HTML. It requires the following arguments:

- **$text** The main text and/or HTML to display
- **$id** The ID of an element such as a <span> or <div>
- **$status** The message text and/or HTML

Variables, Arrays, and Functions

- None

How It Works

Although short and sweet, this is a powerful piece of code. What it does is create the JavaScript necessary to provide onMouseOver and onMouseOut events to *any* HTML element, provided in $text, by getting the contents of the element ID of $id (its innerHTML property) and then saving it in the JavaScript variable PIPHP_temp, before replacing it with the contents of $status.

When the mouse then leaves the area, the contents of PIPHP_temp are replaced back into the innerHTML property of $id.

How to Use It

To use this plug-in, decide on a part of your web page that will contain the status message. In the following example, a <span> with the ID of status is used. Then call the plug-in, passing it some text or HTML to display, and which, when the mouse passes over it, will trigger the status change (in other words, it will be a *hotspot*), the ID of the target element (in this case status), and the status message, like this:

```
echo "The ";
echo PIPHP_StatusMessage('JavaScript', 'status',
   'The mouse is over the word &lsquo;JavaScript&rsquo;');
echo " language is unconnected with the Java language.";
echo "<br /><br /><b>Status message</b>: <span id='status'>" .
   "Nothing to report</span>";
```

This will then display the following:

```
The JavaScript language is unconnected with the Java language.
Status message: Nothing to report
```

But when the mouse passes over the word JavaScript (the hotspot), this changes to the following:

```
The JavaScript language is unconnected with the Java language.
Status message: The mouse is over the word 'JavaScript'
```

However, because you can pass HTML as well as text to it, you can do much more with this plug-in than simply displaying a status message. For example, you could create a photo gallery in which each of the image names is passed to the plug-in, along with the associated HTML to display the photo, like in the following example, which will work if you have the files *camping.jpg, fishing.jpg, hiking.jpg,* and *swimming.jpg* in the current directory:

```
echo "View some recent photos: ";
echo PIPHP_StatusMessage('Camping ', 'photos',
   '<img src=camping.jpg width=640 height=320 />');
echo PIPHP_StatusMessage('Fishing ', 'photos',
   '<img src=fishing.jpg width=640 height=320 />');
echo PIPHP_StatusMessage('Hiking ',  'photos',
   '<img src=hiking.jpg width=640 height=320 />');
echo PIPHP_StatusMessage('Swimming', 'photos',
   '<img src=swimming.jpg width=640 height=320 />');
echo "<br /><span id='photos'>(Photo will appear here)</span>";
```

You can also use HTML in the $text argument, too, so you could place images or other elements there instead of text. You can even take this effect to the extreme and display different subsections of HTML, including images and other content, when the mouse passes over the various hotspots.

There's only one slight drawback to this plug-in, which is that, due to combining the two languages of PHP and JavaScript, it doesn't like any quotation marks, because each language has used up one of the two types. Therefore you should replace any you need to display with HTML entities such as " for a double quotation mark, or ‘ and ’ for left and right single quotation marks, and so on. This means that where you would normally enclose HTML elements within quotes, such as <img src='image.jpg' />, you should ignore them like this: <img src=image.jpg />. But don't worry. Your HTML will still work without them.

The Plug-in

```
function PIPHP_StatusMessage($text, $id, $status)
{
   $target = "getElementById('$id').innerHTML";
   return    "<span onMouseOver=\"PIPHP_temp=$target; " .
             "$target='$status';\" onMouseOut=\"$target=" .
             "PIPHP_temp;\">$text</span>";
}
```

87 Slide Show

If you have a collection of photos that you'd like to display in a smooth fading slide show, then this plug-in is just what you need. With it you simply pass an array of image URLs to it, and the JavaScript code you need to create a slide show is returned by it. Figure 11-8 shows the plug-in being used to display a series of photographs from a Flickr image stream.

About the Plug-in

This plug-in takes an array of image URLs and returns the JavaScript required to display them in a slide show. It requires the following argument:

- **$images** An array of image URLs

Variables, Arrays, and Functions

$count	PHP integer containing the number of URLs in $images
$out	PHP string containing the JavaScript to return
$j	PHP integer counter for iterating through $images
images	JavaScript array containing the image URLs from $images
counter	JavaScript integer for stepping through the images in images
step	JavaScript integer containing the amount to step through opacity values
fade	JavaScript integer containing the opacity amount
delay	JavaScript integer counter that counts up to pause
pause	JavaScript integer containing delay between changing images
startup	JavaScript integer containing the initial startup delay
opacity()	JavaScript function to set the degree of opacity of an image
load()	JavaScript function to load an image from a URL
$()	JavaScript function shorthand for document.getElementById()

FIGURE 11-8 This plug-in can display slideshows of images such as those in a Flickr stream.

How It Works

This plug-in starts by counting the number of images passed in the array $images and assigning the value to $count. Then $out is assigned the string `<script>` to indicate the start of JavaScript code, followed by a JavaScript statement to create a new array called images.

Then more JavaScript code is appended to $out by means of a for loop, which is used to assign each image URL from the PHP $images array into the src property of each element of the JavaScript images array. Then the remaining JavaScript code is added to $out.

Although this is a book on PHP, I'll very briefly explain what the JavaScript code does so that you can modify it if you choose.

At the start, a few variables are initialized that control the code's behavior. They mainly affect timing of the slideshow. Therefore, you can increase the initial value of fade to have less steps during a fade and so speed it up, or you can decrease the value assigned to pause, which represents the number of loops through which the code should cycle before moving onto the next image.

The next three lines of code prepare the slide show by loading the first image in the images array into the HTML elements with the IDs of PIPHP_SS1 and PIPHP_SS2, which must exist in your web page for this plug-in to work. Then an event is set to trigger every 20 milliseconds (thousandths of a second), which will call the function below it, called process().

The process() function is the core of the program and it controls the fading of images by incrementing the variable fade by the amount in step until it reaches 100, during which time it sets the transparencies of the two images so that one starts to become more transparent, while the other becomes more opaque, and so replaces the first.

Then the delay counter begins to increment in a loop, which first sets the invisible image to the same as the currently visible one, and then makes the previously invisible one visible (and the currently visible one invisible). This happens without the user seeing any change but means that a new image can now be loaded into the previously visible (but now invisible) image, ready to be faded in the next time around.

Then we come to the functions. The function opacity() has the commands necessary to change an object's opacity in Internet Explorer and most other browsers. The function load() loads an image into an HTML element, and the function $() is simply a shorthand that many JavaScript programmers use to save on typing document.getElementById(), as that is one of the most common statements you are likely to use in dynamic HTML processing.

How to Use It

To use this plug-in, you need to prepare some HTML such that two elements with the IDs of PIPHP_SS1 and PIPHP_SS2 exactly overlap each other. The plug-in will then place a different image in each of these elements and change the opacities of each to fade between them.

For example, I uploaded a few sample images to my *robinfnixon* Flickr account which the following code will use:

```php
$result = PIPHP_FetchFlickrStream('robinfnixon');
if (!$result[0]) echo "No images returned";
else
{
    $style = "'position:absolute; top:10px; left:10px'";
    echo "<img id='PIPHP_SS1' style=$style>";
    echo "<img id='PIPHP_SS2' style=$style>";
    echo PIPHP_SlideShow($result[1]);
}
```

By calling PIPHP_FetchFlickrStream() (plug-in 74), it saves you having to rummage about and assemble a few photos to try the plug-in with, but you will need to copy the *Fetch Flickr Stream* plug-in into your program, or otherwise include it, to use this example.

If you want to use your own images, then copy some into the same folder as the program and ignore the preceding example. Instead use code such as the following, replacing photo1.jpg with the name of your first image, and so on:

```
$style = "'position:absolute; top:10px; left:10px'";
echo "<img id='PIPHP_SS1' style=$style>";
echo "<img id='PIPHP_SS2' style=$style>";
$images = array('photo1.jpg', 'photo2.jpg', 'photo3.jpg');
echo PIPHP_SlideShow($images);
```

To make this work, the style= attribute of the <img> tag is used to tell the web browser to place each image exactly 10 pixels in from the left, and 10 pixels down from the top of the browser, which makes them overlap each other. The id= attributes then uniquely identify each image so that it can be manipulated by the JavaScript code. Just replace the style details with coordinates of your choosing for the part of the web page in which you want the slideshow to appear. You can even add borders to the images or any other elements you think would present them effectively.

The important thing about this plug-in is that all the images displayed should preferably have the same width and height so that they will all fade into each other neatly. At the very least you can get away with having them all with the same relative dimensions and then force a run-time resize in the image tags, like this:

```
echo "<img id='PIPHP_SS1' style=$style width='320' height='240'>";
echo "<img id='PIPHP_SS2' style=$style width='320' height='240'>";
```

The images will then fade neatly between each other, but any that are enlarged or reduced by these forced widths and heights will not look as good as if they had been properly resized in a graphics program.

The Plug-in

```
function PIPHP_SlideShow($images)
{
    $count = count($images);
    echo "<script>images = new Array($count);\n";

    for ($j=0 ; $j < $count ; ++$j)
    {
        echo "images[$j] = new Image();";
        echo "images[$j].src = '$images[$j]'\n";
    }

    return <<<_END
counter = 0
step    = 4
fade    = 100
delay   = 0
pause   = 250
startup = pause
```

```
load('PIPHP_SS1', images[0]);
load('PIPHP_SS2', images[0]);
setInterval('process()', 20);

function process()
{
    if (startup-- > 0) return;

    if (fade == 100)
    {
        if (delay < pause)
        {
            if (delay == 0)
            {
                fade = 0;
                load('PIPHP_SS1', images[counter]);
                opacity('PIPHP_SS1', 100);
                ++counter;

                if (counter == $count) counter = 0;

                load('PIPHP_SS2', images[counter]);
                opacity('PIPHP_SS2', 0);
            }
            ++delay;
        }
        else delay = 0;
    }
    else
    {
        fade += step;
        opacity('PIPHP_SS1', 100 - fade);
        opacity('PIPHP_SS2', fade);
    }
}

function opacity(id, deg)
{
    var object            = $(id).style;
    object.opacity        = (deg/100);
    object.MozOpacity     = (deg/100);
    object.KhtmlOpacity   = (deg/100);
    object.filter         = "alpha(opacity = " + deg + ")";
}

function load(id, img)
{
    $(id).src = img.src;
}

function $(id)
```

```
    {
        return document.getElementById(id)
    }

    </script>
    _END;
    }
```

⁸⁸ Input Prompt

Sometimes you can make the life of your users easier when filling out web forms by placing a prompt for what is required in the form field itself. Obviously you only want to do that when the field is blank; otherwise, if a field has a value then that's likely to be what the user wanted to enter.

Using this plug-in, whenever you create a form `<input>` element you can specify such a prompt, and it will only appear when the field contains no input. Figure 11-9 shows the plug-in being used to display the string *Required Field: Please enter your Username here* in a field where a username is being requested.

The plug-in is smart enough to note when a field has either been pre-supplied with a value, or if a user has started entering input, in which case it will not replace it with the prompt text. Figure 11-10 shows how it leaves the input well enough alone in such cases.

About the Plug-in

This plug-in creates the HTML and JavaScript required to enable the automatic displaying of a prompt within an input field whenever the field is left blank. It requires the following arguments:

- **$params**   Any additional parameters needed by the tag, including name=, type=, rows=, cols=, name=, size=, value=, and so on

- **$prompt**   The prompt to display

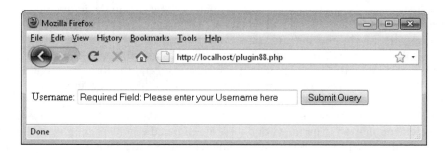

FIGURE 11-9   No text has been entered into the field so the prompt text is displayed.

FIGURE 11-10   If a field already has some text, the plug-in knows to not interfere.

Variables, Arrays, and Functions

$id	PHP string comprising PIPHP_IP_ and a random number
id	JavaScript string containing an input element ID
PIPHP_JS_IP1()	JavaScript function called when an element is given focus
PIPHP_JS_IP2()	JavaScript function called when an element loses focus
$()	JavaScript function shorthand for document.getElementById()

How It Works

So that this plug-in can be used multiple times in a page, it first creates a unique ID in $id, comprising the string PIPHP_IP_ and a random number between 0 and a million. This ID is then used for all the form input elements wherever they are referenced by the HTML and JavaScript that the plug-in assembles.

Next a string of HTML and JavaScript is returned, starting with an HTML <input... tag. The ID in $id is then assigned to the tag, as well as the parameters in $params. Additionally, two events are added to trigger calls to a pair of functions whenever the user selects or deselects the input field. When the user gives the field focus by clicking in it, the onFocus event handler calls PIPHP_JS_IP1(), and when the field loses focus, because the user has removed focus (generally by clicking elsewhere), then the onBlur event handler calls PIPHP_JS_IP2(). In either case, the ID of the input field is passed as the only parameter.

Next the JavaScript is created by opening a <script> tag, and the first statement there calls up PIPHP_JS_IP1() to ensure that the prompt text is displayed if the input field has nothing in it.

Next come the two functions just mentioned. The first one, PIPHP_JS_IP1(), checks the value of the element referred to by the variable id, and if it is the same as the contents of the variable prompt, then the prompt is currently being displayed and so it is removed, ready for the user to enter their own data.

The second function, PIPHP_JS_IP2(), does the inverse of that just mentioned. If the input field identified by id is empty, it inserts the value in the variable prompt into the field.

Finally, the function $() is used as a handy way to save on typing document .getElementById() several times. Then the script is closed with a </script> tag, and the _END; indicates the end of the multiline string, which is then returned.

How to Use It

Use this plug-in as a replacement for creating an `<input>` tag, like this:

```
$prompt = 'Please enter your Username here';
echo "<form method='post' action='program.php'>";
echo "Username: " . PIPHP_InputPrompt("name='uname' type='text'
        size='50'", $prompt);
echo "<input type=submit></form>";
```

In this example an HTML form is created, within which the word `Username:` is displayed, followed by a call to `PIPHP_InputPrompt()`. Then a submit button is added and the form is closed.

Two arguments are passed to the plug-in. First, there are the parameters an `<input>` tag would generally need—in this case, they are a name, the type, and the size, in the string `name='uname' type='text' size='50'`. If required, an initial value could have been defined here by adding `value='a value'` to the string. This would be useful, for example, where a form has already been submitted but is being returned to the user for amending, and where you do have a submitted value for this field. If the user then removes such a predefined value, this plug-in will kick in again and start placing the prompt in the field if it is left empty.

The second argument is the prompt to display, which might be something like *enter your e-mail address*, or *type your name here*, and so on. Just make sure it's not longer than the size of the input window or some of it won't display.

One thing to remember when you use this plug in is that if a user submits the form with the prompt text still visible, then that is the value that will be passed to your program. But this should be easy to catch because you already know the value of your prompt text, likely having it stored in a string such as $prompt, so you can easily check the input received against that value and act accordingly.

Once you start using this plug-in, you should find that the number of successfully submitted forms you receive rises, because you will have added extra assistance for your users that is informational but doesn't distract them from completing your form. But remember that this plug-in only provides an additional prompt to your users and doesn't ensure they actually follow it—for that you need to validate the data received when it arrives at the server.

The plug-in has also been designed to be smart enough to know when it has been called more than once, and will only return the necessary JavaScript functions a single time. This means you can safely use it multiple times within the same document, or even the same form. It manages this by using the `static` PHP variable `$PIPHP_IP_NUM` as a usage counter; a static variable being one that resumes its value when a function is reentered.

The Plug-in

```
function PIPHP_InputPrompt($params, $prompt)
{
    $id = 'PIPHP_IP_' . rand(0, 1000000);

    $out = <<<_END
```

```
<input id='$id' $params
   onFocus="PIPHP_JS_IP1('$id', '$prompt')"
   onBlur="PIPHP_JS_IP2('$id', '$prompt')" />
_END;

   static $PIPHP_IP_NUM;
   if ($PIPHP_IP_NUM++ == 0) $out .= <<<_END
<script>
PIPHP_JS_IP2('$id', '$prompt')

function PIPHP_JS_IP1(id, prompt)
{
   if ($(id).value == prompt) $(id).value = ""
}

function PIPHP_JS_IP2(id, prompt)
{
   if ($(id).value == "") $(id).value = prompt
}

function $(id)
{
   return document.getElementById(id)
}
</script>
_END;
   return $out;
}
```

PLUG-IN 89 Words from Root

Whenever you can save your users a little typing, then you give them yet another reason to use your web site in preference to others. One neat trick is to provide a clickable list of words the user is likely to be entering. For example, Figure 11-11 shows the word part appl entered as part of the GET variable word, and underneath it the first 20 words found in a local dictionary beginning with those letters can be seen.

FIGURE 11-11 The plug-in has returned 20 words beginning with the letters *appl*.

Of course, just displaying a list of words isn't too helpful, and the following plug-in, *Predict Word*, will use some JavaScript to finish off the feature. However, I have still listed this plug-in in its own right because it can often be handy to be able to look up lists of words or phrases based on their first few letters, such as in crossword helper programs, contact directories, and so on, and this routine is flexible enough to deal with both words and phrases.

About the Plug-in

This plug-in takes the first few letters of a word and returns all the words or phrases in the dictionary that begin with those letters, up to a maximum number. It requires the following arguments:

- **$word**   A word root
- **$filename**   The path to a dictionary file
- **$max**   The maximum number of words/phrases to return

Variables, Arrays, and Functions

$dict	String containing a collection of words or phrases separated by \n characters or \r\n pairs
$matches	Array containing all matching words found in $dict
$c	Integer containing either $max or the number of words found, if less
$out	Array of words to return

How It Works

This plug-in loads a file of words or phrases into the string variable $dict. The words or phrases must be separated by a character that isn't a letter or number, or the hyphen or underline character. Typically, the \n character or \r\n pair of characters will do the job, and also make the file easy to load into and edit in a text editor.

The preg_match_all() function is then called with a search regular expression of \b$word[\w]+, which means "starting at any word boundary look for occurrences of the string in $word, followed by any word characters or spaces,"—in other words all letters, digits, hyphens, underlines, and spaces are allowed; anything else indicates a non-word/phrase. This will match any words or phrases in the dictionary file that begin with $word. All the matches found are then placed into the array $matches[0].

The variable $c is then set to either $max or to the number of matches made, whichever is the lower number, using the min() function. Then the array $out is populated with exactly $c words from the $matches[0] array, and that array is returned.

How to Use It

To use this plug-in, pass it the three arguments it requires, a root word, the filename of a dictionary file, and the maximum number of words to return, like this:

```
$list = PIPHP_WordsFromRoot('appl', 'dictionary.txt', 20);
```

The array $list will then contain up to $max words. Or, for the purposes of the next plug-in, *Predict Word,* you would use the following code to read up to two GET arguments from the command line and then return a string, with the words separated by | characters, like this:

```
$out = "";
$max = 5;
if (!isset($_GET['word'])) exit;
if (isset($_GET['max'])) $max = $_GET['max'];
$result = PIPHP_WordsFromRoot($_GET['word'],
    'dictionary.txt', $max);
if ($result != FALSE)
    foreach ($result as $word) $out .= "$word|";
echo substr($out, 0, -1);
```

On a server with the domain myserver.com, running the program program.php, the preceding example code could be called up using a URL such as this:

```
http://myserver.com/program.php?word=appr&max=20
```

By default, five words will be returned, but if a GET argument is passed in the variable max, as in &max=20, then $max will be changed to the supplied value. When output, each word has a | sign after it as a separator, so when the final word has been sent, a call is made to the substr() function to strip the last unwanted | from $out before echoing its contents.

If you download *plug-ins.zip* from the companion web site at *www.pluginphp.com* and extract it, you will find this program in the folder *11,* saved under the filename *wordsfromroot .php.* In that folder, there's also a dictionary file of over 80,000 words called *dictionary.txt.*

The Plug-in

```
function PIPHP_WordsFromRoot($word, $filename, $max)
{
    $dict  = file_get_contents($filename);
    preg_match_all('/\b' . $word . '[\w ]+/', $dict, $matches);
    $c     = min(count($matches[0]), $max);
    $out   = array();
    for ($j = 0 ; $j < $c ; ++$j) $out[$j] = $matches[0][$j];
    return $out;
}
```

PLUG-IN 90   Predict Word

Many more recent applications such as web browsers offer the user the ability to select input from a drop-down list of words or phrases similar to what the user is typing. This predictive technology is also often used for texting on mobile phones. Using this plug-in, you can add the same facility to your web forms, as shown by Figure 11-12.

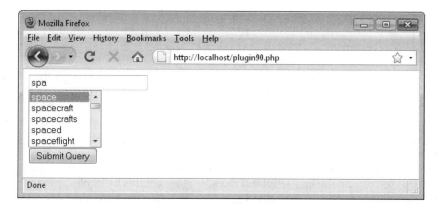

FIGURE 11-12   The plug-in displays a selection of possible words the user may be intending to type.

About the Plug-in

This plug-in creates the HTML and JavaScript required to provide a selection of words or phrases beginning with the letters input so far, from which the user can choose to make a selection. It requires the following arguments:

- **$params**   Any additional parameters needed by the tag, including name=, type=, rows=, cols=, name=, size=, value=, and so on
- **$view**   The maximum number of items to display in the selection box (if there are any more than this, the list becomes scrollable)
- **$max**   The maximum number of items to suggest

Variables, Arrays, and Functions

$id	PHP random number between 0 and 1,000,000
$out	PHP string to be returned by the plug-in
$j	PHP integer loop counter for creating the `<option>` list
PIPHP_JS_CopyWord()	JavaScript function to copy a word to the input
PIPHP_JS_PredictWord()	JavaScript function to display suggested words
PIPHP_JS_GetAjaxRequest2()	JavaScript function to prepare an Ajax request
PIPHP_JS_AjaxRequest()	JavaScript function to perform an Ajax request
$()	JavaScript function shorthand for getElementById()

How It Works

Some of the JavaScript functions in this plug-in are modified versions of those used in plug-in 83, *Get Ajax Request*. As a whole, though, this JavaScript code is too complex to fully explain in a book on PHP, and I don't recommend you try to modify it unless you are very experienced with JavaScript. However, here's a general outline of what it does.

Whenever the user types a letter into the input field, an Ajax request is issued to the program *wordsfromroot.php*, which then returns a list of words that begin with the letters so far entered. Each of these words is then placed in <option> fields of a <select> statement in order to display them in a drop-down list.

If the user then clicks any of these offered words, a function is called to copy the word into the input field, and the list of suggested words is then cleared. In the process, a lot of use is made of hiding and revealing elements using their style.display properties, and the size of the displayed list is also manipulated according to the number of words to show.

Due to appending a random number in $id to all ID names, this function can be successfully reused within a web page, or even the same form since the code is smart enough to realize it has been called one or more additional times and only creates the form elements required, without re-creating the JavaScript functions. It manages this by implementing the static variable counter $PIPHP_PW_NUM, which retains its value between calls to the function.

How to Use It

Use this plug-in as a replacement for a standard <input> tag inside an HTML form, like this:

```
echo "<form method='post'>";
echo PIPHP_PredictWord("name='word' type='text'", 5, 20);
echo "<input type='submit'></form>\n";
```

Here some standard parameters used in an <input> tag have been passed, along with two additional arguments: the maximum number of suggested words to show at a time in the drop-down box (the number of lines on view), and the maximum number of words to suggest in total. If the second parameter is larger, then the drop-down list will become scrollable. In the preceding case, the list will often be scrollable since up to 20 words can be offered, with only 5 displayed at any time.

The supplied *dictionary.txt* file on the companion web site at *www.pluginphp.com* only includes single words, but you can also replace the contents of the file (or use a different one), with a list of useful phrases (perhaps gleaned from extracting common search terms from your log files). Just ensure you don't add any punctuation or you may get unexpected results.

If you use a different PHP program to supply the suggested words or phrases, remember to change the reference in the code to *wordsfromroot.php* to that of the new program.

The Plug-in

```
function PIPHP_PredictWord($params, $view, $max)
{
    $id  = rand(0, 1000000);
    $out = "<input id='PIPHP_PWI_$id' $params" .
           "onKeyUp='PIPHP_JS_PredictWord($view, $max, $id)'><br />" .
           "<select id='PIPHP_PWS_$id' style='display:none' />\n";

    for ($j = 0 ; $j < $max ; ++$j)
        $out .= "<option id='PIPHP_PWO_$j" . "_$id' " .
                "onClick='PIPHP_JS_CopyWord(this.id, $id)'>";

    $out .= '</select>';
    static $PIPHP_PW_NUM;
```

```
    if ($PIPHP_PW_NUM++ == 0) $out .= <<<_END
<script>

function PIPHP_JS_CopyWord(id1, id2)
{
   $('PIPHP_PWI_' + id2).value = $(id1).innerHTML
   $('PIPHP_PWS_' + id2).style.display = 'none';
}

function PIPHP_JS_PredictWord(view, max, id)
{
   if ($('PIPHP_PWI_' + id).value.length > 0)
   {
      PIPHP_JS_GetAjaxRequest2('wordsfromroot.php',
         'word=' + $('PIPHP_PWI_' + id).value +
         '&max=' + max, view, max, id)
      $('PIPHP_PWS_' + id).scrollTop = 0
      $('PIPHP_PWO_0_' + id).selected = true
   }
   else $('PIPHP_PWS_' + id).style.display = 'none'
}

function PIPHP_JS_GetAjaxRequest2(url, params, view, max, id)
{
   nocache = "&nocache=" + Math.random() * 1000000
   request = new PIPHP_JS_AjaxRequest()

   request.onreadystatechange = function()
   {
      if (this.readyState == 4)
         if (this.status == 200)
            if (this.responseText != null)
            {
               a = this.responseText.split('|')
               c = 0

               for (j in a)
               {
                  $('PIPHP_PWO_' + c + '_' + id).
                     innerHTML = a[j]
                  $('PIPHP_PWO_' + c++ + '_' + id).
                     style.display = 'block'
               }

               n = c > view ? view : c
               while (c < max)
               {
                  $('PIPHP_PWO_' + c++ + '_' + id).
                     style.display = 'none'
               }
               $('PIPHP_PWS_' + id).size = n;
               $('PIPHP_PWS_' + id).style.display = 'block'
            }
```

```
// You can remove these two alerts after debugging
            else alert("Ajax error: No data received")
          else alert( "Ajax error: " + this.statusText)
    }

    request.open("GET", url + "?" + params + nocache, true)
    request.send(null)
}

function PIPHP_JS_AjaxRequest()
{
    try
    {
       var request = new XMLHttpRequest()
    }
    catch(e1)
    {
       try
       {
          request = new ActiveXObject("Msxml2.XMLHTTP")
       }
       catch(e2)
       {
          try
          {
             request = new ActiveXObject("Microsoft.XMLHTTP")
          }
          catch(e3)
          {
             request = false
          }
       }
    }
    return request
}

function $(id)
{
    return document.getElementById(id)
}
</script>
_END;
    return $out;
}
```

CHAPTER 12

Diverse Solutions

A number of plug-ins I wanted to include in this book didn't quite fit into any of the categories of the other chapters. So here are the final ten plug-ins which, as the chapter title suggests, offer diverse solutions to a variety of programming problems, including geo-location, "bot" detection, data about books, word and spelling functions, language translation, rounded table borders, and Bing maps.

91 Get Country by IP

Knowing which country a web visitor is from can be extremely useful to a webmaster. For example, a personal ads site could use this information to match people up from the same country, as could an auction or classifieds web site. Or perhaps you have servers in different countries and want to refer visitors to the one nearest to them, or maybe you simply want to show different advertising or other content to different territories.

Whatever the reason, this plug-in, which comes with its own data file, will tell you where a surfer is located, as can be seen from Figure 12-1, in which Google's IP number has been correctly identified as being located in the U.S.

About the Plug-in

This plug-in takes an IP address and then returns the name of the country to which the IP has been allocated. Upon failure, it returns FALSE. It requires the following argument:

- **$ip** An IP address

Variables, Arrays, and Functions

$iptemp	Array containing the four parts of $ip
$ipdec	Integer containing the IP address after conversion to decimal
$file	String containing contents of the file *ips.txt*
$lines	Array of all data lines extracted from $file
$line	String containing a single line from $lines
$parts	Array containing all the parts of $line

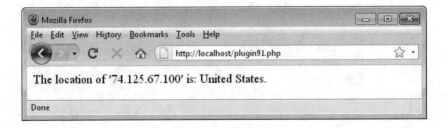

FIGURE 12-1   Provided with google.com's IP number, this plug-in correctly identifies its country.

How it Works

This plug-in takes the four parts of an IP address and converts them into a decimal number. This can be done because all IP addresses actually refer to decimal numbers but are separated out into four parts for reasons of convenience and readability. Therefore the *google.com* IP address of 74.125.67.100 can be turned into its decimal equivalent using the following process:

```
DecimalIP =
    74 * 256 * 256 * 256 +
   125 * 256 * 256 +
    67 * 256 +
   100
```

This results in the values 1241513984, 8192000, 17152, and 100, which add up to 1249723236. And you can prove to yourself that this works by using that number in a URL, like this (go ahead, try it!):

```
http://1249723236
```

Anyhow, what this means is that decimal numbers are a good way to store ranges of IP numbers, which is exactly what has been done in the file *ips.txt*, supplied on the accompanying *www.pluginphp.com* web site. You will find it, along with all the plug-ins in this chapter, inside the folder entitled *12*. The file has over 80,000 lines in it, each one representing the allocation of a range of IP addresses. Each line has three items separated by commas: the start IP address, the end IP address, and the name of the country to which that range is allocated.

So, what the plug-in does is convert `$ip` to its decimal equivalent in `$ipdec` by first extracting the four parts into the array `$iptemp` using the `explode()` function. Then it loads *ips.txt* into the string `$file`, from where all the data lines are extracted into the array `$lines`.

A `foreach` loop is then used to iterate through the array, placing each line of data into the variable `$line`. Then, as long as `$line` contains a string value, it separates out the three items of data in `$line` into the `$parts` array. If `$ipdec` is then found to be equal to or within the two IP addresses in `$parts[1]` and `$parts[2]`, a match has been made and so the associated country name in `$parts[2]` is returned.

If no match is found in the database, then `FALSE` is returned. This will most likely happen if you look up the country for a non-geographic IP address such as 127.0.0.1, for instance, which always refers to the local computer.

How to Use It

To use this plug-in, just pass it an IP address, like this:

```
$ip = '74.125.67.100';
$result = PIPHP_GetCountryFromIP($ip);
if (!$result) echo "Could not identify location for '$ip'.";
else echo "The location of '$ip' is: $result.";
```

Or, to look up the country of the current user, you could use this code to call the plug-in:

```
$result = PIPHP_GetCountryFromIP($_SERVER['REMOTE_ADDR']);
```

Make sure the *ips.txt* file is in the same folder as your program, or modify the plug-in to point to its location.

When using this plug-in, remember that your users may be accessing your web site through a proxy server in a different locality, so you cannot guarantee that a user is actually from the country indicated. The best you can identify is the country in which the final IP at the end of any proxy chain resides. Therefore, you may wish to allow users to manually select their own country if the one you offer is incorrect.

The Plug-in

```
function PIPHP_GetCountryFromIP($ip)
{
    $iptemp = explode('.', $ip);
    $ipdec  = $iptemp[0] * 256 * 256 * 256 +
              $iptemp[1] * 256 * 256 +
              $iptemp[2] * 256 +
              $iptemp[3];
    $file  = file_get_contents('ips.txt');
    if (!strlen($file)) return FALSE;

    $lines = explode("\n", $file);

    foreach($lines as $line)
    {
        $data  = trim($line);
        $parts = explode(',', $data);

        if (strlen($line))
        {
            $parts = explode(',', trim($line));

            if ($ipdec >= $parts[0] && $ipdec <= $parts[1])
                return $parts[2];
        }
    }

    return FALSE;
}
```

Bypass Captcha

The reason you might use a Captcha system, such as plug-in 33, is to prevent your web site from being overwhelmed with posts made by automated "bots." The trouble is, many people find it annoying to fill in a Captcha, so this plug-in is there to help. Using it, your program can make a quick guess at whether the current user is human or not, and if it thinks they *are* human, bypass using a Captcha. Figure 12-2 shows a web page that has been typed in directly and which therefore has no referring page, so it has returned a value of FALSE.

However, the web page shown includes a link which, if it is clicked, will result in creating a referring page that will be sent to the browser. Most "bots" don't send one of these. Also, the page is being viewed in a web browser, so its User Agent string is also being sent to the plug-in. In light of receiving these two items of data, the plug-in returns a value of TRUE and, as Figure 12-3 suggests, it's probably safe to not use a Captcha.

FIGURE 12-2   It appears that the page may have been called up by a "bot," so adding a Captcha is a good idea.

About the Plug-in

This plug-in doesn't take any arguments, but if it thinks the current user is human, it returns TRUE; otherwise, it returns FALSE.

Variables, Arrays, and Functions

`$_SERVER['HTTP_REFERER']`	Array element containing any referring page
`$_SERVER['HTTP_USER_AGENT']`	Array element containing any User Agent string

How It Works

This is another of those short and sweet, yet highly useful plug-ins. All it does is check the values of both `$_SERVER['HTTP_REFERER']` and `$_SERVER['HTTP_USER_AGENT']`. If they both have a value, then it returns FALSE; otherwise, it returns TRUE.

How to Use It

To use this plug-in, just call it and decide what to do based on the result returned, like this:

```
if (!PIPHP_CaptchaBypass())
{
   // Captcha code goes here
}
```

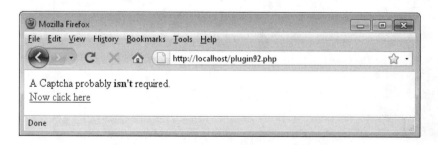

FIGURE 12-3   It looks like a person is using the web site, so there's probably no need for a Captcha.

Just place this code surrounding your call to your Captcha routine, and again around the code where you verify the Captcha once it has been submitted. The code will then only run if the returned value is FALSE, indicating the possibility that the user may be a "bot."

The Plug-in

```
function PIPHP_CaptchaBypass()
{
    if (isset($_SERVER['HTTP_REFERER']) &&
        isset($_SERVER['HTTP_USER_AGENT']))
            return TRUE;
    return FALSE;
}
```

PLUG-IN 93 Get Book from ISBN

If you have a web site that has anything to do with books, you should find this plug-in very useful. With it you can take an ISBN-10 number and it will return both the associated book's title and a thumbnail of its cover. Figure 12-4 shows details being returned for the ISBN-10 of 007149216X, another excellent McGraw-Hill publication.

All books also have an alternate ISBN-13 number, which starts with the digits 978. However, the Amazon web site uses ISBN-10 numbers in its web page URLs and so only ISBN-10 numbers are supported by this plug-in. Amazon web services are also available to handle both the ISBN-10 and ISBN-13 lookups, but they require more code and that you have an Amazon Web Services account—hence, my settling on using this technique to keep the code short and simple.

About the Plug-in

This plug-in searches the *amazon.com* web site for details on a supplied ISBN-10 number. If it finds them, it returns a two-element array, the first of which is the book's title, while the second is the URL to a thumbnail image of the book's cover. It requires the following argument:

- **$isbn** An ISBN-10 number

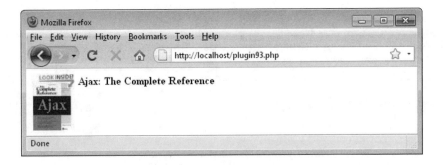

FIGURE 12-4   This plug-in quickly looks up a book's title and also returns its cover.

Variables, Arrays, and Functions

$find	String containing HTML text to find
$url	String containing the URL to load
$page	String containing the contents of $url
$ptr1	Integer pointer to the first occurrence of $find
$ptr2	Integer pointer to subsequent occurrence of " />
$title	String containing the book's title
$image	String containing the URL of a thumbnail image of the book's cover

How It Works

This plug-in loads the contents of $url into the variable $page, returning FALSE if the URL cannot be accessed. The URL comprises the main Amazon web address plus the details required to access details of the book referred to by $isbn.

Then the string in $find is searched for using the strpos() function. If it is located, then a book associated with $isbn has been found and the HTML following will be its title. Therefore, the end of the title is searched for, which is the string " />. Once both strings have been found, their start locations will be in $ptr1 and $ptr2, so using these values, the title is extracted with a call to substr().

The image thumbnail URL is extracted in a similar manner by looking for the string "><img src=", followed by a URL and a double quotation mark.

The two strings are then returned in a two-element array.

How to Use It

To use this plug-in, pass it a ten-digit ISBN number, like this:

```
$isbn = '007149216X';
$result = PIPHP_GetBookFromISBN($isbn);
if (!$result) echo "Could not find title for ISBN '$isbn'.";
else echo "<img src='$result[1]' align='left'><b>$result[0]";
```

The array element $result[0] will be FALSE if no book was found, otherwise it contains the book's title, and $result[1] contains the URL of a thumbnail image of the book's cover.

If you have an Amazon Associates account, this is the perfect place to add a link to it in order to be paid a commission if the book is subsequently purchased.

The Plug-in

```
function PIPHP_GetBookFromISBN($isbn)
{
   $find = '<meta name="description" content="Amazon.com:';
   $url  = "http://www.amazon.com/gp/aw/d.html?a=$isbn";
   $page = file_get_contents($url);
   if (!strlen($page)) return array(FALSE);
```

```
$ptr1 = strpos($page, $find) + strlen($find);
if (!$ptr1) return array(FALSE);

$ptr2  = strpos($page, '" />', $ptr1);
$title = substr($page, $ptr1, $ptr2 - $ptr1);

$find = '"><img src="';
$ptr1  = strpos($page, $find) + strlen($find);
$ptr2  = strpos($page, '"', $ptr1);
$image = substr($page, $ptr1, $ptr2 - $ptr1);

return array($title, $image);
}
```

PLUG-IN 94   Get Amazon Sales Rank

Sometimes it can be interesting to know how well a book is doing at Amazon. With this utility you can find out that information from all six worldwide Amazon web sites. Figure 12-5 shows the plug-in being used to look up the sales rank information for the book used in the previous plug-in.

About the Plug-in

This plug-in takes an ISBN number and the domain of an Amazon web site and then returns the sales rank for that title on that site. Upon success, it returns a number representing the book's popularity, with 1 being the most popular. Upon failure, for example if the book is not found, or if it doesn't have a rank, it returns FALSE. It requires the following arguments:

- **$isbn**   An ISBN-10 number
- **$site**   An Amazon web domain, out of: amazon.com, amazon.ca, amazon.co.uk, amazon.fr, amazon.de, and amazon.co.jp

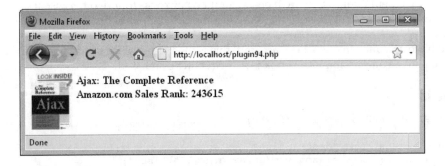

FIGURE 12-5   Using this plug-in, sales rank information has also been returned from Amazon.

Variables, Arrays, and Functions

$url	String containing the URL of the Amazon mobile web site (for speed)
$find	String containing the text to find immediately preceding a Sales Rank
$end	String containing the text to find immediately following a Sales Rank
$page	String containing the contents of $url
$ptr1	Integer pointer to start of $find
$ptr2	Integer pointer to start of $end
$temp	String containing Sales Rank before removing non-digit characters

How It Works

This plug-in extracts sales rank information from five of the six Amazon mobile web sites. The sixth site used however, *amazon.co.jp*, is the main web URL, since its mobile site appears not to provide sales rank information.

The plug-in works by loading the default URL, comprising the value in $site into $url, and the HTML immediately following the sales rank details into $end.

Then a switch statement is used for the different values of $site. In the case of the three English speaking countries, the sites *amazon.com*, *amazon.ca*, and *amazon.co.uk* set the variable $find to the string Sales Rank:, which is what will be searched for in the web page.

The two European web sites, *amazon.fr* and *amazon.de*, replace the string with French and German translations of the phrase "sales rank," while the Japanese web site at *amazon.co.jp* has a different pre– and post–sales rank data string to search for.

With these details prepared, the contents of $url is loaded into $page. If this is unsuccessful, then FALSE is returned. Otherwise, the strpos() function is used to find the first occurrence of $find, the location of which is placed in $ptr1. Again, if it is not found, FALSE is returned.

Next, $ptr2 is given the location of the subsequent occurrence of $end and the string in between the two is extracted into $temp, from where any non-digit characters are removed before returning its value.

How to Use It

To obtain a book's sales rank at a particular Amazon site, just pass the ISBN and domain to the plug-in like this (which should achieve a similar result to that shown in Figure 12-5):

```
echo PIPHP_GetAmazonSalesRank('007149216X', 'amazon.com');
```

Or you could combine this plug-in with the previous one, as follows:

```
$isbn = '007149216X';
$result = PIPHP_GetBookFromISBN($isbn);
if (!$result) echo "Could not find title for ISBN '$isbn'.";
else
{
   echo "<img src='$result[1]' align='left'><b>$result[0]<br>" .
        "Amazon.com Sales Rank: ";
   echo PIPHP_GetAmazonSalesRank($isbn, 'amazon.com');
}
```

If you do combine the pair, make sure both plug-ins are pasted into your code, or are otherwise included.

The Plug-in

```
function PIPHP_GetAmazonSalesRank($isbn, $site)
{
    $url = "http://www.$site/gp/aw/d.html?pd=1" .
           "&l=Product%20Details&a=$isbn";
    $end = '<br />';

    switch(strtolower($site))
    {
        case 'amazon.com':
        case 'amazon.ca':
        case 'amazon.co.uk':
            $find = 'Sales Rank: ';
            break;
        case 'amazon.fr':
            $find = 'ventes Amazon.fr: ';
            break;
        case 'amazon.de':
            $find = 'Verkaufsrang: ';
            break;
        case 'amazon.co.jp':
            $find = '<li id="SalesRank">';
            $url  = "http://$site/gp/product/$isbn";
            $end  = '(<a';
            break;
    }

    $page = file_get_contents($url);
    if (!strlen($page)) return FALSE;

    $ptr1 = strpos($page, $find);
    if (!$ptr1) return FALSE;

    $ptr2 = strpos($page, $end, $ptr1);
    $temp = substr($page, $ptr1, $ptr2 - $ptr1);
    return trim(preg_replace('/[^\d]/', '', $temp));
}
```

PLUG-IN 95   Pattern Match Word

Having a dictionary of 80,000 words at hand, it's a shame not to do more with it, so this and the next plug-in provide more word-related features.

This plug-in will be of use in crossword- or Scrabble game–like scenarios, where you know the number of letters in a word and even have a few letters in place. Given such details, as Figure 12-6 shows, this plug-in will return all possible words in the dictionary that could fit.

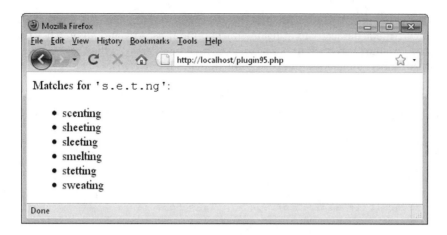

FIGURE 12-6   The plug-in has found six matches for the pattern s.e.t.ng.

About the Plug-in

This plug-in takes a word pattern and then returns a two-element array in which the first is the number of matching words found and the second is an array of the words themselves. On failure, it returns a single-element array with the value FALSE. It requires the following arguments:

- **$word**   A word pattern comprising letters and periods (for unknowns)
- **$dictionary**   The path to a file of words

Variables, Arrays, and Functions

$dict	String containing the contents of $dictionary
$matches[0]	Array containing all the matching words

How It Works

This plug-in takes advantage of PHP's built-in regular expression handling by loading the dictionary file in $dictionary into $dict and then matching its contents against the pattern supplied in $word.

If $dict has no value, the dictionary wasn't found and so a single-element array with the value FALSE is returned. Otherwise, the dictionary contents are loaded into $dict. The dictionary file should contain words separated by non-word characters or sequences of characters. If you use \n or \r\n pairs as separators (as in the supplied *dictionary.txt* file on the *www.pluginphp.com* web site), then the file can be loaded into and edited by most program and text editors.

Before performing the matching, the contents of $word are processed with the preg_replace() function to remove any non-alphabetic or period characters and to convert the entire string to lowercase using the strtolower() function.

A call to the preg_match_all() function is then made, passing the value in $match, surrounded by \b metacharacters to indicate word boundaries. Any and all matches made are then placed into the array in $matches[0]. A two-element array is then returned containing the number of matches found, and the matches themselves.

How to Use It

To use this plug-in, pass it a pattern to match and the path to a file of words, like this:

```
$result = PIPHP_PatternMatchWord('S.e.t.ng', 'dictionary.txt');
if ($result[0] != FALSE)
{
    echo "Matches for <font face='Courier New'>" .
        "'$word'</font>:<br><ul>";
    foreach ($result[1] as $match) echo "<li>$match</li>";
}
```

In this example, as long as $result[0] isn't FALSE, then some matches were made, so a foreach loop iterates through them all in $result[1], displaying them as list elements within an unsorted list, but you could use these words in drop-down lists, with checkboxes, or in a variety of other ways.

If you download the file *plug-ins.zip* from the companion web site at *www.pluginphp.com*, you will find a copy of the *dictionary.txt* file in the folder entitled *12*.

The Plug-in

```
function PIPHP_PatternMatchWord($word, $dictionary)
{
    $dict = @file_get_contents($dictionary);
    if (!strlen($dict)) return array(FALSE);

    $word = preg_replace('/[^a-z\.]/', '', strtolower($word));
    preg_match_all('/\b' . $word . '\b/', $dict, $matches);
    return array(count($matches[0]), $matches[0]);
}
```

96 Suggest Spelling

In Chapter 3, plug-in 8, I introduced a simple spelling checker. Well here's a companion plug-in you could use with it to actually offer suggested replacements for misspelled words. As Figure 12-7 shows, using the same dictionary of words, this plug-in attempts to find the closest matches to a word it is passed, and returns them in order of likelihood.

About the Plug-in

This plug-in takes a word that has been unrecognized and returns the closest matches to it. Upon success, it returns a two-element array, the first of which contains the number of words returned, while the second contains an array of words. On failure, it returns a single-element array with the value FALSE. It requires the following arguments:

- **$word** A word
- **$dictionary** The path to a file of words

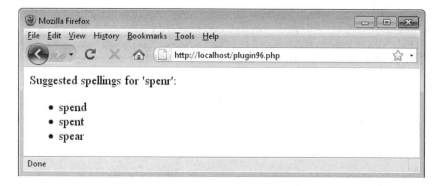

FIGURE 12-7 The plug-in has chosen three possible spelling corrections for the word *spenr*.

Variables, Arrays, and Functions

$count	Static integer containing number of calls to the plug-in
$words	Static array containing words extracted from $dict
$dict	String containing the contents of $dictionary
$possibles	Array containing possible similar words
$known	Array containing all words both on $possibles and $words
$suggested	Array containing all the suggested words
$wordlen	Integer containing the length of $word
$chars	Array containing all the letters of the alphabet
$temp	String containing key extracted from element of $known
$val	String containing value extracted from element of $known

How It Works

The first thing this plug-in does is check whether $word has a value, and if not, it returns a single-element array with the value FALSE.

After that, two variables are declared as *static*. The reason is that this plug-in is built in such a way that it can be called more than once, something that's likely if a section of text has more than one unknown word. Therefore for optimum speed it uses static variables, which retain their value between calls to the function, but outside the function they have no value or a different value. This avoids re-creating large arrays each time the function is called.

The two static variables used are $count, which counts the number of times the function has been called and $words which contains an array of words. If $count has a value of zero, then this is the first time the function has been called and so the contents of $dictionary are loaded into $dict, and as long as the load was successful, the words are split out into the array $words using the explode() function.

On future calls to the function, $count will have a value greater than zero and therefore populating the $words array is unnecessary since $words is a static variable that will remember its contents from the last call. Note that this static value is accessible each time the function is recalled, but only persists during the response to a single web request. Subsequent web requests always start with PHP variables not existing until they are defined.

Next, three arrays are prepared. These are $possibles, which will contain a large number of words the program will make up that are similar to $word. Then there is $known, which will contain all the words in $possibles that also exist in the dictionary of words in $words—in other words, they are proper words, even though they were created by an algorithm. Lastly, there's $suggested, which will be populated with all the words the plug-in wishes to return as suggested replacements for $word.

The variable $wordlen is then set to the length of $word and the array $chars is created out of the 26 letters of the alphabet by using str_split() to split up the provided string.

Next a whole collection of made-up words similar to $word have to be placed in $possibles. Four types of new words are created:

1. The set of words similar to $word but with each letter missing
2. The set of words similar to $word but with each letter substituted with another
3. The set of words similar to $word but with letter pairs swapped
4. The set of words similar to $word but with new letters inserted

This is all achieved within separate for and foreach loops. For a word length of five characters, 295 variations will be created; for six, it's 349, and so on. Most of these will be meaningless gibberish, but because (we assume) the user meant to type something meaningful but probably just made a typo, some of them stand a chance of being real words, and could be what the user intended to type.

To extract the good words, the array_intersect() function is called to return all words that exist in both the $possibles and $words arrays, the result of which is placed in $known, which becomes our set of known real words that could be what the user intended.

Next, all the duplicate occurrences of words in $known are counted up using the array_count_values() function, which returns an array of keys and values in which the key is the word and the value is the number of times it appears in the array. This array is then sorted into reverse order using the arsort() function so that those words that appeared the most frequently come first. That means the most likely candidates will always be at the start of the array, with less and less likely ones further down the array.

A foreach statement then steps through each of the elements to extract just the key in $temp (discarding the value in $val), which is then used to populate the next available element of the array $suggested.

When the loop completes, $suggested contains the list of words the plug-in thinks the user may have meant, in order of likelihood. So a two-element array is returned, the first of which is the number of words returned, while the second is an array containing the words.

How to Use It

When you want to offer alternate spelling suggestions to a user, just call this plug-in with the misspelled word and the path to a file of words, like this:

```
$word = 'spenr';
echo "Suggested spellings for '$word':<br /><ul>";
$results = PIPHP_SuggestSpelling($word, 'dictionary.txt');
if (!$results[0]) echo "No suggested spellings.";
else foreach ($results[1] as $spelling) echo "<li>$spelling</li>";
```

You can call the plug-in multiple times and could therefore use drop-down lists inserted within the text at the occurrence of each unrecognized word, or one of many other methods to offer suggestions for all misspelled words found in a section of text.

Of course, to be truly interactive you ought to rewrite the function in JavaScript and you could then offer interactive spelling management directly within a web page, but that's a plug-in for another book.

The Plug-in

```
function PIPHP_SuggestSpelling($word, $dictionary)
{
    if (!strlen($word)) return array(FALSE);

    static $count, $words;

    if ($count++ == 0)
    {
        $dict = @file_get_contents($dictionary);
        if (!strlen($dict)) return array(FALSE);
        $words = explode("\r\n", $dict);
    }

    $possibles = array();
    $known     = array();
    $suggested = array();
    $wordlen   = strlen($word);
    $chars     = str_split('abcdefghijklmnopqrstuvwxyz');

    for($j = 0 ; $j < $wordlen ; ++$j)
    {
        $possibles[] =    substr($word, 0, $j) .
                          substr($word, $j + 1);

        foreach($chars as $letter)
            $possibles[] = substr($word, 0, $j) .
                          $letter .
                          substr($word, $j + 1);
    }

    for($j = 0; $j < $wordlen - 1 ; ++$j)
        $possibles[] =    substr($word, 0, $j) .
                          $word[$j + 1] .
                          $word[$j] .
                          substr($word, $j +2 );

    for($j = 0; $j < $wordlen + 1 ; ++$j)
        foreach($chars as $letter)
            $possibles[] = substr($word, 0, $j).
                          $letter.
                          substr($word, $j);
```

```
$known = array_intersect($possibles, $words);
$known = array_count_values($known);
arsort($known, SORT_NUMERIC);

foreach ($known as $temp => $val)
    $suggested[] = $temp;

return array(count($suggested), $suggested);
}
```

PLUG-IN 97 — Google Translate

If there's one thing you can be sure of it's that your web site attracts visitors from all around the world. So why not translate parts of your site for them? You could even use the first plug-in in this chapter, number 91, *Get Country from IP*, to determine where a user is from and then offer a translated version of your site accordingly. Figure 12-8 shows this plug-in used to translate the start of the U.S. Declaration of Independence from English into German.

About the Plug-in

This plug-in takes a string of text and converts it from one language to another. Upon success, it returns the translated text. On failure, it returns FALSE. It requires the following arguments:

- **$text**   Text to be translated
- **$lang1**   Source language
- **$lang2**   Destination language

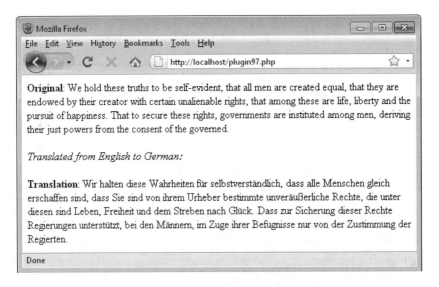

FIGURE 12-8   Translating the start of the U.S. Declaration of Independence into German

The source and destination languages must each be one of the following:

Arabic	Bulgarian	Simplified Chinese	Traditional Chinese	Croatian	Czech
Danish	Dutch	English	Finnish	French	German
Greek	Hindi	Italian	Japanese	Korean	Polish
Portuguese	Romanian	Russian	Spanish	Swedish	

Variables, Arrays, and Functions

`$langs`	Associative array containing languages and their identifiers
`$root`	String containing base Google API URL
`$url`	String containing the final API URL to load
`$json`	String of data returned by the API call
`$result`	JSON object created from parsing `$json`

How It Works

This plug-in makes use of a Google API. It starts by creating the associative array `$langs` in which each of the supported languages is a key, which has a value that will be used by Google to represent the language.

Next the two arguments `$lang1` and `$lang2` are converted to all lowercase strings using the `strtolower()` function; the root of the API URL is defined in `$root`; and the URL to call, based on `$root`, is created in `$url`.

Before proceeding, the associated key values for each of `$lang1` and `$lang2` in the array `$langs` are looked up. If one or the other is not set, as determined by the `isset()` function, then an unknown language was requested and so FALSE is returned.

Next the call to Google's API is made using the `file_get_contents()` function with arguments comprising `$url`, the contents of `$text` after encoding in URL format using the `urlencode()` function, and the pair of language identifiers separated by a `%7C` character. The @ before the function call suppresses any unwanted error messages.

If the call is unsuccessful, then the returned value in `$json` will be empty and so FALSE is returned. Otherwise, `$json` now contains a JSON (JavaScript Object Notation) format string returned by the Google API, which is then parsed using the `json_decode()` function, the result of which is placed in the object `$result`.

The translated text is then extracted from `$result` and returned.

How to Use It

Translating text with this plug-in is as simple as passing it the original text, the language that text was written in, and a language to which the text should be translated, like this:

```
echo      '<html><head><meta http-equiv="Content-Type" ' .
          'content="text/html; charset=utf-8" /></head><body>';
$text = "We hold these truths to be self-evident, that all " .
        "men are created equal, that they are endowed by " .
        "their creator with certain unalienable rights, that " .
        "among these are life, liberty and the pursuit of " .
```

```
          "happiness. That to secure these rights, governments " .
          "are instituted among men, deriving their just powers " .
          "from the consent of the governed.";
$from = 'English';
$to   = 'German';
echo "<b>Original</b>: $text<br /><br />";
echo "<i>Translated from $from to $to:</i><br /><br />";
$result = PIPHP_GoogleTranslate($text, $from, $to);
if (!$result) echo "Translation failed.";
else echo "<b>Translation</b>: $result";
```

Because many languages use accented and other unusual characters, the translated text may require the correct UTF-8 encoding to be in place to ensure it displays correctly. In the preceding example, this is done with the tag:

```
<meta http-equiv="Content-Type" content="text/html; charset=utf-8"/>
```

Some text is then assigned to $text, the two languages to translate from and to are stored in $from and $to, and after a little introductory text, the plug-in is called and its result is placed in $result. Upon failure, an error message is displayed, otherwise the translation is output.

Rather than rely on Google's API every time a non-English user visits your web site, I recommend you cache the first of each translation and serve the copy up on future visits by users of that language. It will keep your web site running fast and keep Google happy.

The Plug-in

```
function PIPHP_GoogleTranslate($text, $lang1, $lang2)
{
    $langs = array(
        'arabic'               => 'ar',
        'bulgarian'            => 'bg',
        'simplified chinese'   => 'zh-cn',
        'traditional chinese'  => 'zh-tw',
        'croatian'             => 'hr',
        'czech'                => 'cs',
        'danish'               => 'da',
        'dutch'                => 'nl',
        'english'              => 'en',
        'finnish'              => 'fi',
        'french'               => 'fr',
        'german'               => 'de',
        'greek'                => 'el',
        'hindi'                => 'hi',
        'italian'              => 'it',
        'japanese'             => 'ja',
        'korean'               => 'ko',
        'polish'               => 'pl',
        'portuguese'           => 'pt',
        'romanian'             => 'ro',
        'russian'              => 'ru',
        'spanish'              => 'es',
        'swedish'              => 'sv');
```

```
$lang1 = strtolower($lang1);
$lang2 = strtolower($lang2);
$root  = 'http://ajax.googleapis.com/ajax/services';
$url   = $root . '/language/translate?v=1.0&q=';

if (!isset($langs[$lang1]) || !isset($langs[$lang1]))
   return FALSE;

$json = @file_get_contents($url . urlencode($text) .
        '&langpair='. $langs[$lang1] . '%7C' .
        $langs[$lang2]);

if (!strlen($json)) return FALSE;

$result = json_decode($json);
return $result->responseData->translatedText;
}
```

PLUG-IN 98 Corner Gif

Displaying content in a table with rounded borders can make it look more professional, but usually you need to create a different set of images to achieve this for each color palette used. This plug-in solves the problem by generating the GIF images needed on the fly, as you can see in Figure 12-9, which shows the top-left corner of a table (enlarged) as returned by the plug-in.

About the Plug-in

This plug-in creates corner and edge GIFs for building a table with rounded borders. Upon success, it returns a GD image containing the constructed GIF. On failure, it returns an unknown value or an unknown image. It requires the following arguments:

- **$corner** An identifier for the image to create, out of: tl, t, tr, l, r, bl, b, and br for top-left, top, top-right, left, right, bottom-left, bottom, and bottom-right

- **$border** The color of the border as a six-digit hexadecimal number

- **$bground** The color of the background as a six-digit hexadecimal number

FIGURE 12-9   A top-left corner GIF for a table (shown enlarged) as created by this plug-in

Variables, Arrays, and Functions

`$data`	Array containing a pixel map for the image
`$image`	GD image to be returned
`$bcol`	GD background color
`$fcol`	GD foreground color
`$tcol`	GD transparent color
`PIPHP_GD_FN1()`	PHP function to convert a six-digit hex number to a GD color

How It Works

When a corner GIF is required, this plug-in uses the pre-populated array in `$data` to create the top-left hand GIF and then rotates it if necessary. It does this by creating a new GD image in `$image` using the `imagecreatetruecolor()` function, and then creating three colors to use, `$bcol`, `$fcol`, and `$tcol` for the background, foreground, and transparent colors, as passed in the arguments `$border` and `$bground`. The image is then filled with the transparent color, ready for the main colors.

The `if (strlen($corner) == 2)` statement simply checks whether a corner piece has been requested by seeing whether `$corner` has one or two letters. If it's two, then a corner is wanted because `$corner` must contain one of the strings `tl`, `tr`, `bl`, or `br`, and so each of the pixels in the image that match those in the `$data` array is populated with either `$bcol` or `$fcol`, depending on whether the array has a value of 1 or 2, with a 0 indicating that a pixel should be left alone as it will be transparent.

If `$corner` has only one letter, then it must contain one of the strings `t`, `l`, `r`, or `b`, so an edge piece was requested and therefore two rectangles are created in the background and foreground colors. Actually, the first rectangle is a line and represents the border, while the other fills in the rest of the area with the background color.

Next a `switch` statement looks at the type of image that was requested in `$corner`, and if necessary, rotates the image before it is returned, with returned images being typically no more than about 50 bytes.

How to Use It

This plug-in is best used to create a self-contained program to return a GIF image, which is what the following code does:

```
$corner  = $_GET['c'];
$border  = $_GET['b'];
$bground = $_GET['f'];
$result = PIPHP_CornerGif($corner, $border, $bground);
if ($result)
{
   header('Content-type: image/gif');
   imagegif($result);
}
```

This code accepts three GET arguments: c, b, and f for corner, border, and fill. It then passes these to the plug-in, and if an image is successfully returned, the correct header to preface sending of a GIF image is output, followed by sending the image in GIF format by calling the imagegif() function.

The preceding example code will be used by the plug-in 99, *Rounded Table*, so type it into a new program file, and then also add the plug-in code below to it, and save the result as *corner.php*, ensuring you also include the opening <?php and closing ?> tags. Alternatively, you can download *plug-ins.zip* from the companion web site at *www.pluginphp.com*, and will find *corner.php* in the */12* folder.

A typical call to the program will then look like the following, which will result in the image displayed in Figure 12-9 (if you enlarge it):

```
corner.php?c=tl&b=444444&f=dedede
```

Here a top-left corner has been requested by the parameter c=tl, the background color has been set to 444444 by the parameter b=444444, and the foreground color has been set to dedede by the parameter f=dedede.

Remember to also paste in or otherwise include the function PIPHP_GD_FN1(), which this plug-in relies on.

The Plug-in

```php
function PIPHP_CornerGif($corner, $border, $bground)
{
    $data  = array(array(0, 0, 0, 0, 0),
                   array(0, 0, 0, 1, 1),
                   array(0, 0, 1, 2, 2),
                   array(0, 1, 2, 2, 2),
                   array(0, 1, 2, 2, 2));

    $image = imagecreatetruecolor(5, 5);
    $bcol  = PIPHP_GD_FN1($image, $border);
    $fcol  = PIPHP_GD_FN1($image, $bground);
    $tcol  = PIPHP_GD_FN1($image, 'ffffff');

    imagecolortransparent($image, $tcol);
    imagefill($image, 0 , 0, $tcol);

    if (strlen($corner) == 2)
    {
        for ($j = 0 ; $j < 5 ; ++$j)
        {
            for ($k = 0 ; $k < 5 ; ++ $k)
            {
                switch($data[$j][$k])
                {
                    case 1:
                        imagesetpixel($image, $j, $k, $bcol); break;
                    case 2:
                        imagesetpixel($image, $j, $k, $fcol); break;
                }
            }
        }
    }
}
```

```
    else
    {
        imagefilledrectangle($image, 0, 0, 4, 0, $bcol);
        imagefilledrectangle($image, 0, 1, 4, 4, $fcol);
    }

    switch($corner)
    {
        case 'tr': case 'r':
            $image = imagerotate($image, 270, $tcol); break;
        case 'br': case 'b':
            $image = imagerotate($image, 180, $tcol); break;
        case 'bl': case 'l':
            $image = imagerotate($image,  90, $tcol); break;
    }

    return $image;
}

function PIPHP_GD_FN1($image, $color)
{
    return imagecolorallocate($image,
        hexdec(substr($color, 0, 2)),
        hexdec(substr($color, 2, 2)),
        hexdec(substr($color, 4, 2)));
}
```

PLUG-IN 99 Rounded Table

With this plug-in, not only do you get the GIFs needed to create rounded table corners in
any colors, you also get the HTML code, too. Figure 12-10 shows it being used to display
some monologue from a Shakespeare play to good effect.

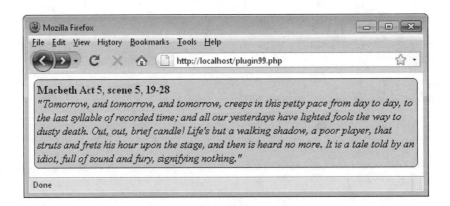

FIGURE 12-10   All the corners of this table have been neatly rounded.

About the Plug-in

This plug-in returns the HTML to use, as well as the corner and edge GIFs, for building a table with rounded borders. It requires the following arguments:

- **$width** The width of the table, use '' for default
- **$height** The height of the table, use '' for default
- **$bground** The table's background color
- **$border** The table's border color
- **$contents** The table's text and/or HTML contents
- **$program** The path to the program to create the GIF images

Variables, Arrays, and Functions

$t1 - $t5	Temporary string variables to avoid string duplication

How It Works

This plug-in returns the HTML required to display the supplied contents of $contents within a table that has rounded borders. If a width and/or height are specified, then the table dimensions are set to those values; otherwise, the browser is left to determine how to size it.

The table is created in nine segments with the eight outer ones each containing either a corner or edge GIF, each of which is created and displayed by the program contained in $program. The inner segment is populated with the string value in $contents.

The various variables $t1 through $t5 are used as shortcuts for repeated sequences to reduce the plug-in in size.

How to Use It

You can use the plug-in in the following manner, which passes the text to display, colors to use, and the path to the program for displaying the GIFs, like this:

```
$contents = "<b>Macbeth Act 5, scene 5, 19-28</b><br />" .
            "<i>&quot;Tomorrow, and tomorrow, and tomorrow, " .
            "creeps in this petty pace from day to day, to " .
            "the last syllable of recorded time; and all our " .
            "yesterdays have lighted fools the way to dusty " .
            "death. Out, out, brief candle! Life's but a " .
            "walking shadow, a poor player, that struts and " .
            "frets his hour upon the stage, and then is heard " .
            "no more. It is a tale told by an idiot, full of " .
            "sound and fury, signifying nothing.&quot</i>";
echo PIPHP_RoundedTable('', '', 'dedede', '444444', $contents,
   'corner.php');
```

In this code segment, the width and height of the table to create are set to the empty string ('') to let the browser choose suitable dimensions. Then a background color of dedede and foreground color of 444444 are passed, followed by the string value in $contents, and the program for displaying the GIFs: corner.php.

As you can see, HTML can also be passed to the plug-in, so you can place an unlimited variety of contents within these rounded border tables.

The Plug-in

```php
function PIPHP_RoundedTable($width, $height, $bground,
   $border, $contents, $program)
{
   if ($width)  $width  = "width='$width'";
   if ($height) $height = "height='$height'";

   $t1 = "<td width='5'><img src='$program?c";
   $t2 = "<td background='$program?c";
   $t3 = "<td width='5' background='$program?c";
   $t4 = "$border&f=$bground' /></td>";
   $t5 = "<td bgcolor='#$bground'>$contents</td>";

   return <<<_END
   <table border='0' cellpadding='0' cellspacing='0'
      $width $height>
   <tr>$t1=tl&b=$t4 $t2=t&b=$t4 $t1=tr&b=$t4</tr>
   <tr>$t3=l&b=$t4 $t5 $t3=r&b=$t4</tr>
   <tr>$t1=bl&b=$t4 $t2=b&b=$t4 $t1=br&b=$t4</tr></table>
_END;
}
```

PLUG-IN 100 Display Bing Map

Maps are as popular as ever, and in a bid to compete with Google, Microsoft's Virtual Earth project is now used for Bing Maps, which has an API that this plug-in makes very easy for you to use. Figure 12-11 shows a scrollable Bing Map, which has been dropped into a web page, with the Bird's Eye view selected.

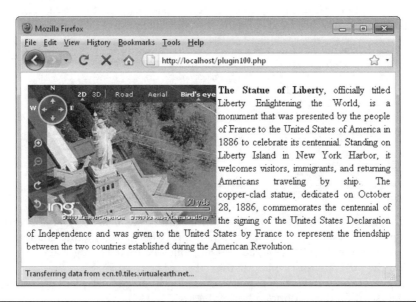

FIGURE 12-11   With this plug-in, you can incorporate Bing maps in your web pages.

About the Plug-in

This plug-in creates the JavaScript and HTML required to embed a scrollable Bing Map into a web page. It requires the following arguments:

- **$lat**   The latitude of a location
- **$long**   The longitude of a location
- **$zoom**   The amount to zoom in by (0 for none, 19 for maximum)
- **$style**   The type of map out of Road or Aerial (exact spelling required)
- **$width**   The width of the map
- **$height**   The height of the map

Variables, Arrays, and Functions

$root	The base part of the API URL

How It Works

Normally, when you wish to include a Bing Map in a web page, you have to call it up from the <body> tag and separately include the JavaScript and a <div> in which to display the map.

But this plug-in removes the need for all that by using PHP to create the JavaScript code to load a map of the correct dimensions exactly where you want it. It does this by attaching automatically to the events required so that only a single call is needed.

The JavaScript is based on the Virtual Earth API and is beyond the scope of this book to explain, other than to say that all the code required is ready made for you, along with a <div> tag in which to display the map.

How to Use It

To insert a Bing Map into a page, just pass this plug-in the location details, zoom level, type of map, and dimensions, like this:

```
$result = PIPHP_DisplayBingMap(40.68913, -74.0446, 18, 'Aerial',
    300, 214);
$text = "<b>The Statue of Liberty</b>, officially titled " .
        "Liberty Enlightening the World, is a monument that " .
        "was presented by the people of France to the United " .
        "States of America in 1886 to celebrate its " .
        "centennial. Standing on Liberty Island in New York " .
        "Harbor, it welcomes visitors, immigrants, and " .
        "returning Americans traveling by ship. The copper-" .
        "clad statue, dedicated on October 28, 1886, " .
        "commemorates the centennial of the signing of the " .
        "United States Declaration of Independence and was " .
        "given to the United States by France to represent " .
        "the friendship between the two countries " .
        "established during the American Revolution.";
echo "<table width='300' height='214' align=left><tr><td>" .
    $result . "</td></tr></table><p align='justify'>$text";
```

The preceding code places the map into a table which is aligned to the left with text flowing around it. You can equally use a <div> or <span> to include it, or just drop a map in without placing it within an element.

The map style should be one of Aerial or Road and the zoom level should be between 0 (for none) and 19 (for maximum). When you need to know the latitude and longitude of a location, you can look it up in a search engine or there are useful web sites such as *www.hmmm.ip3.co.uk/longitude-latitude*.

The Plug-in

```php
function PIPHP_DisplayBingMap($lat, $long, $zoom, $style,
   $width, $height)
{
   if ($style != 'Aerial' && $style != 'Road') $style = 'Road';

   $width  .= 'px';
   $height .= 'px';

   $root = 'http://ecn.dev.virtualearth.net/mapcontrol';
   return <<<_END
<script src = "$root/mapcontrol.ashx?v=6.2"></script>
<script>
if (window.attachEvent)
{
   window.attachEvent('onload',   Page_Load)
   window.attachEvent('onunload', Page_Unload)
}
else
{
   window.addEventListener('DOMContentLoaded', Page_Load, false)
   window.addEventListener('unload', Page_Unload, false)
}

function Page_Load()
{
   GetMap()
}

function Page_Unload()
{
   if (map != null)
   {
      map.Dispose()
      map = null
   }
}

function GetMap()
{
   map = new VEMap('PIPHP_DBM')
   map.LoadMap(new VELatLong($lat, $long),
      $zoom, VEMapStyle.$style, false)
}
</script>
<div id='PIPHP_DBM' style="position:relative;
   width:$width; height:$height;"></div>
_END;
}

?>
```

Index

& (ampersand), 155–157, 257
' (apostrophe), 204
* (asterisk), 47, 215, 246
# (number sign), 220
; (semicolon), 209, 210, 211, 215
@ (at) symbol, 199, 224, 226, 250, 288
| (pipe) symbol, 149, 177, 184, 185, 304

A

absolute URLs, 88–90
accents
    removing, 55–56
    UTF-8 encoding and, 326
acronyms, text speak, 203–206
ActiveX objects, 278–279
Add User to DB plug-in, 208–214
Advanced Packaging Tool (APT) system, 12
Ajax (Asynchronous JavaScript and XML),
    278–287
    GET requests, 285–287
    POST requests, 280–284
Ajax calls, 192
Ajax Request plug-in, 278–280
Amazon sales rank, 316–318
ampersand (&), 155–157, 257
Apache Web Server
    .htaccess files and, 152–153
    Linux systems, 20
    Mac systems, 22, 23
    Windows systems, 6–7, 8
API key, 253, 254, 257
API plug-ins, 236–272
API URL, 197
APIs (application programming interfaces)
    described, 236

Facebook, 284
fetching Flickr streams, 249–251
getting content, 241–243
Google Charts, 236–240
Search Yahoo!, 256–259
Wiki export, 243–248
Yahoo! Answers, 252–255
Yahoo! Stock News, 259–264
apostrophe ('), 204
application programming interfaces. See APIs
APT (Advanced Packaging Tool) system, 12
Aptitude tool, 12, 14
arithmetic operators, 113–114
array_count_values() function, 322
array_intersect() function, 322
array_reverse() function, 182
array_unique() function, 156, 165
arsort() function, 146, 322
aspect ratio, 66
asterisk (*), 47, 215, 246
Asynchronous JavaScript and XML. See Ajax
at (@) symbol, 199, 224, 226, 250, 288
Auto Back Links plug-in, 145–148
auto scrolling, 189–193

B

BB (bulletin board) code, 134–137
BB Code plug-in, 134–137
Bing Maps, 332–334
Bing Search, 256–259
Block User by Cookie plug-in, 230–233
blurring images, 69
books
    Amazon sales rank, 316–318
    ISBN number, 314–316

bots, 118, 121, 288, 312

 tags, 34, 35–36
brightening images, 69
browsers
    mobile, 170–174
    web. *See* web browsers
bulletin board (BB) code, 134–137
Bypass Captcha plug-in, 312–314

▬ C ▬

calculator functionality, 112–114
capitalizing text, 37–39
Caps Control plug-in, 37–39
Caps Lock key, 37–39
Captcha test
    bypassing, 312–314
    creating, 118–122
    verifying, 122–124
cast statement, 48
catch statement, 279
CDATA (character data), 257, 261, 266
CentOS Linux, 16–17
character data (CDATA), 257, 261, 266
charts, 236–240
chat facilities
    auto scrolling, 189–193
    displaying messages, 181–183, 189–193
    posting messages, 183–189
    predictive technology, 304–308
    private messages, 187–191
    text speak acronyms, 203–206
Check Captcha plug-in, 122–124
Check Links plug-in, 92–95, 142–144
client URL. *See CURL entries*
Close Session plug-in, 225–226
code
    HTML. *See* HTML code
    PHP. *See* PHP code
    scope, 29–30
Command Line Client, 211
companion web site, 51, 320
compression, 77, 79
content management, 87–110
    absolute URLs, 88–90
    copyright messages, 100–101
    displaying lists, 103–105

embedded YouTube video, 101–103
extracting links from URLs, 90–92
hit counters, 105–107
listing directories, 95–97
query highlighting, 98–100
referring pages, 98–99, 108–110
relative URLs, 88–90
verifying web site links, 92–95
contrast, 69
Convert Currency plug-in, 272–275
cookies
    blocking users by, 230–233
    deleting, 230
    described, 228
    managing, 228–230
copyright messages, 100–101
Corner Gif plug-in, 327–330
count() function, 106
Count Tail plug-in, 47–49
country, determining, 310–312
Create Captcha plug-in, 118–122
Create Google Chart plug-in, 236–240
Create List plug-in, 103–105
Create Session plug-in, 221–223
Create Short URL plug-in, 148–151
CREATE TABLE command, 210
credit card validatation, 114–117
cropping images, 71–73
Curl Get Contents plug-in, 241–243
curl_close() function, 195, 242
curl_exec() function, 195, 242
curl_init() function, 242
CURLOP_POST option, 195
CURLOP_POSTFIELDS option, 195, 197
CURLOPT_RETURNTRANSFER option, 195
CURLOPT_URL option, 242
CURLOPT_USERAGENT option, 195, 242
CURLOPT_USERPWD option, 195
CURLOP_URL option, 195, 242
curl_setopt() function, 242
currency conversions, 272–275

▬ D ▬

darkening images, 69
databases. *See* MySQL
date() function, 255, 262, 266

dates
    copyright messages, 100–101
    expiration, 114–115
    expiry (cookies), 226, 229
    "friendly" display of, 47–49
Debian Linux, 12–14. *See also* Linux systems
delay counter, 296
diacritic characters, 55–56
dictionary file, 52, 54, 303–304, 318–324
die() function, 77, 158, 192, 213
directories, listing, 95–97
Directory List plug-in, 95–97
disk, saving images to, 64, 78–80
Display Bing Map plug-in, 332–334
display property, 291
<div> tags, 280, 284, 291, 292, 333
Document Object Model (DOM), 91, 164,
    250, 281, 285
document root
    Linux systems, 16, 17
    Mac systems, 20, 24
    Windows systems, 12
DOM (Document Object Model), 91, 164,
    250, 281, 285

E

echo statements, 162, 183
e-mail
    page change notification, 162
    protecting, 287–289
    sending, 131–134
    spam detection, 130–131
    validating addresses, 128–130
e-mail harvesting programs, 287
Embed YouTube Video plug-in, 101–103
embossing images, 69
emoticons, 200–203
error messages. *See also* warnings
    generating, 124–128
    suppressing, 91, 250, 266
    Zend Server CE, 25
eval() function, 112–114
Evaluate Expression plug-in, 112–114
exclusive locks, 180
explode() function
    Caps Control plug-in, 38
    Convert Currency plug-in, 274

Get Guestbook plug-in, 182
Get Yahoo! Stock News plug-in, 261
Page Updated? plug-in, 160
Post to Chat plug-in, 186
Referer Log plug-in, 109
Spell Check plug-in, 52
Suggest Spelling plug-in, 321
Wrap Text plug-in, 35
expressions, evaluating, 112–114

F

Facebook, 176, 280–284
FAT (file allocation table), 180
Fedora Linux, 14, 16–17
Fetch Flickr Stream plug-in, 249–251
Fetch Wiki Page plug-in, 243–248
file allocation table (FAT), 180
file_get_contents() function
    Curl Get Contents plug-in, 241, 242
    Fetch Flickr Stream plug-in, 250
    Get Yahoo! Answers plug-in, 253
    Get Yahoo! News plug-in, 266
    Get Yahoo! Stock News plug-in, 261
    Google Translate plug-in, 325
    Post Ajax Request plug-in, 284
    Search Google Books plug-in, 270
    Search Yahoo! plug-in, 257
    Send Tweet plug-in, 195
file_put_contents() function, 149, 185
files. *See also* HTML files; PHP files
    .htaccess, 152–153
    included, 28–32
    not found, 29
    required, 29
    uploading, 60–64
Flickr image streams, 249–251, 295–299
flock() function, 106, 109, 180
flood control, 178–179, 185–187
flush() function, 191
fonts
    TrueType, 80–83, 118, 120–121
    web browsers and, 80–83
fopen() function, 180
foreach loop, 35, 322
forms
    BB code, 134–137
    Captcha test, 118–124

forms (*cont.*)
evaluating expressions, 112–114
plug-ins for. *See* plug-ins, forms/
user content
predicting words, 304–308
prompting input on, 299–302
sending e-mail, 131–134
spam detection, 130–131
user input in. *See* user input
validating credit cards, 114–117
validating e-mail addresses, 128–130
validating text in, 124–128
Friendly Text plug-in, 39–43
fseek() command, 186
fwrite() function, 180

━━ **G** ━━

GD images, 60, 65, 80, 236–240
GD library, 60, 80
Get Ajax Request plug-in, 285–287
Get Amazon Sales Rank plug-in, 316–318
Get Country by IP plug-in, 310–312
Get Guestbook plug-in, 181–183
Get Links from URL plug-in, 90–92
GET request, 139, 238, 280, 285–286
Get Title from URL plug-in, 144–145
Get Tweets plug-in, 198–200
Get User from DB plug-in, 214–216
Get Yahoo! Answers plug-in, 252–255
Get Yahoo! News plug-in, 264–268
Get Yahoo! Stock News plug-in, 259–264
get_file_contents() function, 145
GFDL (GNU Free Documentation
License), 243
GIF images
Captcha, 120, 123–124
converting to/from different formats,
78–80
converting TrueType fonts to, 80–83,
118, 120–121
corner, 327–330
displaying, 76–78
edge, 327–330
quality setting, 80
rounded corners, 330–332
smileys, 200–203

Gif Text plug-in, 80–83
glob() function, 124
global keyword, 29–30
global scope, 29–30
GNU Free Documentation License
(GFDL), 243
Google AdSense, 32
Google Analytics, 10
Google Books, 268–272
Google Charts, 236–240
Google search engine, 256–259
Google Translate plug-in,
324–327
GRANT command, 212
grayscale images, 69
Guestbook feature, 178–183

━━ **H** ━━

Hash Code, 137–140
hash tokens, 120
header() function, 152
Hit Counter plug-in, 105–107
hit counters, 105–107
hotspots, 293–294
.htaccess files, 152–153
HTML code
converting RSS to, 168–170
converting to RSS, 163–167
correct insertion of tags, 31
enhancing for mobile browsers,
170–174
including, 31–32
inserting, 31–32
for lists, 103–105
HTML files. *See also* files
including, 31–32
inserting, 31–32
inserting snippits from, 31
Linux systems, 16, 17
Mac systems, 20, 24
Windows systems, 12
HTML to Mobile plug-in, 170–174
HTML to RSS plug-in, 163–167
htmlentities() function, 136, 139, 219
HTTP requests, 11

---I---

IF NOT EXISTS clause, 210
if...else pair, 36
<iframe> tag, 186, 284
IIS (Internet Information Server), 6
Image Alter plug-in, 68–71
Image Convert plug-in, 78–80
Image Crop plug-in, 71–73
Image Display plug-in, 76–78
Image Enlarge plug-in, 73–76
image formats, 78–80
image URLs, 295–299
Image Watermark plug-in, 83–86
ImageAlter() function, 120
imagecopyresampled() function, 72
imagecreatefrompng() function, 238
imagecreatetruecolor() function, 72, 238, 328
imagedestroy() function, 238
imagegif() function, 329
images, 59–86. *See also* photos
    altering, 68–71
    aspect ratio, 66
    blurring, 69
    brightening, 69
    Captcha, 118–124
    compression, 77, 79
    contrast, 69
    converting to different formats, 78–80
    cropping, 71–73
    darkening, 69
    displaying, 76–78
    edge detection, 69, 70–71
    embossing, 69
    enlarging, 73–76
    Flickr streams, 249–251, 295–299
    formats, 76–78
    GD, 60, 65, 80, 236–240
    GIF. *See* GIF images
    grayscale, 69
    increasing red/green/blue, 69
    inverting, 69
    JPEG. *See* JPEG images
    modifying, 68–71
    PNG, 76–80, 85, 238, 239
    quality, 66, 76–80
    resizing, 64–68, 73–76
    saving to disk, 64, 78–80
    sharpening, 69
    "sketchifying," 69
    slide shows, 295–299
    smoothing, 73–76
    thumbnail, 66–68
    transforming, 68–71
    uploading, 60–64
    watermarks, 83–86
<img> tag, 173, 297
in_array() function, 149, 152, 179
include command, 28–29
included files, 28–32
included URLs, 32
include_once command, 28–29
indenting paragraphs, 34, 35, 36
INDEX() statement, 210
innerHTML property, 293
input. *See* user input
Input Prompt plug-in, 299–302
Internet Information Server. *See* IIS
Internet plug-ins. *See* plug-ins, Internet
inverting images, 69
IP addresses
    banning users via, 230
    determining country via, 310–312
    determining online presence via, 177
    identifying, 106
is_array() function, 143
ISBN numbers, 314–318
isset() function, 229, 238

---J---

JavaScript. *See* plug-ins, JavaScript
JavaScript Object Notation (JSON), 287, 325
JPEG images
    converting to/from different formats, 78–80
    displaying, 76–78
    resizing, 65
JSON (JavaScript Object Notation), 287, 325
json_decode() function, 325

---L---

LAMP packages, 2
language translation, 324–327

license agreement, Zend Server, 4, 5
links. *See also* URLs
    automatic back links, 145–148
    checking, 90–92
    extracting from URLs, 90–92
    mobile browsers and, 172–173
    obtaining from URLs, 90–92
    verifying in web sites, 92–95, 142–144
Linux systems
    Apache Web Server, 20
    CentOS Linux, 16–17
    Command Line Client, 212
    Debian Linux, 12–14
    document root, 16, 17
    Fedora Linux, 16–17
    HTML files, 16, 17
    installing MySQL, 16–17
    installing Zend Server, 12–17
    passwords, 13, 16
    PHP files, 16, 17
    RHEL Linux, 16–17
    SUSE Linux, 17
    Ubuntu Linux, 14
    uninstalling Zend Server, 14, 16, 17
list() function, 149, 152, 177
lists
    clickable list of words, 302–304
    creating, 103–105
    drop-down, 320, 323
    nested, 246
    ordered/unordered, 246
load() function, 296
LOCK_EX parameter, 180
LOCK_UN parameter, 180
Luhn, Hans Peter, 115
Luhn algorithm, 116

M

Mac systems
    Apache Web Server, 22, 23
    Command Line Client, 212
    passwords, 18–19, 20, 21, 22
Mac systems, Intel
    document root, 20
    HTML files, 20
    installing Zend Server, 18–21

    PHP files, 20
    uninstalling Zend Server, 21
Mac systems, Power PC
    document root, 24
    HTML files, 24
    installing Zend Server, 21–24
    PHP files, 24
Magic Quotes setting, 220
mail() function, 131–134
Make Thumbnail plug-in, 66–68
MAMP packages, 2
MAMP program, installing, 21–24
Manage Cookie plug-in, 228–230
map display, 332–334
mathematical operators, 113–114
md5() checksum, 160
md5() function, 119, 210–211
messaging. *See* chat facilities
Microsoft Virtual Earth, 332–334
Microsoft.XMLHTTP object, 279
mobile browsers, 170–174
mobile phones, 304–308
mod curl facility, 195
Mod Curl library extension, 242
mod rewrite facility, 150, 152, 153
modulus 10 algorithm, 115
mouseover events, 292–294
Msxm12.XMLHTTP object, 279
MySQL
    adding users, 208–214
    case sensitivity, 211
    getting users from, 214–216
    installing from tarball, 17
    installing on Linux, 16–17
    passwords, 210, 216–217
    sanitizing strings, 219–221
    verifying users in, 216–218
MySQL plug-ins, 208–221
MySQL Sanitize String plug-in, 219–221
MySQL Server, 6, 16, 22
mysql_num_rows() function, 210, 215
mysql_query() function, 210, 211, 215
mysql_real_escape_string() function, 220

N

\n (newline) character, 35, 179
Network File System (NFS), 180

new ActiveXObject() command, 279
newline (\n) character, 35, 179
news
    Get Yahoo! Stock News, 259–264
    RSS feeds, 264–268
    Yahoo! News, 264–268
NFS (Network File System), 180
number sign (#), 220
numbers
    appending suffixes to, 47–49
    converting strings to, 48–49
    credit card, 114–117
    decimals, 311
    IP. *See* IP addresses
    ISBN, 314–318

O

ob_flush() function, 191
onClick method, 291
onMouseOut event, 293
onMouseOver event, 293
onreadystatechange event, 281
opacity() function, 296
Open Session plug-in, 223–225
operators
    arithmetic, 113–114
    regular expression, 127, 204
    special, 113–114

P

Page Updated plug-in, 159–163
paragraphs, 34, 35, 36
passwords
    Linux systems, 13, 16
    Mac systems, 18–19, 20, 21, 22
    MySQL, 210, 216–217
    validating, 126
    Windows systems, 8–11
Pattern Match Word plug-in, 318–320
photos. *See also* images
    fetching from Flickr, 249–251
    slide shows, 295–299
PHP code
    correct insertion of tags, 30–31
    correctly inserting, 30–32
    system considerations, 2

PHP files. *See also* files
    including, 28–32
    including from other servers, 32
    Linux systems, 16, 17
    Mac systems, 20, 24
    not found, 29
    Windows systems, 12
PHP sessions. *See* sessions
pipe (|) symbol, 149, 177, 184, 185, 304
pixelation, 73
pixels, 73
plug-ins, 27–32. *See also* plug-ins, listed
    API, 236–272
    chat-related. *See* plug-ins,
      chat/messaging
    content management. *See* plug-ins,
      content management
    cookies, 228–230
    form-related. *See* plug-ins, forms/
      user content
    image handling. *See* plug-ins, image
      handling
    include command, 28–29
    Internet. *See* plug-ins, Internet
    JavaScript. *See* plug-ins, JavaScript
    MySQL, 208–221
    overview, 28
    require command, 29
    saving into program files, 28
    sessions, 221–228
    text-related. *See* plug-ins, text
      processing
    tips for, 28, 30
    use of, 28
plug-ins, chat/messaging
    Get Guestbook, 181–183
    Get Tweets, 198–200
    Post to Chat, 183–189
    Post to Guestbook, 178–181
    Replace Smileys, 200–203
    Replace SMS Talk, 203–206
    Send Direct Tweet, 196–198
    Send Tweet, 194–198
    Users Online plug-in, 176–178
    View Chat, 189–193

plug-ins, content management, 87–110
    Check Links, 90–92
    Create List, 103–105
    Directory List, 95–97
    Embed YouTube Video, 101–103
    Get Links from URL, 90–92
    Hit Counter, 105–107
    Query Highlight, 98–100
    Referer Log, 108–110
    Relative to Absolute URL, 88–90
    Rolling Copyright, 100–101
plug-ins, forms/user content, 111–140
    BB Code, 134–137
    Check Captcha, 122–124
    Create Captcha, 118–122
    Evaluate Expression plug-in, 112–114
    Pound Code, 137–140
    Send E-mail, 131–134
    Spam Catch, 130–131
    Validate Credit Card plug-in, 114–117
    Validate E-mail, 128–130
    Validate Text, 124–128
plug-ins, image handling, 59–86
    Gif Text, 80–83
    Image Alter, 68–71
    Image Convert, 78–80
    Image Crop, 71–73
    Image Display, 76–78
    Image Enlarge, 73–76
    Image Watermark, 83–86
    Make Thumbnail, 66–68
    Resize Image, 64–66
    Upload File, 60–64
plug-ins, Internet, 141–174
    Auto Back Links, 145–148
    Check Links, 92–95, 142–144
    Create Short URL, 148–151
    Get Title from URL, 144–145
    HTML to Mobile, 170–174
    HTML to RSS, 163–167
    Page Updated, 159–163
    RSS to HTML, 168–170
    Simple Web Proxy, 154–159
    Use Short URL, 151–154
plug-ins, JavaScript
    Ajax Request, 278–280
    Get Ajax Request, 285–287

    Input Prompt, 299–302
    Post Ajax Request, 280–284
    Predict Word, 304–308
    Protect E-mail, 287–289
    Slide Show, 295–299
    Status Message, 292–294
    Toggle Text, 290–292
    Words from Root, 302–304
plug-ins, listed
    Add User to DB, 208–214
    Ajax Request, 278–280
    Auto Back Links, 145–148
    BB Code, 134–137
    Block User by Cookie, 230–233
    Bypass Captcha, 312–314
    Caps Control, 37–39
    Check Captcha, 122–124
    Check Links, 92–95, 142–144
    Close Session, 225–226
    Convert Currency, 272–275
    Corner Gif, 327–330
    Count Tail, 47–49
    Create Captcha, 118–122
    Create Google Chart, 236–240
    Create List, 103–105
    Create Session, 221–223
    Create Short URL, 148–151
    Curl Get Contents, 241–243
    Directory List, 95–97
    Display Bing Map, 332–334
    Embed YouTube Video, 101–103
    Evaluate Expression, 112–114
    Fetch Flickr Stream, 249–251
    Fetch Wiki Page, 243–248
    Friendly Text, 39–43
    Get Ajax Request, 285–287
    Get Amazon Sales Rank, 316–318
    Get Country by IP, 310–312
    Get Guestbook, 181–183
    Get Links from URL, 90–92
    Get Title from URL, 144–145
    Get Tweets, 198–200
    Get User from DB, 214–216
    Get Yahoo! Answers, 252–255
    Get Yahoo! News, 264–268
    Get Yahoo! Stock News, 259–264
    Gif Text, 80–83

Google Translate, 324–327
Hit Counter, 105–107
HTML to Mobile, 170–174
HTML to RSS, 163–167
Image Alter, 68–71
Image Convert, 78–80
Image Crop, 71–73
Image Display, 76–78
Image Enlarge, 73–76
Image Watermark, 83–86
Input Prompt, 299–302
Make Thumbnail, 66–68
Manage Cookie, 228–230
MySQL Sanitize String, 219–221
Open Session, 223–225
Page Updated, 159–163
Pattern Match Word, 318–320
Post Ajax Request, 280–284
Post to Chat, 183–189
Post to Guestbook, 178–181
Pound Code, 137–140
Predict Word, 304–308
Protect E-mail, 287–289
Query Highlight, 98–100
Referer Log, 108–110
Relative to Absolute URL, 88–90
Remove Accents, 55–56
Replace Smileys, 200–203
Replace SMS Talk, 203–206
Resize Image, 64–66
Rolling Copyright, 100–101
Rounded Table, 330–332
RSS to HTML, 168–170
Sanitize String, 219–221
Search Google Books, 268–272
Search Yahoo!, 256–259
Secure Session, 226–228
Send Direct Tweet, 196–198
Send E-mail, 131–134
Send Tweet, 194–198
Shorten Text, 57–58
Simple Web Proxy, 154–159
Slide Show, 295–299
Spam Catch, 130–131
Spell Check, 51–55
Status Message, 292–294
Strip Whitespace, 43–45

Suggest Spelling, 320–324
Text Truncate, 49–51
Toggle Text, 290–292
Upload File, 60–64
Use Short URL, 151–154
Users Online, 176–178
Validate Credit Card, 114–117
Validate E-mail, 128–130
Validate Text, 124–128
Verify User in DB, 216–218
View Chat, 189–193
Word Selector, 45–47
Words from Root, 302–304
Wrap Text, 34–37
plug-ins, text processing, 33–58.
    See also text
        Caps Control, 37–39
        Count Tail, 47–49
        Friendly Text, 39–43
        Remove Accents, 55–56
        Shorten Text, 57–58
        Spell Check, 51–55
        Strip Whitespace, 43–45
        Text Truncate, 49–51
        Word Selector, 45–47
        Wrap Text, 34–37
PNG images, 76–80, 85, 238, 239
Post Ajax Request plug-in, 280–284
POST request, 195, 280, 282, 285–286
Post to Chat plug-in, 183–189
Post to Guestbook plug-in, 178–181
Pound Code plug-in, 137–140
Predict Word plug-in, 304–308
predictive technology, 304–308
preg_match() function, 53, 145
preg_match_all() function, 125, 303, 320
preg_replace() function, 50, 135, 165,
    204, 319
process() function, 296
Protect E-mail plug-in, 287–289
pspell module, 51

 Q

queries, 98–100, 211
Query Highlight plug-in, 98–100
query strings, 138, 151. *See also* strings

R

rand() function, 121, 291
rawurlencode() function, 245, 253, 257, 266, 270
Really Simple Syndication. *See* RSS
Referer Log plug-in, 108–110
referring pages, 98–99, 108, 146–147
regular expression operators, 113–114
Relative to Absolute URL plug-in, 88–90
relative URLs, 88–90
Remove Accents plug-in, 55–56
Replace Smileys plug-in, 200–203
Replace SMS Talk plug-in, 203–206
require command, 29, 31
require_once command, 29, 31
resampling, 75
Resize Image plug-in, 64–66
RHEL Linux, 16–17
Rolling Copyright plug-in, 100–101
Rounded Table plug-in, 330–332
RSS (Really Simple Syndication), 163–170
RSS feeds, 163–170
    Flickr streams, 250
    Yahoo! News, 264–268
RSS to HTML plug-in, 168–170
rtrim() function, 36, 182

S

salts, 120, 123, 211, 218
Sanitize String plug-in, 219–221
scope, 29–30
screen scraping, 250
<script> tags, 165, 219, 286, 289, 300
search engines
    Google, 256
    highlighting search terms, 45–47, 98–100
    truncated text, 49–51
    Yahoo!, 256–259
Search Google Books plug-in, 268–272
search queries
    Get Yahoo! News plug-in, 264–268
    Search Google Books plug-in, 268–272
    Search Yahoo! plug-in, 256–259
Search Yahoo! plug-in, 256–259
Secure Session plug-in, 226–228

security
    BB Code and, 135
    closing sessions and, 225–226
    file upload and, 60, 62
    included URLs and, 32
    passwords. *See* passwords
    Secure Session plug-in, 226–228
    Windows Security Alerts, 8, 10
SELECT command, 210
semicolon (;), 209, 210, 211, 215
Send Direct Tweet plug-in, 196–198
Send E-mail plug-in, 131–134
Send Tweet plug-in, 194–198
servers. *See also* web servers
    Apache. *See* Apache Web Server
    including PHP files from, 32
    Internet Information Server, 6
    listing directories on, 95–97
    MySQL Server, 6, 16, 22
    Zend. *See* Zend Server CE
$_SESSION array, 225
session ID, 139, 226
session plug-ins, 221–228
session_destroy() function, 226
session_id() function, 226
session_name() function, 226
sessions
    closing, 225–226
    creating for users, 221–223
    hijacking, 226–228
    opening, 223–225
    secure, 226–228
session_start() function, 222, 224
setcookie() function, 226, 229
set_time_limit() function, 190
sharpening images, 69
short URLs, 148–154
Shorten Text plug-in, 57–58
similar_text() function, 262, 266
Simple Web Proxy plug-in, 154–159
SimpleXML, 250, 258, 261, 266
simplexml_load_string() function
    Get Tweets plug-in, 199
    Get Yahoo! News plug-in, 266
    Get Yahoo! Stock News plug-in, 261
    RSS to HTML plug-in, 169

Search Google Books plug-in, 270
Send Tweet plug-in, 195
sleep() function, 191
Slide Show plug-in, 295–299
smileys
    making thumbnails, 66–68
    replacing in text, 200–203
smoothing images, 73–76
SMS talk, 203–206
spaces
    non-blank, 35
    removing, 36
    white space, 36, 43–45, 165
    wiki pags and, 245
Spam Catch plug-in, 130–131
spam detection
    Captcha test, 118–122
    e-mail, 130–131
special operators, 113–114
Spell Check plug-in, 51–55
spell checking, 51–55, 320–324
Status Message plug-in, 292–294
status messages, 292–294
stock information, 259–264
strings
    converting numbers to, 48–49
    query, 138, 151
    replacing text in, 55–56
    sanitizing, 219–221
    shortening, 57–58
    toggling between, 290–292
    User Agent, 177, 241, 245
Strip Whitespace plug-in, 43–45
stripslashes() function, 220
strip_tags() function
    BB Code plug-in, 136
    Fetch Wiki Page plug-in, 246
    HTML to Mobile plug-in, 173
    HTML to RSS plug-in, 165
    Pound Code plug-in, 139
    Sanitize String plug-in, 219
str_ireplace() function, 138, 201
strpos() function
    Convert Currency plug-in, 274
    Get Amazon Sales Rank plug-in, 317
    Get Book from ISBN plug-in, 315

Post to Chat plug-in, 185–186
Protect E-mail plug-in, 288
str_repeat() function, 35
str_replace() function, 56, 135, 155, 164
strrpos() function, 50
str_split() function, 322
strtolower() function, 262, 319, 325
strtotime() function, 199, 262, 266
strtoupper() function, 261, 274
substr() function
    Get Book from ISBN plug-in, 315
    Protect E-mail plug-in, 288
    Send Tweet plug-in, 195
    Shorten Text plug-in, 58
    Text Truncate plug-in, 50
    Validate E-mail plug-in, 129
    Words from Root plug-in, 304
Suggest Spelling plug-in, 320–324
SUSE Linux, 17
symbols, 113–114

T

tables
    creating, 210
    rounded corners, 327–332
tarball, installing MySQL from, 17
text. See also words
    blanking out, 45–47
    caps control, 37–39
    censoring, 45–47
    fixed-width, 34–37
    "friendly," 39–43
    highlighting in queries, 98–100
    highlighting on web page, 45–47
    indenting paragraphs, 34, 35, 36
    placing in paragraphs, 35
    plug-ins for. See plug-ins,
        text processing
    processing, 33–58
    removing accents, 55–56
    shortening URLs/strings, 57–58
    spell checking, 51–55, 320–324
    status message, 292–294
    toggling on web pages, 290–292
    translating, 324–327
    truncated, 49–51

text. *See also* words (*cont.*)
    underlining, 45–47, 54
    validating, 124–128
    watermarks, 83–86
    whitespace, 36, 43–45, 165
    wrapping, 34–37
text speak acronyms, 203–206
Text Truncate plug-in, 49–51
texting, 304–308. *See also* chat facilities
this keyword, 282
thumbnail images, 66–68
time() function, 191, 229
timestamps, 229, 255
Toggle Text plug-in, 290–292
transforming images, 68–71
translating text, 324–327
trolls, 230–233
TrueType fonts, 80–83, 118, 120–121
truncate() function, 186
truncation process, 49–51
try statement, 279
tweets. *See* Twitter
Twitter
    advantages of, 194
    fetching tweets, 198–200
    logging in to, 194, 196, 198
    sending direct tweets, 196–198
    sending tweets, 194–198
    text speak, 203–206

U

Ubuntu Linux, 12–14.
    See also Linux systems
ucfirst() function, 38, 204
Unix timestamp, 255
unlink() function, 124
Upload File plug-in, 60–64
uploading files/images, 60–64
urlencode() function, 325
URLs. *See also* links
    absolute, 88–90
    failed, 94
    getting links from, 90–92
    getting titles from, 144–145
    image, 295–299
    included, 32
    in programs, 32

referring pages, 98–99, 108–110
relative, 88–90
shortened, 57–58, 148–154
verifying, 90–92, 142–144
web proxies and, 155–159
Use Short URL plug-in, 151–154
User Agent string, 177, 241, 245
user input, 111–140
    caps control, 37–39
    checking for spelling errors, 51–55
    evaluating expressions, 112–114
    prompting, 299–302
    validating, 124–128
users
    active users online, 176–178
    adding to MySQL database, 208–214
    blocking via cookies, 230–233
    closing sessions for, 225–226
    creating sessions for, 221–223
    getting from MySQL database,
      214–216
    opening sessions for, 223–225
    secure sessions, 226–228
    verifying in MySQL database, 216–218
Users Online plug-in, 176–178
UTF-8 characters, 247, 326

V

Validate Credit Card plug-in, 114–117
Validate E-mail plug-in, 128–130
Validate Text plug-in, 124–128
Verify User in DB plug-in, 216–218
videos, YouTube, 101–103
View Chat plug-in, 189–193
Virtual Earth, 332–334

W

WAMP packages, 2
warnings. *See also* error messages
    e-mail, 133
    include command, 29
    suppressing, 91, 199
    timeouts, 190
watermarks, 83–86
web browsers
    cookies. *See* cookies
    fonts and, 80–83

mobile, 170–174
predicting words, 304–308
resizing images, 64–65
simulating, 241–243
testing for non-Microsoft, 279
uploading files, 62
wrapping text in, 34–37
web forms. *See* forms
web pages
    censoring words on, 45–47
    clickable list of words, 302–304
    cookies. *See* cookies
    copyright messages, 100–101
    counting hits, 105–107
    embedding YouTube video in, 101–103
    enhancing for mobile browsers,
        170–174
    extracting titles from, 144–145
    fetching, 241–243
    fonts, 80–83
    highlighting words on, 45–47
    hotspots, 293–294
    inserting into HTML elements,
        280–284
    links to/from. *See* links
    lists on, 103–105
    monitoring for changes, 159–163
    referring data for, 108–110
    referring pages, 98–99, 108, 146–147
    returning links from, 90–92
    statistics from, 105–107
    status messages, 292–294
    toggling text on, 290–292
    tracking IP addresses, 106
    translating, 324–327
    URLs. *See* URLs
    verifying links, 92–95, 142–144
    Wiki, 243–248
web proxy service, 154–159
web servers. *See also* servers
    listing directories on, 95–97
    uploading files to, 60–64
web sites
    APIs. *See* APIs
    companion to book, 51, 320
    cookies. *See* cookies
    copyright messages, 100–101

counting hits, 105–107
creating user sessions, 221–223
determining visitor's country, 310–312
fetching data from, 241–243
Guestbook feature, 178–183
links to/from. *See* links
number of active users online,
    176–178
popularity of, 176–178
proxy service, 154–159
RSS feeds, 163–170
secure sessions, 226–228
statistics, 105–107
translating, 324–327
URLs. *See* URLs
verifying links, 92–95, 142–144
white space, 36, 43–45, 165
Wiki pages, 243–248
Wikipedia, 243–248
Windows Security Alerts, 8, 10
Windows systems
    Command Line Client, 211
    document root, 12
    .htaccess file and, 152
    HTML files, 12
    installing Apache Web Server, 6–7, 8
    installing Zend Server, 2–11
    passwords, 8–11
    PHP files, 12
    uninstalling Zend Server, 8, 11
    upgrading Zend Server, 8
Word Selector plug-in, 45–47
words. *See also* text
    blanking out, 45–47
    breaks in, 49–51
    censoring, 45–47
    clickable list of, 302–304
    highlighting, 45–47
    pattern matching, 318–320
    predicting, 304–308
    removing accents, 55–56
    spell checking, 51–55, 320–324
    translating, 324–327
    underlining, 45–47, 54
Words from Root plug-in, 302–304
Wrap Text plug-in, 34–37
wrapping text, 34–37

━━X━━

XHTML, 155–157, 164
XML (Extensible Markup Language)
    ampersand and, 155–157, 257
    CDATA section, 257, 261, 266
    currency conversions, 272–275
    exporting wiki pages as, 245
    SimpleXML, 250, 258, 261
XML objects, 245
XMLHttpRequest object, 278–286
<xmp> tag, 221
XPath objects, 164

━━Y━━

Yahoo! Answers, 252–255
Yahoo! Finance web site, 259–264
Yahoo! News, 264–268

Yahoo! search engine, 256–259
Yahoo! Stock News, 259–264
YouTube videos, 101–103

━━Z━━

Zend newsletter, 11, 21
Zend Server CE
    described, 2
    error handling, 25
    installing on Linux systems, 12–17
    installing on Windows systems, 2–11
    license agreement, 4, 5
    uninstalling from Linux systems, 14,
      16, 17
    uninstalling from Windows systems,
      8, 11
Zend Server Community Edition. *See* Zend
    Server CE

Cutting-Edge Virtualization Guides

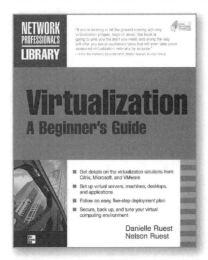

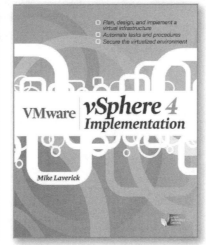

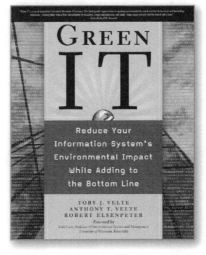

Mokena Community
Public Library District

**Mokena Community
Public Library District**